# MARGARET CAVENDISH, DUCHESS OF NEWCASTLE

# *Political Writings*

EDITED BY
SUSAN JAMES

CAMBRIDGE
UNIVERSITY PRESS

PUBLISHED BY THE PRESS SYNDICATE OF THE UNIVERSITY OF CAMBRIDGE
The Pitt Building, Trumpington Street, Cambridge CB2 1RP, United Kingdom

CAMBRIDGE UNIVERSITY PRESS
The Edinburgh Building, Cambridge, CB2 2RU, UK
40 West 20th Street, New York, NY 10011–4211, USA
477 Williamstown Road, Port Melbourne, VIC 3207, Australia
Ruiz de Alarcón 13, 28014 Madrid, Spain
Dock House, The Waterfront, Cape Town 8001, South Africa

http://www.cambridge.org

First published 2003

Printed in the United Kingdom at the University Press, Cambridge

*Typeface* Ehrhardt 9.5/12 pt.    *System* LATEX 2ε    [TB]

*A catalogue record for this book is available from the British Library*

*Library of Congress Cataloguing in Publication data*
Newcastle, Margaret Cavendish, Duchess of, 1624?–1674.
[Description of a new world, called the blazing world]
Political writings / Margaret Cavendish, Duchess of Newcastle; edited by Susan James.
p.   cm. – (Cambridge texts in the history of political thought)
Includes bibliographical references and index.
Contents: The description of a new world, called the blazing world – Orations of divers
sorts, accommodated of divers places.
Includes bibliographical references and index.
ISBN 0 521 63349 4 – ISBN 0 521 63350 8 (pb)
1. Utopias – Early works to 1800.   2. Great Britain – Politics and government –
Early works to 1800.   3. Great Britain – Social conditions – Early works to 1800.
4. Voyages, Imaginary – Early works to 1800.   5. Political science – Early works to 1800.
I. James, Susan, 1951–   II. Newcastle, Margaret Cavendish, Duchess of, 1624?–1674.
Orations of divers sorts, accommodated to divers places.   III. Title.   IV. Series.
PR3605. N 2A6   2003    823′.4 – dc21   2002041448

ISBN 0 521 63349 4 hardback
ISBN 0 521 63350 8 paperback

CAMBRIDGE TEXTS IN THE
HISTORY OF POLITICAL THOUGHT

———

# MARGARET CAVENDISH
## *Political Writings*

Margaret Cavendish, Duchess of Newcastle, published a wide variety of works including poems, plays, letters, and treatises of natural philosophy, but her significance as a political writer has only recently been recognised. This major contribution to the series of **Cambridge Texts** includes the first ever modern edition of her *Divers Orations* on English social and political life, together with a new student-friendly rendition of her imaginary voyage, *A New World called the Blazing World*. Susan James explains the allusions made in this classic text, and directs readers to the many intellectual debates with which Cavendish engages. Together these two works reveal the character and scope of Margaret Cavendish's political thought. She emerges as a singular and probing writer, who simultaneously upholds a conservative social and political order and destabilises it through her critical and unresolved observations about natural philosophy, scientific institutions, religion, and the relations between men and women.

SUSAN JAMES is Professor of Philosophy at Birkbeck College, London. Her publications include *The Content of Social Explanation* (Cambridge, 1984) and *Passion and Action: The Emotions in Early Modern Philosophy* (Oxford, 1997).

# CAMBRIDGE TEXTS IN THE
# HISTORY OF POLITICAL THOUGHT

*Series editors*

RAYMOND GEUSS

*Reader in Philosophy, University of Cambridge*

QUENTIN SKINNER

*Regius Professor of Modern History in the University of Cambridge*

Cambridge Texts in the History of Political Thought is now firmly established as the major student textbook series in political theory. It aims to make available to students all the most important texts in the history of western political thought, from ancient Greece to the early twentieth century. All the familiar classic texts will be included, but the series seeks at the same time to enlarge the conventional canon by incorporating an extensive range of less well-known works, many of them never before available in a modern English edition. Wherever possible, texts are published in complete and unabridged form, and translations are specially commissioned for the series. Each volume contains a critical introduction together with chronologies, biographical sketches, a guide to further reading, and any necessary glossaries and textual apparatus. When completed the series will aim to offer an outline of the entire evolution of western political thought.

*For a list of titles published in the series, please see end of book*

# Contents

# Preface

The text of *A New World called the Blazing World* contained in this volume was originally edited by Kate Lilley, who included it in her collection, *The Blazing World and Other Writings*, published by Penguin Classics in 1992. I am extremely grateful to Pickering and Chatto, who hold the copyright, for allowing me to use it. Lilley provided forty-one explanatory notes, some of which I have adopted. However, since there is no critical edition of this work, and since it contains allusions and references to a wide range of authors and events, I have added considerably to her annotations. In doing so, I have been aided and inspired by Eileen O'Neill's outstanding edition of *Observations on Experimental Philosophy*, the companion piece to *Blazing World*, now published by Cambridge University Press.

While *Blazing World* has become relatively well known, *Divers Orations* remains less familiar. This is, to the best of my knowledge, the first modern edition. As well as modernising spelling and occasionally altering punctuation, I have numbered individual orations for ease of reference. However, some inconsistencies, for example in titles, have been left. Because it is a relatively self-explanatory work I have added only a few notes, though I hope readers who wish to explore it in greater detail will use the list of Further Reading.

In preparing this pair of texts for publication I have been helped by Shirley Stacey, who gave me comprehensive advice about the various editions of Margaret Cavendish's works; by Virginia Cox, the Academic Librarian of Christ's College Cambridge, who generously allowed me to use the College's copy of *Divers Orations*; by Caroline Murray of Cambridge University Press, who took charge of scanning the text of *Orations*; by Olivia Skinner, who did the same for *Blazing World*; by Jean

Field, who expertly copy-edited the whole volume; by Philip Riley and Janet Hall, who checked the proofs; and by the staff of the Rare Books Room of Cambridge University Library. Together with the General Editors of *Cambridge Texts in the History of Political Thought*, and Richard Fisher, the most patient and considerate of editors, they have made this volume possible.

At the same time, I am deeply grateful for the enthusiasm and advice of several friends and colleagues. I was lucky to be shown something of Antwerp, including the Rubenshuis where Margaret Cavendish lived, by so knowledgeable a guide as Walter Van Herck. Hero Chalmers, Stephen Clucas, Catherine Wilson, and Susan Wiseman have all helped me to try to understand the intellectual milieu in which Cavendish worked, and I have benefited enormously from their writings and conversation. Noel Malcolm has been exceptionally generous with his time and learning, and identified Robert Withers as the source of Cavendish's views about the Ottoman Empire. Raymond Geuss proposed some improvements to an earlier version of the Introduction. He has been, as always, a thoughtful and constructive interlocutor. Julie Sanders, in the manner of a true friend, listened critically and at length, and shared her sensitive grasp of seventeenth-century politics and drama. Most of all, however, I am indebted to Quentin Skinner, who has closely followed the fortunes of this edition. His suggestions, comments, and interest have been a continuing and vital source of encouragement.

# Introduction

## I

Margaret Cavendish was a strikingly prolific writer who, in the course of a comparatively short life, published eleven volumes of work. They include plays, poems, stories, letters, and, unprecedentedly for a female author, three books of natural philosophy. Cavendish's ideas about politics and government are spread through many of these writings, but are concentrated in the two works reprinted here, where the political themes that most absorbed her are intensively explored. These preoccupations arose out of her own experience, which was dramatically shaped by the English Civil War, the execution of King Charles I, the years of Cromwellian rule, and the subsequent restoration of the monarchy. Throughout this period Cavendish lived on the edge of the arena of high politics, and the course of her life was moulded by the fortunes of the Royalist party to which she belonged. The fears and convictions generated by this odyssey form the main elements of her political philosophy which, like the work of many of her conservative contemporaries, focuses on the question of how a monarch can most effectively avoid the dangers of faction and preserve social harmony. A more distinctive feature of Cavendish's writing, however, is her interest in specific forms of social power, a concern which again echoes her own circumstances. The weight she places on a dramaturgical model of political authority, for example, and above all her multifaceted analyses of the hierarchical relations between men and women, reflect her acquaintance with the centre and the margins of English society. The double exclusion of a woman writer who spent the first fifteen years of her adult life in exile is counterbalanced by a familiarity with the ways of power and an aristocratic confidence in her own protected position. To begin to understand this unusual amalgam, and the political views to which it gave rise, it is helpful to know more about her life.

# II

Margaret Cavendish was the youngest child of Elizabeth Lucas, the capable and resourceful widow of Sir Thomas Lucas, an Essex gentleman who died when Margaret was two years old. An apparently uneventful childhood and adolescence spent at her home near Colchester came to an end with the outbreak of the Civil War in 1642, when she and her mother moved to Oxford, the Royalist stronghold to which Charles I had just transferred his court. As her brothers prepared to fight for the king, Margaret became a maid of honour to Queen Henrietta Maria and had to adapt to the claustrophobic and competitive mores of court life. This adjustment was rapidly succeeded by another, for within a year the political situation deteriorated and the queen and her attendants went into exile. Margaret found herself in Paris at the age of twenty-one, in the midst of a troubled community whose expectations and ambitions had been disrupted by civil war.

A few months later, this small band of courtiers was joined by William Cavendish, Marquis of Newcastle. Newcastle was a loyal servant of the Stuarts and an unswerving devotee of the Royalist cause, who had been Governor to the Prince of Wales (the future King Charles II) at the end of the 1630s, and since 1642 had been commanding an army in the north of England. In 1644 he had been heavily defeated at Marston Moor and, together with his brother and two sons who had fought alongside him, immediately left the country.[1] When he arrived in Paris he was fifty-two, a widower with five children, exiled from his estates and cut off from his immense wealth. He immediately set about wooing the young Margaret Lucas with daily letters and poems, and by the end of the year they were married.

Margaret joined a household whose principal members were her husband and his younger brother, Sir Charles Cavendish, both cultivated

---

[1] Edward Hyde, the Earl of Clarendon, later suggested that Newcastle left because he did not enjoy military life and 'was so utterly tired with a condition and employment so contrary to his humour, nature and education', *The History of the Rebellion and Civil Wars in England*, ed. W. Dunn Macray (Oxford, 1888), vol. I, p. 167.

men who kept up with the latest developments in natural philosophy and the arts. Sir Charles, the more professional of the two, had a particular talent for mathematics. Before his exile he had discussed a range of optical and mechanical problems with the circle of scholars surrounding John Pell, among whom was Thomas Hobbes, and had corresponded with several European mathematicians and scientists, including Marin Mersenne.[2] From France, and later from Antwerp, he continued to write to Pell about mathematical problems. Newcastle's intellectual concerns were less specialised, but he nevertheless took a serious interest in scientific developments. In England he had undertaken some chemical experiments with Robert Payne,[3] and since the 1630s had been an important patron of Thomas Hobbes.[4] (He had invited Hobbes to come and live in one of his houses in 1636, and was the dedicatee of Hobbes's first political treatise, *The Elements of Law*.)[5] Newcastle also loved the theatre. As well as writing his own poems and plays, he had commissioned masques from Ben Jonson in the early 1630s as part of the lavish entertainments he had laid on for the king and queen.[6] In 1649 two of his plays were published, and after the Restoration one was performed in London.[7]

Hobbes was already in Paris when the Cavendishes arrived there, and they again took up their habit of discussing his work with him. Charles Cavendish's papers contain detailed notes on *De Corpore* and *De Cive* from this period, while his elder brother, who regularly invited Hobbes to dinner, talked to him about his theory of the passions and encouraged him to

---

[2] See the Biographical Register in Noel Malcolm ed., *The Correspondence of Thomas Hobbes* (Oxford: Oxford University Press, 1994), 2 vols., vol. II, pp. 801–5.

[3] Newcastle mentions these experiments in a short piece appended to Cavendish's *Philosophical and Physical Opinions* (1655).

[4] See Malcolm, *The Correspondence of Thomas Hobbes*, vol. II, pp. 812–15. See Noel Malcolm, 'Robert Payne, the Hobbes Manuscripts and the "Short Tract"' in *Aspects of Hobbes* (Oxford: Clarendon, 2002), pp. 80–145.

[5] Thomas Hobbes, *The Elements of Law, Natural and Politique*, ed. F. Tönnies, new edition with intro. by M. M. Goldsmith (London: Frank Cass and Co., 1969), pp. xv–xvi.

[6] Newcastle entertained Charles I at Welbeck Abbey in 1633 and both Charles I and Henrietta Maria at Bolsover Castle in 1634. Jonson wrote a masque for each occasion. Several other poets, including Richard Brome, John Ford, James Shirley, and later Thomas Shadwell, dedicated works to Newcastle.

[7] Clarendon described him as 'a very fine gentleman, active and full of courage, and most accomplished in those qualities of horsemanship, dancing, and fencing, which accompany a good breeding; in which his delight was. Besides that, he was amorous in poetry and music, to which he indulged the greater part of his time; and nothing could have tempted him out of those paths of pleasure which he enjoyed in a full and ample fortune, but honour, and ambition to serve the king', *History of the Rebellion*, vol. VIII, p. 381.

publish his treatise *Of Libertie and Necessitie*.[8] Newcastle also began to pursue a new form of enquiry when he took up the study of microscopy. While in Paris he owned seven microscopes and telescopes which he subsequently sold to Hobbes.[9] Perhaps with Hobbes's help, the Cavendishes also expanded their intellectual circle. One of their celebrated new acquaintances, and another guest at their table, was Descartes, although according to Margaret he said very little.[10] Nevertheless, Newcastle later plied him with questions about his physics, and Charles Cavendish seems to have mediated in his disputes with Hobbes and Roberval. A further visitor was Gassendi, the champion of Epicurean atomism, described by Hobbes as a man whose knowledge was greater than that of any other mortal and whose virtue was even greater than his knowledge.[11] In addition, Charles Cavendish kept up his connections with Mersenne who, as well as discussing scientific problems with him, lent him books and showed him some curiosities he had brought back from Italy.

When Margaret Cavendish came to publish her own works of natural philosophy, she insisted that she had never had a single conversation with any of these learned men, and had gained all her knowledge from her husband and brothers. She presumably intended this description to encompass Charles Cavendish and her elder brother Lord Lucas, a founding member of the Royal Society who was in London during the two years she spent there between 1651 and 1653. 'Likewise', she writes,

> if they should tell me all the parts of an animal body . . . I conceive it as perfectly to my understanding as if I had seen it dissected . . . for truly I have gathered more by piece-meals than from a full relation, or a methodical education for knowledge; but my fancy will build thereupon and make discourse therefrom, and so of everything they discourse (I say, that is, my husband and brothers); for the singularity of my affections are such that though I have an ill memory [for] . . . anything long that I shall hear from strangers . . . when from my near

---

[8] *De Corpore (On Body)* was published in 1655 and *De Cive (On The Citizen)* appeared in 1642. *Of Libertie and Necessitie*, Hobbes's dispute with John Bramhall, had been drafted in 1646 but was not published until 1654–5.

[9] For further details see Londa Schiebinger, 'Margaret Cavendish, Duchess of Newcastle' in Mary Ellen Waite ed., *A History of Women Philosophers* (Dordrecht: Kluwer Academic Publishers, 1991), 3 vols., vol. III, pp. 1–20.

[10] *Philosophical and Physical Opinions* (1655), sig. B, 3v.

[11] Letter from Hobbes to Gassendi 22 Sept. 1649 in Malcolm, *The Correspondence of Thomas Hobbes*, p. 179.

friends (especially my Lord), whose discourses are lively descriptions,
I cannot forget anything they say, such deep impressions their words
print on my brain.[12]

Even if she did not speak to the great philosophers who came to the
house, and was unable to read works in Latin or Greek, she learned about
the debates they were conducting, and when she developed views of her
own, Descartes and Hobbes were among the authors with whom she engaged.

Alongside his intellectual activities, Newcastle contributed optimisti-
cally to the queen's efforts to rally support for the king, and like other
exiled Royalists Margaret Cavendish presumably believed that she would
soon return to England. However, any confidence she may have had that
life would go on as before must have been shaken by the deaths of her
mother and two of her siblings in 1647. The following year, a more public disaster overtook her when her elder brother, the Royalist general Sir
Charles Lucas, surrendered the besieged city of Colchester to the parliamentary forces and was summarily shot. In the aftermath of the siege,
the family vault at her childhood home was vandalised and the recently
interred bodies of her mother and sister were brutally mutilated. News of
these events was widely circulated in pamphlets and papers, and not sur-
prisingly Margaret became seriously unwell.[13] Over the next two years,
the group of English Royalists gathered around Henrietta Maria watched
their prospects decline, and when in 1649 the king was executed and
a Commonwealth declared, many of them embarked on an uncharted
period of exile which was to last a further eleven years.

One of the most urgent problems facing Newcastle at this juncture was
lack of money, and as his Parisian creditors became increasingly pressing
he decided to move to Antwerp, where he rented a substantial and gracious house which had been built by Rubens. Although he continued to
be intermittently involved in a series of unsuccessful attempts to restore
the English monarchy, he mainly turned his attention to horsemanship.
In the garden of the Rubenshuis he set up a successful riding school where

---

[12] *Philosophical and Physical Opinions* (1655), sig. B, 3v. See also *The World's Olio* (1655),
Epistle sig. E2.r–Ee5.r.

[13] Sir Theodore Mayerne, Margaret's doctor, wrote to Newcastle in May 1648: 'Touching
conception, I know not if in the estate she's in, you ought earnestly to desire it. It is hard
to get children with good courage when one is melancholy, and after they are got and
come into the world, they bring a great deal of pain with them.' Quoted in Douglas Grant,
*Margaret the First* (London: Rupert Hart-Davis, 1957), p. 96.

he demonstrated dressage or 'the art of manage', a popular aristocratic pastime of which he became an internationally acknowledged master, and about which he published a magnificently illustrated book.[14] Margaret Cavendish, meanwhile, began to write. This occupation, as she later indicated, was a familiar one, since in spite of her limited education she had as a child filled sixteen books with her smudged and irregular hand.[15] It seems to have been at this stage, however, that writing started to become for her an intensely satisfying form of retreat, 'a great delight and pleasure to me, as being the only pastime which imploys my idle hours'.[16]

This way of life continued until 1651, when Newcastle's financial affairs took his wife to London. Because he had been impeached by Parliament for his part in the Civil War and excluded from any future amnesty, there was no prospect of his returning to England under a parliamentary government, nor was he able to reclaim his property. Even before his estates were confiscated he was forced to live in what were by his standards desperately straitened circumstances, and Margaret Cavendish's accounts of their exile dwell on his recurrent negotiations with his creditors. When her brother-in-law discovered that his estates were about to be sold, he was persuaded to go to London to compound for them, and it was agreed that Margaret should go too, in the hope that she would be able to claim a pension payable to the wives of Royalists who had lost their property during the war. She duly petitioned the relevant parliamentary committee, but it turned down her request on the grounds that she had not married until after her husband's estates had been confiscated. Mortified, she persuaded her brother, as she later put it, 'to conduct me out of that ungentlemanly place'[17] and it was left to Newcastle's children, brother, and friends to raise money for him wherever they could.

During the two years she spent in London, Cavendish produced 'a book of poems and a little book called my Philosophical Fancies',[18] a playful exposition of Lucretian atomism in verse, influenced, perhaps, by Henry

---

[14] William Cavendish, *La Méthode Nouvelle et Invention Extraordinaire de Dresser les Chevaux* (Antwerp, 1658), illustrated with engravings after Abraham van Diepenbeke. In 1667 Newcastle published a revised version in English, which was translated into French and German.

[15] 'A True Relation' in *Nature's Pictures* (1656), p. 385; *Sociable Letters* (1664), CXXXL.

[16] *Observations on Experimental Philosophy* (1668), Preface sig. b1.v. Cf. *Sociable Letters* (1664), cl.

[17] 'A True Relation', p. 380.     [18] 'A True Relation', p. 382.

More's poem, *Democritus Platonissans*.[19] Returning to Antwerp in 1653, she continued to write, and also gained Newcastle's permission to publish her work. *Poems* and *Philosophical Fancies* appeared in 1653, followed two years later by *The World's Olio*,[20] and a year after that by *Nature's Pictures*, in which she included an autobiographical piece, 'A True Relation of my Birth and Breeding'. In 1655 she also published *Philosophical and Physical Opinions*, her first work of systematic natural philosophy. As she later confided, she was hampered when she first began to read philosophical treatises by her lack of learning (especially of languages) and by her ignorance of the technical terms they employed. It is clear, however, that *Philosophical and Physical Opinions* is grounded on an acquaintance with some of the most up-to-date natural philosophy of the period: with the work of Galileo; with Harvey's account of the circulation of the blood; with mechanical conceptions of bodily motion and perception; with some aspects of the work of Descartes; and with some of Hobbes's objections to Cartesianism. Cavendish entreats her readers to believe 'that whatever is new is my own which I hope all is; for I never had any guide to direct me, not intelligence from any authors to advise me, but writ according to my own natural cogitations'.[21] However, we know that, at least once she began to publish her natural philosophy, she sometimes discussed scientific questions with people outside her family circle, and in 1657 corresponded with the poet and diplomat, Constantijn Huygens. Huygens sent her some small drops of glass formed by putting molten glass into water, and asked if she could tell him why they were liable to explode. This was a widely discussed scientific puzzle at the time, one that Charles II later put to the members of the Royal Society who, like Cavendish, were unable to solve it.[22]

For Newcastle, the late 1650s was also a period of literary activity. Towards the end of it, probably once the death of Oliver Cromwell made

---

[19] Henry More attempts to reconcile atomism and Platonism, and defends the idea that there could be an infinite number of worlds. See *Democritus Platonissans, or, An Essay on the Infinity of Worlds out of Platonick Principles* (1646).

[20] This work contains an attack on monasticism which prompted a response from S. Du Verger. He defends the institution at length in *Du Verger's Humble Reflections upon some Passages of the Right Honourable the Lady Marchioness of Newcastle's Olio, or, An Appeale from her mis-informed to her owne better informed judgement* (London 1657). In many of her subsequent Prefaces, Cavendish acknowledges that her works have excited criticism.

[21] *Philosophical and Physical Opinions* (1655), ch. 209, p. 171.

[22] See Grant, *Margaret the First*, pp. 194–5. The phenomenon of 'Rupert's Drops' was investigated by the Royal Society in 1661.

it seem more likely that Charles II might regain the throne, he wrote his old pupil a letter of advice, explaining how to go about consolidating and maintaining a stable and prosperous kingdom.[23] The optimism implicit in this gesture turned out to be justified, and as soon as the monarchy and the House of Lords were restored in 1660 he set sail for England, leaving his wife in Antwerp to stand surety for him until his creditors were satisfied. She arrived in London a few months later, and after a comparatively short stay, during which it became evident that Newcastle would play no significant role in Charles II's court or government, they retired to his estates. Assuring the king that 'I am in no kind of way displeased, for I am so joyed at your Majesty's happy restoration that I cannot be sad or troubled for any concern to my own particular', he withdrew with Margaret to Welbeck Abbey in Nottinghamshire.[24] While he began to repair his property and returned to his old habit of writing plays, she settled once more to her work, and over the next eight years published six further books: two volumes of plays; *Divers Orations*; *Sociable Letters* (a vivid and sometimes savage commentary on social mores); *Philosophical Letters*; and *Observations on Experimental Philosophy* which appeared in the same volume as its companion piece, *The Description of a New World called The Blazing World*.

In 1665, Newcastle was made a duke and Cavendish accompanied him to London to attend the court. Her reputation as an author, together with her exotic mode of dress, made her something of a public spectacle, and her visit is mentioned in several contemporary letters and diaries. Pepys, for example, records seeing coaches jostling around her carriage as she drove through Hyde Park, and boys and girls running after her as she drove to her house at Clerkenwell.[25] She also became the first woman to visit the Royal Society, which put on a display of experimental curiosities for her benefit, much as the bear men entertain the Empress in *The Blazing World*. Boyle's famous air pump was used to create a vacuum (a challenge to Cavendish, who had denied the possibility of such a thing); a piece of meat was dissolved in sulphuric acid; coloured liquors were mixed together; and a magnet was used to move iron

---

[23] *Ideology and Politics on the Eve of the Restoration: Newcastle's Advice to Charles II*, intro. by Thomas P. Slaughter (Philadelphia: The American Philosophical Society, 1984).

[24] Quoted in Geoffrey Trease, *Portrait of a Cavalier* (London: Macmillan, 1979), p. 183.

[25] Samuel Pepys, 1 May 1667 in *The Diary of Samuel Pepys*, ed. Robert Latham and William Matthews (Berkeley: HarperCollins, 1995), 9 vols., vol. VIII, pp. 196–7.

filings.[26] But whereas the fictional Empress replies sceptically and intelligently to the bear men's claims, the Fellows of the Royal Society seem to have been disappointed, or perhaps reassured, by what they perceived as Cavendish's inarticulate and bewildered responses to their experiments.[27]

Not long after she attained this moment of equivocal recognition, Cavendish's spectacular energy seems to have begun to decline. Back at Welbeck, she wrote and published a biography of her husband and reissued several of her other works, but in the winter of 1673 she fell ill and died. Newcastle, who outlived her by two years, gathered together a collection of letters and poems in her honour.[28] He also wrote the epitaph that adorns her grave in Westminster Abbey, where he describes her as 'a wise, wittie and learned lady, which her many bookes do testifie'.

# III

Cavendish wrote in many literary forms, and as her work developed she increasingly used genres considered unsuitable for women. As she explained, some of her female contemporaries wrote poems and plays, and also 'devotions, or romances, or receipts of medicines, for cookery or confections, or complemental letters, or a copy or two of verses' which 'express our brief wit in our short books'.[29] But very few published systematic philosophical treatises, and no other woman explained in print how her views outshone those of the most celebrated philosophers of the age. In this audacious mood, Cavendish insists that, 'as an honourable dueller will fight only with an honourable and valiant opponent, so I am resolved to argue only with famous and subtle philosophers'.[30] At other moments, however, her confidence wavers. Many of her prefatory epistles ask her dedicatees and readers to take account of the fact that she is not learned, and her awareness that she is likely to be the target of both social and intellectual criticism often prompts her to defend herself in advance.

---

[26] S. I. Mintz, 'The Duchess of Newcastle's Visit to the Royal Society' in *The Journal of English and Germanic Philology* (1952), pp. 168–76. Cavendish equivocates about the vacuum. She denies its existence in *Grounds of Natural Philosophy* (1668), Part 1, ch. 4, but allows the need for it in *Sociable Letters* (1664), clxi.

[27] Pepys, *Diary*, 30 May 1667, vol. VIII, p. 243.

[28] *Letters and Poems in Honour of the Incomparable Princess, Margaret, Duchess of Newcastle* (1676).

[29] *Sociable Letters*, cxii.

[30] *Observations upon Experimental Philosophy* (1668), Preface to the ensuing treatise sig. b3. v.

She is consistent, however, in claiming that she writes to satisfy an extreme and unusual desire for fame. Many people, she allows, will regard this as a disease and many others will condemn her as opinionated and vainglorious; but in her own estimation it is an admirable and honest ambition.

Fame, as Cavendish understands it, is the opposite of oblivion, and consists in being remembered as an honourable person.[31] It can be achieved in a number of ways, but for a woman excluded from heroic actions, public employments, or eloquent pleadings it is most readily attained through authorship.[32] Cavendish began to publish her work and advertise her ambition for fame during the 1650s, at a time when the lives of exiled Royalists were in danger of being forgotten. In her own case, the fact that she had no children after several years of marriage may have increased her anxiety that she would disappear without trace, a fear poignantly expressed at the end of 'A True Relation'. Equally, the reputations of the men to whom she was closest were at a low ebb; national histories had become dangerous reminders of past discord, and her husband had been branded a traitor. Her desire to secure Newcastle's reputation is manifested in the many praises and vindications of him scattered throughout her books, including the appearance of his fictional double in *The Blazing World*. By incorporating him into her work and presenting him as a superlatively honourable man, she both basks in the glory of her association with him and ensures that he is encompassed by whatever fame she acquires.

At the same time, however, she appeals to the strictly gendered nature of honour to justify her role as an author and to fend off the charge that she should be living a more 'feminine' life. While honourable men are required to exemplify a delicate blend of social virtues – to be honest, courageous, prudent, magnanimous, and so on – female honour is primarily a sexual matter and consists above all in chastity.[33] This difference has direct political implications, since it makes way for the view that inconstant women or whores, about whom Cavendish writes with extreme violence, are the ruin of the Commonwealth. Their infidelities, she asserts, 'decay breed', and because men are unwilling to provide for children who may not be their own progeny this in turn 'decays industry'.[34] While she is simultaneously stern about the absolute demands of female honour and eloquent about the sufferings imposed upon women by the sexual double

---

[31] See for example *Divers Orations* (1662), 22.
[32] *Nature's Pictures*, 'An Epistle to my Readers', sig. C1, 1r.
[33] *Sociable Letters*, lx.     [34] *Nature's Pictures*, p. 338.

standard, she also celebrates the fact that many aspects of women's lives do not bear directly on their virtue. As long as they remain chaste, she suggests, women have a certain latitude. In particular, there is nothing dishonourable about a life devoted to writing: it possesses the seriousness appropriate to a married woman and keeps her away from vice; it may provide an improving and profitable entertainment for others; and if it brings its author fame, it enhances an aspect of her honour that she shares with men.

Cavendish was a determined promoter of her own work who sent presentation copies of her books to the Library of the University of Leyden, to several of the Oxford and Cambridge colleges, to the playwright Thomas Shadwell, and to individual philosophers including Glanvill, Charleton, More, Digby, and Hobbes.[35] Her quest for fame made her anxious to win the respect of her powerful male contemporaries, and may also help to explain why she often wrote on what were generally regarded as masculine subjects. Nonetheless, she never produced anything resembling a political treatise and she steered clear of direct engagement with matters of church or state.[36] By way of justification, she claimed that unless you expect to be the favourite of an absolute prince (or, one might add, adviser to the Empress of the Blazing World) the study of a deceiving profession such as politics is a waste of time, especially for women who are not employed in state affairs.[37] Elsewhere, however, she explores the implications of excluding women from political life with characteristic acuity. In a remarkable passage, the author of *Sociable Letters* argues that, because women do not possess the civic rights and duties accorded to men, they are not citizens. Moreover, 'if we be not citizens in the Commonwealth, I know no reason we should be subjects to the Commonwealth; and the truth is we are no subjects, unless it be to our husbands'.[38]

Here, as in her other works, Cavendish avoids discussing political issues in her own voice and creates a distance between author and text which serves both as a precaution and as an opportunity. This is a feature both of *Divers Orations*, which employs the conventions of the art of rhetoric to view each of the issues it discusses from a variety of angles, and of

---

[35] On Cavendish's gift to the University of Leyden see Grant, *Margaret the First*, p. 218; for letters of thanks from other recipients of her work see *Letters and Poems in Honour of the Incomparable Princess, Margaret, Duchess of Newcastle* (1676).

[36] *Philosophical Letters* (1664), Preface to the Reader, sig. b, 1.v; see also pp. 3, 17.

[37] *Philosophical Letters*, Section 1, Letter xiii, p. 47.     [38] *Sociable Letters*, xvi.

*A Description of a New World called the Blazing World*, which depicts an imaginary polity.[39] The latter piece belongs to a popular early-modern genre of utopian writing to which it relates in two specific ways. On the one hand, scientific innovations had led to the revival of a classical discussion as to whether or not the world we inhabit is unique. Cavendish repeatedly addresses this question, and argues that there are many worlds. On the other hand, moralists and political theorists kept up the ancient practice of illuminating the character and worth of an existing society by contrasting it with an imaginary one. Several works of this type are mentioned in *The Blazing World*, and its title seems to allude to yet another of them, a book by Joseph Hall called *The Discovery of a New World. A Description of the South Indies Hitherto Unknown*, which appeared in English in 1605.[40] Cavendish's own fiction tells the story of a virtuous lady who is transported to an exotic and orderly Blazing World, becomes its empress, and with the help of her adviser the Duchess of Newcastle rules it wisely and well.

In both the 1666 and 1668 editions, *The Blazing World* was published together with *Observations on Experimental Philosophy*, a critique of the recently established Royal Society of London which had been incorporated by Charles II in 1662.[41] Cavendish takes issue with the conclusions reached by some of the Society's greatest luminaries, especially Robert Hooke, Henry Power, and Robert Boyle. She criticises their experimental approach, and especially their use of dissection and microscopic observation, claiming that it is far inferior to her more speculative style of philosophising. At the same time, she attacks the corpuscularian assumptions underlying their work. The view that the natural world consists of inanimate material particles is, she argues, much weaker from an explanatory point of view than her own vitalist principles. While *Observations* challenges the Royal Society's philosophical findings, the fictional narrative of *The Blazing World* enables Cavendish to offer a more playful, but also more wide-ranging, commentary on the relationship between scientific investigation and government. Like Charles II, the newly installed empress

---

[39] Although Cavendish does not deign to write romances, her work shares some of the traits of the 'royal romances' published in the middle of the century. See Annabel Patterson, *Censorship and Interpretation: The Conditions of Writing and Reading in Early Modern England* (Madison: University of Wisconsin Press, 1984), pp. 159–202.

[40] And also, perhaps, to the title of a masque by Ben Jonson, *News from a New World Discovered in the Moon*, which had been performed in 1620.

[41] Charles also had a hand in the founding of the Mathematical School at Christ's Hospital in 1673, and the building of the Royal Observatory at Greenwich in 1675.

enthusiastically forms her physicists, chemists, logicians, and other inves-
tigators into learned societies. However, when she quizzes them about
their discoveries she is on the whole disappointed, and eventually decides
to dissolve them on the grounds that their controversies and quarrels are
dangerous to the state. Re-enacting the laws she had started with, the
Empress turns her attention to the defence of her native country, and after a brilliant naval campaign succeeds in subduing the enemies of a king
whom we are allowed to identify as none other than Charles II. The overall
trajectory of the text is therefore a nostalgic one in which the state's support for novel forms of enquiry is abandoned in favour of a government
overwhelmingly concerned with security and conquest. In advocating this
traditional type of polity, and in emphasising the importance of military
glory, it can be read as a plea to the recently restored king to reinstate the
policies of his predecessors, and particularly of Elizabeth I.[42]

*The Blazing World* also explores the character and limits of political
knowledge. When the Empress yearns for a political kabbala – a comprehensive set of insights into the truth about politics – she is informed by
her counsellor, the Duchess of Newcastle, that there is no need for such
a thing, since the only basis of government is reward and punishment.
Cavendish here enables the reader to make several connections. As well
as echoing a view that she elsewhere attributes to her husband[43] and tac-
itly criticising the project of attempting to provide a systematic political
philosophy,[44] she presents government as an art, grounded on simple and
accessible principles and dependent for its success on the skill of rulers
and their advisers. The implication that neither speculative philosophy
nor experimental investigation can contribute anything worthwhile to our
understanding of practical politics underlines her more general view that
all forms of enquiry should be useful, and suggests that the approach of
the Royal Society is irrelevant, if not damaging, to the vital business of
government. A prudent prince, we are encouraged to infer, would do well
to emulate the Empress of the Blazing World and exchange his learned
societies for capable counsellors.

---

[42] Newcastle repeatedly advises Charles II to revert to the policies of Elizabeth I. See
*Newcastle's Advice*, pp. 73, 75. Cf. *The World's Olio* (1655), p. 126.

[43] *Life of the Thrice Noble, High and Puissant Prince William Cavendish, Duke, Marquess and
Earl of Newcastle* (1667), in *The Life of William Cavendish Duke of Newcastle*, ed. C. H.
Firth (London: Routledge, 1907), p. 131.

[44] It is worth remembering that Newcastle was the patron of Hobbes, who wrote no fewer
than three systematic treatises on politics: *Elements of Law*; *De Cive*; and *Leviathan*.

Cavendish's book of orations, like several of her stories and plays,[45] combines fiction with the use of rhetorical conventions in such a way as to provide another means of airing a variety of political and social views without espousing any of them. *Divers Orations* consists of sets of speeches loosely organised into a narrative. We are to imagine ourselves visiting a country on the brink of civil war where we listen to citizens and soldiers talking about the impending hostilities and the restoration of peace. We then hear proceedings in the law courts and the royal council chamber, attend weddings and funerals, join the crowd in the market place, are admitted to a meeting of women, and are treated to the views of country gentlemen. Crossing the border, we travel to a neighbouring state where the government is in crisis, before hearing a final set of orations by scholars. Although many details make it natural to identify this imagined country as England, Cavendish insists that her orations are 'such as may be spoken by any kingdom or government',[46] and by putting them in the mouths of social types rather than individuals she makes them to some degree anonymous. Although she frequently follows the standard practice of writing two speeches on a single topic, each defending one of two opposing views, she sometimes produces three or four on the same subject, and turns her verbal contests into many-sided debates as speakers answer one another back and forth. Defending herself against the complaint that she is unduly forthright, Cavendish claims that her orations are for the most part declamations 'wherein I speak pro and con and determine nothing; and as for that part which contains several pleadings, it is fit and lawful that both parties should bring in their arguments as well as they can'.[47] But by introducing sets of speeches, she both breaks the rules of formal rhetoric and introduces the thought that there are sometimes more than two sides to a question.

A further potential criticism of *Divers Orations*, which Cavendish also tries to fend off, focuses on her ignorance of artificial eloquence – the elaborate conventions governing the composition of speeches, set out in manuals of rhetoric and practised by schoolboys and university students as part of their education.[48] Cavendish admits that she lacks this training,

---

[45] See for example 'The She Anchoret' in *Nature's Pictures* (1656); 'The Female Academy' and 'Youth's Glory and Death's Banquet' in *Plays* (1662).

[46] *Divers Orations*, 'To the Readers of my Works', sig. a.2.r–4.r.

[47] *Sociable Letters*, Preface, sig. C., 2.r.

[48] On this training see Quentin Skinner, *Reason and Rhetoric in the Philosophy of Hobbes* (Cambridge: Cambridge University Press, 1996), Part 1.

but contrasts artificial eloquence unfavourably with its natural counterpart. People whose heads are filled with tropes and conceits are often vanquished in debate by speakers of natural eloquence who, although they follow fewer rules and speak in plainer terms, find that their words flow easily and freely.[49]

Despite her disclaimers, Cavendish in fact reveals a considerable familiarity with artificial eloquence, and especially with Aristotle's *Rhetoric*, which had first been translated into English by Thomas Hobbes and published in 1637.[50] Aristotle distinguishes three types of oration, each with its own function: a demonstrative oration praises or dispraises and aims to prove a thing honourable or dishonourable; a deliberative oration exhorts or dehorts and aims to prove a thing profitable or unprofitable; and a judicial oration accuses or defends and aims to prove a thing just or unjust.[51] Although Cavendish's speeches do not all conform precisely to this classification, she includes many examples of each type and often follows Aristotle's advice about the topics appropriate to each of them. For example, deliberative orations about the business of government will, according to Aristotle, be about levying money, peace and war, the safeguard of the country, and the provisions needed to maintain the state.[52] Cavendish's opening section is duly headed 'Orations to citizens in a chief city concerning peace and war', while Parts I and XIV contain speeches about the pros and cons of levying taxes and the same sections include orations on various aspects of safeguarding the state. In Parts IV and V, Cavendish moves on to judicial orations delivered in courts of law and in the royal council, and here, too, she writes on a pair of themes mentioned by Aristotle – theft and adultery.[53] Finally, she devotes Parts VII and VIII to demonstrative orations, a genre which became important in Renaissance rhetoric in the form of the funeral oration.[54] Funeral speeches were designed both to celebrate the virtue and honour of the deceased and to inspire the audience to imitate their qualities, and although Cavendish keeps to this pattern, she adapts it to her own purposes. Instead

---

[49] *Divers Orations*, 'To the Readers of my Works', sig. a.2–4. See also *Sociable Letters*, clxxv.

[50] Thomas Hobbes, 'A Briefe of the Art of Rhetorique' in John T. Harwood ed., *The Rhetorics of Thomas Hobbes and Bernard Lamy* (Carbondale: Southern Illinois University Press, 1986).

[51] 'Briefe', p. 41.    [52] 'Briefe', pp. 42–3.    [53] 'Briefe', p. 62.

[54] See John M. McManamon, *Funeral Oratory and the Cultural Ideals of Italian Humanism* (Chapel Hill: University of North Carolina Press, 1989); O. B. Hardison, *The Enduring Monument* (Chapel Hill: University of North Carolina Press, 1989).

of remembering an individual, as humanist orators had tended to do, she mainly outlines the virtues appropriate to particular roles, creating portraits of actors who know how to play their parts in public and private life. In this respect, her commemorative speeches are continuous with many of the orations she puts in the mouths of citizens, councillors, kings, or generals, in which they handle volatile or contentious situations with honour and finesse.

Both *The Blazing World* and *Divers Orations* articulate a political position answering to the problems uppermost in the minds of English people who had lived through the Civil War: the justification of war itself; the legitimacy of monarchical government; the significance of social order; the relation between church and state; and the best means to maintain peace and increase prosperity. Cavendish addresses all these issues, but she is less concerned than some of her contemporaries with constitutional questions or with the nature of legitimacy. Confidently Royalist in her assumptions, she mainly concentrates on identifying policies that will enable absolute monarchs to rule successfully and consolidate their power. To achieve this goal, it is not enough to exercise a monopoly of force, in the manner of a Hobbesian sovereign. It is also necessary to promote a particular set of values – a classical conception of virtue which had been revived in the Renaissance – and to win the admiration and love of the people. Some of Cavendish's most intriguing and distinctive discussions are concerned with these latter themes, and open up a broad conception of the practices that are relevant to politics.

According to this picture, the supreme values of a healthy commonwealth are wisdom and above all honour. Communities dedicated to these ends are by no means pacific, since military glory and the fame that accompanies it are essential aspects of the honour code. (Thus, the Empress of the Blazing World attacks the enemies of her native country, and in *Divers Orations* the advantages of war are extolled by generals, kings, and common soldiers alike.) Honourable polities are, however, free from the rancorous envy between citizens that leads to rebellion and civil war, and sustain a social climate in which individuals devote themselves to the collective pursuit of glory and prosperity. As well as celebrating this notion of the good society and exploring its political implications, Cavendish sometimes engages with its critics. To those who protest that honour is a fundamentally aristocratic and elitist value, she replies that it is applicable to everyone. People should be as hospitable as their means allow and should seek the kinds of glory appropriate to their lives. For example, although common soldiers do not achieve as much fame as their commanders, their deeds are remembered by their families and friends.[55] Turning to the conflict between the demands of honour and law, Cavendish sides firmly with the former. She is a staunch defender of duelling even when it is illegal, and deplores the modern habit of fighting with pistols rather than swords.[56] She is equally firm in her view that the law should reflect the differing demands of male and female virtue. In one of her court scenes, two brothers who have murdered their sister because her unchastity has stained their reputation go unpunished on the grounds that they acted as honour required.[57]

Honour is compatible with several types of constitution, and the author of *Sociable Letters* argues that the form of government best adapted to securing it varies with circumstances. Some countries are better off under a monarchy, others under a republic, and still others under the mixed form of government favoured by the Dutch.[58] Usually, however, Cavendish takes the superiority of monarchy for granted, and in the texts reprinted here she produces a series of familiar and deeply conservative arguments for this judgement. Absolute monarchy accords with divine law; it satisfies the requirement that the body politic should have a single head; it is based on ancient rights of conquest; and it answers to the patriarchal claim that, just as children have a natural duty to obey their parents, so subjects are naturally bound to conform to the will of the king.[59] However, while she rehearses these platitudes, Cavendish is not interested in developing them and concentrates instead on the practical business of identifying policies conducive to an honourable peace. Many of the proposals contained in *The Blazing World* and *Divers Orations* implicitly suggest how Charles I might have averted civil war, or indicate how his son might strengthen his kingdom, and the two sets of ideas overlap substantially with those contained in Newcastle's *Advice* to Charles II. For both husband and wife, the recent past contained urgent lessons in the art of government.

Some of the political principles Cavendish defends are conventional features of English absolutist ideology during this period. If society is to be secure, it is vital that the king should possess military supremacy; he must recognise the potential military threat posed by a large capital

---

[55] *Divers Orations*, 21.
[56] *Sociable Letters*, lxviii. As Cavendish mentions here, her father was outlawed by Elizabeth I for killing his opponent in a duel. He went into exile and was only able to return when James I pardoned him in 1604.
[57] *Divers Orations*, 54.    [58] *Sociable Letters*, cxv.    [59] *Divers Orations*, 161–8.

city (as Charles I had failed to do) and take care to maintain control over his army. Equally, if he is to be able to implement his policies, he must fill his treasury, partly through taxation, and partly by encouraging trade and suppressing monopolies. Furthermore, if trade is to flourish he must invest in shipping, on which both prosperity and security depend. Once the seas are safe, merchant adventurers will enrich the commonwealth, thereby increasing their sovereign's independence. These themes are all debated in *Divers Orations*, though the geography and self-sufficiency of the Blazing World conveniently obviate any need for foreign trade or military defences.

At the same time, a monarch must be sure to control print, learning, and religion, all of which are potent sources of faction and rebellion. Cavendish is less adamantly opposed to the wide circulation of printed works than Newcastle who, in his *Advice*, recommends that books about controversial matters should be available only in Latin, and that works liable to encourage dissent should be suppressed. Although two of his wife's orators express this point of view, a third points out that drawing attention to controversial works by censoring them may do more harm than good. This recognition of political complexity is characteristic of Cavendish, and is also echoed in her attitude to learning. While the fictional Duchess of Newcastle advises the Empress of the Blazing World to close down her academies as soon as they threaten to become factious, the Duchess's wisdom is what makes her such a valuable counsellor.

Turning to the pressing issue of religious dissent, Cavendish and Newcastle are united in the view that the power of the sovereign must extend to the church. This point is emphasised in *The Blazing World* when the fictional Duchess argues that, although the power of the Ottoman Emperor appears to be absolute, his greatness is diminished by his inability to alter Mohammedan religion, so that in reality he is governed by priests. In a more local context, however, Cavendish enters what had been a bitter debate about the extent to which preaching should be controlled by the state. Some of the speeches in *Divers Orations* voice support for Newcastle's proposal that the king should exercise direct control over the bishops, who should in turn prescribe the content of sermons, and in her biography of her husband Cavendish praises him for regulating preaching during the Civil War.[60] More expeditiously still, the Empress of the Blazing World avoids all delegation by taking the task of preaching upon

---

[60] *Life of William Cavendish*, p. 11.

herself. In general, however, Cavendish favours religious compromise. She points out that, although absolute liberty leads to factiousness, the imposition of conformity generates fury, and she emphasises that people cannot be forced to hold particular theological beliefs. While it is necessary to suppress sects when they threaten to disrupt security, the most effective way to avoid dissent is to follow the example set in the Blazing World and require only a minimal level of religious conformity. Cavendish's relatively tolerant attitude may have been shaped by her experience of the Netherlands, and was of a piece with the policy that Charles II tried unsuccessfully to impose after the Restoration.[61] It was also consistent with the strikingly heterodox religious views that she herself defended in her philosophical writings. While we can be certain that God exists, she claims, natural reason can teach us virtually nothing about him, so that the detailed theological assertions to be found in established religions are grounded solely on faith.[62]

This agnosticism about theology is allied to a vivid analysis of the significance of devotional practices. Cavendish is keenly aware, for example, that certain styles of preaching can produce what are in her view tasteless and ridiculous emotional responses, and is regularly ironic, and even sarcastic, about the hyperbolical piety of Puritans.[63] However, precisely because people are susceptible to the manner in which ideas are conveyed, she is convinced that the church cannot afford to ignore ceremonial. In the Blazing World, the Empress uses dazzling settings and quasi-magical devices (somewhat akin to the elaborate theatrical effects so popular in Caroline masques) to inspire religious devotion in her subjects. By conducting the rituals of her church herself, she ensures that the worship of the divine sovereign blends conveniently with obeisance to the temporal one, and the dominion of God is identified with that of the state. The link between these domains is created by ceremonies which, together with the related notion of order, play a key role in Cavendish's political philosophy. Through these conventions, ordinary people are transformed into the holders of offices and the bearers of political power, and for want of it 'the state goes down'.[64] Hence Newcastle's rhetorical question to Charles II, 'What is a king more than a subject, but for ceremony and order?'[65]

---

[61] Following the same policy during the 1640s, Newcastle had been criticised by Parliament for allowing Roman Catholics to fight in his army, and had publicly defended himself.
[62] For further details see *Blazing World*, n. to p. 19.
[63] *Sociable Letters*, li, lxxxvi.
[64] *Nature's Pictures*, p. 172. Cf. *Newcastle's Advice*, p. 44.   [65] *Newcastle's Advice*, p. 44.

If a society is to remain stable, so this argument goes, people must be able to recognise those to whom they owe obedience and be willing to obey them. Ceremony creates the first of these conditions by making power visible, and this is why sumptuary laws are an essential ingredient of stability. Cavendish dwells on the need for different ranks to be distinguished by their dress and manners, and worries that the increasingly grand style being adopted by the bourgeoisie in Holland will destabilise the Dutch state.[66] The second condition is met when the trappings of power inspire awe and subservience, and rulers must make use of images of divine splendour to achieve this end. In his *Advice*, Newcastle recommends that Charles II should appear to his people like a god, a suggestion taken to the limit by the Empress of the Blazing World, whose subjects and enemies come to view her as an immortal being.

If ceremony is to have the desired effect, the citizens of a polity must learn to recognise and respond appropriately to performances of power, a disposition generated by custom. Here the theatre plays an important role. One of Cavendish's orators advises a magistrate to set up a company of players at the town's expense, claiming that good players are better than tutors or dancing masters at fashioning the behaviour of young people.[67] Equally, when the Emperor of the Blazing World expresses a wish to put on dramas that will make men wise, the fictional Duchess of Newcastle allows that her own plays would suit the purpose admirably. In answer to the Puritan view that the theatre is profane and corrupting, Cavendish suggests that plays inculcate a habit of responding to performance which carries over into church and state, and also offer images of virtue on which the more and less powerful can model their lives. At the same time, she challenges this argument in some of her own dramas which undercut the very order that ceremony is supposed to maintain. In 'Bel in Campo', for example, the leader of a victorious army of women points out to her troops that they did not know their own powers until they tried them, thus reminding the audience that women may possess capabilities far beyond the ones they are normally expected, or permitted, to exercise.[68]

Cavendish's discussions of the relations between men and women open up vistas which threaten to demolish the social hierarchy she usually defends. On a fictional level, she employs her literary imagination to put aside the constraints of her own social existence and create women such

---

[66] *Sociable Letters*, lxv, xcv. See also *Newcastle's Advice*, pp. 45–6.
[67] *Divers Orations*, 44.     [68] 'Bel in Campo', in *Plays*.

as the Empress and Duchess in *The Blazing World*, who are powerful, childless, untroubled by their devoted but docile husbands, and bound together by conversation and adventure. Such figures recur throughout her writings, but their liberty and resourcefulness contrast starkly with her sombre picture of the condition of living women, whose subjection she sometimes describes as enslavement. Women's suffering is widespread, she claims, but is most intense within marriage, a lottery rightly feared by maids since it exposes them to the risk of physical and psychological torture condoned by the law. The vulnerability of married women, and the failure of the law to treat them as legal subjects, is the theme of some of Cavendish's most striking judicial orations. For instance, a wife who is afraid that her violent husband will kill her asks a court for protection, only to be told by the judge that he has no power to intervene on her behalf because the rights of husbands derive from God and nature. This dark picture of women's condition is, however, only one of the many views that Cavendish offers on the subject. The complexity of her analysis is reflected in the set of female speeches included in *Divers Orations*, in which some women lament their subjection while others extol their power and several examine with varying degrees of scepticism the possibility, as well as the desirability, of social change. By contrast with her attitudes to government, which are largely settled, Cavendish's treatment of the relations between women and men reveals a truly rhetorical ability to see the issue from many points of view.

The works included in this volume address the central political themes that run through Cavendish's writing, but do so in very different styles. *Divers Orations* is relatively straightforward, and I have therefore annotated it lightly. *Blazing World* is a highly allusive fiction that engages with a wide range of seventeenth-century debates. While previous modern editions have mainly left readers to recognise these allusions themselves, I have added a number of notes designed to make Cavendish's text easier to follow, and to provide a guide to the many philosophical and political positions discussed.

# Chronology of Margaret Cavendish

| | |
|---|---|
| 1573 | Birth of Thomas Lucas, Margaret Cavendish's father. |
| 1593 | Birth of William Cavendish, Earl, Marquess, and later Duke of Newcastle. |
| 1595 | Birth of Sir Charles Cavendish, brother of William Cavendish. |
| 1597–1603 | Thomas Lucas outlawed from England by Elizabeth I for killing a relative of Lord Cobham in a duel. |
| Before 1604 | Birth of Margaret's eldest brother Thomas to Elizabeth Leighton, Thomas Lucas's betrothed. |
| 1603 | Death of Elizabeth I; accession of James I, who allows Thomas Lucas to return to England. |
| 1604 | Marriage of Thomas Lucas and Elizabeth Leighton. |
| 1606–17 | Births of John, Mary, Elizabeth, Charles, Anne, and Catherine Lucas, Margaret's siblings. |
| 1618 | Marriage of William Cavendish to Elizabeth Bassett, widow. |
| 1622–30 | Births of Jane, Charles, Elizabeth, Frances, and Henry, children of William and Elizabeth Cavendish. |
| 1623 | Birth of Margaret Lucas, eighth and last child of Thomas and Elizabeth Lucas, of St John's Abbey, Colchester. |
| 1625 | Death of Margaret's father. Death of James I and accession of Charles I. |
| 1633 | William Cavendish entertains Charles I at Welbeck Abbey. Ben Jonson writes a masque for the occasion. |

| | |
|---|---|
| 1634 | William Cavendish entertains Charles I and Queen Henrietta Maria at Bolsover Castle. Jonson provides another masque. |
| 1638 | William Cavendish appointed Governor to Charles, Prince of Wales, then aged seven. |
| 1639 | William Cavendish made Privy Councillor. |
| 1640 | November: opening of Long Parliament. |
| 1641 | William Cavendish implicated in the Army Plot. At Parliament's request, Charles I relieves him of post as Governor to Prince of Wales. |
| | Margaret Lucas's home threatened by local people opposed to the king. |
| 1642 | The court leaves London for Oxford. |
| | The Lucas family's house again attacked; Elizabeth Lucas moves her household to Oxford. |
| | William Cavendish raises an army in the north and takes York. |
| 1643 | April: death of Elizabeth, William Cavendish's wife. |
| | October: William Cavendish created Marquess of Newcastle. |
| | Margaret Lucas joins Queen Henrietta Maria's court in Oxford as maid of honour. |
| 1644 | Henrietta Maria and her court leave for Paris. |
| | William Cavendish's army heavily defeated at Marston Moor. He, his two sons, and Charles Cavendish leave England for Hamburg. |
| 1645 | April: William Cavendish arrives at Henrietta Maria's court in Paris. |
| | December: Margaret Lucas marries William Cavendish. |
| 1646 | May: Charles I captured by Scots. |
| | July: Charles, Prince of Wales arrives in Paris. |
| 1647 | January: Charles I handed over to Parliament. |
| | Deaths of Margaret Cavendish's brother, sister, and mother. |
| | In Paris, William and Charles Cavendish in contact with Hobbes, then tutor in mathematics to the Prince of Wales, and with Descartes, Gassendi, and Mersenne. |

| | |
|---|---|
| 1648 | Charles Lucas, Margaret Cavendish's brother, attempts to hold Colchester against parliamentary army. When Royalists surrender in August, Lucas shot under martial law; Lucas family tomb desecrated. October: Cavendish household moves to Antwerp. December: Charles I tried. |
| 1649 | January: Charles I executed in London. March: Act of Parliament abolishes monarchy. March: Parliament sentences William Cavendish to death for treason and confiscates his estates. Two plays by William Cavendish, *The Country Captain* and *The Variety*, published at The Hague and in London. |
| 1650 | William Cavendish made Privy Councillor to Charles II. Negotiates with the Elector of Brandenburg for troops to attack English Commonwealth. |
| 1651 | Charles II leads Scots into England; defeated by Oliver Cromwell. November: Charles Cavendish returns to London to petition for return of estates. Margaret Cavendish accompanies him to petition for a pension due to wives of Royalists denied right to compound for their estates. Her petition refused. |
| 1652 | Margaret Cavendish stays in England, writing *Poems and Fancies*. |
| 1653 | Margaret Cavendish returns to Antwerp. Publishes *Poems and Fancies* and *Philosophical Fancies*. |
| 1654 | Death of Sir Charles Cavendish, William Cavendish's younger brother. |
| 1655 | Publication of *The World's Olio* (2nd edn 1671) and *Philosophical and Physical Opinions*. |
| 1656 | Publication of *Nature's Pictures* (2nd edn 1671), including 'A True Relation of my Birth and Breeding'. |
| 1658 | Publication at Antwerp of William Cavendish's *La Méthode Nouvelle et Invention Extraordinaire de Dresser les Chevaux*. September: Death of Cromwell. |

| | |
|---|---|
| 1659 | Death of Charles, William Cavendish's eldest son. |
| 1660 | Restoration of Charles II. |
| | May: William Cavendish returns to England; his honours and estates restored. |
| | September: Margaret Cavendish returns to England. William Cavendish made Gentleman of Bedchamber and reappointed Lord Lieutenant of Nottinghamshire. |
| | Retires with Margaret to Welbeck Abbey. |
| 1662 | Publication of *Playes* and *Orations of Divers Sorts*. |
| | Royal Society of London incorporated by Charles II. |
| 1664 | Publication of *Philosophical Letters* amd *Sociable Letters*. |
| 1665 | William Cavendish created Duke of Newcastle. |
| 1666 | Publication of *Observations upon Experimental Philosophy* and *A Description of a New World called the Blazing World* (2nd edn 1668). |
| 1667 | May: Margaret Cavendish attends Royal Society. |
| | Publication of *The Life of the Thrice Noble, High and Puissant Prince William Cavendish, Duke, Marquess and Earl of Newcastle*. |
| 1668 | Publication of *Plays Never Before Printed*. |
| 1673 | December: Death of Margaret Cavendish. Buried in Westminster Abbey. |
| 1676 | Publication of *Letters and Poems in Honour of the Incomparable Princess, Margaret, Duchess of Newcastle*. |
| | Death of William Cavendish. |

# Further reading

Cavendish oversaw the publication of her own works and, until the twentieth century, no further editions were published. The present volume contains the first modern edition of *Divers Orations*. An edition of *The Blazing World*, together with two extracts from *Nature's Pictures*, was produced by Kate Lilley and published by Penguin Books in 1992. Since then, several further anthologies and editions of individual works have appeared. *Paper Bodies: A Margaret Cavendish Reader*, ed. Sylvia Bowerbank and Sara Mendelson (Ontario: Broadview Press, 1999) contains a useful selection and an excellent introduction. The following complete works have been republished: *The Life of the (1st) Duke of Newcastle and Other Writings by Margaret Duchess* (London and Toronto: J. M. Dent and Sons, 1916); *Margaret Cavendish: Sociable Letters*, ed. James Fitzmaurice (New York: Garland, 1997); *The Atomic Poems of Margaret (Lucas) Cavendish*, ed. Leigh Tilman Partington (Women Writers' Resource Project at the Lewis Beck Center, Emory University); *The Convent of Pleasure and Other Plays*, ed. Anne Shaver (Baltimore: Johns Hopkins University Press, 1999); *Grounds of Natural Philosophy*, introduction by Colette V. Michael (West Cornwall, CT: Locust Hill Press, 1996); *Observations upon Experimental Philosophy*, ed. Eileen O'Neill (Cambridge: Cambridge University Press, 2001).

Cavendish wrote an account of her own life, 'A True Relation of my Birth and Breeding', which she published in a collection of short pieces, *Nature's Pictures* (1671). There have been several subsequent biographies, including Douglas Grant, *Margaret the First* (Toronto: University of Toronto Press, 1957) and Kathleen Jones, *A Glorious Fame: The Life of Margaret Cavendish, Duchess of Newcastle 1623–1673* (London:

Bloomsbury, 1988). In 1667 Cavendish published *The Life of the Thrice Noble, High and Puissant Prince William Cavendish, Duke, Marquess and Earl of Newcastle*. This contains information relating to her own life, as does Geoffrey Trease's biography of her husband, *Portrait of a Cavalier: William Cavendish, First Duke of Newcastle* (London: Macmillan, 1979). Letters from Margaret to William are included in *The Phanseys of William Cavendish, Marquis of Newcastle, Addressed to Margaret Lucas*, ed. Douglas Grant (London: Nonsuch, 1956) and in *Letters of Margaret Lucas to her Future Husband*, ed. Richard William Goulding (London: John Murray, 1909). They are reprinted in Anna Battigelli, *Margaret Cavendish and the Exiles of the Mind* (Lexington: University Press of Kentucky, 1998), Appendix B. The judgements of some of her contemporaries can be found in *Letters and Poems in Honour of the Incomparable Princess, Margaret, Duchess of Newcastle* (1676).

Discussions of *Blazing World* often focus on its utopian and feminist themes. See Kate Lilley, 'Blazing Worlds: Seventeenth-Century Women's Writing' in Clare Brant and Diane Purkiss eds., *Women, Texts and Histories 1575–1760* (London and New York: Routledge, 1992); Marina Leslie, 'Gender, Genre and the Utopian Body in Margaret Cavendish's Blazing World', *Utopian Studies* 7.1 (1996), pp. 6–24; Rosemary Kegl, 'Margaret Cavendish, Feminism and the Blazing World' in Valerie Traub, M. Lindsay Kaplan, and Dympna Callaghan eds., *Feminist Readings in Early Modern Culture: Emerging Subjects* (Cambridge: Cambridge University Press, 1996), pp. 119–41; Rachael Trubowitz, 'The Reenchantment of Utopia and the Female Monarchical Self: Margaret Cavendish's Blazing World', *Tulsa Studies in Women's Literature* 11 (1992), pp. 229–46; Lee Cullen Khanna, 'The Subject of Utopia: Margaret Cavendish and her Blazing-World' in Jane A. Donawerth and Carol A. Kolmerten eds., *Utopian and Science Fiction by Women: Worlds of Difference* (Syracuse: Syracuse University Press, 1994), pp. 15–34; Ellayne Fowler, 'Margaret Cavendish and the Ideal Commonwealth', *Utopian Studies*, St Louis, 7.1 (1996), pp. 38–48; Carrie Hintz, 'But One Opinion: Fear of Dissent in Cavendish's New Blazing World', *Utopian Studies*, St Louis, 7.1. (1996), pp. 25–37; Earla A. Wilputte, 'Margaret Cavendish's Imaginary Voyage to "The Blazing World": Mapping a Feminine Discourse' in Donald W. Nichol ed., *Transatlantic Crossings: Eighteenth-Century Explorations* (Newfoundland, 1995), pp. 109–17; Patricia Parker, *Literary Fat Ladies: Gender, Rhetoric, Property* (London, 1987); Mary Baine Campbell, *Wonder and Science: Imagining Worlds in Early Modern Europe* (Ithaca:

Cornell University Press, 1999); Nicole Pohl, ' "Of Mixt natures": Questions of Genre in Margaret Cavendish's *The Blazing World*' in Stephen Clucas ed., *A Princely Brave Woman. Essays on Margaret Cavendish Duchess of Newcastle* (London: Ashgate, 2003). For a useful introduction to the lives of women in the seventeenth century see Jacqueline Eales, *Women in Early Modern England, 1500–1700* (London: UCL Press, 1988).

Some of these studies also consider *Blazing World* as a defence of political absolutism. This theme is further discussed by Oddvar Holmesland, 'Margaret Cavendish's Blazing World: Natural Art and Body Politics', *Studies in Philology* 96 (1999), pp. 457–79; Catherine Gallagher, 'Embracing the Absolute: the Politics of the Female Subject in Seventeenth-Century England', *Genders* 1 (1988), pp. 24–39; Claire Jowitt, 'Imperial Dreams, Margaret Cavendish and the Cult of Elizabeth', *Women's Writing* 4.3 (1997), pp. 84–101.

The political issues broached in *Blazing World* and *Orations* are also treated in some of Cavendish's plays. See Sophie Tomlinson, 'My Brain the Stage: Margaret Cavendish and the Fantasy of Female Performance' in Clare Brant and Diane Purkiss eds., *Women, Texts and Histories 1575–1760* (London and New York: Routledge, 1992), pp. 134–63; Laura J. Rosenthal, *Playwrights and Plagiarists in Early Modern England: Gender, Authorship, Literary Property* (Ithaca and London: Cornell University Press, 1996), pp. 58–104; M. Straznicky, 'Reading the Stage: Margaret Cavendish and Commonwealth Closet Drama', *Criticism. A Quarterly for Literature and the Arts* 37.3 (1996), pp. 355–90; Susan Wiseman, 'Gender and Status in Dramatic Discourse: Margaret Cavendish, Duchess of Newcastle' in Isobel Grundy and Susan Wiseman eds., *Women, Writing, History 1640–1740* (London: B. T. Batsford, 1992), pp. 161–77.

More general discussions of political philosophy in seventeenth-century England can be found in J. P. Sommerville, *Politics and Ideology in England 1603–40*, 2nd edn (Harlow: Longman, 1999); Gordon Schochet, *Patriarchalism in Political Thought* (Oxford: Blackwell, 1975); Margaret R. Sommerville, *Sex and Subjection: Attitudes to Women in Early Modern Society* (London: Arnold, 1995); Richard Tuck, *Philosophy and Government, 1572–1651* (Cambridge: Cambridge University Press, 1993); Paul Seaward, *The Cavalier Parliament and the Reconstruction of the Old Regime, 1661–1667* (Cambridge University Press, 1988) and *The Restoration* (London: Macmillan, 1991). Also relevant is *Ideology and Politics on the Eve of the Restoration: Newcastle's Advice to Charles II*, introd. by

Thomas P. Slaughter (Philadelphia: The American Philosophical Society, 1984).

On Cavendish's thirst for fame see Lilley, 'Blazing Worlds'; James Fitzmaurice, 'Fancy and the Family: Self-Characterisations of Margaret Cavendish', *Huntington Library Quarterly* 53 (1990), pp. 199–209; Jean Gagen, 'Honour and Fame in the Works of the Duchess of Newcastle', *Studies in Philology* 56 (1959), pp. 519–38; Sidonie Smith, 'The Ragged Rout of Self. Margaret Cavendish's True Relation and the Heroics of Self-Disclosure' in *A Poetics of Women's Autobiography. Marginality and the Fictions of Self-Representation* (Bloomington and Indianapolis: Indiana University Press, 1987), pp. 84–101.

Rather little has been written about *Orations*. On Cavendish's use of rhetoric see Jane Donawerth, 'Conversation and the Boundaries of Public Discourse in Rhetorical Theory by Renaissance Women', *Rhetorica* 16.2 (1998), pp. 181–99; Amy Scott Douglas, 'Self-Crowned Laureates: Towards a Historical Revaluation of Margaret Cavendish's Prefaces', *Pretexts: Literary and Cultural Studies* 9.1 (2000), pp. 27–49. On the general topic of rhetoric in early-modern writing see Quentin Skinner, *Reason and Rhetoric in the Philosophy of Hobbes* (Cambridge: Cambridge University Press, 1996), Part I; R. Helgerson, *Self-Crowned Laureates: Spenser, Jonson, Milton and the Literary System* (Berkeley: University of California Press, 1983); Kevin Dunn, *Pretexts of Authority. The Rhetoric of Authorship in the Renaissance Period* (Stanford: Stanford University Press, 1994); John M. McManamon, *Funeral Oratory and the Cultural Ideals of Italian Humanism* (Chapel Hill: University of North Carolina Press, 1989); O. B. Hardison, *The Enduring Monument* (Chapel Hill: University of North Carolina Press, 1989).

On the relations between Cavendish's natural philosophy and her political writings see John Rogers, *The Matter of Revolution: Science, Poetry and Politics in the Age of Milton* (Ithaca and London: Cornell University Press, 1996); Anna Battigelli, *Margaret Cavendish and the Exiles of the Mind* (Lexington: University Press of Kentucky, 1998); Jay Stevenson, 'The Mechanist-Vitalist Soul of Margaret Cavendish', *Studies in English Literature 1500–1900* 36.3 (1996), pp. 527–43; E. Keller, 'Producing Petty Gods: Margaret Cavendish's Critique of Experimental Science', *English Literary History* 64.2 (1997), pp. 447–72.

Cavendish's discussion of natural philosophy in *Blazing World* is part of a wide-ranging and systematic philosophical view developed in several different works, especially *Observations upon Experimental Philosophy*, *Philosophical and Physical Opinions*, and *Philosophical Letters*. On the scientific and philosophical context see Robert Hugh Kargon, *Atomism in England from Hariot to Newton* (Oxford: Oxford University Press, 1966); Michael Hunter, *Science and Society in Restoration England* (Cambridge: Cambridge University Press, 1981).

On Cavendish's position as a woman philosopher see Sarah Hutton, 'Anne Conway, Margaret Cavendish and Seventeenth-Century Scientific Thought' and Frances Harris, 'Living in the Neighbourhood of Science: Mary Evelyn, Margaret Cavendish and the Greshamites' in Lynette Hunter and Sarah Hutton eds., *Women, Science and Medicine, 1500–1700* (Stroud, Gloucestershire: Phoenix Mill, 1997), pp. 198–217; Londa Schiebinger, 'Margaret Cavendish, Duchess of Newcastle' in Mary Ellen Waite ed., *A History of Women Philosophers* (Dordrecht: Kluwer Academic Publishers, 1991), 3 vols., vol. III, pp. 1–20; Eileen O'Neill, 'Disappearing Ink: Early Modern Women Philosophers and their Fate in History' in Janet Kourany ed., *Philosophy in a Feminist Voice* (Princeton: Princeton University Press, 1998).

For more detailed discussions of Cavendish's natural philosophy, see Lisa Sarasohn, 'A World Turned Upside Down. Feminism and the Natural Philosophy of Margaret Cavendish', *Huntington Library Quarterly* 47 (1984), pp. 289–307; Sarah Hutton, 'In Dialogue with Thomas Hobbes. Margaret Cavendish's Natural Philosophy', *Women's Writing* 4.3 (1997), pp. 421–32, and 'Margaret Cavendish and Henry More' in Stephen Clucas ed., *A Princely Brave Woman. Essays on Margaret Cavendish Duchess of Newcastle* (London: Ashgate, 2003), pp. 185–98; Stephen Clucas, 'The Atomism of the Cavendish Circle. A Reappraisal', *The Seventeenth Century* 9.2 (1994), pp. 247–73 and 'The Duchess and the Viscountess: Negotiations between Mechanism and Vitalism in the Natural Philosophies of Margaret Cavendish and Anne Conway', *In-Between: Essays and Studies in Literary Criticism* 9 (2000), pp. 125–36 and 'Variation, Irregularity and Probabilism: Margaret Cavendish and Natural Philosophy as Rhetoric' in Stephen Clucas ed., *A Princely Brave Woman. Essays on Margaret Cavendish Duchess of Newcastle* (London: Ashgate, 2003), pp. 199–209; Susan James, 'The Innovations of Margaret Cavendish', *British Journal for the History of Philosophy* 7.2 (1999), pp. 219–44; Rebecca Merrens, 'A Nature of "Infinite Sense and Reason": Margaret Cavendish's Natural Philosophy and the "Noise" of a Feminised Nature',

*Women's Studies* 2 (1996), pp. 421–38; Jo Wallwork, 'Margaret Cavendish's Response to Hooke's *Micrographia*', *Meridian* 18.1 (2001), pp. 191–200; Mary Baine Campbell, *Wonder and Science: Imagining Worlds in Early Modern Europe* (Ithaca: Cornell University Press, 1999); Jacqueline Broad, *Women Philosophers of the Seventeenth Century* (Cambridge: Cambridge University Press, 2002), pp. 35–64.

The
Description
of a New
World,
Called
The Blazing World.
Written
By the Thrice Noble, Illustrious, and Excellent
Princess,
the Duchess of Newcastle.

# TO THE DUCHESS OF NEWCASTLE, ON HER NEW BLAZING WORLD

Our Elder World, with all their Skill and Arts
Could but divide the World into three Parts:
Columbus then for Navigation fam'd,
Found a new World, America 'tis nam'd:
Now this new World was fou'nd, it was not made,
Only discovered, lying in Time's shade.
Then what are You, having no Chaos found
To make a World, or any such least ground?
But your creating Fancy, thought it fit
To make your World of Nothing, but pure Wit.
Your Blazing-world, beyond the Stars mounts higher,
Enlightens all with a Celestial Fire.

*William Newcastle*

# To the reader[1]

If you wonder, that I join a work of fancy to my serious philosophical contemplations;[2] think not that it is out of a disparagement to philosophy; or out of an opinion, as if this noble study were but a fiction of the mind; for though philosophers may err in searching and enquiring after the causes of natural effects, and many times embrace falsehoods for truths; yet this doth not prove, that the ground of philosophy is merely fiction, but the error proceeds from the different motions of reason, which cause different opinions in different parts, and in some are more irregular than in others; for reason being dividable, because material, cannot move in all parts alike; and since there is but one truth in nature, all those that hit not this truth, do err, some more, some less; for though some may come nearer the mark than others, which makes their opinions seem more probable and rational than others; yet as long as they swerve from this only truth, they are in the wrong: nevertheless, all do ground their opinions upon reason; that is, upon rational probabilities, at least, they think they do: But *fictions* are an issue of man's fancy, framed in his own mind, according as he pleases, without regard, whether the thing he fancies, be really existent without his mind or not; so that reason searches the depth of nature, and enquires after the true causes of natural effects; but fancy creates of its own accord whatsoever it pleases, and delights in its own work. The end of reason, is truth; the end of fancy, is fiction: but mistake me not, when I distinguish *fancy* from reason; I mean not as if fancy were not made by the rational parts of matter; but by *reason* I understand a rational search and enquiry into the causes of natural effects; and by *fancy* a voluntary creation or production of the mind, both being effects, or rather actions

[1] Cavendish printed many prefaces, usually several per work. She uses them to position herself in relation to her various audiences. See Amy Scott Douglas, 'Self-Crowned Laureates: Towards a Historical Revaluation of Margaret Cavendish's Prefaces', *Pretexts: Literary and Cultural Studies* 9.1 (2000), pp. 27–49.

[2] The 1666 and 1668 editions of *The Blazing World* were published together with *Observations on Experimental Philosophy*, a critique of the experimental method advocated by the Royal Society. Cavendish's attack on this approach to natural philosophy is followed by the *Blazing World*, a work of fancy or a fiction. Unlike most seventeenth-century philosophers, who made a firm distinction between reason and fancy, Cavendish stresses their interconnections. By presenting *Observations* and *Blazing World* as 'two worlds' joined at their poles, she encourages her readers to move between philosophy and fiction. See Rosemary Kegl, 'Margaret Cavendish, Feminism and the Blazing World' in Valerie Traub, M. Lindsay Kaplan, and Dympna Callaghan eds., *Feminist Readings in Early Modern Culture: Emerging Subjects* (Cambridge: Cambridge University Press, 1996), pp. 126–34.

of the rational parts of matter; of which, as that is a more profitable and useful study than this, so it is also more laborious and difficult, and requires sometimes the help of fancy, to recreate the mind, and withdraw it from its more serious contemplations.

And this is the reason, why I added this piece of fancy to my philosophical observations, and joined them as two worlds at the ends of their poles; both for my own sake, to divert my studious thoughts, which I employed in the contemplation thereof, and to delight the reader with variety, which is always pleasing. But lest my fancy should stray too much, I chose such a fiction as would be agreeable to the subject treated of in the former parts; it is a description of a new world, not such as Lucian's, or the *French*-man's world in the moon;[3] but a world of my own creating, which I call the *Blazing World*: the first part whereof is *romancical*, the second philosophical, and the third is merely *fancy*, or (as I may call it) *fantastical*, which if it add any satisfaction to you, I shall account my self a happy *creatoress*, if not, I must be content to live a melancholy life in my own world; I cannot call it a poor world, if poverty be only want of gold, silver, and jewels; for there is more gold in it than all the chemists[4] ever did, and (as I verily believe) will ever be able to make. As for the rocks of diamonds, I wish with all my soul they might be shared amongst my noble female friends, and upon that condition, I would willingly quit my part; and of the gold I should only desire so much as might suffice to repair my noble lord and husband's losses:[5] for I am not covetous, but as ambitious as ever any of my sex was, is, or can be; which makes, that though I cannot be *Henry* the Fifth, or *Charles* the Second, yet I endeavour to be *Margaret the First*;[6] and although I have neither power, time nor occasion to conquer the world as *Alexander* and *Caesar* did; yet rather than not to be mistress of one, since Fortune and the Fates would give me none, I have made a world of my own: for which no body, I hope, will blame me, since it is in every one's power to do the like.

---

[3] Lucian of Samosata (*c.*125–200 CE), author of *Vera Historia, An Imaginary Voyage*, trans. Francis Hickes, in *Certain Select Dialogues of Lucian together with his True History* (1634). 'The Frenchman' is probably Savinien Cyrano de Bergerac (1620–55), author of *Histoires comiques contenant les états et empires de la lune* (*Comic Stories containing the States and Empires of the Moon*) (1657), but is possibly a reference to Pierre Borel, *Discours nouveau prouvant la pluralité des mondes* (*New Discourse proving the plurality of worlds*) (Geneva, 1657).
[4] Alchemists.  [5] See Introduction, p. xiv and p. xvi.
[6] On Cavendish's desire for fame see Introduction, p. xviii.

# THE DESCRIPTION OF A NEW WORLD,
# CALLED THE BLAZING WORLD[7]

A merchant travelling into a foreign country, fell extremely in love with a young Lady;[8] but being a stranger in that nation, and beneath her both in birth and wealth, he could have but little hopes of obtaining his desire; however his love growing more and more vehement upon him, even to the slighting of all difficulties, he resolved at last to steal her away; which he had the better opportunity to do, because her father's house was not far from the sea, and she often using to gather shells upon the shore, accompanied not with above two or three of her servants, it encouraged him the more to execute his design. Thus coming one time with a little light vessel, not unlike a packet-boat, manned with some few sea-men, and well victualled for fear of some accidents which might perhaps retard their journey to the place where she used to repair, he forced her away: But when he fancied himself the happiest man of the world, he proved to be the most unfortunate; for Heaven frowning at his theft, raised such a tempest, as they knew not what to do, or whither to steer their course; so that the vessel, both by its own lightness, and the violent motion of the wind, was carried as swift as an arrow out of a bow, towards the North Pole, and in a short time reached the Icy Sea, where the wind forced it amongst huge pieces of ice;[9] but being little, and light, it did by assistance

---

[7] In 1605, Joseph Hall published *The Discovery of a New World. A Description of the South Indies Hitherto Unknown*, by an English Mercury, an English translation of a work which had appeared in Latin. Hall's traveller makes his way to Womaniecoia or Shee-landt, a land ruled by women where the provinces are called Tattlingen, Scoldonna, Blubbertck, etc., and the principal city is called Gospingoa. Cavendish's title may allude to this work. It also more distantly echoes the title of a masque by Ben Jonson, performed in 1620, 'News from a New World Discovered in the Moon'. Since Cavendish's husband, the Marquess of Newcastle, had commissioned two masques from Jonson, it is possible that she had heard of it.

[8] The Lady is referred to throughout by her rank, as she is when she becomes the Empress. Cavendish is deeply concerned with status. Cf. 'Some ladies th'other day did visit me, and in their discourse they spoke of the Duke of D the Marquess of C the Earl of F and Viscount G but I observed that in their discourse, they only gave them the title of a lord; 'tis true a lord is a noble title, but yet the fore-mentioned titles be of higher degrees, by which they ought to be mentioned or named; truly, in my opinion, those men and women that do not give every person their highest titles are either ill-bred, foolish or spiteful, for it is through envy, or a low, base nature, to detract, or take from any one his just rights and dues, but noble, generous and heroic persons will rather give more than what is due than lessen ones due rights', *Sociable Letters*, clxxvi. Cavendish gained the title of Duchess of Newcastle in 1665 when her husband received a dukedom.

[9] In *New Experiments and Observations touching Cold* (1665), Boyle includes reports of voyages to the Arctic. E.g. 'The 17th of May we sailed by many great islands of ice, some of which

7

and favour of the Gods to this virtuous Lady, so turn and wind through those precipices, as if it had been guided by some experienced pilot, and skilful mariner: but alas! those few men which were in it, not knowing whither they went, nor what was to be done in so strange an adventure, and not being provided for so cold a voyage, were all frozen to death, the young Lady only, by the light of her beauty, the heat of her youth, and protection of the gods, remaining alive: neither was it a wonder that the men did freeze to death; for they were not only driven to the very end or point of the Pole of that world, but even to another Pole of another world,[10] which joined close to it; so that the cold having a double strength at the conjunction of those two Poles, was insupportable: at last, the boat still passing on, was forced into another world, for it is impossible to round this world's globe from Pole to Pole, so as we do from East to West; because the Poles of the other world, joining to the Poles of this, do not allow any further passage to surround the world that way; but if any one arrives to either of these Poles, he is either forced to return, or to enter into another world; and lest you should scruple at it, and think, if it were thus, those that live at the Poles would either see two suns at one time, or else they would never want the sun's light for six months together, as it is commonly believed; you must know, that each of these

---

were above two hundred feet high above the water', and 'In June all the sea as far as he could see from the top of a high hill was covered with ice', Michael Hunter and Edward B. Davis eds., *Works of Robert Boyle*, 14 vols. (London: Pickering and Chatto, 1999) (hereafter WRB), vol. IV, p. 353.

[10] The theme of multiple worlds was widely explored in the seventeenth century. See Steven J. Dick, *Plurality of Worlds* (Cambridge: Cambridge University Press, 1982). Aristotle had argued that Earth is unique, but the revival of atomism, together with astronomical discoveries, put this in doubt. Kepler, Galileo, Mersenne, and Descartes among others debated whether other worlds could or did exist, and whether they could be inhabited. For English contributions to this discussion see John Wilkins, *Discovery of a World in the Moone, or, A Discourse Tending to Prove, that 'tis Probable There May be another Habitable World in That Planet* (1638); Walter Charleton, *Physiologia Epicuro-Gassendo-Charletoniana or a Fabric of Science upon the Hypothesis of Atoms* (1654); Henry More, *Democritus Platonissans or an Essay upon the Infinity of Worlds out of Platonic Principles* (1646). Thomas White argued in *De Mundo* that there is only one world. Thomas Hobbes replied that there could be several contiguous worlds. See *Thomas White's De Mundo Examined*, trans. Harold Whitmore Jones (London: Bradford University Press in association with Crosby Lockwood Staples, 1976), pp. 39–46. Cavendish aims to reconcile her own account of matter with the view that there can be many worlds. See *Philosophical and Physical Opinions*, Part 13, chapter 14 and Appendix part 2. In a postscript to this work, Newcastle endorses Galileo's view that the planets are a separate world. See also Anna Battigelli, *Margaret Cavendish and the Exiles of the Mind* (Lexington: University Press of Kentucky, 1998), pp. 53–4.

worlds having its own sun to enlighten it, they move each one in their peculiar circles; which motion is so just and exact, that neither can hinder or obstruct the other; for they do not exceed their tropics, and although they should meet, yet we in this world cannot so well perceive them, by reason of the brightness of our sun, which being nearer to us, obstructs the splendour of the suns of the other worlds, they being too far off to be discerned by our optic perception, except we use very good telescopes, by which skilful astronomers have often observed two or three suns at once.[11]

But to return to the wandering boat, and the distressed Lady, she seeing all the men dead, found small comfort in life; their bodies which were preserved all that while from putrefaction and stench, by the extremity of cold, began now to thaw, and corrupt; whereupon she having not strength enough to fling them over-board, was forced to remove out of her small cabin, upon the deck, to avoid that nauseous smell; and finding the boat swim between two plains of ice, as a stream that runs betwixt two shores, at last perceived land, but covered all with snow: from which came walking upon the ice strange creatures, in shape like bears, only they went upright as men; those creatures coming near the boat, catched hold of it with their paws, that served them instead of hands; some two or three of them entered first; and when they came out, the rest went in one after another; at last having viewed and observed all that was in the boat, they spoke to each other in a language which the Lady did not understand, and having carried her out of the boat, sunk it, together with the dead men.

The Lady now finding herself in so strange a place, and amongst such a wonderful kind of creatures, was extremely stricken with fear, and could entertain no other thoughts, but that every moment her life was to be a sacrifice to their cruelty; but those bear-like creatures, how terrible soever they appeared to her sight, yet were they so far from exercising any cruelty upon her, that rather they showed her all civility and kindness imaginable; for she being not able to go upon the ice, by reason of its slipperiness, they took her up in their rough arms, and carried her into their city, where instead of houses, they had caves under ground; and as

---

[11] Telescopic observations, including those of Galileo, had added weight to the hypothesis that the fixed stars might be suns (and thus the centres of solar systems). Newcastle endorses the first part of this view in his 'Opinion Concerning the Ground of Natural Philosophy' appended to *Physical and Philosophical Opinions*. Cavendish discusses it in *Sociable Letters*, cxi.

soon as they entered the city, both males and females, young and old, flocked together to see this Lady, holding up their paws in admiration; at last having brought her into a certain large and spacious cave, which they intended for her reception, they left her to the custody of the females, who entertained her with all kindness and respect, and gave her such victuals as they were used to eat; but seeing her constitution neither agreed with the temper of that climate, nor their diet, they were resolved to carry her into another island of a warmer temper; in which were men like foxes, only walking in an upright shape, who received their neighbours the bear-men with great civility and courtship, very much admiring this beauteous Lady, and having discoursed some while together, agreed at last to make her a present to the Emperor of their world; to which end, after she had made some short stay in the same place, they brought her cross that island to a large river, whose stream ran smooth and clear, like crystal; in which were numerous boats, much like our foxtraps; in one whereof she was carried, some of the bear- and fox-men waiting on her; and as soon as they had crossed the river, they came into an island where there were men which had heads, beaks, and feathers like wild-geese, only they went in an upright shape, like the bear-men and fox-men; their rumps they carried between their legs, their wings were of the same length with their bodies, and their tails of an indifferent size, trailing after them like a lady's garment; and after the bear- and fox-men had declared their intention and design to their neighbours, the geese- or bird-men, some of them joined to the rest, and attended the Lady through that island, till they came to another great and large river, where there was a preparation made of many boats, much like birds' nests, only of a bigger size; and having crossed that river, they arrived into another island, which was of a pleasant and mild temper, full of woods, and the inhabitants thereof were satyrs, who received both the bear-, fox- and bird-men, with all respect and civility; and after some conferences (for they all understood each other's language) some chief of the satyrs joining to them, accompanied the Lady out of that island to another river, wherein were very handsome and commodious barges; and having crossed that river, they entered into a large and spacious kingdom, the men whereof were of a grass-green complexion, who entertained them very kindly, and provided all conveniences for their further voyage: hitherto they had only crossed rivers, but now they could not avoid the open seas any longer; wherefore they made their ships and tacklings ready to sail over into the island, where the Emperor of their Blazing World (for so it was called) kept his residence; very good navigators they were; and though they had no knowledge of the lodestone, or needle, or pendulous watches,[12] yet (which was as serviceable to them) they had subtle observations, and great practice; insomuch that they could not only tell the depth of the sea in every place, but where there were shelves of sand, rocks, and other obstructions to be avoided by skilful and experienced sea-men: besides, they were excellent augurers, which skill they counted more necessary and beneficial than the use of compasses, cards, watches, and the like; but above the rest, they had an extraordinary art, much to be taken notice of by experimental philosophers, and that was a certain engine,[13] which would draw in a great quantity of air, and shoot forth wind with a great force; this engine in a calm, they placed behind their ships, and in a storm, before; for it served against the raging waves, like canons against an hostile army, or besieged town. It would batter and beat the waves in pieces, were they as high as steeples; and as soon as a breach was made, they forced their passage through, in spite even of the most furious wind, using two of those engines at every ship, one before, to beat off the waves, and another behind to drive it on; so that the artificial wind had the better of the natural; for it had a greater advantage of the waves than the natural of the ships; the natural being above the face of the water, could not without a down-right motion enter or press into the ships, whereas the artificial with a sideward motion did pierce into the bowels of the waves: moreover, it is to be observed, that in a great tempest they would join their ships in battle array, and when they feared wind and waves would be too strong for them, if they divided their ships, they joined as many together as the compass or advantage of the places of the liquid element would give them leave; for their ships were so ingeniously contrived, that they could fasten them together as close as a honey-comb without waste of place,

---

[12] Navigational devices. Loadstone (iron oxide) was used by navigators as a compass. In the 1660s pendulum watches were used for measuring longitude. The results of a trial were reported in the *Philosophical Transactions of the Royal Society* in March 1665, pp. 13–15.

[13] Cf. 'we have . . . engines for multiplying and enforcing of winds, to set also on going divers motions', Francis Bacon, 'The New Atlantis' in *Francis Bacon*, ed. B. Vickers (Oxford: Oxford University Press, 1996), p. 481. Technological expertise contributes to the astonishing quality of the world Cavendish depicts, as to *The New Atlantis* (1627). Cavendish agrees with Bacon that scientific enquiry should be useful. See her dedicatory letter to the Duke of Newcastle in *Observations on Experimental Philosophy*, where she describes him as a virtuoso who owns as many and as good optic glasses as anyone else, but who devotes himself to the noble and heroic art of horsemanship and weapons, the sweet art of poetry and the useful art of architecture. See also the *Preface* for her complaint that viewing minute creatures through a microscope, or sunspots through a telescope, will not give us practical knowledge of gardening, husbandry, or painting.

and being thus united, no wind nor waves were able to separate them. The Emperor's ships were all of gold, but the merchants and skippers of leather; the golden ships were not much heavier than ours of wood, by reason they were neatly made, and required not such thickness, neither were they troubled with pitch, tar, pumps, guns, and the like, which make our wooden ships very heavy; for though they were not all of a piece, yet they were so well soddered,[14] that there was no fear of leaks, chinks, or clefts; and as for guns, there was no use of them, because they had no other enemies but the winds; but the leather ships were not altogether so sure, although much lighter; besides, they were pitched to keep out water.

Having thus prepared and ordered their navy,[15] they went on in despite of calm or storm, and though the Lady at first fancied herself in a very sad condition, and her mind was much tormented with doubts and fears, not knowing whether this strange adventure would tend to her safety or destruction; yet she being withal of a generous spirit, and ready wit, considering what dangers she had passed, and finding those sorts of men civil and diligent attendants to her, took courage, and endeavoured to learn their language; which after she had obtained so far, that partly by some words and signs she was able to apprehend their meaning, she was so far from being afraid of them that she thought her self not only safe but very happy in their company: by which we may see, that novelty discomposes the mind, but acquaintance settles it in peace and tranquillity. At last, having passed by several rich islands and kingdoms, they went towards Paradise,[16] which was the seat of the Emperor; and coming in sight of it, rejoiced very much; the Lady at first could perceive nothing but high rocks, which seemed to touch the skies; and although they appeared not of an equal height, yet they seemed to be all one piece, without partitions; but at last drawing nearer, she perceived a cleft, which was a part of those rocks, out of which she spied coming forth a great number of boats, which

---

[14] Soldered.

[15] The importance of naval power was a central issue in England in the 1660s especially since, during the Dutch War, Dutch ships had managed to overcome English defences and sail into the Medway. Cf. the second part of *Blazing World*. See Bernard Capp, *Cromwell's Navy: The Fleet and the English Revolution, 1648–1660* (Oxford: Clarendon Press, 1989). Newcastle advised Charles II that a flourishing navy is vital for defence, and merchant shipping a key to a secure and prosperous state. *Ideology and Politics on the Eve of the Restoration: Newcastle's Advice to Charles II*, introd. by Thomas P. Slaughter (Philadelphia: The American Philosophical Society, 1984), pp. 9–12, 35–42.

[16] Compare p. 57 where Paradise is identified with the Garden of Eden.

afar off showed like a company of ants, marching one after another; the boats appeared like the holes or partitions in a honey-comb and when joined together, stood as close; the men were of several complexions, but none like any of our world; and when the boats and ships met, they saluted and spake to each other very courteously; for there was but one language in all that world, nor no more than one Emperor,[17] to whom they all submitted with the greatest duty and obedience, which made them live in a continued peace and happiness, not acquainted with other foreign wars or home-bred insurrections. The Lady now being arrived at this place, was carried out of her ship into one of those boats, and conveyed through the same passage (for there was no other) into that part of the world where the Emperor did reside; which part was very pleasant, and of a mild temper: within itself it was divided by a great number of vast and large rivers, all ebbing and flowing, into several islands of unequal distance from each other, which in most part were as pleasant, healthful, rich and fruitful, as nature could make them; and, as I mentioned before, secure from all foreign invasions, by reason there was but one way to enter and that like a labyrinth, so winding and turning among the rocks, that no other vessels but small boats, could pass, carrying not above three passengers at a time: on each side all along this narrow and winding river, there were several cities, some of marble, some of alabaster, some of agate, some of amber, some of coral, and some of other precious materials not known in our world; all which after the Lady had passed, she came to the imperial city, named Paradise, which appeared in form like several islands; for rivers did run betwixt every street, which together with the bridges, whereof there was a great number, were all paved; the city itself was built of gold,

---

[17] Cavendish takes up a longstanding debate about whether self-government or government by one emperor is the most effective means of attaining peace. For classic statements of these two positions see respectively Marsiglio of Padua, *Defensor Pacis* (*The Defender of Peace*) (1324) and Dante Alighieri, *De Monarchia* (*Monarchy*) (*c.*1315). Cavendish's reference to a single language is unusual, although Machiavelli comments on the difficulty of ruling a group of people who do not share a language, *The Prince*, ed. R. Price and Q. Skinner (Cambridge: Cambridge University Press, 1988), ch. 3, pp. 8–10. Some writers also held that true wisdom would only be attained when the confusion of Babel had been overcome and a universal language created. In 1629, Mersenne wrote to Descartes about a universal script, and in *Harmonie Universelle* (1636) sketched a universal, musical language. The same idea was proposed by John Wilkins in *Mercury or the Swift and Secret Messenger* (1641). Later in the 1660s, Wilkins published *Essay towards a Real Character and a Philosophical Language* (1668), and Comenius developed the same idea in *Via Lucis* (*The Way of Light*) (1668), dedicated to the Fellows of the Royal Society. On language in imaginary voyages see James Knowlson, *Universal Language Schemes in England and France 1600–1800* (Toronto: University of Toronto Press, 1975), pp. 112–38.

and their architectures were noble, stately and magnificent, not like our modern, but like those in the Roman's time; for our modern buildings are like those houses which children use to make of cards, one storey above another, fitter for birds, than men; but theirs were more large, and broad, than high; the highest of them did not exceed two storeys, besides those rooms that were under-ground, as cellars, and other offices.[18] The Emperor's palace stood upon an indifferent ascent from the imperial city; at the top of which ascent was a broad arch, supported by several pillars, which went round the palace, and contained four of our English miles in compass: within the arch stood the Emperor's Guard, which consisted of several sorts of men; at every half mile or so was a gate to enter, and every gate was of a different fashion; the first, which allowed a passage from the imperial city to the palace, had on either hand a cloister, the outward part whereof stood upon arches sustained by pillars, but the inner part was close: being entered through the gate, the palace itself appeared in its middle like the aisle of a church,[19] a mile and a half long, and half a mile broad; the roof of it was all arched, and rested upon pillars, so artificially placed, that a stranger would lose himself therein without a guide; at its extreme sides, that is, between the outward and inward part of the cloister, were lodgings for attendants, and in the midst of the palace, the Emperor's own rooms; whose lights were placed at the top of every one, because of the heat of the sun: the Emperor's apartment for state was no more enclosed than the rest; only an imperial throne was in every apartment, of which the several adornments could not be perceived until one entered, because the pillars were so just opposite to one another, that all the adornments could not be seen at once. The first

---

[18] The fire of London in 1666 gave rise to a debate about the style in which the city should be rebuilt. One contributor was John Evelyn, who visited Cavendish during her visit to London in 1667. See his Dedication to Charles II in his translation of Roland Freart, *A Parallel of Architecture both Ancient and Modern*: 'It is from the asymmetries of our buildings, want of decorum and proportion in our houses, that the irregularity of our humours and affections may be shrewdly discerned. But it is from His Majesty's great genius . . . that we may hope to see it all reformed; it being so worthy an imitation of that magnificent Emperor, that touched with the like imagination at the encroachments and deformities of the public edifices and ways, caused a like reformation also; so as we may now affirm of London, as the Poet once of Rome, *Nunc Roma est, nuper magna taberna fuit.*' [Now it is Rome. It used to be a big shop.] The quotation is from Martial, *Epigrams*, Book VII. 61, ed. D. R. Shackleton Bailey, 3 vols. (Cambridge, MA: Harvard University Press, 1993), Book VII, Epigram 60, vol. II, p. 126.

[19] On the Empress as both the religious and civil ruler of the Blazing World cf. Introduction, pp. xxvi–xxviii.

part of the palace was, as the imperial city, all of gold, and when it came to the Emperor's apartment, it was so rich with diamonds, pearls, rubies, and the like precious stones, that it surpasses my skill to enumerate them all. Amongst the rest, the imperial room of state appeared most magnificent; it was paved with green diamonds (for in that world are diamonds of all colours) so artificially, as it seemed but of one piece; the pillars were set with diamonds so close, and in such a manner, that they appeared most glorious to the sight; between every pillar was a bow or arch of a certain sort of diamonds, the like whereof our world does not afford; which being placed in every one of the arches in several rows, seemed just like so many rainbows of several different colours. The roof of the arches was of blue diamonds, and in the midst thereof was a carbuncle, which represented the sun; the rising and setting sun at the East and West side of the room were made of rubies.[20] Out of this room there was a passage into the Emperor's bed-chamber, the walls whereof were of jet, and the floor of black marble; the roof was of mother of pearl, where the moon and blazing stars were represented by white diamonds, and his bed was made of diamonds and carbuncles.

No sooner was the Lady brought before the Emperor, but he conceived her to be some goddess, and offered to worship her; which she refused, telling him, (for by that time she had pretty well learned their language) that although she came out of another world, yet was she but a mortal; at which the Emperor rejoicing, made her his wife, and gave her an absolute power to rule and govern all that world as she pleased.[21] But her subjects, who could hardly be persuaded to believe her mortal, tendered her all the veneration and worship due to a deity.

Her accoutrement after she was made Empress, was as followeth: on her head she wore a cap of pearl, and a half-moon of diamonds just before it; on the top of her crown came spreading over a broad carbuncle, cut in the form of the sun; her coat was of pearl, mixed with blue diamonds, and fringed with red ones; her buskins and sandals were of green diamonds: in her left hand she held a buckler, to signify the defence of her dominions;

---

[20] Precious stones are influentially discussed by Pliny, *Natural History*, Book XXXVII, trans. H. Rackham, 10 vols. (Cambridge, MA: Harvard University Press, 1965), vol. X, pp. 165–333. According to Bruno Latini, the sapphire signifies temperance, the emerald justice, and the diamond fortitude. The carbuncle (which lights up the night) signifies prudence, the greatest of the virtues. *Li livres dou tresor* (Books of Treasure) (1266), II. ii.

[21] Cavendish departs from the standard device of describing an ideal world through the eyes of a visitor. Cf. Thomas More, *Utopia* (1516); Francis Bacon, *New Atlantis* (1627).

which buckler was made of that sort of diamond as has several different colours; and being cut and made in the form of an arch, showed like a rainbow; in her right hand she carried a spear made of a white diamond, cut like the tail of a blazing star, which signified that she was ready to assault those that proved her enemies.[22]

None was allowed to use or wear gold but those of the imperial race, which were the only nobles of the state; nor durst anyone wear jewels but the Emperor, the Empress, and their eldest son,[23] notwithstanding that they had an infinite quantity both of gold and precious stones in that world; for they had larger extents of gold, than our Arabian sands; their precious stones were rocks, and their diamonds of several colours; they used no coin, but all their traffic was by exchange of several commodities.[24]

[22] See also pp. 96f. The heroic female warrior wearing male, martial dress occurs in several of Cavendish's stories and plays. See Battigelli, *Margaret Cavendish*, pp. 18–38. It was realised by Queen Henrietta Maria who, while Cavendish was one of her maids in waiting, marched across England at the head of an army to join Charles I in Oxford and made a triumphal entry into the city. It was also cultivated by Queen Christina of Sweden, who abdicated in 1654 and visited Antwerp while Cavendish was living there. See Susanna Akerman, 'Kristina of Sweden' in Mary Ellen Waithe ed., *A History of Women Philosophers*, 3 vols. (Dordrecht 1991), vol. III: 1600–1900, pp. 221–40. The Empress's magnificence may also allude to Elizabeth I whose reign is represented as a golden age of princely government by Newcastle. See *Advice, passim*. Cavendish surprised Sir Charles Lyttleton by adopting masculine, though not martial, dress in 1665 when cross-dressing, which had been fashionable at Henrietta Maria's court, was nostalgically revived. See Douglas Grant, *Margaret the First* (London: Rupert Hart-Davis, 1957), p. 184. See also Paula R. Backscheider, 'The Cavalier Woman', *Studies in Eighteenth-Century Culture* 24 (1995), pp. 3–27.

[23] The sumptuary laws of the Blazing World are in line with Cavendish's criticism of Holland, where 'the commons strive to out-brave the nobles by their building, garnishing, furnishing, adorning and flourishing in gold and bravery, for even the mechanics in this city, and I believe in the rest, are suffered to have their coaches, lackies, pages, waiting maids, and to wear rich and glorious garments, fashioning themselves in all things like nobles, which causes envy in the nobility and pride in the commonality; . . . this pride and envy causes murmur, and murmur causes faction, which may in time make alteration in the state and government . . . Wherefore the commons should be kept like cattle . . . that is, not to exceed their rank or degree in show and bravery, but to live according to their qualities, and not according to their wealth; and those that will be so presumptuous should be imprisoned and fined great sums . . . [T]his would keep the commons in awe, and the nobles in power to uphold royal government, which is certainly the best and happiest government, that being the most united, by which the people becomes most civil. For democracy is more wild and barbarous than monarchy', *Sociable Letters*, lxv. These sentiments are also rehearsed in Newcastle's *Advice*, pp. 44–9.

[24] See also p. 102. Compare Cavendish's own world with the Blazing World, where gold and jewels are only used by the imperial race and there is no coin, and with More's *Utopia*, where gold and jewels are used only to punish slaves, shame wrong-doers and pacify

Their priests and governors were princes of the imperial blood, and made eunuchs for that purpose;[25] and as for the ordinary sort of men in that part of the world where the Emperor resided, they were of several complexions;[26] not white, black, tawny, olive or ash-coloured; but some appeared of an azure, some of deep purple, some of a grass-green, some of a scarlet, some of an orange colour, etc. which colours and reflections, whether they were made by the bare reflection of light, without the assistance of small particles, or by the help of well-ranged and ordered atoms; or by a continual agitation of little globules; or by some pressing and reacting motion, I am not able to determine. The rest of the inhabitants of that world, were men of several different sorts, shapes, figures, dispositions, and humours, as I have already made mention heretofore; some were bear-men, some worm-men, some fish- or mear-men,[27] otherwise called syrens, some bird-men, some fly-men, some ant-men, some geese-men, some spider-men, some lice-men, some fox-men, some ape-men, some jackdaw-men, some magpie-men, some parrot-men, some satyrs, some giants, and many more, which I cannot all remember;[28] and of these several

infants. Thomas More, *Utopia*, ed. George M. Logan and Robert M. Adams (Cambridge: Cambridge University Press, 1975), p. 64. See also Rosemary Kegl, 'Margaret Cavendish', pp. 128–32.

[25] The reference to eunuchs is presumably to the practices of the Ottoman court. Cavendish appears to draw here on Robert Withers who describes both the role of eunuchs and various conventions designed to prevent faction among the members of the royal family. 'For a Bashaw, having married a daughter or sister of the King, and having sons by them, those sons may not rise above the degree of a Sanjack Begh, or a Capoogee Bashaw, to the end they may be kept under, being allied to the crown; that so, being but in mean places, they may not be apt to rebel. But their brothers, which their fathers begat of slaves, may come to be Bashaws; for they are free from suspicion, in regard they are not of the royal blood', Robert Withers, *A Description of the Grand Signor's Seraglio, or Turkish Emperor's Court*, ed. J. Greaves (London, 1650), reprinted as *The Sultan's Seraglio. An Intimate Portrait of Life at the Ottoman Court*, intro. Godfrey Goodwin (London: Saqi Books, 1996), p. 119. Cavendish seems to have combined these two aspects of Withers's text, itself an unacknowledged translation of a work by Ottavino Bon, the Venetian representative at the Ottoman court from 1604 to 1607.

[26] Cavendish claims that white men and 'Negroes' are both descended from Adam, on the grounds that they have the same 'way of generation'. See *Observations*, p. 115.

[27] Mermen.

[28] On animal men see 'Assaulted and Pursued Chastity' and 'The Drunken Poet' in *Nature's Pictures*, where Cavendish describes Ovid as 'transforming Gods, men and beasts, mingling them all together'. Cavendish draws to some extent on Ben Jonson's *Volpone* (1605), which in turn draws on the conventions of medieval *fabliaux*. Her natural philosophy allows for infinite variety in nature, and for many degrees of perception and knowledge, and contains an account of the material mind which overturns the hierarchical view that humans are superior to other animals. 'For there is only different knowledge belonging to every kind, as to animal kind, vegetable kind, mineral kind, and infinitely more which we are not yet

sorts of men, each followed such a profession as was most proper for the nature of their species, which the Empress encouraged them in, especially those that had applied themselves to the study of several arts and sciences; for they were as ingenious and witty in the invention of profitable and useful arts, as we are in our world, nay, more; and to that end she erected schools, and founded several societies.[29] The bear-men were to be her experimental philosophers, the bird-men her astronomers, the fly-, worm- and fish-men her natural philosophers, the ape-men her chemists, the satyrs her Galenic physicians, the fox-men her politicians, the spider- and lice-men her mathematicians, the jackdaw-, magpie- and parrot-men her orators and logicians, the giants her architects, etc. But before all things, she having got a sovereign power from the Emperor over all the world, desired to be informed both of the manner of their religion and government, and to that end she called the priests and statesmen, to give her an account of either. Of the statesmen she enquired, first, why they had so few laws?[30] To which they answered, that many laws made many divisions, which most commonly did breed factions, and at last break out into open wars. Next, she asked, why they preferred the monarchical form of government before any other? They answered, that as it was natural for one body to have but one head, so it was also natural for a politic body to have but one governor; and that a commonwealth, which had many governors was like a monster with many heads:[31] besides, said they, a monarchy is

---

capable to know . . . so that if a man have different knowledge from a fish, yet the fish may be as knowing as the man', *Philosophical and Physical Opinions*, pp. 113–14. See Susan James, 'The Innovations of Margaret Cavendish', *British Journal for the History of Philosophy* 7.2 (1999), p. 239.

[29] Charles II incorporated the Royal Society of London in 1665. Cf. Bacon's description of Salomon's House or the College of the Six Days' Works. The end of the College is 'the knowledge of Causes, and secret motions of things; and the enlarging of the bounds of Human Empire, to the effecting of all things possible', Bacon, *New Atlantis*, p. 480. Bacon hoped that James I would patronise such a society.

[30] Newcastle also claims that many laws create too many lawyers and promote rebellion, *Advice*, p. 24.

[31] Appeals to the human body as an image of the polity are standard in seventeenth-century political thought. See for example the Introduction to Thomas Hobbes, *Leviathan*, ed. R. Tuck (Cambridge: Cambridge University Press, 1996), Introduction, p. xxv. For an elaborate use of the image see 'Fancy's Monarchy in the Land of Poetry' in *Nature's Pictures*, p. 134. In the same work, Cavendish compares the monarch to the sun: 'For as one sun is sufficient to give light and heat to all the several creatures in the world, so one government is sufficient to give laws and rulers to the several members of a commonwealth' (p. 317). She also draws on a widely held patriarchal view: just as the head of the body stands for the head of state, it also functions as a metaphor for the father, the head of the family, *Sociable Letters*, lxi. See John Rogers, *The Matter of Revolution. Science, Politics and Poetry*

a divine form of government, and agrees most with our religion; for as there is but one God, whom we all unanimously worship and adore with one faith, so we are resolved to have but one Emperor, to whom we all submit with one obedience.

Then the Empress seeing that the several sorts of her subjects had each their churches apart, asked the priests whether they were of several religions? They answered her Majesty, that there was no more but one religion in all that world, nor no diversity of opinions in that same religion; for though there were several sorts of men, yet had they all but one opinion concerning the worship and adoration of God. The Empress asked them, whether they were Jews, Turks, or Christians? We do not know, said they, what religions those are; but we do all unanimously acknowledge, worship and adore the only, omnipotent, and eternal God, with all reverence, submission, and duty. Again, the Empress enquired, whether they had several forms of worship? They answered, no: for our devotion and worship consists only in prayers, which we frame according to our several necessities, in petitions, humiliations, thanksgiving, etc.[32]

*in the Age of Milton* (Ithaca: Cornell University Press, 1996), pp. 16–27; Michele Le Doeuff, *The Social Imaginary* (London: Athlone, 1989). On seventeenth-century patriarchalism see Gordon Schochet, *Patriarchalism in Political Thought* (Oxford: Blackwell, 1975); Carole Pateman, 'The Fraternal Social Contract' in *The Disorder of Women* (Cambridge: Polity, 1989), pp. 33–57; J. P. Sommerville, *Royalists and Patriots. Politics and Ideology in England 1603–40* (Harlow: Longman, 1999), 2nd edn, pp. 29–36.

[32] The view that religious dogmas and practices should be minimal was advocated, particularly in the Netherlands, on the grounds that it fostered peace as opposed to religious war. Members of some more demanding Christian sects regarded it as tantamount to atheism. Cavendish might have heard these issues debated in Antwerp, as well as in England. She defends a minimal natural theology. While all creatures know that God exists, his essence is unknown, *Philosophical Letters*, Part II, I. Her natural philosophy leads her to several radical theological views. Among them are (1) The infinite variety of nature means that different people have different consciences, and thus different beliefs. Since beliefs cannot be altered by force, liberty of conscience should be allowed, as long as it does not prejudice peaceful government, *Grounds of Natural Philosophy*, Appendix, Part I, ch. 12, pp. 248–9. (2) God created matter and could easily have created worlds other than this one. *Philosophical Letters*, Part I, III. (3) There is one soul in infinite nature and every part of rational matter is a particular soul. *Philosophical Letters*, pp. 433f. Such views were often condemned as atheistical, and it is striking that Cavendish is relatively sympathetic to atheism. 'It is better to be an atheist than a superstitious man; for in atheism, there is humanity, and civility, towards man to man; but superstition regards no humanity, and begets cruelty to all things', *The World's Olio*, p. 46. Cavendish's husband and his relatives were patrons of Thomas Hobbes, who held similar views. See Noel Malcolm, 'Hobbes and Spinoza' in J. H. Burns and Mark Goldie eds., *The Cambridge History of Political Thought 1450–1700* (Cambridge: Cambridge University Press, 1991), pp. 543–5. Hobbes was widely regarded as an atheist and in 1666 a motion was brought to the House of Commons in which he was cited as the author of a 'work that tends to Atheism, Blasphemy,

Truly, replied the Empress, I thought you had been either Jews, or Turks, because I never perceived any women in your congregations; but what is the reason, you bar them from your religious assemblies? It is not fit, said they, that men and women should be promiscuously together in time of religious worship; for their company hinders devotion, and makes many, instead of praying to God, direct their devotion to their mistresses. But, asked the Empress, have they no congregation of their own, to perform the duties of divine worship, as well as men? No, answered they: but they stay at home, and say their prayers by themselves in their closets.[33] Then the Empress desired to know the reason why the priests and governors of their world were made eunuchs? They answered, to keep them from marriage: for women and children most commonly make disturbance both in church and state. But, said she, women and children have no employment in church or state. 'Tis true, answered they; but although they are not admitted to public employments, yet are they so prevalent with their husbands and parents, that many times by their importunate persuasions, they cause as much, nay, more mischief secretly, than if they had the management of public affairs.[34]

or Profaneness', *Journals of the House of Commons*, vol. VIII, 1660–7, p. 636, column 2. See Battigelli, *Margaret Cavendish*, pp. 55–71; Lisa Sarasohn, 'A World Turned Upside Down. Feminism and the Natural Philosophy of Margaret Cavendish', *Huntington Library Quarterly* 47 (1984), pp. 289–307; James, 'Innovations of Margaret Cavendish', pp. 229–31.

[33] Cavendish presses this point elsewhere. Cf. 'there ought to be a law that at all public assemblies that are drawn about an oracle, whither such as are to declare the commands of the Gods, or for any other instruction . . . either in the Church, or on theatres, should not be mixed of several sexes, but whither the assembly should be all men, or all women; otherwise a consecrated place may be polluted with wanton eyes and inciting countenances, self whisperings and secret agreements to dangerous meetings . . . by which a Church would become a bawdy house, and the priest, the pimps or procurers, to draw them together; and for the orations concerning the Commonwealth, or for any importunate matter, would be lost, for the ears of the assembly would be stopped by their eyes, at least the hearing of the auditors would be imperfect, and their understanding confounded and their memory dazzled with the splendour of light glances, and fair faces of each sex', 'The She Anchoret' in *Nature's Pictures*, p. 327. On private space see Julie Sanders, ' "The Closet Opened": a reconstruction of "private" space in the writings of Margaret Cavendish' in Stephen Clucas ed., *A Princely Brave Woman. Essays on Margaret Cavendish Duchess of Newcastle* (London: Ashgate, 2003), pp. 127–40.

[34] Withers's account of the Ottoman court notes that 'As for the women, there is no heed taken or reckoning made of their religion at all . . . They never go to church, so that if they happily have a will to pray at the hours of prayer, they do it in their own houses, using the same preparations that men do', Withers, *A Description*, p. 144. Cf. n. 25. See also *Divers Orations*, Part XI.

The Empress having received an information of what concerned both church and state, passed some time in viewing the imperial palace, where she admired much the skill and ingenuity of the architects, and enquired of them, first, why they built their houses no higher than two storeys from the ground? They answered her Majesty, that the lower their buildings were, the less were they subject either to the heat of the sun, to wind, tempest, decay, etc. Then she desired to know the reason, why they made them so thick? They answered, that the thicker the walls were, the warmer were they in winter, and cooler in summer, for their thickness kept out both cold and heat. Lastly, she asked, why they arched their roofs, and made so many pillars? They replied, that arches and pillars, did not only grace a building very much, and caused it to appear magnificent, but made it also firm and lasting.

The Empress was very well satisfied with their answers; and after some time, when she thought that her new founded societies of the virtuosos had made a good progress in their several employments, which she had put them upon, she caused a convocation first of the bird-men, and commanded them to give her a true relation of the two celestial bodies, viz. the sun and moon, which they did with all the obedience and faithfulness befitting their duty.

The sun, as much as they could observe, they related to be a firm or solid stone,[35] of a vast bigness, of colour yellowish, and of an extraordinary splendour; but the moon, they said, was of a whitish colour; and although she looked dim in the presence of the sun, yet had she her own light,[36] and was a shining body of her self as might be perceived by her vigorous appearance in moonshiny nights; the difference only betwixt her own and the sun's light was that the sun did strike his beams in a direct line,[37] but the moon never respected the centre of their world in a right line, but her centre was always excentrical. The spots both in the sun and moon,

---

[35] As opposed to a flame. Newcastle attributes this view to Kepler. See his 'Opinion Concerning the Ground of Natural Philosophy' appended to *Physical and Philosophical Opinions*.

[36] A view defended by Jan Baptista Van Helmont in *Oriatrike or Physick Refined* (London, 1662), XXI. 45, one of the books criticised in Cavendish's *Philosophical Letters*. This view had been opposed by Galileo, who argued that the ashen light of the moon is due to solar rays reflected by the earth. *Dialogue Concerning the Two Chief World Systems, the Ptolemaic and the Copernican* (1623), trans. Stillman Drake (New York: Modern Library, 2001), p. 77. On Van Helmont see Allen G. Debus, *The French Paracelsans* (Cambridge: Cambridge University Press, 1991), pp. 102–15.

[37] A view discussed by Van Helmont, *Oriatrike*, XXI.47.

as far as they were able to perceive, they affirmed to be nothing else but flaws and stains of their stony bodies.[38] Concerning the heat of the sun, they were not of one opinion; some would have the sun hot, in itself,[39] alleging an old tradition, that it should at some time break asunder, and burn the heavens, and consume this world into hot embers, which, said they, could not be done, if the sun were not fiery of itself. Others again said, this opinion could not stand with reason; for fire being a destroyer of all things, the sun-stone after this manner would burn up all the near adjoining bodies: besides, said they, fire cannot subsist without fuel;[40] and the sun-stone having nothing to feed on, would in a short time consume itself; wherefore they thought it more probable that the sun was not actually hot, but only by the reflection of its light; so that its heat was an effect of its light, both being immaterial: but this opinion again was laughed at by others, and rejected as ridiculous, who thought it impossible that one immaterial should produce another; and believed that both the light and heat of the sun proceeded from a swift circular motion of the ethereal globules, which by their striking upon the optic nerve caused light,[41] and their motion produced heat: but neither would this opinion hold; for, said some, then it would follow, that the sight of animals is the cause of light, and that, were there no eyes, there would be no light, which was against all sense and reason. Thus they argued concerning the heat and light of the sun; but which is remarkable, none did say, that the sun

[38] Aristotelian astronomers who regarded the sun as a perfect body rejected the idea that it might be stained. When Christoph Scheiner first observed sunspots in 1611, he argued that they were satellites of the sun. Galileo countered that they were contiguous with the sun, *Dialogue*, pp. 62, 401–3. Cavendish takes the Galileian view. See Michael Hoskin, 'From Geometry to Physics: Astronomy Transferred' in *The Cambridge Concise History of Astronomy* (Cambridge: Cambridge University Press, 1999), pp. 114–18. Galileo also studied the surface of the moon and proposed that its spots were cavities and mountain ranges. *Siderius Nuncius* (*The Sidereal Messenger*) (1610). See Ewen A. Whittaker, 'Selenography in the Seventeenth Century' in M. Hoskin ed., *The General History of Astronomy* (Cambridge: Cambridge University Press, 1989), 4 vols., vol. II, ed. René Taton and Curtis Wilson, pp. 124–5.

[39] See Van Helmont, *Oriatrike*, XIII.24.

[40] This echoes the argument of Newcastle's 'Opinion Concerning the Ground of Natural Philosophy' appended to *Philosophical and Physical Opinions*. Descartes also argues that the sun does not need fuel. *Principles of Philosophy*, III. 22, in *Oeuvres de Descartes*, ed. Charles Adam and Paul Tannery, 11 vols., 2nd edn (Paris: Vrin, 1974–86) (hereafter AT), vol. IX, p. 111.

[41] Hobbes, *De Corpore* IV. 27; *The English Works of Thomas Hobbes*, ed. Sir William Molesworth, 11 vols. (London, 1839–45) (hereafter EW), vol. IV, pp. 448–9.

was a globous, fluid body, and had a swift circular motion;[42] but all agreed it was fixed and firm like a centre,[43] and therefore they generally called it the sun-stone.

Then the Empress asked them the reason, why the sun and moon did often appear in different postures or shapes, as sometimes magnified, sometimes diminished, sometimes elevated, otherwhiles depressed, now thrown to the right, and then to the left? To which some of the bird-men answered, that it proceeded from the various degrees of heat and cold, which are found in the air, from whence did follow a differing density and rarity; and likewise from the vapours that are interposed, whereof those that ascend are higher and less dense than the ambient air, but those which descend are heavier, and more dense. But others did with more probability affirm, that it was nothing else but the various patterns of the air; for like as painters do not copy out one and the same original just alike at all times, so said they, do several parts of the air make different patterns of the luminous bodies of the sun and moon, which patterns, as several copies, the sensitive motions do figure out in the substance of our eyes.[44]

This answer the Empress liked much better than the former, and enquired further, what opinion they had of those creatures that are called the motes of the sun? To which they answered that they were nothing else but streams of very small, rare and transparent particles, through which the sun was represented as through a glass; for if they were not transparent, said they, they would eclipse the light of the sun; and if not rare and of an airy substance, they would hinder flies from flying in the air, at least retard their flying motion: nevertheless, although they were thinner than the thinnest vapour, yet were they not so thin as the body of air, or else they would not be perceptible by animal sight. Then the Empress asked, whether they were living creatures? They answered, yes: because they did increase and decrease, and were nourished by the presence, and starved by the absence of the sun.

Having thus finished their discourse of the sun and moon, the Empress desired to know what stars there were besides? But they answered, that

---

[42] Descartes, *Principles* III. 21, vol. IX, p. 111. See S. Gaukroger, *Descartes' System of Natural Philosophy* (Cambridge: Cambridge University Press, 2002), pp. 15–16.
[43] Although Copernicus published *De revolutionibus* in 1543, a heliocentric view of the planetary system was only gradually established, notably through the work of Kepler and Galileo. The Empress is convinced that the earth moves round the sun. See p. 35.
[44] The view advocated in Cavendish's natural philosophy.

they could perceive in that world none other but blazing stars, and from thence it had the name that it was called the Blazing World; and these blazing stars, said they, were such solid, firm and shining bodies as the sun and moon, not of a globular, but of several sorts of figures, some had tails, and some other kinds of shapes.

After this, the Empress asked them, what kind of substance or creature the air was?[45] The bird-men answered, that they could have no other perception of the air, but by their own respiration: for, said they, some bodies are only subject to touch, others only to sight, and others only to smell; but some are subject to none of our exterior senses: for nature is so full of variety, that our weak senses cannot perceive all the various sorts of her creatures; neither is there any one object perceptible by all our senses, no more than several objects are by one sense. I believe you, replied the Empress; but if you can give no account of the air, said she, you will hardly be able to inform me how wind is made; for they say that wind is nothing but motion of the air. The bird-men answered, that they observed wind to be more dense than air, and therefore subject to the sense of touch; but what properly wind was, and the manner how it was made, they could not exactly tell; some said, it was caused by the clouds falling on each other,[46] and others, that it was produced by a hot and dry exhalation,[47] which ascending, was driven down again by the coldness of the air that is in the middle region, and by reason of its lightness, could not go directly to the bottom, but was carried by the air up and down: some would have it a flowing water of the air;[48] and others again a flowing air moved by the blaze of the stars.[49]

But the Empress seeing they could not agree concerning the cause of wind, asked, whether they could tell how snow was made? To which they answered, that according to their observation, snow was made by a commixture of water, and some certain extract of the element of fire that is under the moon;[50] a small portion of which extract being mixed with

---

[45] The bird-men are interestingly reticent about air. Elsewhere, Cavendish discusses it, as do some of the philosophers whose work she criticises. E.g. Descartes, *Les Météores*, Discours Second, AT, vol. VI, pp. 239–48.

[46] Hobbes, *De Corpore*, IV. 28; EW, vol. I, pp. 470–3.

[47] Van Helmont attributes this view to Aristotle, who discusses wind in *Meteorology* II in J. Barnes ed., *The Complete Works of Aristotle* (Princeton: Princeton University Press, 1984) (hereafter CWA), 359b27–365a12. See *Oriatrike*, XV. 25.

[48] Van Helmont attributes this view to Hippocrates, *Oriatrike*, XIV. 4.

[49] Van Helmont's own view. See *Oriatrike*, XIV. 4.

[50] Scholastic philosophers held that the element of fire was contained by the lunar sphere.

water, and beaten by air or wind, made a white froth called snow, which being after some while dissolved by the heat of the same spirit, turned to water again. This observation amazed the Empress very much; for she had hitherto believed, that snow was made by cold motions, and not by such an agitation or beating of a fiery extract upon water: nor could she be persuaded to believe it until the fish- or mear-men had delivered their observation upon the making of ice, which, they said, was not produced, as some had hitherto conceived, by the motion of the air, raking the superficies of the earth,[51] but by some strong saline vapour arising out of the seas,[52] which condensed water into ice, and the more quantity there was of that vapour, the greater were the mountains or precipices of ice; but the reason that it did not so much freeze in the torrid zone, or under the ecliptic, as near or under the Poles, was, that this vapour in those places being drawn up by the sun beams into the middle region of the air, was only condensed into water, and fell down in showers of rain; when as, under the Poles, the heat of the sun being not so vehement, the same vapour had no force or power to rise so high, and therefore caused so much ice, by ascending and acting only upon the surface of water.

This relation confirmed partly the observation of the bird-men concerning the cause of snow; but since they had made mention that that same extract, which by its commixture with water made snow, proceeded from the element of fire, that is under the moon; the Empress asked them of what nature that elementary fire was;[53] whether it was like ordinary fire here upon earth, or such a fire as is within the bowels of the earth, and as the famous mountains Vesuvius and Etna do burn withal, or whether it was such a sort of fire as is found in flints, etc. They answered, that the elementary fire, which is underneath the sun, was not so solid as any of those mentioned fires; because it had no solid fuel to feed on; but yet it was much like the flame of ordinary fire, only somewhat more thin and fluid; for flame, said they, is nothing else but the airy part of a fired body.

---

[51] Hobbes, *De Corpore*, IV. 28; EW, vol. I, pp. 470–6. His view was criticised by Boyle, 'An Examen of Mr. Hobs's Doctrine, touching Cold' (1665) in WRB, vol. IV, pp. 503–16.

[52] Boyle discusses a series of experiments about freezing water and salt in *New Experiments and Observations touching Cold or an Experimental History of Cold* (1665); WRB, vol. IV, pp. 462f. Cavendish mentions some of these in *Philosophical Letters*, pp. 456–82.

[53] In the Aristotelian and chemical traditions, fire was classified as one of the four elements. Cavendish distinguishes various kinds of fire (cf. *Observations*, p. 120) as does Hobbes, *De Corpore* IV.27; EW, vol. I, pp. 452–4.

Lastly, the Empress asked the bird-men of the nature of thunder and lightning?[54] and whether it was not caused by roves of ice falling upon each other? To which they answered, that it was not made that way, but by an encounter of cold and heat; so that an exhalation being kindled in the clouds, did dash forth lightning, and that there were so many rentings of clouds as there were sounds and cracking noises but this opinion was contradicted by others, who affirmed that thunder was a sudden and monstrous blas, stirred up in the air, and did not always require a cloud; but the Empress not knowing what they meant by blas (for even they themselves were not able to explain the sense of this word) liked the former better; and to avoid hereafter tedious disputes, and have the truth of the phaenomenas of celestial bodies more exactly known, commanded the bear-men, which were her experimental philosophers, to observe them through such instruments as are called telescopes, which they did according to her Majesty's command; but these telescopes caused more differences and divisions amongst them, than ever they had before;[55] for some said, they perceived that the sun stood still, and the earth did move about it, others were of opinion, that they both did move; and others said again, that the earth stood still, and the sun did move; some counted more stars than others; some discovered new stars never seen before;[56] some fell into a great dispute with others concerning the bigness of the stars;[57] some said the moon was another world like their terrestrial globe,

[54] Hobbes argued that thunder and lightning occurred when frozen clouds collide. *De Corpore* IV.28; EW, vol. I, p. 481. Boyle describes the sound of cracking ice as 'icy thunders' and suggests that it occurs when cold ice meets with 'warm exhalations', *New Experiments and Observations touching Cold or an Experimental History of Cold* (1665). WRB, vol. IV, p. 356. Van Helmont argues that the operations of a vital force called 'blas' explain motion and change in natural phenomena. Thunder is a monstrous effect, the 'spiritual blas of the evil spirit', *Oriatrike*, XVI.17. The Empress's criticisms of his view echo those in *Philosophical Letters*, p. 238.

[55] Cavendish attacks the value of telescopes, and above all microscopes, and criticises Henry Power's *Experimental Philosophy* (1663) and Robert Hooke's *Micrographia* (1665). See *Observations*, pp. 50, 135, 200. Her main arguments are rehearsed by the Empress, whose bear-men parody the experimenters of the Royal Society. See Battigelli, *Margaret Cavendish*, pp. 85–113; Catherine Wilson, *The Invisible World: Early Modern Philosophy and the Invention of the Microscope* (Princeton: Princeton University Press, 1995).

[56] For example, Galileo reported his observations of the Milky Way and the moons of Jupiter in *Siderius Nuncius* (*The Sidereal Messenger*) (1610).

[57] Copernicus's generation inherited an ancient consensus as to the sizes and distances of the celestial bodies which was upset by observations made through telescopes. In *Siderius Nuncius* and *Dialogue* Galileo argued that the stars are much smaller than had been believed. See Albert Van Helden, 'The Telescope and Cosmic Dimensions' in René Taton and Curtis

and the spots therein were hills and valleys;[58] but others would have the spots to be the terrestrial parts, and the smooth and glossy parts, the sea: at last, the Empress commanded them to go with their telescopes to the very end of the Pole that was joined to the world she came from, and try whether they could perceive any stars in it; which they did; and being returned to her Majesty, reported that they had seen three blazing-stars appear there, one after another in a short time, whereof two were bright, and one dim; but they could not agree neither in this observation; for some said it was but one star[59] which appeared at three several times in several places; and others would have them to be three several stars; for they thought it impossible, that those three several appearances should have been but one star, because every star did rise at a certain time, and appeared in a certain place, and did disappear in the same place: next, it is altogether improbable, said they, that one star should fly from place to place, especially at such a vast distance, without a visible motion, in so short a time, and appear in such different places, whereof two were quite opposite, and the third side-ways: lastly, if it had been but one star, said they, it would always have kept the same splendour, which it did not; for, as above mentioned, two were bright, and one was dim. After they had thus argued, the Empress began to grow angry at their telescopes, that they could give no better intelligence; for, said she, now I do plainly perceive, that your glasses are false informers,[60] and instead of discovering the truth, deluded your senses; wherefore I command you to break them, and let the bird-men trust only to their natural eyes, and examine celestial objects by the motions of their own sense and reason. The bear-men replied, that it was not the fault of their glasses, which caused such differences in their opinions, but the sensitive motions in their optic organs did not move alike, nor were their rational judgements always regular: to which the Empress answered, that if their glasses were true informers, they would rectify their irregular sense and reason; but, said she, nature has made your sense and reason more regular than art has your glasses, for they are mere deluders, and will never lead you to the knowledge of

Wilson eds., *The General History of Astronomy* (Cambridge: Cambridge University Press, 1989), 4 vols., vol. II, pp. 106–18.

[58] See n. 38.
[59] A reference to debates surrounding the observation of comets in 1572, by Tycho Brahe, and in 1604. John Dee contributed to the first debate. See nn. 101 and 114. See also Victor E. Thoren, 'Tycho Brahe' in René Taton and Curtis Wilson eds., *The General History of Astronomy*, vol. II, pp. 5–7.
[60] Cf. *Observations*, pp. 135–6.

truth; wherefore I command you again to break them; for you may observe the progressive motions of celestial bodies with your natural eyes better than through artificial glasses. The bear-men being exceedingly troubled at her Majesty's displeasure concerning their telescopes, kneeled down, and in the humblest manner petitioned that they might not be broken; for, said they, we take more delight in artificial delusions, than in natural truths. Besides, we shall want employments for our senses, and subjects for arguments; for were there nothing but truth, and no falsehood, there would be no occasion for to dispute, and by this means we should want the aim and pleasure of our endeavours in confuting and contradicting each other; neither would one man be thought wiser than another, but all would either be alike knowing and wise, or all would be fools; wherefore we most humbly beseech your Imperial Majesty to spare our glasses, which are our only delight, and as dear to us as our lives. The Empress at last consented to their request, but upon condition, that their disputes and quarrels should remain within their schools, and cause no factions or disturbances in state, or government.[61] The bear-men, full of joy, returned their most humble thanks to the Empress; and to make her amends for the displeasure which their telescopes had occasioned, told her Majesty, that they had several other artificial optic-glasses, which they were sure would give her Majesty a great deal more satisfaction. Amongst the rest they brought forth several microscopes, by the means of which they could enlarge the shapes of little bodies, and make a louse appear as big as an elephant, and a mite as big as a whale. First of all they showed the Empress a grey drone-fly, wherein they observed that the greatest part of her face, nay, of her head, consisted of two large bunches all covered over with a multitude of small pearls or hemispheres in a trigonal order, which pearls were of two degrees, smaller and bigger; the smaller degree was lowermost, and looked towards the ground; the other was upward and looked sideward, forward and backward: they were all so smooth and polished, that they were able to represent the image of any object, the number of them was in all 14000.[62] After the view of this strange and miraculous

[61] Cf. 'Then no Disputations butt in scooles, nor no bookes of controversey, writt but in Latin, for Else the People would bee overheated with itt, for controversey is a Civil warr with the Pen, which Pulls out the sorde soon afterwards', *Newcastle's Advice*, p. 21.

[62] The drone-fly, charcoal, nettle, flea and louse are illustrated and discussed in Hooke's *Micrographia*. In *Observations*, p. 59, Cavendish challenges his interpretation of his observations as the Empress does here. In 1667, Cavendish attended a meeting of the Royal Society where Hooke and Boyle devised a series of entertainments for her, including viewing objects through a microscope. The event was recorded by Samuel Pepys who was

creature, and their several observations upon it, the Empress asked them what they judged those little hemispheres might be? They answered, that each of them was a perfect eye, by reason they perceived that each was covered with a transparent cornea, containing a liquor within them, which resembled the watery or glassy humour of the eye. To which the Empress replied, that they might be glassy pearls, and yet not eyes, and that perhaps their microscopes did not truly inform them: but they smilingly answered her Majesty, that she did not know the virtue of those microscopes; for they did never delude, but rectify and inform their senses, nay, the world, said they, would be but blind without them, as it has been in former ages before those microscopes were invented.

After this, they took a charcoal, and viewing it with one of their best microscopes, discovered in it an infinite multitude of pores, some bigger, some less; so close and thick, that they left but very little space betwixt them to be filled with a solid body; and to give her Imperial Majesty a better assurance thereof, they counted in a line of them an inch long, no less than 2700 pores; from which observation they drew this following conclusion, to wit, that this multitude of pores was the cause of the blackness of the coal; for, said they, a body that has so many pores, from each of which no light is reflected, must necessarily look black, since black is nothing else but a privation of light, or a want of reflection.[63] But the Empress replied, that if all colours were made by reflection of light, and that black was as much a colour as any other colour; then certainly they contradicted themselves in saying, that black was made by want of reflection. However, not to interrupt your microscopical inspections, said she, let us see how vegetables appear through your glasses; whereupon they took a nettle, and by the virtue of the microscope, discovered that underneath the points of the nettle there were certain little bags or bladders containing a poisonous liquor, and when the points had made way into the interior parts of the skin, they like syringe-pipes served to convey that same liquor into them. To which observation the Empress replied, that if there were such poison

disappointed because he did not 'hear her say anything that was worth hearing, but that she was full of admiration, all admiration', *The Diary of Samuel Pepys*, ed. Robert Latham and William Matthews, 9 vols. (Berkeley: HarperCollins, 1995), 30 May 1667, vol. VIII, p. 243.

[63] The view held by Hobbes, *De Corpore* IV. 27; EW, vol. I, pp. 464–5; Hooke, *Micrographia*, Observation XVI. It was discussed by Boyle in *Experiments and Considerations concerning Colours*, WRB, vol. IV, pp. 70–6. Cavendish argues that colours are bodily motions, and that since motion is an essential quality of body, so is colour. For instance, the mind, being a body, is coloured, *Observations*, pp. 75–9.

in nettles, then certainly in eating of them, they would hurt us inwardly, as much as they do outwardly.[64] But they answered, that it belonged to physicians more than to experimental philosophers, to give reasons hereof; for they only made microscopical inspections, and related the figures of the natural parts of creatures according to the presentation of their glasses.

Lastly, they showed the Empress a flea, and a louse; which creatures through the microscope appeared so terrible to her sight, that they had almost put her into a swoon; the description of all their parts would be very tedious to relate, and therefore I'll forbear it at this present. The Empress after the view of those strangely-shaped creatures, pitied much those that are molested with them, especially poor beggars, which although they have nothing to live on themselves, are yet necessitated to maintain and feed of their own flesh and blood, a company of such terrible creatures called lice, who instead of thanks, do reward them with pains, and torment them for giving them nourishment and food. But after the Empress had seen the shapes of these monstrous creatures, she desired to know whether their microscopes could hinder their biting, or at least show some means how to avoid them? To which they answered, that such arts were mechanical and below that noble study of microscopical observations. Then the Empress asked them whether they had not such sorts of glasses that could enlarge and magnify the shapes of great bodies, as well as they had done of little ones? Whereupon they took one of their best and largest microscopes, and endeavoured to view a whale through it; but alas! the shape of the whale was so big, that its circumference went beyond the magnifying quality of the glass; whether the error proceeded from the glass, or from a wrong position of the whale against the reflection of light, I cannot certainly tell. The Empress seeing the insufficiency of those magnifying-glasses, that they were not able to enlarge all sorts of objects, asked the bear-men whether they could not make glasses of a contrary nature to those they had showed her, to wit, such as instead of enlarging or magnifying the shape or figure of an object, could contract it beneath its natural proportion: which, in obedience to her Majesty's commands, they did; and viewing through one of the best of them, a huge and mighty whale appeared no bigger than a sprat; nay, through some no bigger than a vinegar-eel; and through their ordinary ones, an elephant seemed no bigger than a flea; a camel no bigger than a louse; and an ostrich no bigger than a mite. To

[64] For the same point, see *Observations*, p. 57.

relate all their optic observations through the several sorts of their glasses, would be a tedious work, and tire even the most patient reader, wherefore I'll pass them by; only this was very remarkable and worthy to be taken notice of, that notwithstanding their great skill, industry and ingenuity in experimental philosophy, they could yet by no means contrive such glasses, by the help of which they could spy out a vacuum,[65] with all its dimensions, nor immaterial substances, non-beings, and mixed-beings, or such as are between something and nothing; which they were very much troubled at, hoping that yet, in time, by long study and practice, they might perhaps attain to it.

The bird- and bear-men being dismissed, the Empress called both the syrens, or fish-men, and the worm-men, to deliver their observations which they had made, both within the seas, and the earth. First she enquired of the fish-men whence the saltness of the sea did proceed? To which they answered, that there was a volatile salt in those parts of the earth, which as a bosom contain the waters of the sea, which salt being imbibed by the sea, became fixed; and this imbibing motion[66] was that they called the ebbing and flowing of the sea; for, said they, the rising and swelling of the water, is caused by those parts of the volatile salt as are not so easily imbibed, which striving to ascend above the water, bear it up with such a motion, as man, or some other animal creature, in a violent exercise uses to take breath. This they affirmed to be the true cause both of the saltness, and the ebbing and flowing motion of the sea, and not the jogging of the earth,[67] or the secret influence of the moon,[68] as some others had made the world believe.

After this, the Empress enquired, whether they had observed that all animal creatures within the seas and other waters, had blood?[69] They answered, that some had blood, more or less, but some had none; in

---

[65] Like Hobbes and Descartes, but unlike Boyle, Cavendish denied the possibility of a vacuum. She also denied the existence of immaterial substances, mixed beings, and non-beings. See *Observations*, p. 78.

[66] Aristotle, *Meteorology*, CWA, 356b4–359b26.

[67] Cavendish attributes this view to Galileo. *Philosophical and Physical Opinions*, V, 28. For Galileo's formulation see *Dialogue*, p. 494.

[68] J. Kepler, *New Astronomy* (1609), trans. William H. Donahue (Cambridge: Cambridge University Press, 1992), Author's Introduction, p. 56; Hobbes, *De Corpore*, IV. 26; EW, vol. I, p. 437.

[69] On this debate see Walter Charleton, *Natural History of Nutrition, Life and Voluntary Motion* (1659), Exercitation the Fifth: The Uses of Blood. Cf. *Grounds of Natural Philosophy*, Part 8, ch. 4; *Observations*, pp. 64–6. The view that animal spirits are corporeal motions was held by Descartes and Hobbes.

cray-fishes and lobsters, said they, we perceive but little blood; but in crabs, oysters, cockles, etc. none at all. Then the Empress asked them in what part of their bodies that little blood did reside? They answered, in a small vein, which in lobsters went through the middle of their tails, but in cray-fishes was found in their backs: as for other sorts of fishes, some, said they, had only blood about their gills, and others in some other places of their bodies; but they had not as yet observed any whose veins did spread all over their bodies. The Empress wondering that there could be living animals without blood, to be better satisfied, desired the worm-men to inform her, whether they had observed blood in all sorts of worms? They answered, that as much as they could perceive, some had blood, and some not; a moth, said they, had no blood at all, and a louse had but like a lobster, a little vein along her back: also nits, snails, and maggots, as well as those that are generated out of cheese and fruits, as those that are produced out of flesh, had no blood. But replied the Empress, if those mentioned creatures have no blood, how is it possible they can live; for it is commonly said, that the life of an animal consists in the blood, which is the seat of the animal spirits? They answered, that blood was not a necessary propriety to the life of an animal, and that which was commonly called animal spirits, was nothing else but corporeal motions proper to the nature and figure of an animal. Then she asked both the fish- and worm-men, whether all those creatures that have blood, had a circulation of blood in their veins and arteries? But they answered, that it was impossible to give her Majesty an exact account thereof, by reason the circulation of blood was an interior motion, which their senses, neither of themselves, nor by the help of any optic instrument could perceive; but as soon as they had directed an animal creature to find out the truth thereof, the interior corporeal motions proper to that particular figure or creature were altered. Then said the Empress, if all animal creatures have not blood, it is certain, they have neither all muscles, tendons, nerves, etc. But, said she, have you ever observed animal creatures that are neither flesh, nor fish, but of an intermediate degree between both. Truly, answered both the fish- and worm-men, we have observed several animal creatures that live both in water, and on the earth indifferently, and if any, certainly those may be said to be of such a mixed nature, that is, partly flesh, and partly fish: but how is it possible, replied the Empress, that they should live both in water, and on the earth, since those animals that live by the respiration of air, cannot live within water, and those that live in water, cannot live by the respiration of the air, as experience doth sufficiently witness.[70] They answered her Majesty, that as there were different sorts of creatures, so they had also different ways of respirations; for respiration, said they, was nothing else but a composition and division of parts, and the motions of nature being infinitely various, it was impossible that all creatures should have the like motions; wherefore it was not necessary, that all animal creatures should be bound to live either by the air, or by water only, but according as nature had ordered it convenient to their species. The Empress seemed very well satisfied with their answer, and desired to be further informed, whether all animal creatures did continue their species by a successive propagation of particulars, and whether in every species the off-spring did always resemble their generator or producer, both in their interior and exterior figures? They answered her Majesty, that some species or sorts of creatures, were kept up by a successive propagation of an offspring that was like the producer, but some were not; of the first rank, said they, are all those animals of different sexes, besides several others; but of the second rank are for the most part those we call insects, whose production proceeds from such causes as have no conformity or likeness with their produced effects; as for example, maggots bred out of cheese,[71] and several others generated out of earth, water and the like. But said the Empress, there is some likeness between maggots and cheese; for cheese has no blood, and so neither have maggots, besides, they have almost the same taste which cheese has. This proves nothing, answered they; for maggots have a visible, local, progressive motion, which cheese hath not. The Empress replied, that when all the cheese was turned into maggots, it might be said to have local, progressive motion. They answered, that when the cheese by its own figurative motions was changed into maggots, it was no more cheese. The Empress confessed that she observed nature was infinitely various in her works, and that though the species of creatures did continue, yet their particulars were subject to infinite changes. But since you have informed me, said she, of the various sorts and productions of animal creatures, I desire you to tell me what you have observed of their sensitive perceptions? Truly, answered they, your Majesty puts a very hard question to us, and we shall hardly be able to give

---

[70] These arguments are included in *Observations*, pp. 122–3, 247–8.

[71] In *Observations*, pp. 66–8, Cavendish argues (against her own earlier opinion) that some animals, including maggots, are produced by metamorphosis.

a satisfactory answer to it; for there are many different sorts of creatures, which as they have all different perceptions, so they have also different organs, which our senses are not able to discover, only in an oyster-shell we have with admiration observed, that the common sensorium[72] of the oyster lies just at the closing of the shells, where the pressure and reaction may be perceived by the opening and shutting of the shells every tide.

After all this, the Empress desired the worm-men to give her a true relation how frost was made upon the earth? To which they answered, that it was made much after the manner and description of the fish- and bird-men, concerning the congelation of water into ice and snow, by a commixture of saline and acid particles; which relation added a great light to the ape-men, who were the chemists, concerning their chemical principles, salt, sulphur and mercury. But, said the Empress, if it be so, it will require an infinite multitude of saline particles to produce such a great quantity of ice, frost and snow: besides, said she, when snow, ice and frost, turn again into their former principle, I would fain know what becomes of those saline particles? But neither the worm-men, nor the fish- and bird-men, could give her an answer to it.

Then the Empress enquired of them the reason, why springs were not as salt as the sea is? also, why springs did ebb and flow? To which some answered, that the ebbing and flowing of some springs was caused by hollow caverns within the earth,[73] where the sea-water crowding through, did thrust forward, and draw backward the spring-water, according to its own way of ebbing and flowing; but others said, that it proceeded from a small proportion of saline and acid particles, which the spring-water imbibed from the earth; and although it was not so much as to be perceived by the sense of taste, yet was it enough to cause an ebbing and flowing motion. And as for the spring-water being fresh, they gave, according to their observation, this following reason: there is, said they, a certain heat within the bowels of the earth, proceeding from its swift circular motion upon its own axe, which heat distils the rarest parts of the earth into a fresh and insipid water, which water being through the pores of the earth, conveyed into a place where it may break forth without resistance or obstruction, causes springs and fountains; and these distilled waters within the earth do nourish and refresh the grosser and dryer parts

---

[72] The part of the organism to which diverse sensory stimuli are transmitted. Aristotle, *On the Soul*, Book III.

[73] Van Helmont, *Oriatrike*, IX.57; Descartes, *Les Météores*, Discours III, AT VI, pp. 245–6.

thereof. This relation confirmed the Empress in the opinion concerning the motion of the earth, and the fixedness of the sun, as the bird-men had informed her; and then she asked the worm-men, whether minerals and vegetables were generated by the same heat that is within the bowels of the Earth? To which they could give her no positive answer; only, this they affirmed, that heat and cold were not the primary producing causes[74] of either vegetables or minerals, or other sorts of creatures, but only effects; and to prove this our assertion, said they, we have observed, that by change of some sorts of corporeal motions, that which is now hot, will become cold; and what is now cold, will grow hot; but the hottest place of all, we find to be the centre of the earth: neither do we observe, that the torrid zone does contain so much gold and silver as the temperate; nor is there great store of iron and lead wheresoever there is gold; for these metals are most found in colder climates towards either of the Poles. This observation, the Empress commanded them to confer with her chemists, the ape-men, to let them know that gold was not produced by a violent, but a temperate degree of heat. She asked further, whether gold could not be made by art? They answered, that they could not certainly tell her Majesty, but if it was possible to be done, they thought tin, lead, brass, iron, and silver, to be the fittest metals for such an artificial transmutation. Then she asked them, whether art could produce iron, tin, lead, or silver? They answered, not, in their opinion. Then I perceive, replied the Empress, that your judgements are very irregular,[75] since you believe that gold, which is so fixed a metal, that nothing has been found as yet which could occasion a dissolution of its interior figure, may be made by art, and not tin, lead, iron, copper, or silver, which yet are so far weaker, and meaner metals than gold is. But the worm-men excused themselves, that they were ignorant in that art, and that such questions belonged more properly to the ape-men, which were her Majesty's chemists.

Then the Empress asked them, whether by their sensitive perceptions they could observe the interior corporeal, figurative motions both of vegetables and minerals? They answered, that their senses could perceive them after they were produced, but not before; nevertheless, said they,

---

[74] 'Bodies are formed by heat and cold and . . . these agents work by thickening and solidifying', Aristotle, *Meteorology*, CWA, 384b24–25.

[75] Cf. *Philosophical Letters*, where Cavendish makes light of Van Helmont's claim that quicksilver, treated with a certain powder, will produce gold. 'I myself would turn into a chemist to gain so much as to repair my husband's losses, that his noble family might flourish the better', Part IV, Letter XXIV.

although the interior, figurative motions of natural creatures are not subject to the exterior, animal, sensitive perceptions, yet by their rational perception they may judge of them, and of their productions if they be regular: whereupon the Empress commanded the bear-men to lend them some of their best microscopes; at which the bear-men smilingly answered her Majesty, that their glasses would do them but little service in the bowels of the earth, because there was no light; for, said they, our glasses do only represent exterior objects, according to the various reflections and positions of light; and wheresoever light is wanting, the glasses will do no good. To which the worm-men replied, that although they could not say much of refractions, reflections, inflections, and the like; yet were they not blind, even in the bowels of the earth; for they could see the several sorts of minerals, as also minute animals, that lived there, which minute animal creatures were not blind neither, but had some kind of sensitive perception[76] that was as serviceable to them as sight, taste, smell, touch, hearing, etc. was to other animal creatures: by which it is evident, that nature has been as bountiful to those creatures that live underground, or in the bowels of the earth, as to those that live upon the surface of the earth, or in the air, or in water. But howsoever, proceeded the worm-men, although there is light in the bowels of the earth, yet your microscopes will do but little good there, by reason those creatures that live under ground have not such an optic sense as those that live on the surface of the earth: wherefore, unless you had such glasses as are proper for their perception, your microscopes will not be anyways advantageous to them. The Empress seemed well pleased with this answer of the worm-men; and asked them further, whether minerals and all the other creatures within the earth, were colourless? At which question they could not forbear laughing; and when the Empress asked the reason why they laughed; we most humbly beg your Majesty's pardon, replied they; for we could not choose but laugh, when we heard of a colourless body.[77] Why, said the Empress,

---

[76] On the diversity of forms of sensory perception see *Observations*, pp. 82–3: 'But as for colour, some do mention the example of a blind man, who could discover colours by touch; and truly, I cannot account it a wonder, because colours are corporeal figurative motions, and touch being a general sense, may well perceive by experience . . . some notion of other sensitive perceptions; as, for example, a blind man may know by relation the several touches of water, milk, broth, jelly, vinegar, vitriol, etc., as well as what is hot, cold, rare, dense, hard, soft, or the like; and if he have but his touch, hearing, speaking and smelling, perfectly, he may express the knowledge of his several senses, by one particular sense; or he may express one sense's knowledge by another.'

[77] The worm-men hold that colour is an essential property of bodies, against the view of Galileo, Descartes, and Hobbes who regard colour as a secondary quality. Henry Power

colour is only an accident, which is an immaterial thing, and has no being of itself, but in another body. Those, replied they, that informed your Majesty thus, surely their rational motions were very irregular; for how is it possible, that a natural nothing can have a being in nature? If it be no substance, it cannot have a being, and if no being, it is nothing; wherefore the distinction between subsisting of itself, and subsisting in another body, is a mere nicety, and nonsense,[78] for there is nothing in nature that can subsist of, or by itself, (I mean singly) by reason all parts of nature are composed in one body, and though they may be infinitely divided, commixed and changed in their particulars, yet in general, parts cannot be separated from parts as long as nature lasts; nay, we might as probably affirm, that infinite nature would be as soon destroyed, as that one atom could perish; and therefore your Majesty may firmly believe, that there is no body without colour, nor no colour without body; for colour, figure, place, magnitude, and body, are all but one thing, without any separation or abstraction from each other.

The Empress was so wonderfully taken with this discourse of the wormmen, that she not only pardoned the rudeness they committed in laughing at first at her question, but yielded a full assent to their opinion, which she thought the most rational that ever she had heard yet; and then proceeding in her questions, enquired further, whether they had observed any seminal principles within the earth, free from all dimensions and qualities, which produced vegetables, minerals and the like? To which they answered, that concerning the seeds of minerals, their sensitive perceptions had never observed any; but vegetables had certain seeds out of which they were produced. Then she asked, whether those seeds of vegetables lost their species; that is, were annihilated in the production of their off-spring? To which they answered, that by an annihilation, nothing could be produced, and that the seeds of vegetables were so far from being annihilated in their productions, that they did rather numerously increase and multiply; for the division of one seed, said they, does produce numbers of seeds out of itself. But replied the Empress, a particular part cannot increase of itself.

offers experimental support for the latter position, pointing out that bodies lose their colours when viewed under a microscope, *Experimental Philosophy*, p. 72. Cavendish defends the worm-men's view that colour is an intrinsic property of bodies, *Grounds of Natural Philosophy*, ch. 29; *Philosophical Letters*, Part I, Letter XIX.

[78] The Aristotelian distinction between substances, and accidents or modes, was retained by many defenders of the New Science, e.g. Descartes and Hobbes. The worm-men defend Cavendish's own view that there are no substances in nature other than nature itself. See *Observations*, p. 36.

'Tis true, answered they: but they increase not barely of themselves, but by joining and commixing with other parts, which do assist them in their productions, and by way of imitation form or figure their own parts into such or such particulars.[79] Then, I pray inform me, said the Empress, what disguise those seeds put on, and how they do conceal themselves in their transmutations? They answered, that seeds did no ways disguise or conceal, but rather divulge themselves in the multiplication of their off-spring; only they did hide and conceal themselves from their sensitive perceptions so, that their figurative and productive motions were not perceptible by animal creatures. Again, the Empress asked them, whether there were any non-beings within the earth? To which they answered, that they never heard of any such thing; and that, if her Majesty would know the truth thereof, she must ask those creatures that are called immaterial spirits, which had a great affinity with non-beings, and perhaps could give her a satisfactory answer to this question. Then she desired to be informed, what opinion they had of the beginning of forms?[80] They told her Majesty, that they did not understand what she meant by this expression, for, said they, there is no beginning in nature,[81] no not of particulars, by reason nature is eternal and infinite, and her particulars are subject to infinite changes and transmutations by virtue of their own corporeal, figurative self-motions; so that there's nothing new in nature, nor properly a beginning of any thing. The Empress seemed well satisfied with all those answers, and inquired further, whether there was no art used by those creatures that live within the earth? Yes, answered they: for the several parts of the earth do join and assist each other in composition or framing of such or such particulars; and many times, there are factions and divisions, which cause productions of mixed species; as for example, weeds, instead of sweet flowers and useful fruits; but gardeners and husbandmen use often to decide their quarrels, and cause them to agree;

---

[79] William Harvey, *Disputations Touching the Generation of Animals*, trans. G. Whitteridge (Oxford: Blackwell, 1981), p. 96; Thomas Digby, *Two Treatises* (1645), reprinted New York: Garland, 1978), p. 215. On seventeenth-century views of generation see Catherine Wilson, *The Invisible World*.

[80] According to Aristotle, individual substances are composed of matter and form. *Metaphysics*, CWA, 1042a3–1042b3. The form of a substance explains its properties and powers. Some advocates of the New Science, e.g. Descartes and Hobbes, criticised forms on the same grounds as the worm-men.

[81] This heterodox view conflicts with the Christian dogma that nature came into existence when God created it. Cf. *Philosophical Letters*, II. See James, 'Innovations of Margaret Cavendish', p. 230.

which though it shows a kindness to the differing parties, yet 'tis a great prejudice to the worms, and other animal creatures that live underground; for it most commonly causes their dissolution and ruin, at best they are driven out of their habitations. What, said the Empress, are not worms produced out of the earth? Their production in general, answered they, is like the production of all other natural creatures, proceeding from the corporeal figurative motions of nature; but as for their particular productions, they are according to the nature of their species; some are produced out of flowers, some out of roots, some out of fruits, some out of ordinary earth. Then they are very ungrateful children, replied the Empress, that they feed on their own parents which gave them life. Their life, answered they, is their own, and not their parents; for no part or creature of nature can either give or take away life, but parts do only assist and join with parts,[82] either in the dissolution or production of other parts and creatures.

After this, and several other conferences, which the Empress held with the worm-men, she dismissed them; and having taken much satisfaction in several of their answers, encouraged them in their studies and observations. Then she made a convocation of her chemists, the ape-men, and commanded them to give her an account of the several transmutations which their art was able to produce. They began first with a long and tedious discourse concerning the primitive ingredients of natural bodies, and how, by their art, they had found out the principles out of which they consist. But they did not all agree in their opinions; for some said, that the principles of all natural bodies were the four elements, fire, air, water, earth, out of which they were composed:[83] others rejected this elementary commixture, and said, there were many bodies out of which none of the four elements could be extracted by any degree of fire whatsoever; and that, on the other side, there were divers bodies, whose resolution by fire reduced them into more than four different ingredients; and these affirmed, that the only principles of natural bodies were salt, sulphur, and mercury:[84] others again declared, that none of the forementioned could be

---

[82] Cf. *Philosophical and Physical Opinions*, p. 17.

[83] See Aristotle, *On the Heavens*, Books III and IV, and subsequent Aristotelians, e.g. Digby, *Two Treatises*, First Treatise, ch. 4. Cf. *Observations*, pp. 227–9.

[84] The view of Paracelsus and subsequent chemists. See Allen G. Debus, *The English Paracelsans* (London: Oldbourne, 1965), pp. 26–9. Cf. *Observations*, p. 231. Both Aristotelian and chemical views are criticised by Boyle. *The Sceptical Chemist* (1661), WRB, vol. II, pp. 215–442.

called the true principles of natural bodies, but that by their industry and pains which they had taken in the art of chemistry, they had discovered, that all natural bodies were produced but from one principle, which was water;[85] for all vegetables, minerals and animals, said they, are nothing else, but simple water distinguished into various figures by the virtue of their seeds. But after a great many debates and contentions about this subject, the Empress being so much tired that she was not able to hear them any longer, imposed a general silence upon them, and then declared herself in this following discourse:

I am too sensible of the pains you have taken in the art of chemistry, to discover the principles of natural bodies, and wish they had been more profitably bestowed upon some other, than such experiments; for both by my own contemplation, and the observations which I have made by my rational and sensitive perception upon nature, and her works, I find, that nature is but one infinite self-moving body,[86] which by the virtue of its self-motion, is divided into infinite parts, which parts being restless, undergo perpetual changes and transmutations by their infinite compositions and divisions. Now, if this be so, as surely, according to regular sense and reason, it appears not otherwise; it is in vain to look for primary ingredients, or constitutive principles of natural bodies, since there is no more but one universal principle of nature, to wit, self-moving matter, which is the only cause of all natural effects.[87] Next, I desire you to consider, that fire is but a particular creature, or effect of nature, and occasions not only different effects in several bodies, but on some bodies has no power at all; witness gold, which never could be brought yet to change its interior figure by the art of fire; and if this be so, why should you be so simple as to believe that fire can show you the principles of nature? and that either the four elements, or water only, or salt, sulphur, and mercury, all which are no more but particular effects and creatures of nature, should be the primitive ingredients or principles of all natural bodies? Wherefore, I will

---

[85] Van Helmont, *Oriatrike*, VIII.17; Robert Fludd, *Mosaicall Philosophy. Grounded on the Essential Truth or Eternal Sapience* (London, 1659), p. 48. On Fludd see Debus, *The English Paracelsans*, pp. 105–27. Cf. *Observations*, pp. 205, 229.

[86] Cavendish's own view. Cf. *Observations*, p. 137.

[87] Philosophers with an interest in the New Science were generally sceptical about the Aristotelian and Paracelsan accounts of the elements. Nevertheless, the view that the principle of all natural creatures is salt is defended by Nicolas Le Fèvre, *A Compleat Body of Chemistry* (London, 1664), Joseph Duchesne [Quercatanus], *The Practice of Chymicall and Hermeticall Physicke* trans. Thomas Timmes (London, 1605) and William Newcastle, Appendix to Margaret Cavendish, *Philosophical and Physical Opinions*.

not have you to take more pains, and waste your time in such fruitless attempts, but be wiser hereafter, and busy yourselves with such experiments as may be beneficial to the public.

The Empress having thus declared her mind to the ape-men, and given them better instructions than perhaps they expected, not knowing that her Majesty had such great and able judgement in natural philosophy, had several conferences with them concerning chemical preparations, which for brevity's sake, I'll forbear to rehearse: amongst the rest, she asked, how it came, that the imperial race appeared so young, and yet was reported to have lived so long; some of them two, some three, and some four hundred years?[88] and whether it was by nature, or a special divine blessing? To which they answered, that there was a certain rock in the parts of that world, which contained the golden sands, which rock was hollow within, and did produce a gum that was a hundred years before it came to its full strength and perfection; this gum, said they, if it be held in a warm hand, will dissolve into an oil, the effects whereof are the following:[89] it being given every day for some certain time to an old decayed man, in the bigness of a little pea, will first make him spit for a week or more; after this, it will cause vomits of phlegm, and after that it will bring forth by vomits, humours of several colours: first of a pale yellow, then of a deep yellow, then of a green, and lastly of a black colour; and each of these humours have a several taste, some are fresh, some salt, some sour, some bitter, and so forth; neither do all these vomits make them sick, but they come out on a sudden and unawares, without any pain or trouble to the patient: and after it hath done all these mentioned effects, and cleared both the stomach and several other parts of the body, then it works upon the brain, and brings forth of the nose such kind of humours as it did out of the mouth, and much after the same manner; then it will purge by stool, then by urine, then by sweat, and lastly by bleeding at the nose, and the emeroids; all which effects it will perform within the space of six weeks, or a little more; for it does not work very strongly, but gently, and by degrees: lastly, when it has done all this, it will make the body break

---

[88] Cavendish also argues that it is possible for a human who has lost certain properties 'to be repeated' and have them restored. *Grounds of Natural Philosophy*, Part VII, ch. 11.

[89] Alchemists searched for the elixir of life. John Thornborough, Bishop of Bristol, presented such an elixir to James I: 'he presented a precious extraction to King James, reputed to be a great preserver of health, and prolonger of life. He conceived by such helps to have added to his vigorous vivacity, though I think a merry heart, whereof he had a great measure, was his best elixir to that purpose', Thomas Fuller, *The Worthies of England*, ed. John Freeman (London: Allen and Unwin, 1952), p. 165. James died at the age of sixty-one.

out into a thick scab, and cause both hair, teeth and nails to come off;
which scab being arrived to its full maturity, opens first along the back,
and comes off all in a piece like an armour, and all this is done within the
space of four months. After this the patient is wrapped into a cere-cloth,
prepared of certain gums and juices, wherein he continues until the time
of nine months be expired from the first beginning of the cure, which is
the time of a child's formation in the womb. In the meanwhile his diet
is nothing else but eagle's-eggs, and hind's-milk; and after the cere-cloth
is taken away, he will appear of the age of twenty, both in shape, and
strength. The weaker sort of this gum is sovereign in healing of wounds,
and curing of slight distempers. But this is also to be observed, that none
of the imperial race does use any other drink but lime-water, or water
in which lime-stone is immersed; their meat is nothing else but fowl of
several sorts, their recreations are many, but chiefly hunting.

This relation amazed the Empress very much; for though in the world
she came from, she had heard great reports of the philosopher's stone,[90]
yet had she not heard of any that had ever found it out, which made her
believe that it was but a chimera; she called also to mind, that there had
been in the same world a man who had a little stone which cured all kinds
of diseases outward and inward, according as it was applied; and that a
famous chemist had found out a certain liquor called alkahest,[91] which by
the virtue of its own fire, consumed all diseases; but she had never heard
of a medicine that could renew old age, and render it beautiful, vigorous
and strong: nor would she have so easily believed it, had it been a medicine
prepared by art; for she knew that art, being nature's changeling, was not
able to produce such a powerful effect, but being that the gum did grow
naturally, she did not so much scruple at it; for she knew that nature's
works are so various and wonderful, that no particular creature is able to
trace her ways.

The conferences of the chemists being finished, the Empress made an
assembly of her Galenical Physicians,[92] her herbalists and anatomists; and
first she enquired of her herbalists the particular effects of several herbs
and drugs, and whence they proceeded? To which they answered, that
they could, for the most part, tell her Majesty the virtues and operations

---

[90] Sought by alchemists who believed that it would turn other substances to gold. Cf. *Observations*, p. 241.
[91] The name, probably coined by Paracelsus, of the universal solvent sought by alchemists.
[92] Followers of Galen of Pergamum (129?–199 CE).

of them, but the particular causes of their effects were unknown; only thus much they could say, that their operations and virtues were generally caused by their proper inherent, corporeal, figurative motions, which being infinitely various in infinite nature, did produce infinite several effects. And it is observed, said they, that herbs and drugs are as wise in their operations, as men in their words and actions; nay, wiser; and their effects are more certain than men in their opinions; for though they cannot discourse like men, yet have they sense and reason, as well as men; for the discursive faculty is but a particular effect of sense and reason in some particular creatures, to wit, men, and not a principle of nature, and argues often more folly than wisdom. The Empress asked, whether they could not by a composition and commixture of other drugs, make them work other effects than they did, used by themselves?[93] They answered, that they could make them produce artificial effects, but not alter their inherent, proper and particular natures.

Then the Empress commanded her anatomists to dissect such kinds of creatures as are called monsters.[94] But they answered her Majesty, that it would be but an unprofitable and useless work, and hinder their better employments; for when we dissect dead animals,[95] said they, it is for no other end, but to observe what defects or distempers they had, that we may cure the like in living ones, so that all our care and industry concerns only the preservation of mankind; but we hope your Majesty will not preserve monsters, which are most commonly destroyed, except it be for novelty; neither will the dissection of monsters prevent the errors of nature's irregular actions; for by dissecting some, we cannot prevent the production of others; so that our pains and labours will be to no purpose, unless to satisfy the vain curiosities of inquisitive men. The Empress replied, that such dissections would be very beneficial to experimental

[93] Influenced by Paracelsus, English physicians accepted the use of some chemical remedies in England from the end of the sixteenth century. More wholeheartedly, Van Helmont aimed to replace the Galenic corpus with a medicine based on chemistry. See Debus, *The English Paracelsans*, pp. 181–3.

[94] Dissections of deformed, newborn animals were reported at meetings of the Royal Society. For discussion of a 'monstrous birth' see *Proceedings*, June 1667, pp. 479–80. Cf. *The World's Olio*, III. 1.

[95] Dissection was practised by some of the natural philosophers discussed in *Philosophical Letters*, e.g. Descartes and Harvey, and was part of the experimental approach favoured by the Royal Society. The Empress's anatomists take Cavendish's own view. See *Philosophical Letters*, Part I, Letter XXXIII; *Observations*, p. 225.

philosophers. If experimental philosophers, answered they, do spend their time in such useless inspections, they waste it in vain, and have nothing but their labour for their pains.

Lastly, her Majesty had some conferences with the Galenic physicians about several diseases, and amongst the rest, desired to know the cause and nature of apoplexy, and the spotted plague.[96] They answered, that a deadly apoplexy was a dead palsy of the brain, and the spotted plague was a gangrene of the vital parts, and as the gangrene of outward parts did strike inwardly; so the gangrene of inward parts, did break forth outwardly; which is the cause, said they, that as soon as the spots appear, death follows; for then it is an infallible sign, that the body is throughout infected with a gangrene, which is a spreading evil; but some gangrenes do spread more suddenly than others, and of all sorts of gangrenes, the plaguey-gangrene is the most infectious; for other gangrenes infect but the next adjoining parts of one particular body, and having killed that same creature, go no further, but cease; whenas, the gangrene of the plague, infects not only the adjoining parts of one particular creature, but also those that are distant; that is, one particular body infects another, and so breeds a universal contagion. But the Empress being very desirous to know in what manner the plague was propagated and became so contagious, asked, whether it went actually out of one body into another? To which they answered, that it was a great dispute amongst the learned of the profession, whether it came by a division and composition of parts, that is, by expiration and inspiration; or whether it was caused by imitation: some experimental philosophers, said they, will make us believe, that by the help of their microscopes, they have observed the plague to be a body of little flies, like atoms, which go out of one body into another, through the sensitive passages;[97] but the most experienced and wisest of our society, have rejected this opinion as a ridiculous fancy, and do for the

---

[96] Cf. *Grounds of Natural Philosophy*, Part 10, ch. 2, and *Observations*, pp. 245–7. On theories of contagion see Wilson, *The Invisible World*, pp. 140–61.

[97] Walter Charleton records an observation made in Rome that 'there was a kind of insect in the air, which being put upon a man's hand, would lay eggs scarcely discernible without a microscope; which eggs being for an experiment given to be snuffed up by a dog, the dog fell into a distemper accompanied by all the symptoms of the plague'. Thomas Birch, *History of the Royal Society*, vol. II, p. 69. Athanasius Kircher claimed to be able to see the animate 'seeds' of 'worms' through a microscope and argued that they were the cause of plague, *Scrutinium physico-medicum contagiosae luis, quae pestis dicitur* (*A Physico-Medical Enquiry of the Contagious Plague which is called the Pest*) (Rome, 1658).

most part believe, that it is caused by an imitation of parts,[98] so that the motions of some parts which are sound, do imitate the motions of those that are infected, and that by this means, the plague becomes contagious and spreading.

The Empress having hitherto spent her time in the examination of the bird-, fish-, worm- and ape-men, etc. and received several intelligences from their several employments; at last had a mind to divert herself after her serious discourses, and therefore she sent for the spider-men, which were her mathematicians, the lice-men, which were her geometricians, and the magpie-, parrot- and jackdaw-men, which were her orators and logicians. The spider-men came first, and presented her Majesty with a table full of mathematical points, lines and figures of all sorts of squares, circles, triangles, and the like; which the Empress, notwithstanding that she had a very ready wit, and quick apprehension, could not understand; but the more she endeavoured to learn, the more was she confounded: whether they did ever square the circle,[99] I cannot exactly tell, nor whether they could make imaginary points and lines;[100] but this I dare say, that their points and lines were so slender, small and thin, that they seemed next to imaginary. The mathematicians were in great esteem with the Empress, as being not only the chief tutors and instructors in many arts, but some of them excellent magicians[101] and informers of spirits, which was the reason their characters were so abstruse and intricate, that the Empress knew not what to make of them. There is so much to learn in

---

[98] Cavendish's own view.

[99] In 1645 Charles Cavendish, Margaret's brother-in-law, was involved in a controversy between the mathematicians John Pell and Christian Longborg about squaring the circle. Hobbes's claim to have squared the circle, published in *De Corpore* (1655), was contested by John Wallis and Seth Ward, professors of geometry and astronomy at Oxford. Their acrimonious dispute dragged on until 1678. See Douglas M. Jesseph, *The Squaring of the Circle. The War between Hobbes and Wallis* (Chicago: Chicago University Press, 1993).

[100] Euclidean mathematicians regarded points and lines as immaterial. See, e.g., Clavius's definition of a line: '(m)athematicians also, in order to teach us the true understanding of the line imagine a point . . . to be moved from one place to another. Now since the point is absolutely indivisible, there will be left behind by this imaginary motion a certain path lacking in all breadth', Christopher Clavius, *Opera Mathematica* (Mainz, 1612), 5 vols., vol. I, p. 13. Hobbes's opposition to this view was contested by Wallis. See Jesseph, *The Squaring of the Circle*, pp. 76–81. The Empress sides with Hobbes.

[101] John Dee (1527–1608) published a 'Mathematical Preface' to Henry Billingsley's translation of Euclid's *Elements of Geometry* (1570). He was accused of sorcery and acquitted by the Court of Star Chamber in the 1550s. In 1604 he petitioned King James I to be formally cleared of the charge of being a magician. See n. 114.

your art, said she, that I can neither spare time from other affairs to busy myself in your profession; nor, if I could, do I think I should ever be able to understand your imaginary points, lines and figures, because they are non-beings.

Then came the lice-men, and endeavoured to measure all things to a hair's breadth, and weigh them to an atom; but their weights would seldom agree, especially in the weighing of air,[102] which they found a task impossible to be done; at which the Empress began to be displeased, and told them, that there was neither truth nor justice in their profession; and so dissolved their society.

After this the Empress was resolved to hear the magpie-, parrot- and jackdaw-men, which were her professed orators and logicians; whereupon one of the parrot-men rose with great formality, and endeavoured to make an eloquent speech before her Majesty; but before he had half ended, his arguments and divisions being so many, that they caused a great confusion in his brain, he could not go forward, but was forced to retire backward, with the greatest disgrace both to himself, and the whole society; and although one of his brethren endeavoured to second him by another speech, yet was he as far to seek as the former. At which the Empress appeared not a little troubled, and told them, that they followed too much the rules of art, and confounded themselves with too nice formalities and distinctions; but since I know, said she, that you are a people who have naturally voluble tongues, and good memories; I desire you to consider more the subject you speak of, than your artificial periods, connexions and parts of speech, and leave the rest to your natural eloquence; which they did, and so became very eminent orators.

Lastly, her Imperial Majesty being desirous to know, what progress her logicians had made in the art of disputing, commanded them to argue upon several themes or subjects; which they did; and having made a very nice discourse of logistical terms and propositions, entered into a dispute by way of syllogistical arguments,[103] through all the figures and

---

[102] Boyle did a series of experiments relating to the vacuum in the 1660s, and his air pump was one of the Royal Society's showpieces. 'New Experiments Physico-Mechanical Touching the Spring in the Air and its Effects' (1660) in WRB, vol. I, pp. 141–300. Hobbes replied in *Dialogus Physicus* (1661) and Boyle responded in 1662. See Steven Shapin and Simon Shaffer, *Leviathan and the Air Pump. Hobbes, Boyle and the Experimental Life* (Princeton: Princeton University Press, 1985).

[103] Parody of the syllogism, a mode of formal reasoning which was the mainstay of Aristotelian argument and remained central to seventeenth-century logic. E.g., it is treated at length by Antoine Arnauld and Pierre Nicole in *Logic or the Art of Thinking*, ed. Jill Vance Buroker

modes: one began with an argument of the first mode of the first figure, thus:

> Every politician is wise:
> Every knave is a politician,
> Therefore every knave is wise.

Another contradicted him with a syllogism of the second mode of the same figure, thus:

> No politician is wise:
> Every knave is a politician,
> Therefore no knave is wise.

The third made an argument in the third mode of the same figure, after this manner:

> Every politician is wise:
> Some knaves are politicians,
> Therefore some knaves are wise.

The fourth concluded with a syllogism in the fourth mode of the same figure, thus:

> No politician is wise:
> Some knaves are politicians,
> Therefore some knaves are not wise.

After this they took another subject, and one propounded this syllogism:

> Every philosopher is wise:
> Every beast is wise,
> Therefore every beast is a philosopher.

But another said that this argument was false, therefore he contradicted him with a syllogism of the second figure of the fourth mode, thus:

> Every philosopher is wise:
> Some beasts are not wise,
> Therefore some beasts are not philosophers.

(Cambridge: Cambridge University Press, 1996), Part III. The art of formal disputation displayed by the Empress's logicians was a key part of the university curriculum. On the view that formal logic impedes rather than advances reasoning see, e.g., Philip Sidney, 'The Defense of Poesie' in *The Prose Works*, ed. A. Feuillerat (Cambridge: Cambridge University Press, 1962), vol. III, pp. 13–14.

Thus they argued, and intended to go on, but the Empress interrupted them: I have enough, said she, of your chopped logic, and will hear no more of your syllogisms; for it disorders my reason, and puts my brain on the rack; your formal argumentations are able to spoil all natural wit; and I'll have you to consider, that art does not make reason, but reason makes art; and therefore as much as reason is above art, so much is a natural rational discourse to be preferred before an artificial: for art is, for the most part, irregular, and disorders men's understandings more than it rectifies them, and leads them into a labyrinth whence they'll never get out, and makes them dull and unfit for useful employments; especially your art of logic, which consists only in contradicting each other, in making sophisms, and obscuring truth, instead of clearing it.

But they replied [to] her Majesty, that the knowledge of nature, that is, natural philosophy, would be imperfect without the art of logic, and that there was an improbable truth which could no otherwise be found out than by the art of disputing. Truly, said the Empress, I do believe that it is with natural philosophy, as it is with all other effects of nature; for no particular knowledge can be perfect, by reason knowledge is dividable, as well as composable; nay, to speak properly, nature herself cannot boast of any perfection, but God himself; because there are so many irregular motions in nature, and 'tis but a folly to think that art should be able to regulate them, since art itself is, for the most part, irregular. But as for improbable truth, I know not what your meaning is; for truth is more than improbability; nay, there is so much difference between truth and improbability, that I cannot conceive it possible how they can be joined together.[104] In short, said she, I do no ways approve of your profession; and though I will not dissolve your society, yet I shall never take delight in hearing you any more; wherefore confine your disputations to your

---

[104] Some supporters of the New Science opposed the scholastic view that natural philosophy must reach conclusions that are certain, and argued instead that it should aim to establish claims that are probable. This view was held, e.g., by Boyle, Glanvill, and Charleton. Cavendish agrees, though she does not think their experimental approach is the best way to arrive at probable claims. 'Though we are all but guessers, yet he that brings the most probable and rational arguments, does come nearer to the truth than those whose ground is only fancy without reason', *Observations*, p. 269. See Stephen Clucas, 'Variation, Irregularity and Probabilism: Margaret Cavendish and Natural Philosophy as Rhetoric' in *A Princely Brave Woman. Essays on Margaret Cavendish, Duchess of Newcastle* (London: Ashgate, 2003), pp. 199–209; Barbara J. Shapiro, *Probability and Certainty in Seventeenth-century England: A Study of the Relationships between Natural Science, Religion, History, Law and Literature* (Princeton: Princeton University Press, 1983); Henry G. van Leeuwen, *The Problem of Certainty in English Thought, 1630–1690* (The Hague: Nijhoff, 1963).

schools,[105] lest besides the commonwealth of learning, they disturb also divinity and policy, religion and laws, and by that means draw an utter ruin and destruction both upon church and state.

After the Empress had thus finished the discourses and conferences with the mentioned societies of her virtuosos, she considered by herself the manner of their religion, and finding it very defective, was troubled, that so wise and knowing a people should have no more knowledge of the divine truth; wherefore she consulted with her own thoughts, whether it was possible to convert them all to her own religion, and to that end she resolved to build churches, and make also up a congregation of women, whereof she intended to be the head herself, and to instruct them in several points of her religion.[106] This she had no sooner begun, but the women, which generally had quick wits, subtle conceptions, clear understandings, and solid judgements, became, in a short time, very devout and zealous sisters; for the Empress had an excellent gift of preaching, and instructing them in the articles of faith; and by that means, she converted them not only soon, but gained an extraordinary love of all her subjects throughout that world. But at last, pondering with herself the inconstant nature of mankind, and fearing that in time they would grow weary, and desert the divine truth, following their own fancies, and living according to their own desires, she began to be troubled that her labours and pains should prove of so little effect, and therefore studied all manner of ways to prevent it. Amongst the rest, she called to mind a relation which the bird-men made her once, of a mountain that did burn in flames of fire – and thereupon did immediately send for the wisest and subtlest of her worm-men, commanding them to discover the cause of the eruption of that same fire; which they did; and having dived to the very bottom of the mountain, informed her Majesty, that there was a certain sort of stone, whose nature was such, that being wetted, it would grow excessively hot, and break forth into a flaming-fire, until it became dry, and then it ceased from burning. The Empress was glad to hear this news, and forthwith desired the worm-men to bring her some of that stone, but be sure to keep it secret: she sent also for the bird-men, and asked them whether they could not get her a piece of the sun-stone? They answered, that it

---

[105] Cf. n. 61.

[106] Cf. Newcastle's advice to Charles II. 'Neyther can a Prince bee Soverayne so much as in civill Matters, so long as any other besides himselfe, Eyther abroade, or att home, Doth claim, and Exercise a soveraynety over the same subjects, though in pretence it bee but in Eclesiasticis only.' *Advice*, p. 13. See also Hobbes, *Leviathan*, ch. 29, p. 225.

was impossible, unless they did spoil or lessen the light of the world: but, said they, if it please your Majesty, we can demolish one of the numerous stars of the sky, which the world will never miss.

The Empress was very well satisfied with this proposal, and having thus employed these two sorts of men, in the meanwhile built two chapels[107] one above another; the one she lined throughout with diamonds, both roof, walls and pillars; but the other she resolved to line with the star-stone; the fire-stone she placed upon the diamond-lining, by reason fire has no power on diamonds; and when she would have that chapel where the firestone was, appear all in a flame, she had by the means of artificial-pipes, water conveyed into it, which by turning the cock, did, as out of a fountain, spring over all the room, and as long as the fire-stone was wet, the chapel seemed to be all in a flaming fire.

The other chapel, which was lined with the star-stone,[108] did only cast a splendorous and comfortable light; both the chapels stood upon pillars, just in the middle of a round cloister which was dark as night; neither was there any other light within them, but what came from the fire- and star-stone; and being everywhere open, allowed to all that were within the compass of the cloister, a free prospect into them; besides, they were so artificially contrived[109] that they did both move in a circle about their own centres, without intermission, contrary ways. In the chapel which was lined with the fire-stone, the Empress preached sermons of terror to the wicked, and told them of the punishments for their sins, to wit, that after this life they should be tormented in an everlasting fire. But in the other chapel lined with the star-stone, she preached sermons of comfort to those that repented of their sins, and were troubled at their own wickedness; neither did the heat of the flame in the least hinder her; for the fire-stone did not cast so great a heat but the Empress was able to endure it, by reason the water which was poured on the stone, by its own self-motion turned into a flaming fire, occasioned by the natural motions of the stone, which made the flame weaker than if it had been fed by some other kind of

[107] Henrietta Maria, the Catholic queen of Charles I, had built a magnificent chapel at Somerset House, lit by four hundred candles. See Battigelli, *Margaret Cavendish*, p. 17.

[108] Pliny mentions a fire stone, *Natural History*, Book XXXVII. xlvii, and a star stone, Book XXXVII. xxv. Ed. W. H. S. Jones (Cambridge, MA: Harvard University Press, 1966), vol. X, pp. 239, 271.

[109] In the theatre, and in the courts of kings and princes, mechanically produced effects designed to evoke wonder and admiration were highly prized during the seventeenth century. Nevertheless, this account of the use of artifice to sustain religious belief is unusual.

fuel; the other chapel where the star-stone was, although it did cast a great light, yet was it without all heat, and the Empress appeared like an angel in it; and as that chapel was an emblem of Hell, so this was an emblem of Heaven. And thus the Empress, by art, and her own ingenuity, did not only convert the Blazing World to her own religion, but kept them in a constant belief, without enforcement or blood-shed; for she knew well, that belief was a thing not to be forced or pressed upon the people,[110] but to be instilled into their minds by gentle persuasions; and after this manner she encouraged them also in all other duties and employments, for fear, though it makes people obey, yet does it not last so long, nor is it so sure a means to keep them to their duties, as love.[111]

Last of all, when she saw that both church and state was now in a well-ordered and settled condition, her thoughts reflected upon the world she came from; and though she had a great desire to know the condition of the same, yet could she advise no manner of way how to gain any knowledge thereof; at last, after many serious considerations, she conceived that it was impossible to be done by any other means, than by the help of immaterial spirits; wherefore she made a convocation of the most learned, witty and ingenious of all the forementioned sorts of men, and desired to know of them, whether there were any immaterial spirits in their world. First, she enquired of the worm-men, whether they had perceived some within the earth? They answered her Majesty, that they never knew of any such creatures; for whatsoever did dwell within the earth, said they, was embodied and material. Then she asked the fly-men, whether they had observed any in the air? for you having numerous eyes, said she, will be more able to perceive them, than any other creatures. To which they answered her Majesty, that although spirits, being immaterial, could not be perceived by the worm-men in the earth, yet they perceived that such creatures did lodge in the vehicles of the air.[112] Then the Empress asked, whether they could speak to them, and whether they did understand

---

[110] 'But as for Conscience, and holy Notions, they being Natural, cannot be altered by force, without a Free-will; so that the several societies, or communicants, commit an Error, if not a sin, to endeavour to compel their brethren to any particular opinion', *Grounds of Natural Philosophy*, Appendix, First Part, ch. 12.

[111] Cavendish echoes the Ciceronian view that subjects are more likely to obey the sovereign out of love than fear, Cicero, *De Officiis*, Book 2, vii. 23–4. Machiavelli parodies this view in *The Prince* and Hobbes emphasises fear over love in *Leviathan*. Cf. Newcastle's view; 'butt I should wish your Majestie to Governe by Both, Love and feare, mixed together as occation Serves', *Advice*, p. 68.

[112] Attacking the mechanism of Hobbes and Descartes, Henry More advocates what he describes as the Platonist view that souls have three kinds of vehicles: aerial, aetherial,

each other? The fly-men answered, that those spirits were always clothed in some sort or other of material garments; which garments were their bodies, made for the most part, of air; and when occasion served, they could put on any other sort of substances; but yet they could not put these substances into any form or shape, as they pleased. The Empress asked the fly-men, whether it was possible that she could be acquainted, and have some conferences with them? They answered, they did verily believe she might. Hereupon the Empress commanded the fly-men to ask some of the spirits, whether they would be pleased to give her a visit? This they did; and after the spirits had presented themselves to the Empress, (in what shapes or forms, I cannot exactly tell) after some few compliments that passed between them, the Empress told the spirits that she questioned not, but they did know how she was a stranger in that world, and by what miraculous means she was arrived there; and since she had a great desire to know the condition of the world she came from, her request to the spirits was, to give her some information thereof, especially of those parts of the world where she was born, bred, and educated, as also of her particular friends and acquaintance; all which, the spirits did according to her desire; at last, after a great many conferences and particular intelligences, which the spirits gave the Empress, to her great satisfaction and content, she enquired after the most famous students, writers, and experimental philosophers in that world, which they gave her a full relation of; amongst the rest she enquired whether there were none that had found out yet the Jews' Cabbala?[113] Several have endeavoured it, answered the spirits, but those that came nearest (although themselves denied it) were one Dr Dee and one Edward Kelly[114] the one representing

and terrestrial, *Immortality of the Soul* (1658), Book 2, ch. 14. Much of Cavendish's description of spirits is a play on More's view, which she criticises in *Philosophical Letters*.

[113] Sources of ancient wisdom – mystical Hebrew texts, particularly the *Sohar*, and also the *Corpus Hermeticum* – aroused great interest during the Renaissance. Some seventeenth-century Christian authors continued to believe that, by studying these keys to the wisdom given by God to Moses on Mt Sinai, it would be possible to reconcile Judaism and Christianity. This in turn would make way for the conversion of Jews and pagans to the Christian religion, itself a precondition of the millennium. A compilation of kabbalistic texts, the *Kabbala Denudata*, was published in two volumes in 1677 and 1684 by Baron Christian Von Rosenruth (1636–89), assisted by Francis Mercury Van Helmont (1614–98), the son of the Jan Baptiste Van Helmont (1577–1644) whose work Cavendish criticises. See Alison Coudert, 'A Cambridge Platonist's Kabbalist Nightmare', *Journal of the History of Ideas* 36 (1975), pp. 633–52.

[114] John Dee, mathematician and magician, was admired throughout Europe and respected by Elizabeth I, who consulted him and encouraged him to attend her court. The kabbala, especially the hermetic tradition revived by Marsilio Ficino, played an important role

Moses, and the other Aaron; for Kelly was to Dr Dee, as Aaron to Moses;[115] but yet they proved at last but mere cheats, and were described by one of their own country-men, a famous poet, named Ben Jonson, in a play called *The Alchemist*,[116] where he expressed Kelly by Capt. Face, and Dee by Dr Subtle, and their two wives by Doll Common, and the widow; by the Spaniard in the play, he meant the Spanish ambassador, and by Sir Epicure Mammon, a Polish lord. The Empress remembered that she had seen the play, and asked the spirits whom he meant by the name of Ananias? Some zealous brethren, answered they, in Holland, Germany, and several other places. Then she asked them, who was meant by the druggist? Truly, answered the spirits, we have forgot, it being so long since it was made and acted. What replied the Empress, can spirits forget? Yes, said the spirits; for what is past, is only kept in memory, if it be not recorded. I did believe, said the Empress, that spirits had no need of memory, or remembrance, and could not be subject to forgetfulness. How can we, answered they, give an account of things present, if we had no memory, but especially of things past, unrecorded if we had no remembrance? Said the Empress, by present knowledge and understanding. The spirits answered, that present knowledge and understanding was of actions or things present, not of past. But, said the Empress, you know what is to come, without memory or remembrance, and therefore you may know what is past without memory and remembrance. They answered, that their foreknowledge was only a prudent and subtle observation made by a comparing of things or actions past, with those that are present, and that remembrance was nothing else but a repetition of things or actions past.[117]

in Dee's magic, and in 1564 he published a new kabbala designed to reveal the secrets of the entire creation, *Monas Hieroglyphica*. During the 1580s, he used the kabbala to communicate with angels. His most successful medium was Edward Kelley (1555–95), widely suspected of having duped Dee. See Peter French, *John Dee. The World of an Elizabethan Magus* (London: Routledge, 1972).

[115] Aaron, Moses's elder brother, appears in the Bible as Moses's mouthpiece, Exodus 7: 1.

[116] Ben Jonson, *The Alchemist* (1610). William Newcastle was a patron of Jonson and employed him in the 1630s to write masques for two occasions when the king visited Newcastle's estates: Charles I's visit to Welbeck in 1633; and the summer progress of Charles and Henrietta Maria in 1634, when they stayed at Bolsover Castle. See Cedric C. Brown, 'Courtesies of Place and Arts of Diplomacy in Ben Jonson's Last Two Entertainments for Royalty', *The Seventeenth Century* 9.2 (1994), pp. 147–71; Nick Rowe, ' "My Best Patron": William Cavendish and Jonson's Caroline Dramas', *The Seventeenth Century* 9.2 (1994), pp. 197–212.

[117] Prudence is the virtue that allows you to know the future by understanding the past. See e.g. Thomas Aquinas, *Summa Theologiae*, ed. and trans. The Dominican Fathers,

Then the Empress asked the spirits, whether there was a threefold Cabbala? They answered, Dee and Kelly made but a two-fold Cabbala, to wit, of the Old and New Testament, but others might not only make two or three, but threescore Cabbalas, if they pleased. The Empress asked, whether it was a traditional, or merely a scriptural, or whether it was a literal, philosophical, or moral Cabbala? Some, answered they, did believe it merely traditional, others scriptural, some literal, and some metaphorical; but the truth is, said they, 'twas partly one, and partly the other; as partly a traditional, partly a scriptural, partly literal, partly metaphorical. The Empress asked further, whether the Cabbala was a work only of natural reason, or of divine inspiration? Many, said the spirits, that write Cabbalas pretend to divine inspirations, but whether it be so, or not, it does not belong to us to judge; only this we must needs confess, that it is a work which requires a good wit, and a strong faith, but not natural reason; for though natural reason is most persuasive, yet faith is the chief that is required in Cabbalists. But, said the Empress, is there not divine reason, as well as there is natural? No, answered they: for there is but a divine faith, and as for reason it is only natural; but you mortals are so puzzled about this divine faith, and natural reason, that you do not know well how to distinguish them, but confound them both, which is the cause you have so many divine philosophers who make a gallimaufry[118] both of reason and faith. Then she asked, whether pure natural philosophers were Cabbalists?[119] They answered, no; but only your mystical or divine philosophers, such as study beyond sense and reason. She enquired further, whether there was any Cabbala in God, or whether God was full of Ideas? They answered, there could be nothing in God, nor could God be full of any thing, either forms or figures, but of himself; for God is the perfection of all things, and an unexpressible Being, beyond the conception of any creature, either natural or supernatural. Then I pray inform me, said the

---

30 vols. (London, 1964–80), vol. XXXVI, IIa IIae, Qu. 47. Cavendish here touches on a seventeenth-century debate as to whether prophecy or foreknowledge is divinely inspired. Elsewhere, she argues that 'prophecies are somewhat of the nature of dreams, whereof some may prove true by chance, but for the most part, they are false', *Grounds of Natural Philosophy*, Part 7, ch. 12. Cf. Hobbes, *Leviathan*, ch. 36, p. 292.

[118] Medley, mixture.

[119] Some authors argued that the kabbala could overcome the distinction between natural reason and divine faith. E.g. Henry More defends the possibility of a kabbala (i.e. a particularly enlightening theory) capable of reconciling natural philosophy and Christianity. In *Conjectura Cabbalistica* (1653) he argues that the Book of Genesis anticipates the natural philosophy of Descartes. See Coudert, 'A Cambridge Platonist's Kabbalist Nightmare', pp. 646–7.

Empress, whether the Jews', or any other Cabbala, consist in numbers?[120] The spirits answered, no: for numbers are odd, and different, and would make a disagreement in the Cabbala. But said she again, is it a sin then not to know or understand the Cabbala? God is so merciful, answered they, and so just, that he will never damn the ignorant, and save only those that pretend to know him and his secret counsels by their Cabbalas, but he loves those that adore and worship him with fear and reverence, and with a pure heart. She asked further, which of these two Cabbalas was most approved, the natural, or theological? The theological, answered they, is mystical, and belongs only to faith; but the natural belongs to reason. Then she asked them, whether divine faith was made out of reason? No, answered they, for faith proceeds only from a divine saving grace, which is a peculiar gift of God. How comes it then, replied she, that men, even those that are of several opinions, have faith more or less? A natural belief, answered they, is not a divine faith. But, proceeded the Empress, how are you sure that God cannot be known? The several opinions you mortals have of God, answered they, are sufficient witnesses thereof. Well then, replied the Empress, leaving this inquisitive knowledge of God, I pray inform me, whether you spirits give motion to natural bodies? No, answered they; but, on the contrary, natural material bodies give spirits motion; for we spirits, being incorporeal, have no motion but from our corporeal vehicles, so that we move by the help of our bodies, and not the bodies by the help of us; for pure spirits are immoveable.[121] If this be so, replied the Empress, how comes it then that you can move so suddenly at a vast distance? They answered, that some sorts of matter were more pure, rare, and consequently more light and agile than others; and this was the reason of their quick and sudden motions: then the Empress asked them, whether they could speak without a body, or bodily organs? No, said they; nor could we have any bodily sense, but only knowledge. She asked, whether they could have knowledge without body? Not a natural, answered they, but a supernatural knowledge, which is a far better knowledge than a natural. Then she asked them, whether they had a general or universal

---

[120] Kabbalists used permutations of the letters of the Hebrew alphabet in their contemplation of celestial and supercelestial mysteries. Some, including Dee, favoured a method called gematria, in which numerical values were assigned to Hebrew letters and the resulting collections of numbers were calculated to derive the mysteries of the universe. See French, *John Dee*, pp. 103–12.

[121] The spirits defend Cavendish's view that motion is a property of bodies and bodies alone, against the view, held for example by Henry More, that incorporeal spirits are self-moving. See More, *The Immortality of the Soul*, Book 1, ch. 7.

knowledge? They answered, single or particular created spirits, have not; for not any creature, but God himself, can have an absolute and perfect knowledge of all things. The Empress asked them further, whether spirits had inward and outward parts? No, answered they; for parts only belong to bodies, not to spirits. Again, she asked them, whether their vehicles were living bodies? They are self-moving bodies,[122] answered they, and therefore they must needs be living; for nothing can move itself, without it hath life. Then, said she, it must necessarily follow, that this living, self-moving body gives a spirit motion, and not that the spirit gives the body, as its vehicle, motion. You say very true, answered they, and we told you this before. Then the Empress asked them, of what forms of matter those vehicles were? They said they were of several different forms; some gross and dense, and others more pure, rare, and subtle. Then she enquired, whether immaterial spirits were not of a globous figure? They answered, figure and body were but one thing; for no body was without figure, nor no figure without body; and that it was as much nonsense to say, an immaterial figure, as to say an immaterial body. Again, she asked, whether spirits were not like water, or fire? No, said they, for both fire and water are material; and we are no more like fire or water, than we are like earth; nay, were it the purest and finest degree of matter, even above the heavens; for immaterial creatures cannot be likened or compared to material; but, as we said before, our vehicles being material, are of several degrees, forms and shapes. But if you be not material, said the Empress, how can you be generators of all creatures? We are no more, answered they, the generators of material creatures, than they are the generators of us spirits. Then she asked, whether they did leave their vehicles? No, answered they; for we being incorporeal, cannot leave or quit them; but our vehicles do change into several forms and figures, according as occasion requires. Then the Empress desired the spirits to tell her, whether man was a little world?[123] They answered, that if a fly or worm was a little world, then man was so too. She asked again, whether our forefathers had been as wise, as men

---

[122] Many philosophers, including Descartes, believed that bodies could be moved only by the impact of other bodies, except that in humans, the soul or mind has the power to move the body via its volitions. Cavendish's spirits challenge both views.

[123] The claim that man is a microcosm is widespread in early modern writing. E.g. John Dee, 'The description of him who is the lesse world; and from the beginning called the microcosmos' (*Mathematical Preface* 1570); King James I, 'The divers parts of our microcosme or little world within ourselves' (*Counterblast*, 1604). It is rejected by Van Helmont. 'The name therefore of microcosm . . . is poetical, heathenish and metaphorical, but not natural or true' (*Oriatrike*, p. 323).

were at present, and had understood sense and reason, as well as they did now? They answered, that in former ages they had been as wise as they are in this present, nay, wiser; for, said they, many in this age do think their forefathers have been fools, by which they prove themselves to be such. The Empress asked further, whether there was any plastic power in nature?[124] Truly, said the spirits, plastic power is a hard word, [it] signifies no more than the power of the corporeal, figurative motions of nature. After this, the Empress desired the spirits to inform her where the Paradise was, whether it was in the midst of the world as a centre of pleasure? or whether it was the whole world, or a peculiar world by itself, as a world of life, and not of matter; or whether it was mixed, as a world of living animal creatures? They answered, that Paradise was not in the world she came from, but in that world she lived in at present; and that it was the very same place where she kept her court, and where her palace stood, in the midst of the imperial city. The Empress asked further, whether in the beginning and creation of the world, all beasts could speak? They answered, that no beasts could speak, but only those sorts of creatures which were fish-men, bear-men, worm-men, and the like, which could speak in the first age, as well as they do now. She asked again, whether they were none of those spirits that frighted Adam out of the Paradise, at least caused him not to return thither again? They answered they were not. Then she desired to be informed, whither Adam fled when he was driven out of the Paradise? Out of this world, said they, you are now Empress of, into the world you came from. If this be so, replied the Empress, then surely those Cabbalists are much out of their story, who believe the Paradise to be a world of life only, without matter; for this world, though it be most pleasant and fruitful, yet it is not a world of mere immaterial life, but a world of living, material creatures. Without question, they are, answered the spirits; for not all Cabbalas are true. Then the Empress asked, that since it is mentioned in the story of the creation of the world, that Eve was tempted

---

[124] Plastic or vital powers in nature were posited by various opponents of mechanism including Ralph Cudworth and Henry More. See More, *The Immortality of the Soul*; Ralph Cudworth, *The True Intellectual System of the Universe* (1678), *The Digression concerning the Plastick Life of Nature, or an Artificial, Orderly and Methodical Nature*, Book I, ch. 3, section xxxviii. Reprinted in C. A. Patrides, *The Cambridge Platonists* (Cambridge: Cambridge University Press, 1969), pp. 288–325. They continued to be discussed by experimental philosophers. On the relation between Cavendish and Cudworth see Stephen Clucas, 'The Duchess and the Viscountess: negotiations between mechanism and vitalism in the natural philosophies of Margaret Cavendish and Anne Conway', *In-Between: Essays and Studies in Literary Criticism* 9 (2000), pp. 125–36.

by the serpent, whether the Devil was within the serpent, or whether the serpent tempted her without the Devil?[125] They answered, that the Devil was within the serpent. But how came it then, replied she, that the serpent was cursed? They answered, because the Devil was in him: for are not those men in danger of damnation which have the Devil within them, who persuades them to believe and act wickedly? The Empress asked further, whether light and the heavens were all one. They answered, that the region which contains the lucid natural orbs, was by mortals named Heaven; but the beatifical Heaven, which is the habitation of the blessed angels and souls, was so far beyond it, that it could not be compared to any natural creature. Then the Empress asked them, whether all matter was fluid at first? They answered, that matter was always as it is; and that some parts of matter were rare, some dense, some fluid, some solid, etc. Neither was God bound to make all matter fluid at first. She asked further, whether matter was immovable in itself. We have answered you before, said they, that there is no motion but in matter, and were it not for the motion of matter, we spirits, could not move, nor give you any answer to your several questions. After this, the Empress asked the spirits, whether the universe was made within the space of six days, or whether by those six days, were meant so many decrees or commands of God? They answered her, that the world was made by the all powerful decree and command of God; but whether there were six decrees or commands, or fewer, or more, no creature was able to tell. Then she enquired, whether there was no mystery in numbers?[126] No other mystery, answered the spirits, but reckoning or counting, for numbers are only marks of remembrance. But what do you think of the number four, said she, which Cabbalists make such ado withal, and of the number of ten, when they say that ten is all, and that all numbers are virtually comprehended in four? We think, answered they, that Cabbalists have nothing else to do but to trouble their heads with such useless fancies; for naturally there is no such thing as prime or

---

[125] Cavendish recounts a discussion about witches between her husband and Thomas Hobbes, which, she says, Hobbes later incorporated in *Leviathan*. Hobbes pointed out that witches confess to being possessed by the devil. Newcastle replied that they confess because they have the erroneous belief that they have made a compact with the devil, *Life of the Thrice Noble, High and Puissant Prince William Cavendish*, pp. 144–5; cf. *Leviathan*, ch. 12, pp. 76–7. In her discussions of More and Van Helmont (who both believed in demonic possession) Cavendish denies that there are witches, *Philosophical Letters*, III. xvi.

[126] Cf. Hobbes, who describes names as 'Markes, or Notes of remembrance', *Leviathan*, ch. 4, p. 25.

all in numbers; nor is there any other mystery in numbers, but what man's fancy makes; but what men call prime, or all, we do not know, because they do not agree in the number of their opinion. Then the Empress asked, whether the number of six was a symbol of matrimony, as being made up of male and female, for two into three is six. If any number can be a symbol of matrimony, answered the spirits, it is not six, but two; if two may be allowed to be a number: for the act of matrimony is made up of two joined in one. She asked again, what they said to the number of seven? whether it was not an emblem of God, because Cabbalists say, that it is neither begotten, nor begets any other number. There can be no emblem of God, answered the spirits; for if we do not know what God is, how can we make an emblem of him? Nor is there any number in God, for God is the perfection himself, but numbers are imperfect; and as for the begetting of numbers, it is done by multiplication and addition; but subtraction is as a kind of death to numbers. If there be no mystery in numbers, replied the Empress, then it is in vain to refer the creation of the world to certain numbers, as Cabbalists do. The only mystery of numbers, answered they, concerning the creation of the world is, that as numbers do multiply, so does the world. The Empress asked, how far numbers did multiply? The spirits answered, to infinite. Why, said she, infinite cannot be reckoned nor numbered.[127] No more, answered they, can the parts of the universe; for God's creation, being an infinite action, as proceeding from an infinite power, could not rest upon a finite number of creatures; were it never so great. But leaving the mystery of numbers, proceeded the Empress, let me now desire you to inform me, whether the suns and planets were generated by the heavens, or ethereal matter? The spirits answered, that the stars and planets were of the same matter which the heavens, the ether, and all other natural creatures did consist of; but whether they were generated by the heavens or ether, they could not tell: if they be, said they, they are not like their parents; for the sun, stars, and planets, are more splendorous than the ether, as also more solid and constant in their motions: but put the case, the stars and planets were generated by the heavens, and the ethereal matter; the question then would be, out of what these are generated or produced? If these be created out of nothing, and not generated out of something, then it is probable the sun, stars and planets are so too; nay, it

---

[127] The classical view of the infinite as inexhaustible and incomplete was upheld by Hobbes, who argued that we can have 'no idea or conception of anything we call infinite', *Leviathan*, ch. 3, p. 23. It was challenged by Wallis in his controversy with Hobbes. See Jesseph, *The Squaring of the Circle*, pp. 173–88.

is more probable of the stars and planets, than of the heavens, or the fluid ether, by reason the stars and planets seem to be further off from mortality, than the particular parts of the ether; for no doubt but the parts of the ethereal matter alter into several forms, which we do not perceive of the stars and planets. The Empress asked further, whether they could give her information of the three principles of man, according to the doctrine of the Platonists; as first of the intellect, spirit, or divine light: 2. of the soul of man herself: and 3. of the image of the soul, that is, her vital operation on the body? The spirits answered, that they did not understand these three distinctions, but that they seemed to corporeal sense and reason, as if they were three several bodies, or three several corporeal actions; however, said they, they are intricate conceptions of irregular fancies. If you do not understand them, replied the Empress, how shall human creatures do then? Many, both of your modern and ancient philosophers, answered the spirits, endeavour to go beyond sense and reason, which makes them commit absurdities; for no corporeal creature can go beyond sense and reason; no not we spirits, as long as we are in our corporeal vehicles. Then the Empress asked them, whether there were any atheists in the world?[128] The spirits answered, that there were no more atheists than what Cabbalists make. She asked them further, whether spirits were of a globous or round figure?[129] They answered, that figure belonged to body, but that they being immaterial had no figure. She asked again, whether spirits were not like water or fire? They answered, that water and fire was material, were it the purest and most refined that ever could be; nay, were it above the heavens: but we are no more like water or fire, said they, than we are like earth; but our vehicles are of several forms, figures and degrees of substances. Then she desired to know, whether their vehicles were made of air? Yes, answered the spirits, some of our vehicles are of thin air. Then I suppose, replied the Empress, that those airy vehicles, are your corporeal summer suits. She asked further, whether the spirits had not ascending and descending motions, as well as other creatures? They answered, that properly there was no ascension or descension in infinite nature, but only in relation to particular parts; and as for us spirits, said

---

[128] Cavendish defines atheists narrowly, as people who do not believe that God exists. She argues that there are no atheists because all creatures have innate knowledge of the existence, though not the nature, of God, and worship him in their own way. See *Philosophical Letters*, III. xx; *Observations*, pp. 216–17, 219–20.

[129] For the view that the primary and most perfect figures of nature are globular see *Observations*, p. 204.

they, we can neither ascend nor descend without corporeal vehicles; nor can our vehicles ascend or descend, but according to their several shapes and figures, for there can be no motion without body. The Empress asked them further, whether there was not a world of spirits, as well as there is of material creatures? No, answered they; for the word world implies a quantity or multitude of corporeal creatures, but we being immaterial, can make no world of spirits.[130] Then she desired to be informed when spirits were made? We do not know, answered they, how and when we were made, nor are we much inquisitive after it; nay, if we did, it would be no benefit, neither for us, nor for you mortals to know it. The Empress replied, that Cabbalists and divine philosophers said, men's rational souls were immaterial,[131] and stood as much in need of corporeal vehicles, as spirits did. If this be so, answered the spirits, then you are hermaphrodites of nature; but your Cabbalists are mistaken, for they take the purest and subtlest parts of matter for immaterial spirits. Then the Empress asked, when the souls of mortals went out of their bodies, whether they went to Heaven or Hell, or whether they remained in airy vehicles? God's justice and mercy, answered they, is perfect, and not imperfect; but if you mortals will have vehicles for your souls and a place that is between Heaven and Hell, it must be Purgatory, which is a place of purification, for which action fire is more proper than air, and so the vehicles of those souls that are in Purgatory cannot be airy, but fiery, and after this rate there can be but four places for human souls to be in, viz. Heaven, Hell, Purgatory and this world;[132] but as for vehicles, they are but fancies, not real truths.

---

[130] For a defence of the view that the whole world is material see *Philosophical and Physical Opinions*, pp. 93–100.

[131] Aristotelian philosophers distinguish three souls: the vegetative soul responsible for digestion and generation, found in humans, animals, and vegetables; the sensitive soul responsible for sense, imagination, and emotion, found in humans and animals; and the rational soul responsible for reasoning and volition, found only in humans. Cf. *Observations*, pp. 271–2. Thomas Aquinas had attempted to reconcile this view with the Christian doctrine of the immortality of the soul by arguing that only the rational or intellectual soul is immortal. Christian theologians and natural philosophers frequently equated immortality with immateriality. Hence the standard view that rational souls are immaterial. Cavendish disagrees. In her view, the finer parts of matter are responsible for our capacities to reason and will, and there is no immaterial soul. This view is open to interpretation as a form of materialism, and it is striking that Cavendish's spirits immediately qualify it, claiming that vehicles 'are fancies, not real truths'. See also *Observations*, pp. 221–4.

[132] Purgatory, the home of souls that will be saved at Judgement Day but which are sinful enough to be punished in the meantime, is a feature of Roman Catholic doctrine, not officially accepted by the Church of England. See Peter Marshall, 'Fear, Purgatory and Polemic' in William Naphy and Penny Roberts eds., *Fear in Modern Societies* (Manchester:

Then the Empress asked them, where Heaven and Hell was? Your saviour Christ, answered the spirits, has informed you, that there is Heaven and Hell, but he did not tell you what, nor where they are; wherefore it is too great a presumption for you mortals to enquire after it; if you do but strive to get into Heaven, it is enough, though you do not know where or what it is, for it is beyond your knowledge and understanding. I am satisfied, replied the Empress, and asked further, whether there were any figures or characters in the soul? They answered, where there was no body, there could be no figure. Then she asked them, whether spirits could be naked? and whether they were of a dark, or a light colour? As for our nakedness, it is a very odd question, answered the spirits; and we do not know what you mean by a naked spirit; for you judge of us as of corporeal creatures; and as for colour, said they, it is according to our vehicles; for colour belongs to body, and as there is no body that is colourless, so there is no colour that is bodiless. Then the Empress desired to be informed, whether all souls were made at the first creation of the world?[133] We know no more, answered the spirits, of the origin of human souls, than we know of ourselves. She asked further, whether human bodies were not burdensome to human souls? They answered, that bodies made souls active, as giving them motion; and if action was troublesome to souls, then bodies were so too. She asked again, whether souls did choose bodies? They answered, that Platonics believed, the souls of lovers lived in the bodies of their beloved; but surely, said they, if there be a multitude of souls in a world of matter, they cannot miss bodies; for as soon as a soul is parted from one body, it enters into another; and souls having no motion of themselves, must of necessity be clothed or embodied with the next parts of matter. If this be so, replied the Empress, then I pray inform me, whether all matter

---

Manchester University Press, 1997), pp. 150–66. Hobbes argues that there is no scriptural warrant for Purgatory, *Leviathan*, ch. 44, p. 426 but several English writers countenance something very like it. E.g. More argues in *Immortality of the Soul* that sinful souls are punished after death, either by the pangs of conscience or by devils. Joseph Glanvill proposes that, once punished, souls have another chance of salvation. See *Lux Orientalis or an Enquiry into the Opinion of the Eastern Sages concerning the praeexistnce of Souls* (London, 1662). See D. P. Walker, *The Decline of Hell. Seventeenth Century Discussions of Eternal Torment* (London: Routledge, 1964), pp. 127–36.

[133] Three main views about the origin of the soul were debated in England in the middle of the seventeenth century. (1) God creates a new soul for each human body. (2) Traduction, i.e. the souls of parents 'emit' a new soul for their child. (3) God creates all souls at once, so that they pre-exist the bodies with which they are later united. (3) is defended by More, *Immortality of the Soul*, Book 2, chs. 12 and 13, and by Glanvill in *Lux Orientalis*.

be soulified? The spirits answered, they could not exactly tell that; but if it was true, that matter had no other motion but what came from a spiritual power, and that all matter was moving, then no soul could quit a body, but she must of necessity enter into another soulified body, and then there would be two immaterial substances in one body. The Empress asked, whether it was not possible that there could be two souls in one body? As for immaterial souls, answered the spirits, it is impossible; for there cannot be two immaterials in one inanimate body, by reason they want parts, and place, being bodiless; but there may be numerous material souls in one composed body, by reason every material part has a material natural soul; for nature is but one infinite self-moving, living and self-knowing body, consisting of the three degrees of inanimate, sensitive and rational matter, so intermixed together, that no part of nature, were it an atom, can be without any of these three degrees; the sensitive is the life, the rational the soul, and the inanimate part, the body of infinite nature.[134] The Empress was very well satisfied with this answer, and asked further, whether souls did not give life to bodies? No, answered they; but spirits and divine souls have a life of their own, which is not partable, being purer than a natural life; for spirits are incorporeal, and consequently indivisible. But when the soul is in its vehicle, said the Empress, then methinks she is like the sun, and the vehicle like the moon. No, answered they, but the vehicle is like the sun, and the soul like the moon; for the soul hath motion from the body, as the moon has light from the sun. Then the Empress asked the spirits, whether it was an evil spirit that tempted Eve, and brought all the mischiefs upon mankind, or whether it was the serpent? They answered, that spirits could not commit actual evils. The Empress said they might do it by persuasions. They answered, that persuasions were actions; but the Empress not being contented with this answer, asked whether there was not a supernatural evil? The spirits answered, that there was a super-natural good, which was God; but they knew of no supernatural evil that was equal to God.[135] Then she desired to know, whether evil spirits were reckoned amongst the beasts of the field? They answered, that many beasts of the field were harmless creatures, and very serviceable for man's use; and though some were accounted fierce and cruel, yet did they exercise their cruelty upon other creatures, for the most part, to no other end, but

---

[134] Cf. *Philosophical and Physical Opinions*, Part I, pp. 3–4. See also James, 'Innovations of Margaret Cavendish', pp. 225–31.

[135] Manicheanism, the view that there are two supernatural powers, one good and the other evil, was a heresy.

to get themselves food, and to satisfy their natural appetite; but certainly, said they, you men are more cruel to one another, than evil spirits are to you; and as for their habitations in desolate places, we having no communion with them, can give you no certain account thereof. But what do you think, said the Empress, of good spirits? may not they be compared to the fowls of the air? They answered, there were many cruel and ravenous fowls as well in the air, as there were fierce and cruel beasts on earth, so that the good are always mixed with the bad. She asked further, whether the fiery vehicles were a Heaven, or a Hell, or at least a Purgatory to the souls? They answered, that if the souls were immaterial, they could not burn, and then fire would do them no harm; and though Hell was believed to be an undecaying and unquenchable fire, yet Heaven was no fire. The Empress replied, that Heaven was a light. Yes, said they, but not a fiery light. Then she asked, whether the different shapes and sorts of vehicles, made the souls and other immaterial spirits, miserable, or blessed? The vehicles, answered they, make them neither better, nor worse, for though some vehicles sometimes may have power over others, yet these by turns may get some power again over them, according to the several advantages and disadvantages of particular natural parts. The Empress asked further, whether animal life came out of the spiritual world, and did return thither again? The spirits answered, they could not exactly tell; but if it were so, then certainly animal lives must leave their bodies behind them, otherwise the bodies would make the spiritual world a mixed world, that is, partly material, and partly immaterial; but the truth is, said they, spirits being immaterial, cannot properly make a world; for a world belongs to material, not to immaterial creatures. If this be so, replied the Empress, then certainly there can be no world of lives and forms without matter? No, answered the spirits, nor a world of matter without lives and forms, for natural lives and forms cannot be immaterial, no more than matter can be immovable. And therefore natural lives, forms and matter, are inseparable. Then the Empress asked, whether the first man did feed on the best sorts of the fruits of the earth, and the beasts on the worst? The spirits answered, that unless the beasts of the field were barred out of the manured fields and gardens, they would pick and choose the best fruits as well as men; and you may plainly observe it, said they, in squirrels and monkeys, how they are the best choosers of nuts and apples, and how birds do pick and feed on the most delicious fruits, and worms on the best roots, and most savoury herbs; by which you may see, that those creatures live and feel better than men do, except you will say, that artificial cookery is better and more wholesome than the natural. Again, the Empress asked, whether the first man gave names to all the several sorts of fishes in the sea, and fresh waters? No, answered the spirits, for he was an earthly, and not a watery creature, and therefore could not know the several sorts of fishes. Why, replied the Empress, he was no more an airy creature than he was a watery one, and yet he gave names to the several sorts of fowls and birds of the air. Fowls answered they, are partly airy, and partly earthly creatures, not only because they resemble beasts and men in their flesh, but because their rest and dwelling places are on earth; for they build their nests, lay their eggs, and hatch their young, not in the air, but on the earth. Then she asked, whether the first man did give names to all the various sorts of creatures of the earth?[136] Yes, answered they, to all those that were presented to him; or he had knowledge of that is, to all the prime sorts; but not to every particular; for of mankind, said they, there were but two at first, and as they did increase, so do their names. But, said the Empress, who gave the names to the several sorts of fish? The posterity of mankind, answered they. Then she enquired, whether there were no more kinds of creatures now, than at the first creation? They answered, that there were no more nor fewer kinds of creatures than there are now; but there were, without question, more particular sorts of creatures now, than there were then. She asked again, whether all those creatures that were in Paradise were also in Noah's Ark? They answered, that the principal kinds had been there, but not all the particulars. Then she would fain know, how it came, that both spirits and men did fall from a blessed into so miserable a state and condition they are now in. The spirits answered, by disobedience. The Empress asked, whence this disobedient sin did proceed? But the spirits desired the Empress not to ask them any such questions, because they went beyond their knowledge. Then she begged the spirits to pardon her presumption, for, said she, it is the nature of mankind to be inquisitive. Natural desire of knowledge, answered the spirits, is not blameable, so you do not go beyond what your natural reason can comprehend. Then I'll ask no more, said the Empress, for fear I should commit some error;

---

[136] 'And Adam gave names to all cattle, and to the fowl of the air, and to every beast of the field', Genesis 2: 20. The view that Adam did not name all the animals is shared by Hobbes. 'The first author of speech was God himself, that instructed Adam to name such creatures as he presented to his sight . . . But this was sufficient to direct him to add more names, as the experience and use of the creatures should give him occasion', *Leviathan*, ch. 4, p. 24. It was contested by Van Helmont, who argues that God brought Adam one animal of each kind from all the parts of the earth, and returned them to their natural habitats once they had been named, *Oriatrike* XXIII. 1.

but one thing I cannot but acquaint you withal: what is that, said the spirits? I have a great desire, answered the Empress, to make a Cabbala. What kind of Cabbala asked the spirits? The Empress answered, the Jews' Cabbala. No sooner had the Empress declared her mind, but the spirits immediately disappeared out of her sight; which startled the Empress so much, that she fell into a trance, wherein she lay for some while; at last being come to herself again, she grew very studious, and considering with herself what might be the cause of this strange disaster, conceived at first, that perhaps the spirits were tired with hearing and giving answers to her questions, but thinking by herself, that spirits could not be tired, she imagined that this was not the true cause of their disappearing, till after diverse debates with her own thoughts, she did verily believe that the spirits had committed some fault in their answers, and that for their punishment they were condemned to the lowest darkest vehicles.[137] This belief was so fixed in her mind, that it put her into a very melancholic humour; and then she sent both for her fly- and worm-men, and declared to them the cause of her sadness. 'Tis not so much, said she, the vanishing of those spirits that makes me melancholic, but that I should be the cause of their miserable condition, and that those harmless spirits should, for my sake, sink down into the black and dark abyss of the earth. The worm-men comforted the Empress, telling her, that the Earth was not so horrid a dwelling, as she did imagine; for, said they, not only all minerals and vegetables, but several sorts of animals can witness, that the earth is a warm, fruitful, quiet, safe and happy habitation; and though they want the light of the sun, yet are they not in dark, but there is light even within the earth, by which those creatures do see that dwell therein. This relation settled her Majesty's mind a little; but yet she being desirous to know the truth, where, and in what condition those spirits were, commanded both the fly- and worm-men to use all labour and industry to find them out, whereupon the worm-men straight descended into the earth, and the fly-men ascended into the air. After some short time, the worm-men returned, and told the Empress, that when they went into the earth, they enquired of all the creatures they met withal, whether none of them had perceived such or such spirits, until at last coming to the very centre of the earth, they were truly informed, that those spirits had stayed some time there, but at last were gone to the antipodes on the other side of

---

[137] More argues that as souls go through various stages of purification they move from terrestrial to celestial vehicles, *Immortality of the Soul*, Book 2, ch. 29.

the terrestrial globe, diametrically opposite to theirs. The fly-men seconded the worm-men, assuring her Majesty, that their relation was very true; for, said they, we have rounded the earth, and just when we came to the antipodes, we met those spirits in a very good condition, and acquainted them that your Majesty was very much troubled at their sudden departure, and feared they should be buried in the darkness of the earth: whereupon the spirits answered us, that they were sorry for having occasioned such sadness and trouble in your Majesty; and desired us to tell your Majesty, that they feared no darkness; for their vehicles were of such a sort of substance as cats'-eyes, glow-worms' tails, and rotten wood, carrying their light along with them; and that they were ready to do your Majesty what service they could, in making your Cabbala. At which relation the Empress was exceedingly glad, and rewarded both her fly- and worm-men bountifully.

After some time, when the spirits had refreshed themselves in their own vehicles, they sent one of their nimblest spirits, to ask the Empress, whether she would have a scribe, or whether she would write the Cabbala herself? The Empress received the proffer which they made her, with all civility; and told him, that she desired a spiritual scribe. The spirit answered, that they could dictate, but not write, except they put on a hand or arm, or else the whole body of man. The Empress replied, how can spirits arm themselves with gauntlets of flesh? As well, answered he, as man can arm himself with a gauntlet of steel. If it be so, said the Empress, then I will have a scribe. Then the spirit asked her, whether she would have the soul of a living or a dead man? Why, said the Empress, can the soul quit a living body, and wander or travel abroad?[138] Yes, answered he, for according to Plato's doctrine, there is a conversation of souls, and the souls of lovers live in the bodies of their beloved. Then I will have, answered she, the soul of some ancient famous writer, either of Aristotle, Pythagoras, Plato, Epicurus, or the like. The spirit said, that those famous men were very learned, subtle, and ingenious writers, but they were so wedded to their own opinions, that they would never have the patience to be scribes. Then, said she, I'll have the soul of one of the most famous modern writers,

---

[138] The migration of souls was defended by English Platonist philosophers. E.g., More claims that the soul can leave the body and return to it, and that when the soul is out of its body, the body goes on as before, *Immortality of the Soul*, Book 2, ch. 15. A cult of Platonic love was fashionable in the court of Henrietta Maria in the 1640s, and Cavendish unites the souls of lovers in several works, e.g. 'The Propagating Souls' in *Nature's Pictures*, p. 133. See Battigelli, *Margaret Cavendish*, pp. 25–37.

as either of Galileo, Gassendus, Descartes, Helmont, Hobbes, H. More, etc.[139] The spirit answered, that they were fine ingenious writers, but yet so self-conceited, that they would scorn to be scribes to a woman. But, said he, there's a lady, the Duchess of Newcastle, which although she is not one of the most learned, eloquent, witty and ingenious, yet is she a plain and rational writer, for the principle of her writings, is sense and reason, and she will without question, be ready to do you all the service she can. This lady then, said the Empress, will I choose for my scribe, neither will the Emperor have reason to be jealous, she being one of my own sex. In truth, said the spirit, husbands have reason to be jealous of platonic lovers, for they are very dangerous, as being not only very intimate and close, but subtle and insinuating. You say well, replied the Empress; wherefore I pray send me the Duchess of Newcastle's soul; which the spirit did; and after she came to wait on the Empress, at her first arrival the Empress embraced and saluted her with a spiritual kiss; then she asked her whether she could write? Yes, answered the Duchess's soul, but not so intelligibly that any reader whatsoever may understand it, unless he be taught to know my characters; for my letters are rather like characters, than well-formed letters. Said the Empress, you were recommended to me by an honest and ingenious spirit. Surely, answered the Duchess, the spirit is ignorant of my handwriting. The truth is, said the Empress, he did not mention your handwriting; but he informed me that you writ sense and reason, and if you can but write so that any of my secretaries may learn your hand, they shall write it out fair and intelligible. The Duchess answered, that she questioned not but it might easily be learned in a short time. But, said she to the Empress, what is it that your Majesty would have written? She answered, the Jews' Cabbala. Then your only way for that is, said the Duchess, to have the soul of some famous Jew; nay, if your Majesty please, I scruple not, but you may as easily have the soul of Moses, as of any other. That cannot be, replied the Empress, for no mortal knows where Moses is. But, said the Duchess, human souls are immortal, however, if this be too difficult to be obtained, you may have the soul of one of the chief rabbis or sages of the tribe of Levi, who will truly instruct you in that mystery; whenas, otherwise, your Majesty will be apt to mistake, and a thousand to one, will commit gross errors. No, said the Empress,

---

[139] Cavendish critically discusses the work of Descartes, Van Helmont, Hobbes, More, and Charleton in *Philosophical Letters*. Gassendi, who knew William and Charles Cavendish in Paris, was an Epicurean whose work was introduced into England by Charleton.

for I shall be instructed by spirits. Alas! said the Duchess, spirits are as ignorant as mortals in many cases; for no created spirits have a general or absolute knowledge, nor can they know the thoughts of men, much less the mysteries of the great creator, unless he be pleased to inspire into them the gift of divine knowledge. Then, I pray, said the Empress, let me have your counsel in this case. The Duchess answered, if your Majesty will be pleased to hearken to my advice, I would desire you to let that work alone, for it will be of no advantage either to you, or your people, unless you were of the Jews' religion; nay, if you were, the vulgar interpretation of the holy scripture would be more instructive, and more easily believed, than your mystical way of interpreting it;[140] for had it been better and more advantageous for the salvation of the Jews, surely Moses would have saved after ages that labour by his own explanation, he being not only a wise, but a very honest, zealous and religious man: wherefore the best way, said she, is to believe with the generality the literal sense of the scripture, and not to make interpretations every one according to his own fancy, but to leave that work for the learned, or those that have nothing else to do; neither do I think, said she, that God will damn those that are ignorant therein, or suffer them to be lost for want of a mystical interpretation of the scripture. Then, said the Empress, I'll leave the scripture, and make a philosophical Cabbala.[141] The Duchess told her, that sense and reason would instruct her of nature as much as could be known; and as for numbers, they were infinite, but to add nonsense to infinite, would breed a confusion, especially in human understanding. Then, replied the Empress, I'll make a moral Cabbala. The only thing, answered the Duchess, in morality, is but to fear God, and to love his neighbour, and this needs no further interpretation. But then I'll make a political Cabbala, said the Empress. The Duchess answered, that the chief and only ground in government, was but reward and punishment, and required no further Cabbala;[142] but, said she, if your Majesty were resolved to make a Cabbala, I would advise you, rather to make a poetical or romancical Cabbala, wherein you can use metaphors, allegories, similitudes, etc. and interpret them as you please. With that

---

[140] Henry More was among those who held that kabbalism was unnecessarily complex and made faith more difficult. He also objected that kabbalistic teachings were incompatible with Christianity because they were materialist and pantheist. See Coudert, 'A Cambridge Platonist's Kabbalist Nightmare', p. 648.

[141] Cf. n. 119.

[142] Cavendish attributes the view that government should be by just rewards and punishments to her husband, *Life of the Thrice Noble, High and Puissant Prince William Cavendish*, Part IV, LI.

the Empress thanked the Duchess, and embracing her soul, told her she would take her counsel: she made her also her favourite, and kept her sometime in that world, and by this means the Duchess came to know and give this relation of all that passed in that rich, populous, and happy world;[143] and after some time the Empress gave her leave to return to her husband and kindred into her native world, but upon condition, that her soul should visit her now and then; which she did, and truly their meeting did produce such an intimate friendship between them, that they became platonic lovers, although they were both females.

One time, when the Duchess her soul was with the Empress, she seemed to be very sad and melancholy; at which the Empress was very much troubled, and asked her the reason of her melancholic humour? Truly said the Duchess to the Empress (for between dear friends there's no concealment, they being like several parts of one united body) my melancholy proceeds from an extreme ambition. The Empress asked, what the height of her ambition was? The Duchess answered, that neither she herself, nor no creature in the world was able to know either the height, depth or breadth of her ambition; but said she, my present desire is, that I would be a great princess. The Empress replied, so you are; for you are a princess of the fourth or fifth degree; for a duke or duchess is the highest title or honour that a subject can arrive to, as being the next to a king's title; and as for the name of a prince or princess, it belongs to all that are adopted to the crown; so that those that can add a crown to their arms, are princes, and therefore a duke is a title above a prince; for example, the Duke of Savoy, the Duke of Florence, the Duke of Lorraine, as also kings' brothers are not called by the name of princes, but dukes, this being the higher title. 'Tis true, answered the Duchess, unless it be kings' eldest sons, and they are created princes. Yes, replied the Empress, but no sovereign does make a subject equal to himself, such as kings' eldest sons partly are: and although some dukes be sovereign, yet I never heard that a prince by his title is sovereign, by reason the title of a prince is more a title of honour, than of sovereignty; for, as I said before, it belongs to all that are adopted to the crown. Well, said the Duchess, setting aside this dispute, my ambition is, that I would fain be as you are, that is, an Empress of

---

[143] Cavendish here identifies herself with the fictional Duchess of Newcastle. Elsewhere, she protests that she has not read the political parts of Hobbes's *Leviathan* because women have no reason to study politics unless they are queens or are the favourites of absolute princes. *Philosophical Letters* XIII. In *Blazing World*, the Duchess acquires a reason to learn about politics.

a world, and I shall never be at quiet until I be one. I love you so well, replied the Empress, that I wish with all my soul, you had the fruition of your ambitious desire, and I shall not fail to give you my best advice how to accomplish it; the best informers are the immaterial spirits, and they'll soon tell you, whether it be possible to obtain your wish. But, said the Duchess, I have little acquaintance with them, for I never knew any before the time you sent for me. They know you, replied the Empress; for they told me of you, and were the means and instrument of your coming hither: wherefore I'll confer with them, and enquire whether there be not another world, whereof you may be Empress as well as I am of this? No sooner had the Empress said this, but some immaterial spirits came to visit her, of whom she enquired, whether there were but three worlds in all, to wit, the Blazing World where she was in, the world which she came from, and the world where the Duchess lived? The spirits answered, that there were more numerous worlds than the stars which appeared in these three mentioned worlds. Then the Empress asked, whether it was not possible, that her dearest friend the Duchess of Newcastle, might be Empress of one of them? Although there be numerous, nay, infinite worlds, answered the spirits, yet none is without government.[144] But is none of these worlds so weak, said she, that it may be surprised or conquered? The spirits answered, that Lucian's world of lights,[145] had been for some time in a snuff, but of late years one Helmont had got it, who since he was Emperor of it, had so strengthened the immortal parts thereof with mortal out-works, as it was for the present impregnable. Said the Empress, if there be such an infinite number of worlds, I am sure, not only my friend, the Duchess, but any other might obtain one. Yes, answered the spirits, if those worlds were uninhabited; but they are as populous as this, your Majesty governs. Why, said the Empress, it is not impossible to conquer a world. No, answered the spirits, but, for the most part, conquerors seldom enjoy their conquest, for they being more feared than loved, most commonly come to an untimely end.[146] If you will but direct me, said the Duchess to the spirits, which world is easiest to be conquered, her Majesty will assist me with means, and I will trust to fate and fortune; for I had rather die in the adventure of

---

[144] I.e. none of them are in a state of nature. Cavendish here distances herself from questions about the origins of political society.

[145] 'We came to a city called Lychnopolis . . . and arriving there, not a man was to be seen, but lights in great number running to and fro', Lucian, *True History*, p. 120.

[146] See n. 158. Cf. *Blazing World*, 'The Second Part'; *The World's Olio*, I. 3, 'A Tyrannical Power Never Lasts'.

noble achievements, than live in obscure and sluggish security; since by
the one, I may live in a glorious fame[147] and by the other I am buried in
oblivion. The spirits answered, that the lives of fame were like other lives;
for some lasted long, and some died soon. 'Tis true, said the Duchess;
but yet the shortest-lived fame lasts longer than the longest life of man.
But, replied the spirits, if occasion does not serve you, you must content
yourself to live without such achievements that may gain you a fame:
but we wonder, proceeded the spirits, that you desire to be Empress of a
terrestrial world, whenas you can create your self a celestial world if you
please. What, said the Empress, can any mortal be a creator? Yes, answered
the spirits; for every human creature can create an immaterial world fully
inhabited by immaterial creatures, and populous of immaterial subjects,
such as we are, and all this within the compass of the head or scull; nay,
not only so, but he may create a world of what fashion and government he
will, and give the creatures thereof such motions, figures, forms, colours,
perceptions, etc. as he pleases, and make whirlpools, lights, pressures and
reactions, etc. as he thinks best; nay, he may make a world full of veins,
muscles, and nerves, and all these to move by one jolt or stroke: also he
may alter that World as often as he pleases, or change it from a natural
world, to an artificial; he may make a world of ideas, a world of atoms,[148] a
world of lights, or whatsoever his fancy leads him to. And since it is in your
power to create such a world, what need you to venture life, reputation
and tranquillity, to conquer a gross material world? For you can enjoy no
more of a material world than a particular creature is able to enjoy, which
is but a small part, considering the compass of such a world; and you may
plainly observe it by your friend the Empress here, which although she
possesses a whole world, yet enjoys she but a part thereof; neither is she
so much acquainted with it, that she knows all the places, countries and
dominions she governs. The truth is, a sovereign monarch has the general
trouble; but the subjects enjoy all the delights and pleasures in parts; for
it is impossible, that a kingdom, nay, a country should be enjoyed by one
person at once, except he take the pains to travel into every part, and endure the inconveniencies of going from one place to another; wherefore,
since glory, delight and pleasure lives but in other men's opinions, and
can neither add tranquillity to your mind, nor give ease to your body, why

---

[147] See Introduction, p. xviii.
[148] Cavendish writes about a world of atoms in *Poems and Fancies*, pp. 52–7. Her early
philosophy followed Epicurus's atomism, and his view that there are infinite worlds. Cf.
*Observations*, p. 262.

should you desire to be Empress of a material world, and be troubled with the cares that attend your government? whenas by creating a world within yourself, you may enjoy all both in whole and in parts[149] without control or opposition, and may make what world you please, and alter it when you please, and enjoy as much pleasure and delight as a world can afford you? You have converted me, said the Duchess to the spirits, from my ambitious desire; wherefore I'll take your advice, reject and despise all the worlds without me, and create a world of my own. The Empress said, if I do make such a world, then I shall be mistress of two worlds, one within, and the other without me. That your Majesty may, said the spirits; and so left these two ladies to create two worlds within themselves: who did also part from each other, until such time as they had brought their worlds to perfection. The Duchess of Newcastle was most earnest and industrious to make her world, because she had none at present; and first she resolved to frame it according to the opinion of Thales,[150] but she found herself so much troubled with demons, that they would not suffer her to take her own will, but forced her to obey their orders and commands; which she being unwilling to do, left off from making a world that way, and began to frame one according to Pythagoras's doctrine;[151] but in the creation thereof, she was so puzzled with numbers, how to order and compose the several parts, that she having no skill in arithmetic was forced also to desist from the making of that world. Then she intended to create a world

---

[149] For the view that imagination is not restricted by time or space see, e.g., Hobbes's claim that imagination is able to 'fly from one Indies to another, and from Heaven to Earth, and to penetrate the hardest matter and obscurest places, into the future and herselfe, and all this in a point of time'. *The Answer of Mr. Hobbes to Sir William D'Avenant's Preface before Gondibert* in Sir William Davenant's *Gondibert*, ed. David Gladish (Oxford, 1971), p. 49.

[150] In *Observations*, Cavendish includes a series of 'Observations on the Opinions of Some Ancient Philosophers', based on Thomas Stanley, *The History of Philosophy* (1655–62). According to Stanley, Thales holds 'that nature is full of demons and spiritual substances'. See *Observations*, p. 250.

[151] 'Alexander . . . says that he found in the Pythagorean Memoirs the following tenets . . . The principle of all things is the monad or unit; arising from this monad the undefined dyad or two serves as a material substratus to the monad, which is cause; from the monad and the undefined dyad spring numbers; from numbers points; from points, lines; from lines, plane figures; from plane figures, solid figures; from solid figures, sensible bodies, the elements of which are four, fire, water, earth and air; these elements interchange and turn into one another completely, and combine to produce a universe animate, intelligent, spherical, with the earth at its centre', Diogenes Laertius, *Lives of Eminent Philosophers*, trans. D. Hicks (Loeb Classical Library, Cambridge, MA: Harvard University Press, 1979), vol. II, VIII. 25–7.

according to the opinion of Plato;[152] but she found more trouble and difficulty in that, than in the two former; for the numerous Ideas having no
other motion but what was derived from her mind, whence they did flow
and issue out, made it a far harder business to her, to impart motion to
them, than puppet-players have in giving motion to every several puppet;
in so much, that her patience was not able to endure the trouble which
those ideas caused her; wherefore she annihilated also that world, and
was resolved to make one according to the opinion of Epicurus;[153] which
she had no sooner begun, but the infinite atoms made such a mist, that it
quite blinded the perception of her mind; neither was she able to make a
vacuum as a receptacle for those atoms, or a place which they might retire
into; so that partly for the want of it, and of a good order and method, the
confusion of those atoms produced such strange and monstrous figures,
as did more affright than delight her, and caused such a chaos in her mind,
as had almost dissolved it. At last, having with much ado cleansed and
cleared her mind of these dusty and misty particles, she endeavoured to
create a world according to Aristotle's opinion; but remembering that her
mind, as most of the learned hold, was immaterial, and that according
to Aristotle's principle, out of nothing, nothing could be made; she was
forced also to desist from that work, and then she fully resolved, not to
take any more patterns from the ancient philosophers, but to follow the
opinions of the moderns; and to that end, she endeavoured to make a world
according to Descartes' opinion;[154] but when she had made the ethereal
globules, and set them a-moving by a strong and lively imagination, her
mind became so dizzy with their extraordinary swift turning round, that it
almost put her into a swoon; for her thoughts, by their constant tottering,
did so stagger, as if they had all been drunk: wherefore she dissolved that
world, and began to make another, according to Hobbes' opinion;[155] but
when all the parts of this imaginary world came to press and drive each
other, they seemed like a company of wolves that worry sheep, or like so
many dogs that hunt after hares; and when she found a reaction equal

[152] Cf. *Observations*, p. 253.

[153] Atomist philosopher whose views were revived and adapted in the seventeenth century
by Gassendi and Charleton. The Duchess's problems with an Epicurean world echo her
objections to atomism in *Physical and Philosophical Opinions*, Second Epistle to the Reader.
See also *Observations*, pp. 263–4.

[154] Descartes's theory of vortices, *Principles of Philosophy*, III, in *Oeuvres de Descartes* ed.
Charles Adam and Paul Tannery, 11 vols., 2nd edn (Paris, 1974–86), vol. VIII, pp. 80–202.

[155] Hobbes, *De Corpore* IV.25; EW, pp. 387–410. Cavendish raises this objection to Hobbes's
corpuscularianism in *Philosophical Letters*, I. xviii.

to those pressures, her mind was so squeezed together, that her thoughts could neither move forward nor backward, which caused such an horrible pain in her head, that although she had dissolved that world, yet she could not, without much difficulty, settle her mind, and free it from that pain which those pressures and reactions had caused in it.

At last, when the Duchess saw that no patterns would do her any good in the framing of her world; she resolved to make a world of her own invention, and this world was composed of sensitive and rational self-moving matter;[156] indeed, it was composed only of the rational, which is the subtlest and purest degree of matter; for as the sensitive did move and act both to the perceptions and consistency of the body, so this degree of matter at the same point of time (for though the degrees are mixed, yet the several parts may move several ways at one time) did move to the creation of the imaginary world; which world after it was made, appeared so curious and full of variety, so well ordered and wisely governed, that it cannot possibly be expressed by words, nor the delight and pleasure which the Duchess took in making this world of her own.

In the meantime the Empress was also making and dissolving several worlds in her own mind, and was so puzzled, that she could not settle in any of them; wherefore she sent for the Duchess, who being ready to wait on the Empress, carried her beloved world along with her, and invited the Empress's soul to observe the frame, order and government of it. Her Majesty was so ravished with the perception of it, that her soul desired to live in the Duchess's world; but the Duchess advised her to make such another world in her own mind; for, said she, your Majesty's mind is full of rational corporeal motions, and the rational motions of my mind shall assist you by the help of sensitive expressions, with the best instructions they are able to give you.

The Empress being thus persuaded by the Duchess to make an imaginary world of her own, followed her advice and after she had quite finished it, and framed all kinds of creatures proper and useful for it, strengthened it with good laws, and beautified it with arts and sciences; having nothing else to do, unless she did dissolve her imaginary world, or made some alterations in the Blazing World she lived in, which yet she could hardly do, by reason it was so well ordered that it could not be mended; for it was governed without secret and deceiving policy; neither was there any ambition, factions, malicious detractions, civil dissensions, or home-bred

---

[156] I.e. a world conforming to Cavendish's own philosophy.

quarrels, divisions in religion, foreign wars, etc. but all the people lived in a peaceful society, united tranquillity, and religious conformity; she was desirous to see the world the Duchess came from, and observe therein the several sovereign governments, laws and customs of several nations. The Duchess used all the means she could, to divert her from that journey, telling her, that the world she came from, was very much disturbed with factions, divisions and wars; but the Empress would not be persuaded from her design; and lest the Emperor, or any of his subjects should know of her travel, and obstruct her design, she sent for some of the spirits she had formerly conversed withal, and enquired whether none of them could supply the place of her soul in her body at such a time, when she was gone to travel into another world? They answered, yes, they could; for not only one, said they, but many spirits may enter into your body, if you please. The Empress replied, she desired but one spirit to be viceroy of her body in the absence of her soul, but it must be an honest and ingenious spirit; and if it was possible, a female spirit. The spirits told her, that there was no difference of sexes amongst them;[157] but, said they, we will choose an honest and ingenious spirit, and such a one as shall so resemble your soul, that neither the Emperor, nor any of his subjects, although the most divine, shall know whether it be your own soul, or not: which the Empress was very glad at, and after the spirits were gone, asked the Duchess, how her body was supplied in the absence of her soul? who answered Her Majesty, that her body, in the absence of her soul, was governed by her sensitive and rational corporeal motions. Thus those two female souls travelled together as lightly as two thoughts into the Duchess her native world; and which is remarkable, in a moment viewed all the parts of it, and all the actions of all the creatures therein, especially did the Empress's soul take much notice of the several actions of human creatures in all the several nations and parts of that world, and wondered that for all there were so many several nations, governments, laws, religions, opinions, etc. they should all yet so generally agree in being ambitious, proud, self-conceited, vain, prodigal, deceitful, envious, malicious, unjust, revengeful, irreligious, factious, etc. She did also admire, that not any particular state, kingdom or common-wealth, was contented with their own shares, but endeavoured to encroach upon their neighbours, and that their greatest glory was in plunder and slaughter, and yet their victories less than their expenses, and their losses more than their gains, but their being overcome in a manner their utter

---

[157] Cf. More's claim that the soul is hermaphroditic. *Immortality of the Soul*, Book 2, ch. 2.

ruin. But that she wondered most at, was, that they should prize or value dirt more than men's lives,[158] and vanity more than tranquillity; for the Emperor of a world, said she, enjoys but a part, not the whole; so that his pleasure consists in the opinions of others. It is strange to me, answered the Duchess, that you should say thus, being yourself, an Empress of a world, and not only of a world, but of a peaceable, quiet, and obedient world. 'Tis true, replied the Empress, but although it is a peaceable and obedient world, yet the government thereof is rather a trouble, than a pleasure; for order cannot be without industry, contrivance and direction; besides, the magnificent state, that great Princes keep or ought to keep, is troublesome.[159] Then by your Majesty's discourse, said the Duchess, I perceive that the greatest happiness in all worlds consists in moderation:[160] no doubt of it, replied the Empress; and after these two souls had visited all the several places, congregations and assemblies both in religion and state, the several courts of judicature, and the like, in several nations, the Empress said, that of all the monarchs of the several parts of that world, she had observed the Grand Signior was the greatest, for his word was a law, and his power absolute.[161] But the Duchess prayed the Empress to pardon her that she was of another mind; for, said she, he cannot alter Mahomet's laws and religion; so that the law and church do govern the Emperor, and not the Emperor them. But, replied the Empress, he has

---

[158] An influential discussion of the pros and cons of conquest is found in Erasmus, *Querela Pacis* (1517). The issue was much debated when England became a conquering power during the 1650s. See David Armitage, *The Ideological Origins of the British Empire* (Cambridge: Cambridge University Press, 2000).

[159] See Introduction, pp. xxvii–xxviii; Newcastle's *Advice*, pp. 45–6, 59.

[160] Cf. the Aristotelian view that virtue, and hence happiness, lies in the mean. Aristotle, *Nicomachean Ethics*, Book II, 1106a14–1108b10.

[161] Praise for the Grand Signor is unusual, as he is usually presented as a tyrant whose word is law. Robert Withers says of the Grand Mufti that 'he is amongst them as an archbishop is with us, for he is the Primate over the church', and adds that 'although this Muftee hath not an absolute rule over the other Muftees of other parts of the King's dominions; yet by his policy he ever prevails with the Grand Seignor, and effecteth whatsoever he undertakes, especially when he hath the Vizir Azem to his friend, who in degree, dignity and authority is his superior'. The Empress's response to the Duchess's judgement also echoes Withers's claims that the Grand Mufti is chosen by the Grand Signor himself, and that all senior judges, including the grand Mufti, are changed every three years. Withers, *A Description of the Grand Signor's Seraglio*, pp. 129, 131. See also n. 25. The question of whether the sovereign should be above the law was much debated in seventeenth-century political philosophy. A strong version of Cavendish's view that a ruler should be in a position to make and change law was influentially voiced by Hobbes, who describes the view that 'he that hath the Sovereign Power is subject to the Civill Lawes' as 'repugnant to the nature of a Commonwealth', *Leviathan*, ch. 29, p. 224.

power in some particulars; as for example, to place and displace subjects in their particular governments of church and state, and having that, he has the command both over church and state, and none dares oppose him. 'Tis true, said the Duchess; but if it pleases your Majesty, we will go into that part of the world whence I came to wait on your Majesty, and there you shall see as powerful a monarch as the Grand-Signior; for though his dominions are not of so large extent, yet they are much stronger, his laws are easy and safe, and he governs so justly and wisely, that his subjects are the happiest people of all the nations or parts of that world. This monarch, said the Empress, I have a great mind to see: then they both went, and in a short time arrived into his dominions; but coming into the metropolitan city, the Empress's soul observed many gallants go into a house, and enquired of the Duchess's soul, what house that was? She told her, it was one of the theatres where comedies and tragedies were acted. The Empress asked, whether they were real? No, said the Duchess, they are feigned. Then the Empress desired to enter into the theatre, and when she had seen the play that was acted, the Duchess asked her how she liked that recreation? I like it very well, said the Empress; but I observe, that the actors make a better show than the spectators, and the scenes a better than the actors, and the music and dancing is more pleasant and acceptable than the play itself; for I see, the scenes stand for wit, the dancing for humour, and the music is the chorus. I am sorry, replied the Duchess, to hear your Majesty say so; for if the wits of this part of the world should hear you, they would condemn you. What, said the Empress, would they condemn me for preferring a natural face before a sign-post, or a natural humour before an artificial dance, or music before a true and profitable relation? As for relation, replied the Duchess, our poets defy and condemn it into a chimney-corner, fitter for old women's tales, than theatres. Why, said the Empress, do not your poets' actions comply with their judgements? for their plays are composed of old stories, either of Greek or Roman, or some new-found world. The Duchess answered her Majesty, that it was true; that all or most of their plays were taken out of old stories, but yet they had new actions, which being joined to old stories, together with the addition of new prologues, scenes, music and dancing, made new plays.

After this, both the souls went to the court, where all the royal family was together, attended by the chief of the nobles of their dominions, which made a very magnificent show; and when the soul of the Empress viewed the King and Queen, she seemed to be in amaze, which the Duchess's soul perceiving, asked the Empress how she liked the King, the Queen, and all the royal race? She answered, that in all the monarchs she had seen in that world, she had not found so much majesty and affability mixed so exactly together, that none did overshadow or eclipse the other; and as for the Queen, she said, that virtue sat triumphant in her face, and piety was dwelling in her heart, and that all the royal family seemed to be endued with a divine splendour: but when she had heard the King discourse, she believed, that Mercury and Apollo[162] had been his celestial instructors; and my dear lord and husband, added the Duchess, has been his earthly governor.[163] But after some short stay in the court, the Duchess's soul grew very melancholy; the Empress asking the cause of her sadness? she told her, that she had an extreme desire to converse with the soul of her noble lord and dear husband, and that she was impatient of a longer stay. The Empress desired the Duchess to have but patience so long, until the King, the Queen, and the royal family were retired, and then she would bear her company to her lord and husband's soul who at that time lived in the country some 112 miles off; which she did: and thus these two souls went towards those parts of the kingdom where the Duke of Newcastle was.

But one thing I forgot all this while, which is, that although thoughts are the natural language of souls, yet by reason souls cannot travel without vehicles, they use such language as the nature and propriety of their vehicles require, and the vehicles of those two souls being made of the purest and finest sort of air, and of a human shape; this purity and fineness was the cause that they could neither be seen nor heard by any human creature; whenas, had they been of some grosser sort of air, the sound of that air's language would have been as perceptible as the blowing of Zephyrus.[164]

And now to return to my former story; when the Empress's and Duchess's soul were travelling into Nottinghamshire, for that was the place where the Duke did reside; passing through the forest of Sherwood,

---

[162] Mercury, the messenger of the Gods and patron of orators; Apollo, the God of music and poetry.

[163] Newcastle was governor or tutor to the Prince of Wales (later King Charles II) from 1638 to 1641 and in 1638 wrote a *Letter of Instruction to Prince Charles for his Studies, Conduct and Behaviour*, Royal Letters in the Harleian MSS 6988 art. 68. Also printed in Henry Ellis, *Original Letters Illustrative of English History*, 1st series, 3 (London, 1825), p. 288. After the English court went into exile in 1645, he secured Hobbes a position as tutor in mathematics to the Prince of Wales.

[164] One of the four winds.

the Empress's soul was very much delighted with it, as being a dry, plain and woody place, very pleasant to travel in both in Winter and Summer; for it is neither much dirty, not dusty at no time: at last they arrived at Welbeck,[165] a house where the Duke dwelled, surrounded all with wood, so close and full, that the Empress took great pleasure and delight therein, and told the Duchess she never had observed more wood in so little a compass in any part of the kingdom she had passed through; the truth is, said she, there seems to be more wood on the seas, she meaning the ships, than on the land.[166] The Duchess told her, the reason was, that there had been a long Civil War in that kingdom, in which most of the best timber-trees and principal palaces were ruined and destroyed; and my dear lord and husband, said she, has lost by it half his woods, besides many houses, land, and movable goods; so that all the loss out of his particular estate, did amount to above half a million of pounds. I wish, said the Empress, he had some of the gold that is in the Blazing World, to repair his losses. The Duchess most humbly thanked her Imperial Majesty for her kind wishes; but, said she, wishes will not repair his ruins: however, God has given my noble lord and husband great patience, by which he bears all his losses and misfortunes. At last, they entered into the Duke's house, an habitation not so magnificent, as useful; and when the Empress saw it, Has the Duke, said she, no other house but this? Yes, answered the Duchess, some five miles from this place, he has a very fine castle, called Bolsover.[167] That place then, said the Empress, I desire to see. Alas! replied the Duchess, it is but a naked house, and unclothed of all furniture. However, said the Empress, I may see the manner of its structure and building. That you may, replied the Duchess: and as they were thus discoursing, the Duke came out of the house into the court, to see his horses of manage;[168] whom

---

[165] Welbeck Abbey in Nottinghamshire, one of Newcastle's estates.

[166] In 1662 the Royal Society discussed the planting and preservation of timber in view of the needs of the Commissioners for the Navy. John Evelyn's contribution developed into *Sylva or a Discourse of Forest Trees and the Propagation of Timber in his Majesty's Dominions* (1664). Evelyn remarks that 'there is nothing which seems more fatally to threaten a *weakening* if not a *dissolution* of the strength of this famous and flourishing nation, than the sensible and notorious decay of her wooden walls, when . . . the present navy shall be worn out and impaired' and criticises the destruction of woodland during the Civil War, p. 121. Cavendish attributes the same criticism to her husband, along with Evelyn's admiration for oak, *Life of the Thrice Noble, High and Puissant Prince William Cavendish*, Book IV, XXXVI.

[167] Bolsover Castle, an estate belonging to Newcastle, was partly destroyed during the Civil War.

[168] Newcastle, an outstanding horseman, published two books about the art of manage or dressage: *La Méthode Nouvelle et Invention Extraordinaire de dresser les Chevaux* (Antwerp,

when the Duchess's soul perceived, she was so overjoyed, that her aerial vehicle became so splendorous, as if it had been enlightened by the sun; by which we may perceive, that the passions of souls or spirits can alter their bodily vehicles. Then these two ladies' spirits went close to him, but he could not perceive them; and after the Empress had observed the art of manage, she was much pleased with it, and commended it as a noble pastime, and an exercise fit and proper for noble and heroic persons; but when the Duke was gone into the house again, those two souls followed him; where the Empress observing, that he went to the exercise of the sword, and was such an excellent and unparalleled master thereof, she was as much pleased with that exercise, as she was with the former:[169] but the Duchess's soul being troubled, that her dear lord and husband used such a violent exercise before meat, for fear of overheating himself, without any consideration of the Empress's soul, left her aerial vehicle, and entered into her lord. The Empress's soul perceiving this, did the like: and then the Duke had three souls in one body; and had there been but some such souls more, the Duke would have been like the Grand Signior in his seraglio, only it would have been a platonic seraglio. But the Duke's soul being wise, honest, witty, complaisant and noble, afforded such delight and pleasure to the Empress's soul by her conversation, that these two souls became enamoured of each other; which the Duchess's soul perceiving, grew jealous at first, but then considering that no adultery could be committed amongst Platonic lovers, and that Platonism was divine, as being derived from divine Plato, cast forth of her mind that Idea of jealousy. Then the conversation of these three souls was so pleasant, that it cannot be expressed; for the Duke's soul entertained the Empress's soul with scenes, songs, music, witty discourses, pleasant recreations, and all kinds of harmless sports; so that the time passed away faster than they expected. At last, a spirit came and told the Empress, that although neither the Emperor, nor any of his subjects knew that her soul was absent; yet the Empress's soul was so sad and melancholy, for want of his own beloved soul, that all the imperial court took notice of it. Wherefore he advised the Empress's soul to return into the Blazing World, into her own body she left there; which both the Duke's and Duchess's soul was very sorry for,

---

1658); *A New Method and Extraordinary Invention to Dress Horses and Work Them According to Their Nature* (1667). He advises Charles II 'to ride your Horses of manage, twice a weeke, which will incourage Noble men, to Doe the Like', *Advice*, p. 61.

[169] In a dedicatory letter to her husband, Cavendish describes him as employing most of his time in the noble and heroic art of horsemanship and weapons, *Observations*, p. 4.

and wished, that if it had been possible, the Empress's soul might have stayed a longer time with them; but seeing it could not be otherwise, they pacified themselves: but before the Empress returned into the Blazing World, the Duchess desired a favour of her, to wit, that she would be pleased to make an agreement between her noble lord, and Fortune. Why, said the Empress, are they enemies?[170] Yes, answered the Duchess, and they have been so ever since I have been his wife; nay, I have heard my lord say, that she hath crossed him in all things ever since he could remember. I am sorry for that, replied the Empress, but I cannot discourse with Fortune without the help of an immaterial spirit, and that cannot be done in this world, for I have no fly- nor bird-men here, to send into the region of the air, where for the most part, their habitations are. The Duchess said, she would entreat her lord to send an attorney or lawyer, to plead his cause. Fortune will bribe them, replied the Empress, and so the Duke may chance to be cast; wherefore the best way will be for the Duke to choose a friend on his side, and let Fortune choose another, and try whether by this means it be possible to compose the difference. The Duchess said, they will never come to an agreement, unless there be a judge or umpire to decide the case. A judge, replied the Empress, is easy to be had, but to get an impartial judge, is a thing so difficult, that I doubt we shall hardly find one; for there is none to be had neither in nature, nor in Hell, but only from Heaven, and how to get such a divine and celestial judge I cannot tell: nevertheless, if you will go along with me into the Blazing World, I'll try what may be done. 'Tis my duty, said the Duchess, to wait on your Majesty, and I shall most willingly do it, for I have no other interest to consider. Then the Duchess spake to the Duke concerning the difference between him and Fortune, and how it was her desire that they might be friends. The Duke answered, that for his part, he had always with great industry, sought her friendship, but as yet he could never obtain it, for she had always been his enemy: however, said he, I'll try, and send my two friends, Prudence and Honesty, to plead my cause. Then these two friends went with the Duchess and the Empress into the Blazing World; (for it is to be observed, that they are somewhat like spirits, because they are immaterial, although their actions are corporeal:) and after their arrival there,

---

[170] In many of her works Cavendish constructs her husband as a paragon of nobility who has suffered cruelly at the hands of Fortune. See particularly *The Life of the Thrice Noble, High and Puissant Prince William Cavendish*.

when the Empress had refreshed herself, and rejoiced with the Emperor, she sent her fly-men for some of the spirits, and desired their assistance, to compose the difference between Fortune, and the Duke of Newcastle. But they told her Majesty, that Fortune was so inconstant, that although she would perhaps promise to hear their cause pleaded, yet it was a thousand to one, but she would never have the patience to do it: nevertheless, upon her Majesty's request, they tried their utmost, and at last prevailed with Fortune so far, that she chose Folly, and Rashness, for her friends, but they could not agree in choosing a judge; until at last, with much ado, they concluded, that Truth should hear, and decide the cause. Thus all being prepared, and the time appointed, both the Empress's and Duchess's soul went to hear them plead; and when all the immaterial company was met Fortune standing upon a golden globe,[171] made this following speech:

> Noble Friends, We are met here to hear a cause pleaded concerning the difference between the Duke of Newcastle, and myself and though I am willing upon the persuasions of the ambassadors of the Empress, the immaterial spirits, to yield to it, yet it had been fit, the Duke's soul should be present also, to speak for herself, but since she is not here, I shall declare myself to his wife, and his friends, as also to my friends, especially the Empress, to whom I shall chiefly direct my speech. First, I desire, your Imperial Majesty may know, that this Duke who complains or exclaims so much against me, hath been always my enemy; for he has preferred Honesty and Prudence before me, and slighted all my favours; nay, not only thus, but he did fight against me, and preferred his innocence before my power. His friends Honesty and Prudence, said he most scornfully, are more to be regarded, than inconstant Fortune, who is only a friend to fools and knaves; for which neglect and scorn, whether I have not just reason to be his enemy, your Majesty may judge yourself.

After Fortune had thus ended her speech, the Duchess's soul rose from her seat, and spake to the immaterial assembly in this manner:

> Noble Friends, I think it fit, by your leave, to answer Lady Fortune in the behalf of my noble lord and husband, since he is not here himself; and since you have heard her complaint concerning the choice my lord

---

[171] In Renaissance iconography, Fortune is sometimes shown standing on a globe to indicate her unsteadiness and inconstancy.

made of his friends, and the neglect and disrespect he seemed to cast upon her; give me leave to answer, that, first concerning the choice of his friends, he has proved himself a wise man in it; and as for the disrespect and rudeness, her Ladyship accuses him of, I dare say, he is so much a gentleman, that I am confident he would never slight, scorn or disrespect any of the female sex in all his lifetime; but was such a servant and champion for them, that he ventured life and estate in their service; but being of an honest, as well as an honourable nature, he could not trust Fortune with that which he preferred above his life, which was his reputation, by reason Fortune did not side with those that were honest and honourable, but renounced them; and since he could not be of both sides, he chose to be of that which was agreeable both to his conscience, nature and education; for which choice Fortune did not only declare herself his open enemy, but fought with him in several battles; nay, many times, hand to hand; at last, she being a powerful princess, and as some believe, a deity, overcame him, and cast him into a banishment, where she kept him in great misery, ruined his estate, and took away from him most of his friends; nay, even when she favoured many that were against her, she still frowned on him; all which he endured with the greatest patience, and with that respect to Lady Fortune, that he did never in the least endeavour to disoblige any of her favourites, but was only sorry that he, an honest man, could find no favour in her court; and since he did never injure any of those she favoured, he neither was an enemy to her Ladyship, but gave her always that respect and worship which belonged to her power and dignity, and is still ready at any time honestly and prudently to serve her; he only begs her Ladyship would be his friend for the future, as she hath been his enemy in times past.

As soon as the Duchess's speech was ended, Folly and Rashness started up, and both spake so thick and fast at once, that not only the assembly, but themselves were not able to understand each other: at which Fortune was somewhat out of countenance, and commanded them either to speak singly, or be silent: but Prudence told her Ladyship, she should command them to speak wisely, as well as singly; otherwise, said she, it were best for them not to speak at all: which Fortune resented very ill, and told Prudence, she was too bold; and then commanded Folly to declare what she would have made known: but her speech was so foolish, mixed with such nonsense, that none knew what to make of it; besides, it was so tedious, that Fortune bid her to be silent, and commanded Rashness to speak for her, who began after this manner:

> Great Fortune; The Duchess of Newcastle has proved herself, according to report, a very proud and ambitious lady, in presuming to answer you her own self, in this noble assembly without your command, in a speech wherein she did not only contradict you, but preferred Honesty and Prudence before you; saying, that her lord was ready to serve you honestly and prudently; which presumption is beyond all pardon; and if you allow Honesty and Prudence to be above you, none will admire, worship or serve you; but you'll be forced to serve yourself, and will be despised, neglected and scorned by all; and from a deity, become a miserable, dirty, begging mortal in a churchyard porch, or nobleman's gate: wherefore to prevent such disasters, fling as many misfortunes and neglects on the Duke and Duchess of Newcastle, and their two friends, as your power is able to do; otherwise Prudence and Honesty will be the chief and only moral deities of mortals.

Rashness having thus ended her speech, Prudence rose and declared herself in this manner:

> Beautiful Truth, Great Fortune, and you the rest of my noble friends; I am come a great and long journey in the behalf of my dear friend the Duke of Newcastle, not to make more wounds, but, if it be possible, to heal those that are made already. Neither do I presume to be a deity; but my only request is, that you would be pleased to accept of my offering, I being an humble and devout supplicant, and since no offering is more acceptable to the gods, than the offering of peace; in order to that, I desire to make an agreement between Fortune, and the Duke of Newcastle.

Thus she spake, and as she was going on, up started Honesty (for she has not always so much discretion as she ought to have) and interrupted Prudence.

> I came not here, said she, to hear Fortune flattered, but to hear the cause decided between Fortune and the Duke; neither came I hither to speak rhetorically and eloquently, but to propound the case plainly and truly; and I'll have you know, that the Duke, whose cause we argue, was and is my foster-son; for I Honesty bred him from his childhood, and made a perpetual friendship betwixt him and Gratitude, Charity

and Generosity; and put him to school to Prudence, who taught him wisdom, and informed him in the rules of Temperance, Patience, Justice, and the like; then I put him into the University of Honour, where he learned all honourable qualities, arts, and sciences; afterward I sent him to travel through the world of actions, and made Observation his governor; and in those travels, he contracted a friendship with Experience; all which, made him fit for Heaven's blessings, and Fortune's favours: but she hating all those that have merit and desert, became his inveterate enemy, doing him all the mischief she could, until the god of Justice opposed Fortune's malice and passed him out of those ruins she had cast upon him: for this god's favourites were the Duke's champions; wherefore to be an enemy to him, were to be an enemy to the god of Justice: in short, the true cause of Fortune's malice to this Duke, is, that he would never flatter her; for I Honesty, did command him not to do it, or else he would be forced to follow all her inconstant ways, and obey all her unjust commands, which would cause a great reproach to him: but, on the other side, Prudence advised him not to despise Fortune's favours, for that would be an obstruction and hindrance to his worth and merit; and he to obey both our advice and counsels, did neither flatter nor despise her, but was always humble and respectful to her, so far as honour, honesty and conscience would permit: all which I refer to Truth's judgement, and expect her final sentence.

Fortune hearing thus Honesty's plain speech, thought it very rude, and would not hearken to Truth's judgement, but went away in a passion: at which, both the Empress and Duchess were extremely troubled, that their endeavours should have no better effect: but Honesty chid the Duchess, and said, she was to be punished for desiring so much Fortune's favours; for it appears, said she, that you mistrust the gods' blessings: at which the Duchess wept, answering Honesty, that she did neither mistrust the gods' blessings, nor rely upon Fortune's favours; but desired only that her lord might have no potent enemies. The Empress being much troubled to see her weep, told Honesty in anger, she wanted the discretion of Prudence; for though you are commendable, said she, yet you are apt to commit many indiscreet actions, unless Prudence be your guide. At which reproof Prudence smiled, and Honesty was somewhat out of countenance; but they soon became very good friends: and after the Duchess's soul had stayed some time with the Empress in the Blazing World, she begged leave of her to return to her lord and husband; which the Empress granted her, upon condition she should come and visit her as often as conveniently she could, promising that she would do the same to the Duchess.

Thus the Duchess's soul, after she had taken her leave of the Empress, as also of the spirits, who with great civility, promised her, that they would endeavour in time to make a peace and agreement between Fortune and the Duke, returned with Prudence and Honesty into her own world: but when she was just upon her departure, the Empress sent to her, and desired that she might yet have some little conference with her before she went; which the Duchess most willingly granted her Majesty, and when she came to wait on her, the Empress told the Duchess, that she being her dear Platonic friend, of whose just and impartial judgement, she had always a very great esteem, could not forbear, before she went from her, to ask her advice concerning the government of the Blazing World; for, said she, although this world was very well and wisely ordered and governed at first, when I came to be Empress thereof; yet the nature of women, being much delighted with change and variety, after I had received an absolute power from the Emperor, did somewhat alter the form of government from what I found it; but now perceiving that the world is not so quiet as it was at first, I am much troubled at it; especially there are such contentions and divisions between the worm-, bear- and fly-men, the ape-men, the satyrs, the spider-men, and all others of such sorts, that I fear they'll break out into an open rebellion, and cause a great disorder and the ruin of the government; and therefore I desire your advice and assistance, how I may order it to the best advantage, that this world may be rendered peaceable, quiet and happy, as it was before. Whereupon the Duchess answered, that since she heard by her Imperial Majesty, how well and happily the world had been governed when she first came to be Empress thereof, she would advise her Majesty to introduce the same form of government again, which had been before;[172] that is, to have but one sovereign, one religion, one law, and one language, so that all the world might be as one united family, without divisions; nay, like God, and his blessed saints and angels;[173] otherwise, said she, it may in time prove as unhappy, nay, as miserable a world as that is from which I came,[174] wherein are more sovereigns than

---

[172] Perhaps a nostalgic recommendation to return to the governments of Charles I and his predecessors.

[173] This adapts a standard French absolutist trope that there should be 'une foi, une loi, un roi'. Note the addition of one language.

[174] Cavendish is pessimistic about the possibility of achieving lasting peace. 'If men do not naturally agree, Art cannot make unity amongst them, or associate them into one Body

worlds, and more pretended governors than governments, more religions than gods, and more opinions in those religions than truths; more laws than rights, and more bribes than justices, more policies than necessities, and more fears than dangers, more covetousness than riches, more ambitions than merits, more services than rewards, more languages than wit, more controversy than knowledge, more reports than noble actions, and more gifts by partiality, than according to merit; all which, said she, is a great misery, nay, a curse, which your blessed Blazing World never knew, nor 'tis probable, will never know of, unless your Imperial Majesty alter the government thereof from what it was when you began to govern it: and since your Majesty complains much of the factions of the bear-, fish-, fly-, ape- and worm-men, the satyrs, spider-men, and the like, and of their perpetual disputes and quarrels, I would advise your Majesty to dissolve all their societies;[175] for 'tis better to be without their intelligences, than to have an unquiet and disorderly government. The truth is, said she, wheresoever is learning, there is most commonly also controversy and quarrelling; for there be always some that will know more, and be wiser than others; some think their arguments come nearer to truth, and are more rational than others; some are so wedded to their own opinions, that they never yield to reason; and others, though they find their opinions not firmly grounded upon reason, yet for fear of receiving some disgrace by altering them, will nevertheless maintain them against all sense and reason, which must needs breed factions in their schools, which at last break out into open wars, and draw sometimes an utter ruin upon a state or government. The Empress told the Duchess, that she would willingly follow her advice, but she thought it would be an eternal disgrace to her,

---

Politick, and so rule them . . . The truth is, Man rules an Artificial Government, and not Government man, just like as a Watch-Maker rules his Watch, and not the Watch the Watch-maker', *Philosophical Letters*, Part I, xiii. Battigelli argues that Cavendish is more Hobbesian than Hobbes, in that she agrees with him about the difficulty of establishing secure government, but has no confidence in his solution. Battigelli, *Margaret Cavendish*, pp. 83–4.

175 On the pernicious effects of philosophy on church and state see also *Philosophical Letters*, Part IV, Letter XX; *Newcastle's Advice*, p. 21. Cavendish distinguishes controversy in philosophy from controversy in families, states, or divinity. While she avoids the latter – 'I shun, as much as I can, not to discourse of either church or state'– she presents philosophical debate as less dangerous; 'Lawyers are friends though they contradict one another at the bar. So with philosophers, whose opinions are like their clients and who have clients not for wealth but fame', *Philosophical Letters*. Prefatory Letter to William Cavendish. See Battigelli, *Margaret Cavendish*, pp. 89–90; Shapin and Schaffer, *Leviathan*, pp. 110–224.

to alter her own decrees, acts and laws. To which the Duchess answered, that it was so far from a disgrace, as it would rather be for her Majesty's eternal honour, to return from a worse to a better, and would express and declare her to be more than ordinary wise and good; so wise, as to perceive her own errors, and so good, as not to persist in them, which few did; for which, said she, you will get a glorious fame in this world, and an eternal glory hereafter; and I shall pray for it so long as I live. Upon which advice, the Empress's soul embraced and kissed the Duchess's soul with an immaterial kiss, and shed immaterial tears, that she was forced to part from her, finding her not a flattering parasite, but a true friend; and, in truth, such was their Platonic friendship, as these two loving souls did often meet and rejoice in each other's conversation.

# THE SECOND PART OF THE DESCRIPTION OF
# THE NEW BLAZING WORLD

The Empress having now ordered and settled her government to the best advantage and quiet of her Blazing World, lived and reigned most happily and blessedly, and received oftentimes visits from the immaterial spirits, who gave her intelligence of all such things as she desired to know, and they were able to inform her of: one time they told her, how the world she came from, was embroiled in a great war, and that most parts or nations thereof made war against that kingdom, which was her native country, where all her friends and relations did live, at which the Empress was extremely troubled; insomuch that the Emperor perceived her grief by her tears, and examining the cause thereof, she told him that she had received intelligence from the spirits, that that part of the world she came from, which was her native country, was like to be destroyed by numerous enemies that made war against it. The Emperor being very sensible of this ill news, especially of the trouble it caused to the Empress, endeavoured to comfort her as much as possibly he could, and told her, that she might have all the assistance which the Blazing World was able to afford. She answered, that if there were any possibility of transporting forces out of the Blazing World, into the world she came from, she would not fear so much the ruin thereof: but, said she, there being no probability of effecting any such thing, I know not how to show my readiness to serve my native country. The Emperor asked, whether those spirits that gave her intelligence of this war, could not with all their power and forces assist her against those enemies? She answered, that spirits could not arm themselves, nor make any use of artificial arms or weapons; for their vehicles were natural bodies, not artificial: besides, said she, the violent and strong actions of war, will never agree with immaterial spirits; for immaterial spirits cannot fight, nor make trenches, fortifications, and the like. But, said the Emperor, their vehicles can; especially if those vehicles be men's bodies, they may be serviceable in all the actions of war. Alas, replied the Empress, that will never do; for first, said she, it will be difficult to get so many dead bodies for their vehicles, as to make up a whole army, much more to make many armies to fight with so many several nations; nay, if this could be, yet it is not possible to get so many dead and undissolved bodies in one nation; and for transporting them out of other nations, it would be a thing of great difficulty and improbability: but put the case, said she, all these difficulties could be overcome, yet there is one obstruction or hindrance which can no ways be avoided; for although those dead and undissolved bodies did all die in one minute of time, yet before they could rendezvous, and be put into a posture of war, to make a great and formidable army, they would stink and dissolve; and when they came to a fight, they would moulder into dust and ashes, and so leave the purer immaterial spirits naked: nay, were it also possible, that those dead bodies could be preserved from stinking and dissolving, yet the souls of such bodies would not suffer immaterial spirits to rule and order them, but they would enter and govern them themselves, as being the right owners thereof, which would produce a war between those immaterial souls, and the immaterial spirits in material bodies; all which would hinder them from doing any service in the actions of war, against the enemies of my native country. You speak reason, said the Emperor, and I wish with all my soul I could advise any manner or way, that you might be able to assist it; but you having told me of your dear Platonic friend the Duchess of Newcastle, and of her good and profitable counsels, I would desire you to send for her soul, and confer with her about this business.

The Empress was very glad of this notion of the Emperor, and immediately sent for the soul of the said Duchess, which in a minute waited on Her Majesty. Then the Empress declared to her the grievance and sadness of her mind, and how much she was troubled and afflicted at the news brought her by the immaterial spirits, desiring the Duchess, if possible, to assist her with the best counsels she could, that she might show the greatness of her love and affection which she bore to her native country. Whereupon the Duchess promised Her Majesty to do what lay in her power; and since it was a business of great importance, she desired some time to consider of it; for, said she, great affairs require deep considerations; which the Empress willingly allowed her. And after the Duchess had considered some little time, she desired the Empress to send some of her syrens or mear-men, to see what passages they could find out of the Blazing World, into the world she came from; for said she, if there be a passage for a ship to come out of that world into this; then certainly there may also a ship pass through the same passage out of this world into that. Hereupon the mear-men or fish-men were sent out; who being many in number, employed all their industry, and did swim several ways; at last having found out the passage, they returned to the Empress, and told her, that as their Blazing World had but one Emperor, one government, one religion, and one language, so there was but one passage into that world, which was so little, that no vessel bigger than a packet-boat could go through; neither was that passage always open, but sometimes quite frozen up. At which relation both the Empress and Duchess seemed somewhat troubled, fearing that this would perhaps be an hindrance or obstruction to their design.

At last the Duchess desired the Empress to send for her shipwrights, and all her architects, which were giants; who being called, the Duchess told them how some in her own world had been so ingenious, and contrived ships that could swim under water,[176] and asked whether they could do the like? The giants answered, they had never heard of that invention; nevertheless, they would try what might be done by art, and spare no labour or industry to find it out. In the meantime, while both the Empress and Duchess were in a serious council, after many debates, the Duchess desired but a few ships to transport some of the bird-, worm- and bear-men. Alas! said the Empress, what can such sorts of men do in the other world? especially so few? They will be soon destroyed, for a musket will destroy numbers of birds at one shot. The Duchess said, I desire Your Majesty will have but a little patience, and rely upon my advice, and you shall not fail to save your own native country, and in a manner become mistress of all that world you came from. The Empress, who loved the Duchess as her own soul, did so; the giants returned soon after, and told Her Majesty, that they had found out the art which the Duchess had mentioned, to make such ships as could swim under water; which the Empress and Duchess were both very glad at, and when the ships were made ready, the Duchess told the Empress, that it was requisite that Her Majesty should go her self in body as well as in soul; but, I, said she, can only wait on Your Majesty after a spiritual manner, that is, with my soul. Your soul, said the Empress, shall live with my soul, in my body;

---

[176] The inhabitants of Salomon's House have 'ships and boats for going under water and brooking of seas', Bacon, *New Atlantis*, p. 486. Cornelius Drebbel built a submarine and sailed it on the Thames in the early 1620s. Constantijn Huygens, who knew Cavendish in Antwerp, wrote 'it is not hard to imagine what would be the usefulness of this bold invention in time of war; if in this manner . . . enemy ships lying safely at anchor could be secretly attacked and sunk unexpectedly'. Quoted in Alex Roland, *Underwater Warfare in the Age of Sail* (Bloomington: University of Indiana Press, 1978), pp. 23–4. Cf. Marin Mersenne, 'Peut-on faire des navires, et des bateaux qui nagent entre deux eaux?' ('Is it possible to make ships and boats that will sail underwater?') in *Questions inouyes* (1634) (Paris: Fayard, 1985), p. 59. John Wilkins discusses 'the making of a ship, wherein men may safely swim under water'. Such an invention 'may be of very great advantage against a navy of enemies, who by this means may be undermined in the water and blown up', John Wilkins, *Mathematicall Magic or the Wonders that may be performed by Mechanical Geometry* (London, 1648), pp. 178, 187.

for I shall only desire your counsel and advice. Then said the Duchess, Your Majesty must command a great number of your fish-men to wait on your ships; for you know that your ships are not made for cannons, and therefore are no ways serviceable in war; for though by the help of your engines they can drive on, and your fish-men may by the help of chains or ropes, draw them which way they will, to make them go on, or fly back, yet not so as to fight: and though your ships be of gold, and cannot be shot through, but only bruised and battered; yet the enemy will assault and enter them, and take them as prizes; wherefore your fish-men must do you service instead of cannons. But how, said the Empress, can the fish-men do me service against an enemy, without cannons and all sorts of arms? That is the reason, answered the Duchess, that I would have numbers of fish-men, for they shall destroy all your enemy's ships, before they can come near you. The Empress asked in what manner that could be? Thus, answered the Duchess: - Your Majesty must send a number of worm-men to the Burning Mountains (for you have good store of them in the Blazing World) which must get a great quantity of the fire-stone, whose property, you know, is, that it burns so long as it is wet; and the ships in the other world being all made of wood, they may by that means set them all on fire; and if you can but destroy their ships, and hinder their navigation, you will be mistress of all that world, by reason most parts thereof cannot live without navigation.[177] Besides, said she, the fire-stone will serve you instead of light or torches; for you know, that the world you are going into, is dark at nights (especially if there be no moon-shine, or if the moon be overshadowed by clouds) and not so full of blazing-stars as this world is, which make as great a light in the absence of the sun, as the sun doth when it is present; for that world hath but little blinking stars, which make more shadows than light, and are only able to draw up vapours from the earth, but not to rarify or clarify them, or to convert them into serene air.

This advice of the Duchess was very much approved, and joyfully embraced by the Empress, who forthwith sent her worm-men to get a good quantity of the mentioned fire-stone. She also commanded numbers of fish-men to wait on her under water, and bird-men to wait on her in the air; and bear- and worm-men to wait on her in ships, according to the Duchess's advice; and indeed the bear-men were as serviceable to her as the north-star; but the bird-men would often rest themselves upon the

[177] See n. 15.

decks of the ships; neither would the Empress, being of a sweet and noble nature, suffer that they should tire or weary themselves by long flights; for though by land they did often fly out of one country into another, yet they did rest in some woods, or on some grounds, especially at night, when it was their sleeping time: and therefore the Empress was forced to take a great many ships along with her, both for transporting those several sorts of her loyal and serviceable subjects, and to carry provisions for them: besides, she was so wearied with the petitions of several others of her subjects who desired to wait on Her Majesty, that she could not possibly deny them all; for some would rather choose to be drowned, than not tender their duty to her.

Thus after all things were made fit and ready, the Empress began her journey, I cannot properly say, she set sail, by reason in some part, as in the passage between the two worlds (which yet was but short) the ships were drawn under water by the fish-men with golden chains, so that they had no need of sails there, nor of any other arts, but only to keep out water from entering into the ships, and to give or make so much air as would serve for breath or respiration, those land animals that were in the ships; which the giants had so artificially contrived, that they which were therein found no inconveniency at all: and after they had passed the Icy Sea, the golden ships appeared above water, and so went on until they came near the kingdom that was the Empress's native country; where the bear-men through their telescopes discovered a great number of ships which had beset all that kingdom, well rigged and manned.

The Empress before she came in sight of the enemy, sent some of her fish- and bird-men to bring her intelligence of their fleet; and hearing of their number, their station and posture, she gave order that when it was night, her bird-men should carry in their beaks some of the mentioned fire-stones, with the tops thereof wetted; and the fish-men should carry them likewise, and hold them out of the water; for they were cut in the form of torches or candles, and being many thousands, made a terrible show; for it appeared as if all the air and sea had been of a flaming fire; and all that were upon the sea, or near it, did verily believe, the time of judgement, or the last day was come, Which made them all fall down, and pray.

At the break of day, the Empress commanded those lights to be put out, and then the naval forces of the enemy perceived nothing but a number of ships without sails, guns, arms, and other instruments of war; which ships seemed to swim of themselves, without any help or assistance: which sight put them into a great amaze; neither could they perceive that those ships were of gold, by reason the Empress had caused them all to be coloured black, or with a dark colour; so that the natural colour of the gold could not be perceived through the artificial colour of the paint, no not by the best telescopes. All which put the enemy's fleet into such a fright at night, and to such wonder in the morning, or at day time, that they knew not what to judge or make of them; for they knew neither what ships they were, nor what party they belonged to, insomuch that they had no power to stir.

In the meanwhile, the Empress knowing the colours of her own country, sent a letter to their general, and the rest of the chief commanders, to let them know, that she was a great and powerful princess, and came to assist them against their enemies; wherefore she desired they should declare themselves, when they would have her help and assistance.

Hereupon a council was called,[178] and the business debated; but there were so many cross and different opinions, that they could not suddenly resolve what answer to send the Empress; at which she grew angry, insomuch that she resolved to return into her Blazing World, without giving any assistance to her countrymen: but the Duchess of Newcastle entreated Her Majesty to abate her passion; for, said she, great councils are most commonly slow, because many men have several opinions: besides, every councillor striving to be the wisest, makes long speeches, and raises many doubts, which cause retardments. If I had long speeched councillors, replied the Empress, I would hang them, by reason they give more words, than advice. The Duchess answered, that Her Majesty should not be angry, but consider the differences of that and her Blazing World;

---

[178] Cavendish here contributes to a debate about the role of councils in government. Cf. 'Then they asked if a tyrant king were not worse than a factious council? She said no, for said she, a tyrant king might make good laws and keep peace, and maintain supreme power and authority; but a factious council, said she, will break all laws, do no justice, keep no peace, obstruct authority and overthrow supreme power, but, said she, that kingdom is happiest that lives under a tyrant prince, for when the people are afraid of their prince there is peace, but when the prince is afraid of the people there is war; and there is no misery like a civil war, and there is no greater sign that a king is afraid of his people than when he advances those that are, or seem to be his enemies; thus subjects in general live happier under a tyrant but not particular courtiers or busy prating fools or factious knaves, when a facile king causeth more trouble and distraction and greater ruin by his soft, easy nature than a cruel tyrant with executions, severe laws or heavy taxes. For the greatest tyrant that ever was will not destroy all his subjects or take away all subsistence, for his own sake; for if he did, he would destroy his power and ruin his monarchy', 'The She Anchoret' in *Nature's Pictures*, p. 327.

for, said she, they are not both alike; but there are grosser and duller understandings in this, than in the Blazing World.

At last a messenger came out, who returned the Empress thanks for her kind proffer, but desired withal to know from whence she came, and how, and in what manner her assistance could be serviceable to them? The Empress answered, that she was not bound to tell them whence she came; but as for the manner of her assistance, I will appear, said she, to your navy in a splendorous light, surrounded with fire. The messenger asked at what time they should expect her coming? I'll be with you, answered the Empress, about one of the clock at night. With this report the messenger returned; which made both the poor councillors and sea-men much afraid; but yet they longed for the time to behold this strange sight.

The appointed hour being come, the Empress appeared with garments made of the star-stone, and was born or supported above the water, upon the fish-men's heads and backs, so that she seemed to walk upon the face of the water, and the bird- and fish-men carried the fire-stone, lighted both in the air, and above the waters.

Which sight, when her countrymen perceived at a distance, their hearts began to tremble; but coming something nearer, she left her torches, and appeared only in her garments of light, like an angel, or some deity, and all kneeled down before her, and worshipped her with all submission and reverence: but the Empress would not come nearer than at such a distance where her voice might be generally heard, by reason she would not have that of her accoutrements anything else should be perceived, but the splendour thereof; and when she was come so near that her voice could be heard and understood by all, she made this following speech:

> Dear Country-men, for so you are, although you know me not; I being a native of this kingdom, and hearing that most part of this world had resolved to make war against it, and sought to destroy it, at least to weaken its naval force and power; have made a voyage out of another world, to lend you my assistance against your enemies. I come not to make bargains with you, or to regard my own interest, more than your safety; but I intend to make you the most powerful nation of this world; and therefore I have chosen rather to quit my own tranquillity, riches and pleasure, than suffer you to be ruined and destroyed. All the return I desire, is but your grateful acknowledgement, and to declare my power, love and loyalty to my native country; for although I am now a great and absolute princess and empress of a whole world, yet I acknowledge that once I was a subject of this kingdom, which is but

a small part of this world; and therefore I will have you undoubtedly
believe, that I shall destroy all your enemies before this following
night, I mean those which trouble you by sea; and if you have any by
land, assure your self I shall also give you my assistance against them,
and make you triumph over all that seek your ruin and destruction.

Upon this declaration of the Empress, when both the General, and
all the commanders in their several ships had returned their humble and
hearty thanks to Her Majesty for so great a favour to them, she took her
leave and departed to her own ships. But, good Lord! what several opinions
and judgements did this produce in the minds of her country-men; some
said she was an angel; others, she was a sorceress; some believed her a
goddess; others said the devil deluded them in the shape of a fine lady.

The morning after, when the navies were to fight, the Empress appeared
upon the face of the waters, dressed in her imperial robes, which were all
of diamonds and carbuncles; in one hand she held a buckler, made of one
entire carbuncle, and in the other hand a spear of one entire diamond;
on her head she had a cap of diamonds, and just upon the top of the
crown, was a star made of the star-stone, mentioned heretofore, and a
half-moon made of the same stone, was placed on her forehead; all her
other garments were of several sorts of precious jewels; and having given
her fish-men directions how to destroy the enemies of her native country,
she proceeded to effect her design. The fish-men were to carry the fire-
stones in cases of diamonds (for the diamonds in the Blazing World are
in splendour so far beyond the diamonds of this world, as pebble-stones
are to the best sort of this world's diamonds) and to uncase or uncover
those fire-stones no sooner but when they were just under the enemy's
ships, or close at their sides, and then to wet them, and set their ships on
fire, which was no sooner done, but all the enemy's fleet was of a flaming
fire; and coming to the place where the powder was, it straight blew them
up;[179] so that all the several navies of the enemies, were destroyed in a
short time: which when her countrymen did see, they all cried out with
one voice, that she was an angel sent from God to deliver them out of the
hands of their enemies: neither would she return into the Blazing World,

---

[179] Cf. 'When Henery the forth king of france your Royal Grand father, began to Increase
his shipping [Queen Elizabeth] sent him word, to Disiste, for she would not loose her
prorogative of the narrow seas, and did Assure him if he did not, Disist, shee would
burn his shipps in their Havens', *Newcastle's Advice*, p. 10. On Elizabeth I as a model for
Cavendish's heroines see Claire Jowitt, 'Imperial Dreams? Margaret Cavendish and the
Cult of Elizabeth' in Emma L.E. Rees ed., *Women's Writing* 4.3 (1997), pp. 383–99.

until she had forced all the rest of that world to submit to that same nation.

In the meantime, the General of all their naval forces sent to their sovereign to acquaint him with their miraculous delivery and conquest, and with the Empress's design of making him the most powerful monarch of all that world. After a short time, the Empress sent her self to the sovereign of that nation to know in what she could be serviceable to him; who returning her many thanks, both for her assistance against his enemies, and her kind proffer to do him further service for the good and benefit of his nations (for he was King over several kingdoms) sent her word, that although she did partly destroy his enemies by sea, yet they were so powerful, that they did hinder the trade and traffic of his dominions. To which the Empress returned this answer, that she would burn and sink all those ships that would not pay him tribute; and forthwith sent to all the neighbouring nations, who had any traffic by sea, desiring them to pay tribute to the King and sovereign of that nation where she was born; but they denied it with great scorn. Whereupon she immediately commanded her fish-men to destroy all strangers' ships that trafficked on the seas; which they did according to the Empress's command; and when the neighbouring nations and kingdoms perceived her power, they were so discomposed in their affairs and designs, that they knew not what to do: at last they sent to the Empress, and desired to treat with her, but could get no other conditions than to submit and pay tribute to the said King and sovereign of her native country, otherwise, she was resolved to ruin all their trade and traffic by burning their ships. Long was this treat, but in fine, they could obtain nothing, so that at last they were forced to submit; by which the King of the mentioned nations became absolute master of the seas, and consequently of that world; by reason, as I mentioned heretofore, the several nations of that world could not well live without traffic and commerce, by sea, as well as by land.

But after a short time, those neighbouring nations finding themselves so much enslaved, that they were hardly able to peep out of their own dominions without a chargeable tribute, they all agreed to join their forces against the King and sovereign of the said dominions; which when the Empress received notice of, she sent out her fish-men to destroy, as they had done before, the remainder of all their naval power, by which they were soon forced again to submit, except some nations which could live without foreign traffic, and some whose trade and traffic was merely by land;

these would no ways be tributary to the mentioned King. The Empress sent them word, that in case they did not submit to him, she intended to fire all their towns and cities, and reduce them by force, to what they would not yield with a good will. But they rejected and scorned Her Majesty's message, which provoked her anger so much, that she resolved to send her bird- and worm-men thither, with order to begin first with their smaller towns, and set them on fire (for she was loath to make more spoil than she was forced to do) and if they remained still obstinate in their resolutions, to destroy also their greater cities. The only difficulty was, how to convey the worm-men conveniently to those places; but they desired that her Majesty would but set them upon any part of the earth of those nations, and they could travel within the earth as easily, and as nimbly as men upon the face of the earth; which the Empress did according to their desire.

But before both the bird- and worm-men began their journey, the Empress commanded the bear-men to view through their telescopes what towns and cities those were that would not submit; and having a full information thereof, she instructed the bird- and bear-men what towns they should begin withal; in the meanwhile she sent to all the princes and sovereigns of those nations, to let them know that she would give them a proof of her power, and check their obstinacies by burning some of their smaller towns; and if they continued still in their obstinate resolutions, that she would convert their smaller loss into a total ruin. She also commanded her bird-men to make their flight at night, lest they be perceived. At last when both the bird- and worm-men came to the designed places, the worm-men laid some fire-stones under the foundation of every house, and the bird-men placed some at the tops of them, so that both by rain, and by some other moisture within the earth, the stones could not fail of burning. The bird-men in the meantime having learned some few words of their language, told them, that the next time it did rain, their towns would be all on fire; at which they were amazed to hear men speak in the air; but withal they laughed when they heard them say that rain should fire their towns, knowing that the effect of water was to quench, not produce fire.

At last a rain came, and upon a sudden all their houses appeared of a flaming fire, and the more water there was poured on them, the more they did flame and burn; which struck such a fright and terror into all the neighbouring cities, nations and kingdoms, that for fear the like should happen to them, they and all the rest of the parts of that world granted the Empress's desire, and submitted to the monarch and sovereign of her native country, the King of EFSI;[180] save one, which having seldom or never any rain, but only dews, which would soon be spent in a great fire, slighted her power: the Empress being desirous to make it stoop, as well as the rest, knew that every year it was watered by a flowing tide, which lasted some weeks; and although their houses stood high from the ground, yet they were built upon supporters which were fixed into the ground. Wherefore she commanded both her bird- and worm-men to lay some of the fire-stones at the bottom of those supporters, and when the tide came in, all their houses were of a fire, which did so rarefy the water, that the tide was soon turned into vapour, and this vapour again into air; which caused not only a destruction of their houses, but also a general barrenness over all their country that year, and forced them to submit as well as the rest of the world had done.

Thus the Empress did not only save her native country, but made it the absolute monarchy of all that world; and both the effects of her power and her beauty did kindle a great desire in all the greatest princes to see her; who hearing that she was resolved to return into her own Blazing World, they all entreated the favour, that they might wait on Her Majesty before she went. The Empress sent word, that she should be glad to grant their requests; but having no other place of reception for them, she desired that they should be pleased to come into the open seas with their ships, and make a circle of a pretty large compass, and then her own ships should meet them, and close up the circle, and she would present her self to the view of all those that came to see her:[181] which answer was joyfully received by all the mentioned princes, who came, some sooner, and some later, each according to the distance of his country, and the length of the voyage. And being all met in the form and manner aforesaid, the Empress appeared upon the face of the water in her imperial robes; in some part of her hair she had placed some of the star-stone, near her face, which added such a lustre and glory to it, that it caused a great admiration in all that

---

[180] Charles II's full title was 'King of England, France, Scotland and Ireland'. (The Stuarts maintained their claim to the kingdom of France.)

[181] Cf. the scene in Bacon's *New Atlantis* where ships are arranged in a circle around a pillar of divine light. 'But when the boats were come within about sixty yards of the pillar they found themselves all bound . . . so as the boats stood all as in a theatre, beholding this light, as an heavenly sign', *New Atlantis*, p. 464. On Bacon and Cavendish see Sylvia Bowerbank and Sara Mendelson, *Paper Bodies. A Margaret Cavendish Reader* (Peterborough, Ontario: 2000).

were present, who believed her to be some celestial creature, or rather an uncreated goddess, and they all had a desire to worship her, for surely, said they, no mortal creature can have such a splendid and transcendent beauty, nor can any have so great a power as she has, to walk upon the waters, and to destroy whatever she pleases, not only whole nations, but a whole world.

The Empress expressed to her own countrymen, who were also her interpreters to the rest of the princes that were present, that she would give them an entertainment at the darkest time of night; which being come, the fire-stones were lighted, which made both air and seas appear of a bright shining flame, insomuch that they put all spectators into an extreme fright, who verily believed, they should all be destroyed; which the Empress perceiving, caused all the lights of the fire-stones to be put out, and only showed herself in her garments of light: the bird-men carried her upon their backs into the air, and there she appeared as glorious as the sun. Then she was set down upon the seas again, and presently there was heard the most melodious and sweetest consort of voices, as ever was heard out of the seas, which was made by the fish-men; this consort was answered by another, made by the bird-men in the air, so that it seemed as if sea and air had spoke and answered each other by way of singing dialogues, or after the manner of those plays that are acted by singing voices.[182]

But when it was upon break of day, the Empress ended her entertainment, and at full daylight all the princes perceived that she went into the ship wherein the prince and monarch of her native country was, the King of EFSI with whom she had several conferences; and having assured him of the readiness of her assistance whensoever he required it, telling him withal, that she wanted no intelligence, she went forth again upon the waters, and being in the midst of the circle made by those ships that were present, she desired them to draw somewhat nearer, that they might hear her speak; which being done, she declared her self in this following manner:

[182] Opera developed in Italy at the beginning of the seventeenth century and reached Paris in 1645. Davenant, one of the dramatists employed by the Earl of Newcastle, had planned to stage opera in England in 1639, but it was not until the 1650s that the first English operas were performed. See Susan Wiseman, *Drama and Politics in the English Civil War*, pp. 124–36. On the use of opera to inculcate civic virtue see James R. Jacob and Timothy Raylor, 'Opera and Obedience: Thomas Hobbes and *A Proposition of Advancement of Moralitie* by Sir William Davenant', *The Seventeenth Century* 6.1 (1991), pp. 205–33.

Great, heroic, and famous monarchs: I came hither to assist the King of EFSI against his enemies, he being unjustly assaulted by many several nations, which would fain take away his hereditary rights and prerogatives of the narrow seas; at which unjustice Heaven was much displeased; and for the injuries he received from his enemies, rewarded him with an absolute power, so that now he is become the head-monarch of all this world; which power, though you may envy, yet you can no ways hinder him; for all those that endeavour to resist his power, shall only get loss for their labour, and no victory for their profit. Wherefore my advice to you all is, to pay him tribute justly and truly, that you may live peaceably and happily, and be rewarded with the blessings of Heaven, which I wish you from my soul.

After the Empress had thus finished her speech to the princes of the several nations of that world, she desired that their ships might fall back, which being done, her own fleet came into the circle, without any visible assistance of sails or tide; and herself being entered into her own ship, the whole fleet sunk immediately into the bottom of the seas, and left all the spectators in a deep amazement; neither would she suffer any of her ships to come above the waters until she arrived into the Blazing World.

In time of the voyage, both the Empress's and Duchess's soul were very gay and merry, and sometimes they would converse very seriously with each other: amongst the rest of their discourses, the Duchess said, she wondered much at one thing, which was, that since Her Majesty had found out a passage out of the Blazing World into the world she came from, she did not enrich that part of the world where she was born, at least her own family, when as yet she had enough to enrich the whole world. The Empress's soul answered, that she loved her native country and her own family as well as any creature could do, and that this was the reason why she would not enrich them; for said she, not only particular families or nations, but all the world, their natures are such, that much gold, and great store of riches makes them mad, insomuch as they endeavour to destroy each other for gold, or riches' sake. The reason thereof is, said the Duchess, that they have too little gold and riches, which makes them so eager to have it. No, replied the Empress's soul, their particular covetousness is beyond all the wealth of the richest world, and the more riches they have, the more covetous they are, for their covetousness is infinite; but, said she, I would there could a passage be found out of the Blazing World into the world whence you came, and I would willingly give you as much riches as you desired. The Duchess's soul gave Her Majesty humble thanks for her great favour, and told her that she was not covetous, nor desired any more wealth than what her lord and husband had before the Civil Wars; neither, said she, should I desire it for my own, but my lord's posterity's sake. Well, said the Empress, I'll command my fish-men to use all their skill and industry to find out a passage into that world which your lord and husband is in. I do verily believe, answered the Duchess, that there will be no passage found into that world; but if there were any, I should not petition Your Majesty for gold and jewels, but only for the elixir that grows in the midst of the golden sands, for to preserve life and health; but without a passage it is impossible to carry away any of it, for whatsoever is material, cannot travel like immaterial beings such as souls and spirits are; neither do souls require any such thing that might revive them, or prolong their lives, by reason they are unalterable: for were souls like bodies, then my soul might have had the benefit of that natural elixir that grows in your Blazing World. I wish earnestly, said the Empress, that a passage might be found, and then both your lord and yourself should neither want wealth, nor long life; nay, I love you so well, that I would make you as great and powerful a monarchess as I am of the Blazing World. The Duchess's soul humbly thanked Her Majesty, and told her, that she acknowledged and esteemed her love beyond all things that are in nature.

After this discourse they had many other conferences, which for brevity's sake I'll forbear to rehearse. At last, after several questions which the Empress's soul asked the Duchess, she desired to know the reason why she did take such delight when she was joined to her body, in being singular both in accoutrements, behaviour and discourse? The Duchess's soul answered, she confessed that it was extravagant, and beyond what was usual and ordinary; but yet her ambition being such, that she would not be like others in any thing if it were possible; I endeavour, said she, to be as singular as I can; for it argues but a mean nature to imitate others; and though I do not love to be imitated if I can possibly avoid it; yet rather than imitate others, I should choose to be imitated by others; for my nature is such, that I had rather appear worse in singularity, than better in the mode. If you were not a great lady, replied the Empress, you would never pass in the world for a wise lady; for the world would say your singularities are vanities. The Duchess's soul answered, she did not at all regard the censure of this or any other age concerning vanities; but, said she, neither this present, nor any of the future ages can or will truly say that I am not virtuous and chaste; for I am confident, all that were or are acquainted with me, and all the servants which ever I had, will or can upon their oaths declare my actions no otherwise than virtuous; and certainly there's none, even of the meanest degree, which have not their spies and witnesses, much more those of the nobler sort, which seldom or never are without attendants, so that their faults (if they have any) will easily be known, and as easily divulged: wherefore happy are those natures that are honest, virtuous and noble, not only happy to themselves, but happy to their families. But, said the Empress, if you glory so much in your honesty and virtue, how comes it that you plead for dishonest and wicked persons in your writings? The Duchess answered, it was only to show her wit, not her nature.

At last the Empress arrived into the Blazing World, and coming to her imperial palace, you may sooner imagine than expect that I should express the joy which the Emperor had at her safe return; for he loved her beyond his soul; and there was no love lost, for the Empress equalled his affection with no less love to him. After the time of rejoicing with each other, the Duchess's soul begged leave to return to her noble lord; but the Emperor desired, that before she departed, she would see how he had employed his time in the Empress's absence; for he had built stables and riding-houses, and desired to have horses of manage, such as, according to the Empress's relation, the Duke of Newcastle had:[183] the Emperor enquired of the Duchess, the form and structure of her lord and husband's stables and riding-house. The Duchess answered His Majesty, that they were but plain and ordinary; but said she; had my lord wealth, I am sure he would not spare it, in rendering his buildings as noble as could be made. Hereupon the Emperor showed the Duchess the stables he had built, which were most stately and magnificent; among the rest there was one double stable that held a hundred horses on a side, the main building was of gold, lined with several sorts of precious materials; the roof was arched with agates, the sides of the walls were lined with cornelian, the floor was paved with amber, the mangers were mother of pearl, the pillars, as also the middle aisle or walk of the stables, were of crystal; the front and gate was of turquoise, most neatly cut and carved. The riding-house was lined with sapphires, topazes, and the like; the floor was all of golden sand, so finely sifted, that it was extremely soft, and not in the least hurtful to

---

[183] In 1622 Newcastle built stables at Welbeck Abbey to a design by John Smythson, and later built stables at Bolsover Castle. His stables and horsemanship were praised by Ben Jonson (*Epigram* LIII). See Cedric C. Brown, 'Courtesies of Place and Arts of Diplomacy in Ben Jonson's Last Two Entertainments for Royalty', *The Seventeenth Century*, 9.4 (1994), pp. 150, 221.

the horses' feet, and the door and frontispiece was of emeralds, curiously carved.

After the view of these glorious and magnificent buildings, which the Duchess's soul was much delighted withal, she resolved to take her leave; but the Emperor desired her to stay yet some short time more, for they both loved her company so well, that they were unwilling to have her depart so soon: several conferences and discourses passed between them; amongst the rest the Emperor desired her advice how to set up a theatre for plays. The Duchess confessed her ignorance in this art, telling His Majesty that she knew nothing of erecting theatres or scenes, but what she had by an immaterial observation when she was with the Empress's soul in the chief city of E[184] entering into one of their theatres, whereof the Empress could give as much account to His Majesty as herself. But both the Emperor and Empress told the Duchess, that she could give directions how to make plays. The Duchess answered, that she had as little skill to form a play after the mode, as she had to paint, or make a scene for show. But you have made plays, replied the Empress:[185] yes, answered the Duchess, I intended them for plays, but the wits of these present times condemned them as incapable of being represented or acted, because they were not made up according to the rules of art; though I dare say, that the descriptions are as good as any they have writ. The Emperor asked, whether the property of plays were not to describe the several humours, actions and fortunes of mankind? 'Tis so, answered the Duchess: why then, replied the Emperor, the natural humours, actions and fortunes of mankind, are not done by the rules of art: but said the Duchess, it is the art and method of our wits to despise all the descriptions of wit, humour, actions and fortunes that are without such artificial rules. The Empress asked, are those good plays that are made so methodically and artificially? The Duchess answered, they were good according to the judgement of the age, or mode of the nation, but not according to her judgement; for truly, said she, in my opinion, their plays will prove a nursery of whining lovers, and not an

[184] The chief city of England, i.e. London.
[185] Cavendish published a volume of plays in 1662. William Newcastle also wrote plays, as did two of his daughters. See Lisa Hopkins, 'Play Houses: Drama at Bolsover and Welbeck', *Early Theatre* 2 (1999), pp. 25–44; Lynn Hulse ed., *Dramatic Works by William Cavendish*, Malone Society Reprints (Oxford, 1996). Newcastle advised Charles II to provide 'a masque each Twelve-tide, and weekly plays', *Advice*, p. 60. See Margaret J. M. Ezell, ' "To be your Daughter in your Pen": The Social Functions of Literature in the Writings of Lady Elizabeth Brackley and Lady Jane Cavendish' in *Huntington Library Quarterly* 53 (1990), pp. 199–209.

academy or school for wise, witty, noble, and well-behaved men. But I, replied the Emperor, desire such a theatre as may make wise men; and will have such descriptions as are natural, not artificial. If Your Majesty be of that opinion, said the Duchess's soul, then my plays may be acted in your Blazing World, when they cannot be acted in the Blinking World of Wit; and the next time I come to visit Your Majesty, shall endeavour to order Your Majesty's theatre, to present such plays as my wit is capable to make. Then the Empress told the Duchess, that she loved a foolish farce,[186] added to a wise play. The Duchess answered, that no world in nature had fitter creatures for it than the Blazing World; for, said she, the louse-men, the bird-men, the spider- and fox-men, the ape-men and satyrs appear in a farce extraordinary pleasant.

Hereupon both the Emperor and Empress entreated the Duchess's soul to stay so long with them, till she had ordered her theatre, and made plays and farces fit for them; for they only wanted that sort of recreation; but the Duchess's soul begged Their Majesties to give her leave to go into her native world; for she longed to be with her dear lord and husband, promising, that after a short time she would return again. Which being granted, though with much difficulty, she took her leave with all civility and respect, and so departed from Their Majesties.

After the Duchess's return into her own body, she entertained her lord (when he was pleased to hear such kind of discourses) with foreign relations: but he was never displeased to hear of the Empress's kind commendations, and of the characters she was pleased to give of him to the Emperor. Amongst other relations she told him all what had passed between the Empress, and the several monarchs of that world whither she went with the Empress; and how she had subdued them to pay tribute and homage to the monarch of that nation or kingdom to which she owed both her birth and education. She also related to her lord what magnificent stables and riding-houses the Emperor had built, and what fine horses were in the Blazing World, of several shapes and sizes, and how exact their shapes were in each sort, and of many various colours, and fine marks, as if they had been painted by art, with such coats or skins, that they had a far greater gloss and smoothness than satin; and were there but a passage out of the Blazing World into this, said she, you should not only have some of

---

[186]  The printed text has 'verse'. Kate Lilley, the original editor, adopted the marginal authorial emendations in the Bodleian copy of 1668, and substituted 'farce' both here and later in the paragraph.

those horses, but such materials, as the Emperor has, to build your stables and riding-houses withal; and so much gold, that I should never repine at your noble and generous gifts. The Duke smilingly answered her, that he was sorry there was no passage between those two worlds; but said he, I have always found an obstruction to my good fortunes.

One time the Duchess chanced to discourse with some of her acquaintance, of the Empress of the Blazing World, who asked her what pastimes and recreations Her Majesty did most delight in? The Duchess answered, that she spent most of her time in the study of natural causes and effects, which was her chief delight and pastime, and that she loved to discourse sometimes with the most learned persons of that world; and to please the Emperor and his nobles, who were all of the royal race, she went often abroad at night to take the air, but seldom in the daytime, always at night, if it might be called night; for, said she, the nights there are as light as days, by reason of the numerous blazing-stars, which are very splendorous, only their light is whiter than the sun's light; and as the sun's light is hot, so their light is cool, not so cool as our twinkling star-light, nor is their sun-light so hot as ours, but more temperate; and the part of the Blazing World that the Empress resides, is always clear, and never subject to any storms, tempests, fogs or mists, but has only refreshing dews that nourish the earth; the air of it is sweet and temperate, and, as I said before, as much light as in the sun's absence, as in its presence, which makes that time we call night, more pleasant there than the day; and sometimes the Empress goes abroad by water in barges, sometimes by land in chariots, and sometimes on horseback; her royal chariots are very glorious; the body is one entire green diamond; the four small pillars that bear up the top-cover, are four white diamonds, cut in the form thereof; the top of the roof of the chariot is one entire blue diamond, and at the four corners are great springs of rubies; the seat is made of cloth of gold, stuffed with amber-gris beaten small; the chariot is drawn by twelve unicorns, whose trappings are all chains of pearl;[187] and as for her barges, they are only of gold. Her guard of state (for she needs none for security, there being no rebels or enemies) consists of giants, but they seldom wait on Their Majesties abroad, because their extraordinary height and bigness does hinder their prospect. Her entertainment when she is upon the water, is the music of the fish- and bird-men, and by land are horse- and

---

[187] Cf. the chariot of one of the Fathers of Salomon's House, described by Bacon, *New Atlantis*, p. 479.

foot-matches; for the Empress takes much delight in making race-matches with the Emperor, and the nobility; some races are between the fox- and ape-men, which sometimes the satyrs strive to outrun, and some are between the spider-men and lice-men. Also there are several flight-matches, between the several sorts of bird-men, and the several sorts of fly-men; and swimming-matches between the several sorts of fish-men. The Emperor, Empress and their nobles, take also great delight to have collations; for in the Blazing World, there are most delicious fruits of all sorts, and some such as in this world were never seen nor tasted; for there are most tempting sorts of fruit: after their collations are ended, they dance; and if they be upon the water, they dance upon the water, there lying so many fish-men close and thick together, as they can dance very evenly and easily upon their backs, and need not fear drowning. Their music, both vocal and instrumental, is according to their several places: upon the water it is of water instruments, as shells filled with water, and so moved by art, which is a sweet and delightful harmony; and those dances which they dance upon the water, are, for the most part such as we in this world call swimming dances, where they do not lift up their feet high: in lawns or upon plains they have wind instruments, but much better than those in our world; and when they dance in the woods they have horn instruments, which although they are a sort of wind instruments, yet they are of another fashion than the former, in their houses they have such instruments as are somewhat like our viols, violins, theorboes, lutes, citherns, guitars, harpsichords, and the like, but yet so far beyond them, that the difference cannot well be expressed; and as their places of dancing and their music is different, so is their manner or way of dancing. In these, and the like recreations, the Emperor, Empress, and the nobility pass their time.

# THE EPILOGUE TO THE READER

By this poetical description, you may perceive, that my ambition is not only to be Empress, but Authoress of a whole world; and that the worlds I have made, both the Blazing and the other Philosophical World, mentioned in the first part of this description, are framed and composed of the most pure, that is, the rational parts of matter, which are the parts of my mind; which creation was more easily and suddenly effected, than the conquests of the two famous monarchs of the world, Alexander and Caesar: neither have I made such disturbances, and caused so many dissolutions of particulars, otherwise named deaths, as they did; for I have destroyed but some few men in a little boat, which died through the extremity of cold, and that by the hand of justice, which was necessitated to punish their crime of stealing away a young and beauteous Lady. And in the formation of those worlds, I take more delight and glory, than ever Alexander or Caesar did in conquering this terrestrial world; and though I have made my Blazing World, a peaceable world, allowing it but one religion, one language, and one government; yet could I make another world, as full of factions, divisions, and wars, as this is of peace and tranquillity; and the rational figures of my mind might express as much courage to fight, as Hector and Achilles had; and be as wise as Nestor, as eloquent as Ulysses, and as beautiful as Helen. But I esteeming peace before war, wit before policy, honesty before beauty; instead of the figures of Alexander, Caesar, Hector, Achilles, Nestor, Ulysses, Helen, etc. chose rather the figure of honest Margaret Newcastle, which now I would not change for all this terrestrial world; and if any should like the world I have made, and be willing to be my subjects, they may imagine themselves such, and they are such, I mean, in their minds, fancies or imaginations; but if they cannot endure to be subjects, they may create worlds of their own, and govern themselves as they please: but yet let them have a care, not to prove unjust usurpers, and to rob me of mine; for concerning the Philosophical World, I am Empress of it myself; and as for the Blazing World, it having an Empress already, who rules it with great wisdom and conduct, which Empress is my dear Platonic friend; I shall never prove so unjust, treacherous and unworthy to her, as to disturb her government, much less to depose her from her imperial throne, for the sake of any other; but rather choose to create another world for another friend.

ORATIONS of DIVERS SORTS,
Accommodated to DIVERS PLACES.
Written by the thrice Noble,
Illustrious and excellent Princess,
the Lady Marchioness
OF
*NEW CASTLE.*
LONDON,
Printed *Anno Dom. 1662.*

# TO THE LADY MARCHIONESS OF NEWCASTLE

## On her Book of Orations

Were all the Grecian Orators alive,
And swarms of Latines, that did daily strive
With their perfum'd and oily tongues to draw
The deceiv'd people to their Will and Law,
Each word so soft and gentle, every peece
As it were spun still from the Golden fleece,
How short would all this be, did you but look
On this admired Ladies witty Book!
All Europ's Universities, no doubt,
Will study English now, the rest put out.

W. Newcastle.

# TO HIS EXCELLENCY THE LORD MARQUIS OF NEWCASTLE

*My Lord,*

I have mentioned in my other Books that I think it not fit I should dedicate unto your Lordship the single parts of my works before I dedicate all the parts in the whole; yet I cannot choose but declare to the world how happy I and my works are in your approvement, which makes the pastime of my writing very delightful; besides, it makes me confident and resolute to put them to the press, and so to the public view, in despite of these critical times and censorious age which is apt to find fault with every action, let it be never so innocent or harmless, or with any work although good and profitable, yet they will fling spiteful aspersions on them: But I have heard your Lordship say that most men believe themselves not wise if they find no fault with their neighbours' actions, and that it is as easy to find fault as it is hard to do well. It seems such men have more evil in their natures than justice in their censures; but your Lordship, who is full of truth and generosity, reason and knowledge, will give your opinion clearly and uprightly, and my works having your approbation, I regard not the dislike of other men, for I have dedicated myself and all my actions to your Lordship, as becomes

Your Lordship's honest wife and humble servant
*M. Newcastle.*

# To the readers of my works

I know not how to please all that are pleased to read my works; for do what I can, some will find fault; and the worst is that those faults or imperfections I accuse myself of in my Prefatory Epistles, they fling back with a double strength against my poor harmless works, which shows their malice and my truth. And as for my plays, which they say are not made up so exactly as they should be, as having no plots, designs, catastrophes and such like I know not what, I expressed in the Epistles prefixed before my plays that I had not skill nor art to form them as they should be, for that work was like a tailor's work to make clothes.[1] But many that find such faults are not so good as a tailor, but mere botchers or brokers, to patch and set several old and new pieces together to make up a play, which I never did; for I thank my Fates, all is not only new but my own, what I have presented to the world. But this age is so censorious that the best poets are found fault with, wherefore it is an honour to my writings which are so much inferior to theirs; neither can their dislikes deter me from writing, for I write to please myself rather than to please such crabbed readers. Yet all my readers have not been so cross nor cruel, for there are many to whom my endeavours and works are acceptable, and the more honour it is to my works, as being approved and known by worthy and judicious men and noble persons. But many men have more ill natures to find faults with their neighbours than virtue to mend faults in themselves; also they are apt to censure other men's wit, and yet have none of their own. The truth is, they are a sort of persons that in plays prefer plots before wit and scenes before humours; in poems, rhyme before similizing and numbers before distinguishing; in theology, faction before faith and sophistry before truth; in philosophy, old authors before new truths and opinions before reason; and in orations, they prefer artificial connections before natural eloquence. All which makes them foolish, censorious and unjust judges. Wherefore I desire these my orations may not be read by such humoured men, but by the just and wise, which will be a satisfaction to me.

'Tis probable, had I been a learned scholar, I might have written my orations more short than I have done, but yet some of them are so short that had they been shorter they would not have been of force to persuade, whereas the intention of an orator, or use of orations, is to persuade the auditors to be of the orator's opinion or belief, and it is not probable that forcible arguments or persuasions can be contained in two or three lines of

---

[1] For a later defence of *Orations*, see the Preface to *Sociable Letters* and Letter clxxv.

words. Also, had I been a learned scholar, I might have written them more compendiously and not so loose, but I affect freedom and ease, even in my works of writings. Besides, I have observed that whatsoever is bound or knit close is difficult to disclose, and for writings, whatsoever is very compendious requires some study to conceive and understand the sense and design of the author's meaning. But I hope that defect or want of learning will not blemish my work, nor obstruct the sense of my orations, nor puzzle the understanding of the reader. Only one thing more I desire my noble readers, as to observe that most of my orations are general orations, *viz.* such as may be spoken in any kingdom or government; for I suppose that in all, at least in most kingdoms and governments there are soldiers, magistrates, privy-counsellors, lawyers, preachers, and university scholars.

We have, it is true, gotten a foolish custom both in our writing and speaking, to endeavour more to match or marry words together than to match and marry sense and reason together, which is strange we should prefer shadows before substances, or the spig or tap before the liquor. For words are but to convey the sense of an oration to the ears, and so into the understanding of the hearers, like as spouts do wine into bottles. And who that is wise will regard what the vessel is, so it be wholesome and clean? For should not we believe those to be fools that had rather have foul water out of a golden vessel, than pure wine out of earthen or wooden vessels? The like may be said for words and sense, for who that is wise would choose choice words before profitable reasons? Wherefore, Noble Readers, let me advise you to leave this custom in writing and speaking, or rather be silently wise than foolish in rhetoric.

I have endeavoured in this book to express perfect orators that speak perfect orations, as to cause their auditors to act or believe according to the orator's opinion, judgement, design, or desire. But before I did put this my book forth, know, Noble Readers, I did enquire to find whether any person had composed and put out a whole book of pure and perfect orations. But I could neither hear of nor see any such works of any person that composed and set forth to the public view a book of pure orations, composed out of one orator's own fancy, wit, and eloquence. 'Tis true, I have heard of single orations made by single persons in single parts;[2] also I have seen orations mixed with history, wherein the substance of the

---

[2] Orations made on particular occasions, for example by princes, ambassadors, bishops or scholars, were regularly published in the seventeenth century.

history is the ground of their orations.[3] Also I have seen two translations called orations, but they are rather orations in name than in reality, for their nature is history: the one contains relations of several countries;[4] in the other are relations from several princes of their actions or fortunes or both, expressed in an orator's style; yet those are not perfect or right orations, but adulterated, or rather hermaphrodites.[5] But perchance my readers will say I understand not true orations. If I do not, I am sorry for [it], and ask their pardon for speaking what I understand not. But I desire, Noble Readers, you will not think or believe I speak to illustrate my own works, and to detract from the works of others; for upon my conscience, I speak and write as I believe, and if I commit an error in this belief I ask your pardon, and if you excuse me I shall take it for a favour and obligation.

I have written orations and speeches of all sorts, and in all places fit for orations, speeches or particular discourses; and first imagining myself and you to be in a metropolitan city, I invite you into the chief market place, as the most populous place where usually orations are spoken, at least they were so in older times; and there you shall hear orations concerning peace and war. But the generality of the people being more apt to make war than to keep peace, I desire you to arm yourselves, supposing you to be of the masculine sex and of valiant heroical natures, to enter into the field of war; and since wars bring ruin and destruction to one or some parties if not to all, and loss causes men to desire peace, out of war I bring you into great disorders caused by the ruins wars have made, which I am sorry for, yet it must be so, the Fates have decreed it. And misery causing men to be prudent and industrious, by which they come to flourish again, at least their successors, and to show you their industry, I bring you out of the field of war into a new-built city, where you must stay the building

---

3 Perhaps Cavendish has in mind something like the works of Sallust, published in an English translation in 1629: *The Works of Caius Crispus Salustius contayning the conspiracie of Catiline, The Warre of Iugurth. Various bookes of historicall fragments. II orations to Caesar for the institution of a common-wealth and one against Cicero*, translated by William Crosse (London, 1629).

4 Perhaps James Howells Esq., *A German Diet, or the Balance of Europe wherein the power and weakness . . . of all the kingdoms and states of Christendom are impartially poiz'd: at a solemn convention of som German princes in sundry elaborate orations pro and con* (London, 1653).

5 Perhaps Thomas Norton, *Orations of Arsanes agaynst Philip, the trecherous kyng of Macedone: of the Embassadors of Venice against the prince that under crafty league with Scandeberg, layed snare for Christendome; and of the Christian Duke Mahumetes confederate: with a notable example of God's vengeance upon a faithlesse Kyng, Quene, and her children* (London, 1560). Norton notes that 'The 1st [oration] of Arsanes the Persian is made after the mater of the hystorie as it is repeated in Iustine's Epitome of the hystorie written by Trogus Pompeius . . . The second containying 2 Orations . . . are fathefully tra[n]slated out of Marinus Bartelius.'

of it, for it will be built soon, having many labourers; and after it is built, there being a large market place, you may stand or sit with ease and hear the orations that are there spoken. And by reason there are some causes or cases to be pleaded, I shall endeavour to persuade you, after some time of refreshment at your own homes, to go into the courts or halls of judicature. After these causes are judged, or at least pleaded, I shall desire you to adorn yourselves fit for the court, then to wait upon the King's Majesty, and if you be privy councillors or have any business or petitions at the council table, by the king's permission you may enter into the council chamber. But great monarchs having many subjects, whereof some are more active than wise, and more apt to complain than to obey, you may hear the petitions of the subjects and the speeches or orations of the sovereign. And after a good agreement, unity, and love, you may rest yourselves in peace until such time as your charity calls you forth to visit the sick, and when as death hath released those sick persons of their pains, humanity will persuade you to wait on their dead corpse to the grave, and after some tears showered on their graves, and having dried your eyes and heard some sermons of reproof and instructions, you will be invited as bridal guests to see some men and women united in holy matrimony. After the wedding ceremonies are ended, you may, as formerly you have done, go into the market place again, and hear what orations there are spoken, wherein one short oration concerning the liberty of women hath so angered that sex, as after the men's orations are ended they privately assemble together, where three or four take the place of an orator and speak to the rest. The only difficulty will be to get undiscovered amongst them to hear their private conventicles; but if you regard not what women say, you may ride to a country market town and hear a company of gentlemen associate together their discourse and pastime; and if you like not their pastime, then you may walk into the fields of peace to receive the sweet and healthful air, or to view the curious and various works of nature, and for variety of pastime you may stand or sit under a spreading tree and hear the country clowns or peasants speak concerning their own affairs and course of life. In which shady place, sweet air, and happiness of peace I leave you, unless you will travel to see the government or rather disorders in other states or kingdoms, to which observation I will wait upon you. And when all is in peace, before we return home, we will, if you please, enter some of their colleges, and hear some school-arguments, after which return I shall kiss your hands and take my leave.

*M. Newcastle.*

# The Table of all Orations and Speeches contained in this Book

*A Prefatory Oration*        *page* 129

## PART I

*Orations to Citizens in a Chief City concerning Peace and War*

## PART II

*Orations in the Field of War*

## PART III

*Orations to Citizens in the Market Place, after a Long time of War*

## PART VI

*Orations in Courts of Majesty, from Subjects to their King, and from the King to his Subjects*

## PART VII

*Speeches of Dying Persons*

## PART IX

### *Marriage Orations*

## PART X

### *Orations to Citizens in the Market Place*

## PART XI

### *Female Orations*

## PART XII

### *Nine Orations in Country Market Towns, where Country Gentlemen meet*

## PART XV

### *Scholastical Orations*

### A Prefatory Oration

Worthy Countrymen,

*You know that there is difference between orations of fancy and orations of business, as also difference between orations of public employments and private divertisements; the one sort requires rational persuasions, the other only eloquent expressions. And as there are different subjects of orations, so there are different places for orations; and the subjects of my orations being of the most serious and most concernable actions and accidents amongst mankind, and the places most common and public, it hath caused me to write my orations rather to benefit my auditors than to delight them. But by reason I have not been bred, being a woman, to public affairs, associations, or negotiations, it is not to be expected I should speak or write wisely. The truth is, it were more easy and more proper for one of my sex to speak or write wittily than wisely; but 'tis probable my auditors will think or judge that I have done neither. Yet I can assure you, noble auditors, I have done my endeavour, and my desire was and is that every several oration may be acceptable to your minds, profitable to your lives, and delightful to your hearing.*

# ORATIONS TO CITIZENS IN A CHIEF CITY CONCERNING PEACE AND WAR

## PART I

1 *An Oration for War*

Be not offended, *Noble Citizens*, if I labour to persuade my country to make heroic wars, since it is neither safe, profitable, nor honourable for it to live in sluggish peace: for in peace you become ignorant of the arts in war, and living sluggishly you lose the courage of men and become effeminate, and having neither skill nor courage, you cannot expect safety: for should you chance to have enemies, you would not have abilities to help yourselves, having neither experience by practice, nor courage by use and custom; for custom and use work much upon the natures of men. And as for arms, in times of peace they lie like garments out of fashion, never worn but despised and laughed at as ridiculous things, and men of action, like as arms, they jeer and make a mock of. Thus, martial men and arms in time of peace are scorned, although in time of wars they only are a kingdom's safety, to guard it from their enemies. Indeed, peace spoils both youth and age, it makes the one sort covetous, the other wanton: for aged men study only to get wealth; the young men how to spend it. Besides, it makes the poor men rich men's asses, and rich men poor men's burdens. Also peace makes old men fools, and young men cowards: for in long times of peace grave counsels are mere gossiping meetings, rather ideally to talk than wisely to advise. They propound many things but resolve not any, debate not, but conclude, and sometimes find faults, but never help to mend them. The truth is, for the most part they rather make errors than help to rectify defects, and in wars they had rather suffer calamity than stir for necessity; neither will they believe they are in danger until their enemies be at their gates. And as for youth, peace quenches out their heroic spirits and noble ambitions: for their only ambition is their mistress's favours, and they will go to no other wars, but *Venus*,[6] where *Cupid* is general, where they only make love-skirmishes, and are shot through their hearts with glances from their mistress's eyes. Thus peace makes men like beasts: for in peace they feed like swine, sport like apes, live like goats, and may be brought to the shambles like silly sheep. Nay, it makes men not only live but die like beasts, having neither spirits, skill nor conduct to defend

[6] The Goddess of Love.

themselves or fight an enemy. And how should it be otherwise, when as the young men are only armed with vanity, march with pride, entrench with luxury, fight with *Bacchus*,[7] and are overcome by *Venus*? Thus we may observe that all which causes peace and takes away the courage of young vigorous men, rots their bodies with excess, and corrupts their blood with idleness, by which their spirits are quenched, their strengths weakened, their minds softened and their natures become effeminate, which makes their lives vacant, and when they die, they are buried in oblivion: for fame lives in heroic actions. And surely it is better for noble men to have fame than wealth, and for young gallants to have honour than gay clothes; and more honour to have scars than black patches, to fight with an enemy than to dance with a lady, to march to a battle than to tread a measure. And for the meaner sort, it is better for them to wear honourable arms than to bear slavish burdens; and how happy is that man that can raise himself from a low birth to a glorious renown? Thus from the noblest to the meanest, war is the way to advance them to honour, if the common soldiers fight with courage and the nobles command and direct with skill, for which their posterity will glory in their valours, poets will sing their praises, historians write their acts, and fame keep their records, that after ages may know what heroic men they were; and as for kingdoms, those are safest that are protected by *Mars*.[8]

## 2  *An Oration for Peace*

*Noble Citizens*,

The oration that was last spoken unto you hath stirred your spirits and encumbered your thoughts with wars, and your desire for war is such that you will not only seek for enemies, but make enemies to fight with, which is neither heroic nor just, to fight with those that have done you no injury or wrong; and what can be a more unworthy act than to assault peaceable neighbours? It cannot be called an honourable war, but a base outrage; like as pirates at sea, so you will be robbers at land, taking that from others which you have no right to. But say you have some slight injuries done you, if you were wise you had better wink at small faults than make wars, which will exhaust your treasures, waste your strength, depopulate your nation and leave your lands unmanured. Besides, wars corrupt all good manners, nay, even good natures, making the one rude and the other cruel;

---

[7] The God of Wine.    [8] The God of War.

and though long wars may make men martial, skilful, and may heighten their courage, yet neither skill nor courage can always bear away victory, especially from a powerful enemy, unless fortune be on their side. The truth is, fortune is the chief actor and decider in wars; and who that are wise will trust their goods, lives and liberties to fortunes disposal if they may choose? Wherefore they are either fools or mad that will make war when they may live in peace. And give me leave to tell you that it is not the way to keep our country safe, to make wars abroad, but to make our country strong with forts on the frontiers, and ships on the seas that beat on our shores, and to practice our men with training, not fighting; and it is easier to keep out an enemy than to conquer an enemy's kingdom: for at home we have all provisions needful and near at hand, when in a foreign country we shall be to seek. But say good fortune may enrich us, yet ill fortune will absolutely ruin us: I answer, war enriches few, for it makes spoil of all; the truth is, war is a great devourer, for it consumes almost all that is consumable, wheresoever it comes, and is like a glutton that eats much and yet is very lean; for most commonly the under soldiers are very poor, and the commanders only rich in fame, yet not unless they have good fortune; otherwise if they have ill fortune they are usually scorned, at least but pitied, but never praised. Wherefore it is neither courage nor conduct that gets fame in the wars, but fortune that gives it, and she many times gives glorious fame to cowards and fools, and blemishes, at least obscures the worth and merit, of wise and valiant men. Wherefore, let me persuade you not to follow unjust and inconstant fortune to the wars, but to live at home in peace with *Minerva*[9] and *Pallas*.[10] The one will defend you, the other will employ you, and both will make you happy in present life and will give you fame and renown according to your desert, that your memory may live in after-ages.

3  *An Oration against War*

*Dear Countrymen,*
I perceive, all this nation, or the most part, their minds are hot and their spirits inflamed through an over-earnest desire to be in war, which expresses you have surfeited with the delicious fruits of peace, which hath made your reason, judgement and understanding sick and faint, so that it desires a change, as from rest to trouble, from plenty to scarcity, from

[9] The Goddess of Wisdom.    [10] Pallas Athena, Goddess of War.

palaces to tents, from safety to danger, from gay apparel to bloody wounds, from freedom to slavery, all which war will bring upon you. The truth is, war is more likely to kill you than cure your surfeit: for war is a dangerous physic, and the more dangerous by reason your enemies must be your physicians. But let me advise you to cure your selves with temperance and prudence, by which you will flourish with wealth, and grow strong with wisdom: for wealth and wisdom is the health and strength of a common-wealth which will preserve it from destruction. For what is the strength of a kingdom but riches and wise government? And what exhausts the one and confounds the other more than war? Which for the most part is in Fortune's power, to order as she pleases, and Fortune in wars hath power to puzzle the wise and impoverish the rich. Wherefore, *noble countrymen*, do not make your selves beggars and fools in warring actions, and ruin not your country through the ambition of pre-eminence or applause, or through the ill nature of revenge; but be wise and rich with peace, by which you will become impregnable against your enemies and happy amongst yourselves; for certainly war is better to hear of than to feel; for though in wars you may covet much yet in the end enjoy but little, you may have high designs but you are not sure to have prosperous success, and instead of being conquerors be conquered, instead of being masters become slaves. But to conclude, it were more happy to lie peaceable in the grave with our forefathers than to live in the turmoils of war with our enemies.

4 *An Oration persuading to the Breach of Peace with their Neighbour-Nation*

*Dear Countrymen*,
Our neighbours, the *U. G.*, have done us many injuries contrary to the articles of agreement made betwixt our nation, by which they have broken the peace; but yet we, out of laziness or fearful natures, suffer them to make riots and never stir against them, when we are so far from being abusers as we suffer our selves to be abused. 'Tis true, the first shows us to be honest men, but the last proves us to be fools, if not cowards, which, if our enemies know, (for now they are but a proving, making a trial of us,) they will overcome us without resistance and will enslave us in our own territories, so that we shall labour for our enemies, and have no profit our selves. Thus whilst we sit still we shall have a yoke cast on us, we shall be bound in fetters, and they enjoy their own and our liberties, which rather than suffer or yield to, were a thousand times better to dye; wherefore, bethink your selves and consider the danger; be not so surprised as not to

be able to help yourselves; and if you be wise and valiant, as I hope you are, you will be watchful and active; let not your enemies tread you into the earth like dull worms, or drive you into bondage like silly sheep into a pinfold, but rather be as the subtle serpents and dreadful lions, to take your advantages and make them your prey; suffer them not to be your vultures, but be their eagles, let them not feed on our ruins, but be you their emperors to command them, make them march under your banners, and suffer them not to lead you as slaves.

5 *An Oration against the Breaking of Peace with their Neighbour-Nation*

*Dear Countrymen,*

I perceive you desire, or rather are resolved, to be no longer in peace but to make war on the *U. G.* for some slight injuries, which perchance could not be avoided: for there is no friendship between man and man, or the dearest natural affections betwixt brethren, or parents and children, or husbands and wives, but will give some occasions, either by words or actions or both, to take exceptions, and to be angry with each other; and should they for some small offences or indiscreet actions break off all bonds of friendship or natural affection, or should they endeavour to destroy each others lives, this would be inhumane, unnatural, uncharitable, unjust, and irreligious; and if near and dear friends cannot live without exceptions and faults, much less can two several nations under two several governments. And give me leave to tell you that if it be not wicked, yet it will be very unwise to hazard your lives, liberties, possessions and habitations, in war, only to be revenged for some few abuses or faults that should rather be winked at than taken notice of; but should you be victorious, though it is probable you may be overcome, yet you will be in the end of the war but like chemists,[11] who to make some grains of gold spend many thousand or at least hundred pounds and ruin their estates and posterity through covetousness; so will you, through anger and desire of revenge, lose many thousand lives and impoverish the state; but experience will tell you that anger and rashness for the most part cause repentance, whereas patience and discretion many times bring men out of great evils; and though wars begin flauntingly and boastingly, yet commonly they end miserably and dejectedly, at least of one side if not on both, and the soldiers are more certain to have wounds or death than victory and spoils: and though

---

[11] Alchemists.

covetousness and revenge is their hire, yet loss and slavery is many times their reward; they advance with hopes but draw back with doubts, and are oppressed with fears. But you imagine you shall be victorious, otherwise you would not make war, for imagination can easily and suddenly conquer all the world; yet you will find it not so in action as in thought. It is one thing to fight a battle in the brain and an other thing to fight a battle in the field: and if I might advise you, you should fight only with thoughts and not with arms, with supposed not with real enemies. But to conclude, this warlike preparation or resolution is not only inconsiderable and foolish, but mad, as to leave and forsake your delicious pleasures, sweet delights, happy contents, dear friends and safe habitations, which you enjoy in peace, to put your selves into many inconveniences, much troubles, great hazards, dangerous adventures, and uncertain successes in wars.

6 *An Oration to prevent Civil War*

*Noble Citizens, and Dear Countrymen,*
Give me leave to tell you, I do foresee a civil war, if not timely hindered or prevented; the chief signs of this war are vanity, pride, luxury, ambition, corruption, extortion, envy, faction and poverty. As for vanity, pride, and luxury, they are amongst our young nobles; envy, ambition, and faction amongst our states-men; corruption and extortion amongst our magistrates and officers, and poverty is amongst our commons, as also in our common and public treasury; all which will bring our city and kingdom to ruin if the disorders and grievances be not timely rectified. Wherefore *noble citizens* and *dear countrymen*, prevent your own ruin by reforming your own state both of public and private misdemeanors; but the chief rectifiers must be the statesmen, magistrates, and officers; for wise statesmen and good magistrates will not only endeavour to abolish vanity and luxury by their frugal examples, but by their wise and severe laws; for without strict and severe laws, wise government cannot be; also wise statesmen and honest magistrates will endeavour to fill the public treasury by just and regular means, and not their private purses by extortion and corruption, for the one relieves the poor, the other starves them, and not only relieves the poor but is a means to supply the public wants, to guard the public state, and to keep the public peace; all which makes wise and honest statesmen and magistrates to be provident to enrich, and sparing to spend the public treasure, that the public state may have means and wealth for necessary occasions. Also wise statesmen and magistrates will

employ the common people to keep them from want and idleness, which will keep them in order and peace; but the greatest good, and greatest scarcity in a commonwealth is wise statesmen and just magistrates, which are free from private interest and ambition of particular power, not making their self designs the general ruin: but such men, if any such there be, ought to be chosen out from the rest of the people, to govern and rule so that prudence, fortitude, justice and temperance, as also charity, love, and unity, may be the bond and security of the public weal, which I pray the gods to give you, and bless you with peace, plenty, and tranquillity.

7  *An Oration to send out Colonies*

*Noble citizens, and Dear Countrymen,*
Give me leave to tell you that both the young and aged men in this nation spend their times idly; the one sort sleeps away their time, the other plays it away. But it may be said that rest is proper for aged men, and pleasure for young men; I answer, rest to the bodies of aged men doth well, and action for young men; but aged men might employ their brains in counsels, and young men their arms in wars; for aged brains are wisest and young men's bodies strongest, and both may be employed in the service of this nation. But this nation is like a man that increases his issue and doth not increase his estate: for this nation grows populous, but the men not industrious to enlarge it. The truth is, we have more men than means to maintain them or business to employ them, which makes them idle, having nothing to husband or manage, and idleness will in time make them evil; wherefore, if some of the wise aged men send not some of the young strong men to make wars abroad, to employ or enrich them or to destroy them, they will make wars at home and destroy themselves and others for want of wealth and employment: for this nation is like a body over-grown, or rather full of humours, which requires evacuation.[12] Wherefore, send some to sea, others to march by land, to seek new habitations and to conquer nations; and men of fortune will be more willing to go than you to send them if you

---

[12] In his advice to Charles II, William Newcastle, Cavendish's husband, proposes to the King that foreign wars would enrich his kingdom, busy his people, 'vent the over-plus that would be burden to the kingdom' and make the people warlike. *Ideology and Politics on the Eve of the Restoration. Newcastle's Advice to Charles II*, ed. Thomas P. Slaughter (Philadelphia: The American Philosophical Society, 1984), p. 75. On colonisation see S. S. Webb, *The Governors-General: The English Army and the Definition of Empire* (Chapel Hill, NC: University of North Carolina Press, 1979) and David Armitage, *The Ideological Origins of the British Empire* (Cambridge: Cambridge University Press, 2000), ch. 6.

help them with necessaries to begin the war; and they having nothing to lose, nor nothing to live on, will fight without fear and therefore probably destroy their enemies without favour, that they may come to be absolute conquerors.

## 8 *An Oration concerning Shipping*

*Noble Citizens, and Dear Countrymen,*
You know that this country is an island, and therefore it is well to put you in mind of the proverb which says take care of your ships and look well to your tacklings, otherwise you can have no safety: for the strength of an island are ships which are the guard to defend it, not empty unrigged ships in your havens but good strong ships well manned on the seas; for to have ships only in your havens will be no security; besides, it spoils both ships and mariners for want of use and practice. Thus the close havens destroy more ships and mariners than the open seas: for that which makes good mariners is navigation, and the more storms they have been in the more experience they have gained. It is true, 'tis a laborious and dangerous profession, but yet it is expedient, both for security and profit to those that inhabit an island; for islands commonly have more men than land, and therefore require provisions from abroad besides many things for pleasure and delight. But though islands be not so spacious as continents, yet they are for the most part richer, for shipping of burdens is profitable, although shipping of war is chargeable; and perchance you will say that the charge of the one sort eats out the profit of the other, unless you can make them serve for both, as for traffic and for war, which in my opinion cannot well be done; for ships for war will be too heavy and unwieldy for burden, and too big for speed as also too slow for flight; for merchants do seldom fight if they can possibly lye, not only that their wealth makes them fearful, but their rich freights would be spoiled, although they should not be taken from them. But howsoever, safety is to be preferred before wealth, wherefore ships of war are to be considered before ships of burdens, and that there be good mariners and ship-masters for both; and not only to repair ships, but to build ships yearly, that you may be so strong as to be masters of the seas;[13] also to pay well your poor laborious mariners and careful and skilful ship-masters, who keep you in safety and bring

---

[13] During the 1660s, shipping was widely regarded as vital to England's defences, especially after the Dutch War. See *Blazing World*, n. 15. Newcastle advises Charles II that shipping is the key to his power, and urges him to support merchant shipping, such as the coal

you riches and foreign rarities and curiosities for pleasure and delight; although they be but poor themselves, and have less or as little pleasure as riches, being for the most part accompanied with dangers and fears as much as with want and necessity; the truth is, they often times endure great extremities; for in a storm they fight for life, and in a calm they starve for want; for they fight not like those that fight at land, as men with men, but they fight with the blustering winds and raging waves where, although they get the victory, yet they are sure to be losers, their ships being wounded and their tacklings tattered and torn, and every thing out of order; besides, their spirits are spent and their limbs sore, and their whole bodies wearied and tyr'd with labour, having nothing to refresh them but joy that they were not drowned. Wherefore, mariners deserve more pay and thanks than land-soldiers, who fight with men equal to them, not with the elements above and beneath them, as wind and water, which are strong, fierce, and devouring: besides, when land-soldiers get a victory, they are enriched with the spoil, refreshing themselves with luxurious pleasures, sporting and feasting, whereas poor mariners and seamen are forced to fast rather than to feast, having never much plenty, but after a storm more scarcity, their provision being spoiled by their enemies, the elements. But to conclude, the seamen want pay and their ships repairing, for which you must disburse a sufficient sum of money to mend the one and to relieve the other, who deserve not only pay, but reward to encourage them.[14]

## 9  *An Oration for Contribution*

*Noble citizens, and Dear Countrymen,*

It seems you are covetous but not prudent, that you are so loath to raise, and so slow to pay contribution-money towards the maintenance of the army, which is to fight not only for your lives and liberties, but to protect your goods, and that every man may without disturbance enjoy his own: but you are so covetous that rather than you would part with some, you

---

ships of Newcastle, which can be converted into war ships if necessary. *Newcastle's Advice*, pp. 9–11.

[14] Throughout the 1650s there were disturbances about seamen's pay. See Bernard Capp, *Cromwell's Navy: The Fleet and the English Revolution, 1648–1660* (Oxford: Clarendon Press, 1989), pp. 277–82. These continued after the Restoration, when the government was perpetually short of money for maintaining its sizeable navy. See Paul Seaward, *The Restoration* (Basingstoke: Macmillan, 1991), pp. 18–20.

will endanger the whole; and as you are covetous, so you are fearful, for you will neither maintain poor soldiers that are willing to fight for you, nor yet go to the wars to fight for your selves; you fear your enemies, and yet will take no care to overcome them. And give me leave to tell you that your covetousness and fear doth make you treacherous; for if you will neither help with your purse nor your person, you betray your country to the enemies power, also your old parents, tender wives, and young children, that cannot help themselves, all which you betray to slavery, leaving them for a prey to the enemy; and not only your fertile country, and shiftless friends, and near allies, but your own lives; for it seems by your covetousness and cowardliness that you had rather have your throats cut than part with your money or fight in your own defence, which is a strange madness, as to be afraid to dye, and yet to take no care to provide for your safety, nor to have courage to fight for your lives. The best that can be said or thought of you is that you rely upon base hopes, as that the enemy may spare your lives to enslave your persons: but I can only say this, that either you must fight your selves, or maintain others, or else others will take what you have to maintain themselves, to defend their country.

10  *An Oration to persuade a City not to yield to their Enemies*

*Worthy Citizens,*

I do not doubt your courage in resisting and fighting your enemies, nor your patience in sufferance, nor your care in watching, nor your industry in labouring, nor your prudence in ordering, and all for the defence of your city which is besieged by your enemies, which you endeavour to keep out by all possible means, sparing neither your limbs nor your lives; nor do I fear the power of your enemies, for whilst your courages, strengths, patience and industries be united together, it is more probable you will raise the siege, than the enemies take this city; for though your victuals be scarce and your ammunition wasted, yet your temperance doth supply the scarcity of the one, and your courage the want of the other; only that I fear will make you yield upon any conditions is the love to your wives, daughters, mothers, kinswomen, and female friends, and not so much their safety, for so long as your lives last you will defend them, but if you yield to your enemies by yielding to the women's effeminate fears, if your enemies do not say or think you base cowards they will say or think you facile fools. For give me leave to tell you that, though men of honour, as valiant men, will fight for the safety and protection of women, not only for those that are near allied to them but for those that are neither of their country nor kin; yet no man that would keep the reputation of valour will quit that honour for a woman's sake, no, although it be to save his daughter, wife, or mother from their enemies: for a gallant man dreads more the name of a coward than any thing in the world; and it is no dishonour to a man to have his wife taken and abused by his enemy when he could not honourably help her; for force is no dishonour, but a base free act; for a man cannot be forced to be a coward, nor a chaste woman to be a whore, they may both have misfortunes, injuries, and hateful abuses done to them, but not wicked, base, or ignoble minds. Wherefore, let me persuade you for your own honour's sake not to yield through the women's desires; let not their tears move you, nor their entreaties persuade you; for if you yield, though upon the assurance of your lives and liberties, where will you wander to seek an habitation? For if you could not keep your own city and wealth, it is not likely you will get the like from other men; alas your neighbours will shut their gates and doors against you, for poverty and misfortune hath not many friends or hosts, for few are so hospitable as to entertain either; and you will not only find charity cold, but those that have envied you in your prosperity will despise you in your adversity, and what masculine spirits can bear such misery as neglect, want and scorn, and the infamy of yielding courages? Wherefore, it is better to die in the defence of your own city and be renowned for your valour and constancy in after-ages, wherein your lives, acts and deaths will be mentioned to your honour and renown.

11  *An Oration for those that are Slain in the Wars and brought home to be Buried*

*Worthy Citizens,*

You lament over the corpse of your friends slain in the wars, shedding your tears and breathing your sighs on their hearses. 'Tis true, they are natural showers and Zephyrus's[15] airs of loving affections and passionate hearts; yet give me leave to tell you, you have more cause to rejoice than grieve: first, that their death begets their renowns, and [it] is an honour to their memory to die in the service of their country; for all men that have worth and merit would willingly, nay gladly, die to save their country, or for the honour of their country, and all wise men will gladly quit a present, frail

---

[15] Zephyrus, one of the four winds.

and uncertain life to live eternally in the memory of the present and future ages, in whose memories their actions live like glorified bodies and purified souls; for thus they become from terrestrial to be celestial. The next cause you have to rejoice is that their bodies are brought home as a witness of their victory, and their deaths are their triumphs, which are adorned and set out with numerous and glorious praises; besides, they have the happiness to be inurned with their forefathers, where by a natural instinct or sympathy they may mutually intermix and perchance transmigrate together; and since they fought valiantly and died honourably, they shall be buried happily and will be remembered eternally, and have an everlasting fame, rejoice with music, bells and bonfires and offer unto the gods oblations of thanksgiving.

# ORATIONS IN THE FIELD OF WAR
## Part II

12  *An Oration from a Besieged City, ready to yield or else to be taken*

I am come here to entreat you, that are our over-powerful enemies, to be
our merciful saviours, that though you are determined to destroy our city
and possess our goods, yet you would be pleased to spare the lives of the
inhabitants; for what profit will it be to destroy numbers of defenceless
and powerless persons only to satisfy your fury, which will be satisfied
with time better than with blood? For though our blood may quench
your present rage, yet it may afterwards clog your consciences and cause a
sorrowful repentance, which may disturb the peace of your minds, wherein
your thoughts will be in a perpetual war: for to kill us after our submission,
and when we have made a satisfaction for our faults in yielding up our city
and goods without any further resistance, our deaths will be but murders;
so that you will blemish your conquest, from being noble and generous
conquerors to be cruel and inhumane murderers; whereas the sparing of
our lives will be acceptable to god, nature, and mankind, and the trumpet
of your fame will sound sweetly and harmoniously in the ears of after-
ages, where you will get as much love and praises for your clemency
and mercy, as admiration and renown for your valours and conducts;
whereas your cruelty will sound so harshly with such discords as it will
beget dislike, and so much hate as to bury all your valour and wisdom in
Fortune's partial and unjust favours, ascribing that to her she had no right
to challenge.[16]


13  *A Common Soldiers Oration to take the City by Force*

*Fellow Soldiers,*

We have been long at the siege of this city where we have not only been
obedient to our commanders, careful, watchful, and laborious, as also
valiant in assaulting, regarding not our limbs nor lives, but we have patiently endured want of victuals, and yet for all this, the town being ready
to be taken, our commanders intend to rob us of the spoils which by
the law of arms ought to be ours as a reward; for those that venture

---

[16] During the Civil War Margaret Cavendish's husband had raised two sieges in the north
of England, and her brother, General Lucas, surrendered the besieged city of Colchester
to the Parliamentary forces in 1648.

most ought to have the greatest shares in the conquest, and the common
soldiers venturing more than the commanders ought to have the spoil: for
though they direct, yet it is we that fight and win the victory. Wherefore
let us not suffer them to make a composition, but enter the town by
force and plunder it, otherwise the commanders, or rather the general
alone, will be the only gainer, and all the rest losers; and shall one man go
away with the wealth when as the poor common soldiers are naked and
almost starved for want? Shall our sick and wounded friends that cannot
remove, or be removed, nor help themselves, be left as a prey to those
which they have helped to conquer with the loss of their blood and limbs?
For no doubt but those new-made friends will be their deadly enemies,
and cut their throats when we are gone and left them. Thus we shall
betray our friends and lose our shares if they make peace and enter not
the town by assault: for to take a town by force is a gain to the common
soldiers, but little or none to the general or great commanders; but to take
a town by composition is a gain to the general and chief commanders,
but not to the common soldiers; for we shall lie without the gates whilst
they are received in triumph, where they will feast whilst we do fast, and
will be enriched with treasures, but we remain in want.

14 *An Oration to those Soldiers that are against an Agreement with the Citizens*

*Fellow Soldiers,*
Let me tell you that you speak against your own profit when you speak
against compounding and agreeing with the besieged citizens: for it is
not only human and charitable, generous and noble, to spare the lives of
yielding and conquered enemies, but profitable; for their lives will serve
you and their industry maintain you; wherefore it is better to spare their
lives and make peace with them, also to take their money and spare their
cumbersome and combustible goods, which will trouble your carriage and
hinder your march; neither can you make so much profit of them as they
will give you for them. And as for their city and lives, it were a great folly
to kill and destroy them to no purpose, unless to satisfy your bloody minds
and furious rage; for death and destruction will bring you not any profit;
but if you give them their lives and let their city stand, they will give you
a constant and settled contribution towards your maintenance, also they
will be surgeons, physicians, and nurses to our sick and wounded soldiers,
by which means they may recover their former health and strength again
and be able to do their country more service; but if they be left behind us,

and none to take care of them, nor men to help them, nor houses to lodge in, they must of necessity perish in great misery; and we have no reason to fear they will be cruel to them because they know we shall return to revenge their cruelty: besides, they will be very careful of them, and kind and helpful to them, to keep peace and to merit our favours; for conquerors are always flattered, obeyed, and served with ceremony, industry, and fidelity, so long as Fortune favours them. Thus you know by what I have spoken that it is the best for the common soldiers and commanders to spare the city and citizens. And now give me leave to tell you that you are unjust judges of me, your general's, actions, and evil censurers and malicious accusers, to accuse my prudence for my soldiers of covetousness for my self, and my careful love for my sick and wounded soldiers of an insensible and cruel neglect, whereas you might more truly accuse me for using too much clemency to my mutinous and rebellious soldiers, winking at their faults and pardoning their crimes when they ought to have been severely punished, by which they would have been better taught, and I obeyed: for severe generals make humble, obedient, industrious, laborious, patient, and courageous soldiers, whereas a compliant general quite spoils them; but I have showed mercy to offenders, love and care to the wounded, sick, tired, and weary, and I have been bountiful to the well-deservers; all which I am forced to remember you of because you have forgotten, at least are unwilling to take any notice thereof; yet I perceive it is the nature of most of mankind, especially mean births, low fortunes, and brute breedings, to be ungrateful, malicious, revengeful, and inhumane.

15  *An Oration to Soldiers after the Loss of a Battle*

*Fellow Soldiers,*

I perceive you are dejected at your ill fortune, for Fortune is a thief, robbing some to give partially to others; wherefore we soldiers, whom she busies her self most with, to show her power and agility, ought to be so careful and watchful as to lock and barricade out Fortune's malice, giving her no advantage, if you can possibly hinder her from taking any. Yet was it neither for want of conduct or valour that we won not the victory, but heaven and earth was against us: for the sun, wind and dust beat on our faces; for you endeavouring to get the side of the wind went against the sun-beams, so that with the sun-beams and the glittering dust that flew up by the motion of the wind, we could not see, neither to assault our enemies nor to defend our selves, nay, we were so blinded as to mistake our friends for our foes, and our foes for our friends; which tempestuous wind had it been before we began to fight, we might have prevented the mischief it did us, some way or other; but the wind did rise when we were so engaged, as we could not help ourselves; the truth was, it blew so fully against the main part of our battalion, and with that violent force, as it pressed the former ranks so much back that they did disturb the hinder ranks and so disordered them, till at last it blew them quite away; for they were forced to turn their backs and to fly for their lives, and when that part of the army fled, others had no hearts to stay; but do not mistake so as to believe that the divine power was against us, but only the elements, and they were against us more by chance than malice. Wherefore take courage again, and rouse up your dejected spirits, and repine not for that we could not foresee to avoid: for I make no doubt but the next time we encounter our enemies we shall not only get the reputation you think you have lost, but we shall add to what we formerly had and pull down the haughty pride of our enemies that now seem to insult on our misfortunes.

16 *An Oration to Soldiers in Necessity*

*My Good Soldiers,*

I cannot much blame your murmuring and complaining words and speeches, by reason our camp is vexed and tormented with scarcity, sickness, and inconveniences; and although we cannot tell how to mend or help ourselves in these extremities, yet it troubles our patience and somewhat alters your natures, at least divulges them more, making you forward, testy, cholerick; and forward minds, and testy thoughts are apt to send forth out of the mouth lamenting words and complaining speeches. Yet give me leave to tell you, it expresseth you have partaken too much of your mothers natures, which is not so well for soldiers, who should be no ways effeminate; for women naturally are impatient, fretting, chasing and complaining without cause. I do not deny but you at this present have great cause, and therefore some reason for what you speak: yet I hope, though you speak like your mothers, you will act like your fathers. Wherefore give me leave to remember you of *Caesar*'s soldiers, for surely you could not choose but hear of them, their fame being so great and sounding so loud, for their patience, sufferance, hardiness, industry, carefulness, watchfulness, valours and victories; yet were they no more than men, and I hope you are not less than men; but there are two sorts of courages, and they, as the story says, had them both, as fortitude in suffering and valour in acting, which made them so fortunate in overcoming as to conquer the most part of the world; and though I cannot hope you will conquer all the world, yet I hope you will have victory over your enemies. So shall you be masters and not slaves.

17  *An Encouraging Oration to Fearful Soldiers*

*Fellow soldiers, and Dear Countrymen,*
I perceive by your dejected countenances and drooping spirits, you are afraid of your enemies; but I am more afraid of your fears than of the enemies power; for fear makes powerful armies powerless, and [as] a little body with a great spirit is stronger and more vigorous than a great body and a little spirit, so a little army with great courages is more forcible than a great or numerous army full of faint hearts and cowardly fears. Wherefore consider, there are but three ways. The one is to run away, but remember you cannot run from shame or disgrace, though you may run from your enemy; another way is, you may yield up yourselves to the enemy, but then you must yield up your liberties with your persons and become their slaves, in which slavery you live in scorn, are used as beasts, and die as cowards; the third and last way, which is the best, is to fight your enemy, which if you overcome, you will have the honour of victory and the profit of the spoils, and if you be killed, you die uncon- quered; for courage is never overcome nor gallant heroic actions never die, and their fames will be their perpetual triumphs, which may last eternally. Wherefore, my good soldiers fight valiantly for life, victory, and glory.

18  *An Oration to Soldiers that fled from their Enemies*

What shall I call you? For I cannot call you fellow soldiers, because you have degraded your selves of that honourable title by running away, which shows you have but effeminate spirits or souls, though masculine bodies; nor can I call you dear countrymen; for you have unnaturalised your selves by betraying your country with your cowardly fears, to the power of their enemies; nor can I call you my good friends, for you did forsake me in danger and left me to death, had not Fortune rescued me; so that you cannot challenge, nor I cannot give you, any other names but base cowards and traitors, which words cannot but sound grievously, sadly, and scornfully to your own, your friend's, and enemies' hearing: and that which will heighten your reproach is that you were not forced nor necessitated to fly, as being overcome or overpowered; for you fled not only before you had tried your enemies force, but when in all probability you should have had the victory, having all the advantages of your side and against your enemies that could be, as ground, place, wind, sun, form, order, and number of men, and yet to run away; O horrid shame to all posterity! The truth is, I am so out of countenance in your behalf, and so sorrowful for you, as I cannot choose but blush for shame and weep for grief when I look upon you, to see so many able and strong yet heartless men, that have soiled your bright arms with disgrace, instead of the blood of your enemies. Wherefore, you may now pull off your arms, since you have coats of dishonour to wear, and break your swords, for the tongues of reproach are unsheathed against you, which will wound your reputations and kill your renowns, and your infamy will live in after-ages eternally.

19  *An Oration to Run-away Soldiers who Repent their fault*

Sorrowful penitents, (for so you seem by your countenances and your words, the one being sad, the other full of promises), I must confess it becomes you well, for you have been great cowards and fearful run-aways, which are faults that cannot be enough lamented, but your actions may be amended, and so you may have a pardon and your disgrace taken off with some valiant and courageous exploits against your enemies, where I, your general, who am one of *Mars*'s high priests, shall guide and direct you the way; and you may rely upon me; for I am well learned and practised in the mystery of war. But pray be not as a flock of sheep, making me as a parish-priest, as only to talk and you to run away; for then I shall curse you instead of blessing you; and though it be requisite you should be as meek sheep in *Jove*'s temple, yet you must be as raging lions in *Mars*'s field, and the prayers you make to *Mars* must be for victory and fame; but let me tell you, you must implore *Pallas*'s help, and *Fortune*'s favour; and therefore fight valiantly and fiercely, and take your advantages prudently, stick closely and fight orderly, and leave the rest to Fortune; which if you do thus as I advise you, your actions will wipe out all former faults and take away all your reproach or disgrace, so clean as if they had never been, especially if you have the victory.

20  *A Mutinous Oration to Common Soldiers, by a Common Soldier*

*Fellow Soldiers,*

Give me leave to tell you that although you have proved your valours in the battles you have fought and the assaults you have made, yet you have not proved yourselves wise, to leave your native country and peaceable habitations only to fight with foreigners, who are as industrious, valiant, and active to overcome and kill you as you to overcome and kill them; and what do we fight and hazard our lives for? Not for riches; for what we get we are subject to lose again, and should we get riches, we should soon consume them, having no settled abiding to thrive upon the stock or to get out use of the principal, nor to have any returns by traffic or commerce, but those spoils we can get are only cumbersome goods which we are forced to fling away in times or places of danger, or when we make sudden or long marches; and albeit we could easily and safely carry them along with us, yet we should make but small profit of them and get little ready money for them, although they were not spoiled in the carriage. By this we may know the wars will not enrich us; and as for fame, common soldiers are never mentioned, although they are the only fighters, but thousands of them, when killed, are buried in oblivion's grave, and no other burial they have; for their slain bodies for the most part lie and rot above ground or are devoured by carrion-birds or ravenous beasts; but the fame or renown is given to the general alone; some under-commanders may chance to be slightly mentioned but not gloriously famed; and if you can neither get wealth nor honour in or by the wars, why should you be soldiers? Wherefore, let us return home, and rather be ploughmen in our own country than soldiers in a foreign nation, rather feed with our own labours than starve at our general's command, and rather choose to die peaceably than to live in the war, wherein is nothing to be gotten but scars and wounds; where we may lose our limbs and lives, but not make our fortunes.

21  *An Oration to stay the Soldiers from a Mutinous return from the Wars*

*Fellow Soldiers, and Dear Countrymen,*

The soldier that spoke to persuade you to mutiny, as to leave the wars dishonourably, by his speech any man of courage would believe he were a coward: for no man of courage would leave an enemy in the field, for that would be as bad as running away; and will you, who have gotten honourable renown by the wars, quit that renown for disgrace? Shall the speech of a cowardly, idle, base man persuade you more than your reputations? Can any man live, act, or die more honestly than in the service of his country? Besides, it will not only be a disgrace to you, and also a disgrace to your country to leave the wars, but you will endanger your country; for no question but your enemies will follow you at the heels, so that instead of carrying home victory and spoils, you will carry home danger and perchance ruin, betraying your country by faction, mutiny, or cowardly fears. Thus, although you came out of your country soldiers, you will return traitors. But should they not follow you, they would scorn you, and your friends would despise you at your return, and what is worse than to be scorned and despised of enemies and friends? When as by your gallant actions the one would be afraid, the other proud of you. And let me tell you, to be a soldier is the noblest profession; for it makes mean men as princes, and those princes that are not soldiers are as mean men; and though fame doth not mention every particular soldier, but generally all together, yet the memory of every particular soldier and their particular actions never die, as long as their successors live; for their children mention their fore-fathers valiant actions with pride, pleasure, and delight, and glory that they descended from such worthy ancestors; and as for scars gotten in the wars, they are such graces and becoming marks as they woo and win a mistress and gain her favour sooner than wealth, title, or beauty doth. But I hope you will neither show yourselves cowards nor prove yourselves traitors, by leaving the war when you ought to follow it.

22 *A Generals Oration to his Mutinous Soldiers*[17]

*Fellow Soldiers,*
I hear you murmur, complain, and speak against me, forgetting your respects, obedience, duty, and fidelity to me your general; for which I am sorry, not for myself, but for my soldiers; for I am never the worse

[17] During the English Civil War the speeches made by generals to their armies were printed and circulated, so that Cavendish could easily have read them. For example, addressing his army in 1642, the Earl of Newcastle remarked that to use encouragement to men of fortitude is an implicit diminution of their valour. 'I shall not therefore so much undervalue yours, as to intrude an exhortation upon your courages, only . . . perform these orders.' *Orders and Institutions of War made and ordained by his Majesty and by him delivered to his General his Excellence the Earl of Newcastle, with the said earl's speech to the army at the delivery and publishing the said Orders prefixt* (1642).

for my soldiers being evil; but I am sorry, my soldiers are not what they ought to be; and though I do not wonder at the disobedience of my common soldiers, yet I cannot but wonder at the baseness of my officers and under-commanders; for though inferior men have inferior minds, rude and wild natures, and barbarous manners, yet men of quality usually have generous, and noble minds, gentle natures, and civil manners, and of all men, gallant soldiers have the noblest minds and ought to have the reformedest manners; for though heroic men fight in blood to kill their enemies, yet they will spill their blood and sacrifice their lives for their friends, country, or country-men, as also for honour, generosity, and fame, and they will rather choose to endure all kind or manner of torments and to die a thousand, nay millions of deaths if it could be, than to do one act of dishonour, or that is not fit for a man of honour to do; indeed heroic and honourable men are petty gods, whereas other men are beasts, the one having celestial natures, the other terrestrial. But by your mutinous speeches, I perceive I have not those gallant, noble, generous, and valiant soldiers as I thought I had in this my army, which I am sorry for, especially that there is none like myself; for I utterly renounce all actions or thoughts that ought not be to be done by worthy men or to be inherent in worthy men; I hate treachery as I hate cowardliness, and I hate cowardliness as I hate disgrace or infamy, and I hate infamy worse than oblivion; for oblivion is the hell of meritorious and gallant men; and as I prefer after-memory, which is fame, before present life, which fame is the heaven wherein worthy and honourable men and actions are glorified and live to all eternity, so would I have my soldiers there to live and be glorified; which desire expresses that I love my soldiers equal with my self; and as I do prefer honour and fame before sensual pleasures or life, so I have always preferred my soldiers lives before my own; for I never endeavoured to save my own life when my soldiers lives were in danger, but have put my person in the same danger they were in, nay, I have ventured one more danger than they have done; for I have led them singly to the face and front of their enemies; neither have I been idle when as my soldiers have taken pains, but to the contrary I have taken pains when as they have been idle; for my person hath not only been employed in ordering, appointing, and directing of every particular, but I have marched on foot with the infantry, whilst the cavalry hath rid easily on horses or the chief commanders have rid lazily in their wagons; as also I have taken pains in teaching, ordering, and marshalling my soldiers, as well as time, place, and opportunity would give me leave; and my body hath not only laboured, but my mind and thoughts were always and at all times busily employed for the affairs of the army, and for my soldiers advantage, contriving the best as how to prevent the worst. Thus my thoughts have laboured for you continually, keeping me waking whilst you have slept and rested in ease. Neither did I ever rob my soldiers of their spoils, but was pleased to distribute my share amongst them; nor did I ever make a scarcity of your victuals through my luxury; nor have I ever brought my soldiers into want through my imprudence; for whatsoever want or loss you have had, it came merely from Fortune, whose power the wisest and valiantest cannot always and at all times withstand. But yet the common soldiers and under-commanders for the most part accuse their generals, laying the disfavour of Fortune to their general's charge, although it is not in any man's power to avoid Fortune's malice, unless men could divine what would fall out against all reason or probability; and though wise men may imagine such chances, yet they will never order their affairs or designs, or any action against reason, sense, and probability; besides, foolery and knavery cause loss and misery without Fortune's help, making more disorder and confusion than the wisest men can rectify. But I will not trouble you with many more words nor reproofs; for neither words, reproofs, nor persuasions will do any good on a mutinous and rebellious army, who hath more strength to do evil than honesty to do good; more fury to mutiny than courage to fight; more envy to their leaders than love to their own honours. I add only this, your baseness I abhor, your rudeness I scorn, your malice I despise, your designs I slight, and your intended cruelty I fear not.

23 *A Commanders Refusing Speech to Mutinous Soldiers, who Deposed their General, and would Choose him in his place*

*Fellow Soldiers,*

You have forcibly against my will proclaimed me your general, and because I sent you word I would not command you, you sent me a threatening message that although you at first chose me through your love and kind-ness, yet now, whereas I did slight your love, you would force me to take that charge upon me; but let me tell you, I care not for your favour nor I fear not your anger, as being neither a knave nor a coward; for to be a friend to mutinous soldiers is to be a knave, to fear them is to be a coward, and to be chosen general to a rebellious army, is a dishonour; wherefore I, preferring honour before life, will rather die than be your general. But who gave you authority to depose your general and to make another? Or what right have you to take away and give commissions? You will answer, by force of arms, or rather force of rebels; for arms are, or ought to be, for justice, right, truth, or honour, not for injustice, wrong, injury, falsehood, and dishonour; and strong arms and courageous hearts do not agree with mad heads and wild passions; but you, by your disobedience seem to be cowards; for valour is obedient, nay, valiant men will obey unreasonable commands rather than oppose their commanders, and choose rather to die obediently than to live disobediently; but your actions have showed you to be rebellious cowards; for which I am not only ashamed that you are my countrymen or fellow soldiers, but hate you as enemies to honour and honesty; and therefore, if it lay in my power, I would destroy you as being unworthy to live.

24  *A Generals Oration to his Evil-designing Soldiers*

*Fellow Soldiers,*
I have not called you together to persuade you to fight your enemies, for I perceive you are turned cowards, and cowards are deaf to all persuasions of adventures: nor do I go about to persuade you to patience, although it be the part of good soldiers to suffer patiently as well as to fight vigorously, also to be patient with painful labours; but I perceive, patience and industry, that accompany valour, have also forsaken you. Nor shall I persuade you to stick close to me as to defend my life from the enemies, although I have been more careful to defend your lives with skill and knowledge in war and arms than you have been to defend my life with your strength and courages. And give me leave to tell you that the renown you have gotten in the wars hath been gained as much by my conduct as your valours. Thus I neither persuade you to fight, to suffer, nor to help me in time of need; but my desire is to persuade you not to bury the renown you have gotten in these wars in the grave of treachery, nor to cast down your glorious acts from the palace of fame into the pit of infamy, which you will do if you put your evil designs into acts; for I perceive well by your secret meetings and gatherings in companies together without order, and by your whisperings into each others ears, as also by your murmuring, complaints, and exclamations, you intend some evil, but in what manner you will execute your evil designs I cannot tell; I suppose it is either that you will desert me, or make peace with the enemy without me on dishonourable terms, or that you will betray me to the enemy and deliver

me into their hands; or else it is that you have conspired to murder me with your own hands, either of which will be unworthy for good soldiers to do. Wherefore I would, if I could, dissuade you for your own sakes, and not for mine, not to do such acts as to cause honest men to hate you, valiant men to despise you, wise men not to trust you, your enemies to scorn you, your country to exclaim against you, your acquaintance to shun you, your friends to grieve for you, your posterity to be ashamed of you and disgraced by you; for when after-ages shall mention you, your posterity, if they have any worth or merit, will hang down their heads for shame to hear of your evil deeds; all which will be, if you be mutinous conspirers, traitors, or cowards; but if neither honour, honesty, fidelity nor love can dissuade you from your base, treacherous, and wicked designs, or that your design is against me, here I offer my self to you to dispose of my person and life as you please; for I am neither ashamed to suffer, nor afraid to die, knowing I have not done anything that a man of honour ought not to do; and as fear hath no power over my mind, so force hath no power over my will, for I shall willingly die.

### 25 *An Oration to Soldiers, who have Killed their General*

Barbarous soldiers, or rather cruel murderers, you that have inhumanely killed your general, your careful, painful, prudent, valiant, loving and kind general, ought to be generally killed; but death would be too great a mercy and happiness for such wretches as you are, for you deserve such torments and afflictions as are above all expressions, and your bloody action hath made you appear to me so horrid, that methinks life is terrible because you live, and death is amiable since our general is dead, and honour lives in the grave with him, and baseness lives in the world with you, devils possess your souls in your living bodies, when as angels have born away his soul from his lifeless corpse to be crowned with everlasting glory. You shall not need to fear your enemies now, for surely they will fly you, not for fear you should kill them but for fear you should infect them, they fear not your courage but your wickedness; neither shall you fear oblivion, for you will be infamous and the very report of your murdering act will cause a trembling of limbs and chilliness of spirit to all the hearers, and you will not only be scorned, hated, and cursed, but prayers will be offered against you, and men will bless themselves from you as from a plague or evil spirit. Thus your enemies will despise you, your friends renounce you, honest men exclaim against you, men of honour shun you, good fortune forsake you, heaven shut all mercy from you, your conscience torment you, insomuch that you will be ashamed to live and afraid to dye.

### 26  *An Oration to Soldiers which repent the Death of their General*

Penitent soldiers, (for so you seem by your tears, sighs, groans, and sorrowful complaints,) I cannot forbid you to weep, for your fault requires great and many showers of tears to wash away your crime; indeed there is no other way to purge your souls and to cleanse your consciences from the stains of your general's blood but by penitent tears. Wherefore, let me advise you to go to his urn and there humbly on your knees, lamenting your sorrow, pray to heaven for pardon; then make him a statue and carry his image in your ensigns, and set his statue under your banner; thus make him that was your general your saint, and let his memory be famous by your valour, that his enemies may know the power of his name is able to destroy them, so will you make him victorious in his grave, and appease his angry ghost.

### 27  *An Oration to Distressed Soldiers*

*Dear Countrymen,*

You know we are a people that have been conquered and made slaves to our enemies, which slavery we did patiently endure a long time, but at last we had an impatient desire of liberty, and had our prudence been according to our desires, no doubt but we should have gained it, but our over-hasty desires have put us into a greater misery; for now we are not only like to lose our liberties again, but our lives, or to live in worse bondage than we did before, which we had better die than endure. But since we were not so wise for ourselves to prevent our danger as we were just to our selves to endeavour our liberty, yet we must not leave endeavouring our own good so long as life lasts; wherefore, we must consider what is best to be done in this extremity. First, we have of our selves a great body, though not so well armed as I wish we were, yet so as we are not left naked to our enemies; but though we have a great number, yet our enemies have a greater number, and though we be armed, yet our enemies are better armed. The worst of all is that we are in a place of such disadvantage as either we must starve, or yield ourselves, or fight it out at all hazards; as for starving, it is a lingering and painful death, and to yield will be a miserable and painful life, wherefore to fight it out at all hazards will be best for us to choose; for death is the end of misery, and pain is not felt in a raging or acting fury; and if we resolve, let the worst come to the worst, we can but die, and that we must do in time, had we no other enemies than what are natural, as sickness and age; and these hopes we have that desperate men in desperate adventures have many times good fortune, and those that are desperate want no courage, but they are apt to be careless of conduct; wherefore let me advise you to listen to direction, and be careful to obey your instructions; for if we should overcome our enemies we should not only save our lives, which we give for lost, but we should have our liberties, and also honour, power, and wealth too, whereas our enemies only venture their lives to keep us in subjection, which will cause them to fight but faintly; for where there is neither profit nor honour to be gained, they will sooner run away than venture their lives in the battle, so that our poverty will defend us and our necessity help to fight for us; prudence shall guide us, and then perchance Fortune may favour us. Wherefore, let us assault our enemies before they expect us, and endeavour to overcome them before they are ready to fight with us; for if we take them unprepared we shall find them without defence, and in such disorder as we shall destroy them without hazard.

# ORATIONS TO CITIZENS IN THE MARKET PLACE

## PART III

28 *An Oration to a Dejected People, ruined by War*

*Unfortunate Citizens and Countrymen,*

You now seem to be as much cast down and dejected in your misery as you were puffed up with pride in your prosperity, in which prosperity you were so confident, and so careless of your security, as you would neither believe your danger nor provide for your safety, insomuch that you murmured and mutinied against all assessments and payments, although it were to keep the kingdom in peace and to strengthen it against foreign force; but now you do not murmur at small taxes but mourn for your great losses, not for your security but your ruin; your vanity is vanished, your pride humbled, and plenty and prosperity fled from you; where are your brave furnishings, your gay adornings? Your far-fetched curiosities, and your curious rarities? Your numerous varieties and rich treasures? All plundered and gone. Where are your chargeable buildings, your stately palaces, your delightful theatres, your pleasant bowers? All burnt to ashes. Where are your races of horses, your fleecy flocks, your lowing herds, your feathered poultry, and your full-stored barns? All ruined and gone. Where are your rich merchandises and your thriving trades? All spoiled. Where are your wise laws? All broken. Your sporting recreations? All ceased. Your ancestors' monuments? All pulled down, and your fathers' bones and ashes dispersed. Where are your comrades, companions, and acquaintance? Most of them killed. Where are your beautiful wives, daughters, sisters, and mistresses? The enemy enjoys them, and your country is desolate, ruined, and forlorn; and you that are left are miserable. But what was the cause of your misery? Your pride, envy, factions, luxury, vanity, vice, and wickedness; for you would neither be instructed, advised, persuaded nor ruled; you neglected the service of the gods, disobeyed the orders of your governors, trampled down the laws of the nation and despised your magistrates, and did all what you would; which brought this confusion, and so a destruction, in which destruction you must have patience, for patience will mediate and qualify your misery.

29 *A Comforting Oration to a dejected People, ruined by War*

*Noble Citizens and Dear Countrymen,*
I confess, our condition is miserable and our lives unhappy, in that we are
so unfortunate as to be overcome by our enemies and impoverished by our
losses; but yet it was uncharitable, nay inhumane, for the former orator
to open our wounded thoughts with repetition of our losses, and to rub
our sore minds with bitter and salt reproaches; for if we have committed
faults I am sure we have been sufficiently punished for them, and if the
gods be just, as we believe they are, our loss and misery hath made them
a satisfaction, for which I hope they are pacified; and though we ought
to repent of our past disobedience to the divine and national laws, yet we
have no reason to repent of our past lawful pleasures; for who that is wise
will not make use of his riches and liberties whilst he hath them? For were
it not madness for fear of a dearth to starve our selves in plenty? For fear
of an enemy to make our selves slaves in prosperity? This were as much
as if we should take away our own lives before their natural time, because
we know we shall die; no, *Dear Countrymen*, it is soon enough to quit
pleasure, liberty, and life when we can enjoy them no longer; and since
our fortune is bad we must endeavour with industry to amend it, and if
we cannot we must suffer patiently and please our selves with hopes; for
hope is a food the mind delights to feed on, and entertains it self with
pleasing imaginations: and those are fools that will trouble their minds for
that which cannot be helped; for shall we have not only enemies without
us but also within us? Shall we torture our minds with grief, sorrow, fear,
and despair for our misfortunes? No, *Dear Countrymen*, let us wipe the
tears from our eyes and defy Fortune's malice, and when she knows we
regard not her frowns she may chance to favour us, for she is of the female
gender, whose nature is such as the more they are neglected or despised,
the kinder they are.

30 *An Oration for Rebuilding a City ruined by War*

*Unfortunate Citizens*; for so I may call you, having been ruined by wars and
spoiled by our enemies; for our city is not only burned to the ground and
all our goods plundered, but many of our citizens and countrymen killed,
and we that remain are preparing with our wives and children to seek new
habitations and acquaintance in foreign countries, from which I would, if
I could, dissuade you, since our enemies are gone and not like to return;

for though they had the victory and won our city, yet it was with such loss to them as will force them to keep peace for a long time, not being able to make wars any longer; for their valiantest and most experienced soldiers are killed, and most of the flower of their youth; besides, they have spoiled and lost many of their horses and have wasted and spent abundance of ammunition and arms; all which considered, they have not gained much by this war; indeed, war makes more spoil than profit; for though we are ruined, yet our enemies are not much enriched; but leaving them, let us consider what is the best for ourselves in these our misfortunes, and to be industrious to repair our losses; my advice is not to separate, but to keep in an united body together, and to rebuild our city. For shall we be worse citizens than the ants or pismires, which will rebuild their hill or mound over their heads whensoever it is pulled down, either by beast, men, or birds, and though it be often pulled down, and the dust dispersed, yet they will bring new earth, or gather up the relics of the former faith to rebuild, and will never leave rebuilding so long as they live. And certainly, they are very wise in so doing. The like for men; for it is better, as the wisest way, to unite in a commonwealth, than to live dispersed and to wander about like vagabonds, or to live with strangers in foreign lands, or to be governed by unknown or new laws, or to marry with strangers that mix or corrupt their generations. For those men are happiest that live in their native countries with their natural friends, are governed by their ancient laws, marry into their own tribes or natives, increase their own breed, continue their own races, uphold their own families, and are buried with or by their forefathers. Wherefore, *Good Citizens*, be industrious to rebuild your city, whereby and wherein you may be as happy and flourishing as formerly you were; but if through a dejected discontent you leave your city in its ruins, 'tis probable you will live unhappy and in slavery all your lives, as also your posterity after you.

31  *An Oration for Building a Church*

*Noble Citizens, and Dear Countrymen,*
You have built many streets of houses, but never a church, which shows you think more of the world than you do of heaven; you take more care for your bodies than your souls; for you build stately palaces to live in but not a church to pray in, rooms to feast in, not churches to fast in, to unite in riot, not to unite in religion, to talk extravagantly, not to pray piously, to rejoice in evil, not to rejoice in thanksgiving. But the nature of mankind is

such that they spend foolishly and spare foolishly, they will spend to their own hurt and spare to their own hurt, they fear evil but never endeavour to avoid punishment, they repent what is past but never take warning for what is to come; as for spending their means, they will spend so much as to make themselves sick and poor, with surfeiting, feasting, drunken drinking, pocky whoring, covetous gaming, vain shows, idle sports and the like; and when they spare, they are so miserable as not to allow themselves necessaries, so that they make themselves unhappy through want and yet have more than enough to spend; also they fear pain and sickness, but will not endeavour to avoid either; for men drink so much as they are sure to be so sick as to vomit, and will eat such meat, or drink such drinks, as they are sure to have painful fits of the gout after them. But it may be said that the enticing appetite is so persuading and over-ruling as they cannot forebear; but some men will drink when they are not dry, and eat when they are not hungry or have any desire thereto, but will drink merely for company, or being persuaded by others, or out of a humour, and so for eating. Which is strange, that men should be persuaded to suffer and endure great pain for the sake of idle company, or through the persuasion of fools, or out of a foolish or mad humour. Likewise all men are loath to die, and yet most men will venture their lives unnecessarily or for very small occasions; and all men are afraid of damnation, and yet they will not endeavour salvation, nay, they will venture damnation for a trifle, yea, for nothing: as for example they will lie, swear, and forswear when they are not provoked or have any occasion to swear, lie, and forswear; and for worldly riches, men are so covetous and greedy as they will extort, cozen, steal, murder, and venture soul, body, and life for it, yet when they have it, they spend it as if they did not care for it, nay, as if they did hate such riches; and not any man would willingly be poor, yet they will spend their wealth so foolishly as neither to have pleasure, thanks, nor fame for it. The truth is that by men's actions it could not be believed that mankind had rational souls; for though many men will speak wisely, yet most act foolishly or rather madly, so that men's rational souls live more in their words than in their deeds. But if you have rational souls and a saving belief, you ought to build a church, wherein you may gather together to repent your sins, to pray for forgiveness, to promise amendment, and to reform your lives, also to hear instructions and to give good examples to each other, and to accustom yourselves to devotion; so shall you become holy men. Besides, churches ought to be built not only for the souls of the living but for the bodies of the dead, wherein they may be inurned decently, humanly, and religiously.

32  *An Oration persuading the Citizens to erect a Statue in Honour of a Dead Magistrate*

*Noble Citizens,*

N., who is now dead, was the wisest, justest, and honestest magistrate that a commonwealth could desire or have; and as he served the commonwealth justly, so he ought to be rewarded honourably, for he did well deserve it; but his death must not be an excuse for ungratefulness, for honours are given to the dead as well as to the living; for men's good works live after them although their bodies die, and living men are benefited thereby; but should the benefit cease with their death, yet men ought not to forget the good they have received; for those are very unthankful, unworthy, and base men that will not acknowledge what they have had, but only respect the present good; indeed such men are worse than beasts, and ought to live and die in oblivion, whereas virtuous, worthy, honourable, and noble men ought to live free, and be remembered after their lives, and those that have done wise, or ingenious, or good, or profitable, or valiant, or great works, deeds, or acts, ought to be remembered in the minds of men, mentioned by the tongues of men, and figured by the hands of art, so as to live in the minds, ears, and eyes of living men; as for their merits to be praised, their acts recorded and their bodies figured to the life, not only pencilled, but carved, or cast in moulds, as carved in stone, or cast in metal, that all ages may not only hear of their name, read of their acts, but see their figures, all which are due rights and right honours to the memory of worthy deceased men; wherefore, this worthy deceased man, who was a wise and just magistrate, ought at the commonwealth's charge to have his statue in stone or metal, and to be set up in the most publick place in the city, that every particular person may think of him and remember his acts when they see his figure, which will not only be a due honour to him that is dead, but an encouragement to those that live after him, to imitate and follow his example, and that such magistrates and ministers of state that are employed after him may do as he hath done, as to be just, prudent, careful and industrious, which the gods grant for the sake of the commonwealth.[18]

---

[18] See Nigel Llewellyn, 'Honour in Life, Death and in the Memory: Funeral Monuments in Early Modern England' in *Transactions of the Royal Historical Society* VI (Cambridge: Cambridge University Press, 1996), pp. 179–200.

33 *An Accusing Oration for Refusing the Office of a Magistrate, and so Neglecting the Service of the Commonwealth*

*Noble Citizens,*

I have assembled you at this time to make a complaint against D. D. who, being chosen a magistrate, as believing him to be one of the ablest men for his wisdom amongst us and so fittest to be employed in the service and affairs of the commonwealth, hath refused the office and employment, choosing rather to live idly than to take pains and labour to do good, for which he ought to be punished either in body or estate; for it is not only an obstruction to the affairs of the commonwealth, but a dangerous example; for if all the wisest men should refuse the employment and management of state-affairs, leaving the government only to fools, the commonwealth would be quickly brought to ruin, in which ruin the wise men would suffer as much as other men; wherefore, for their own sakes as well as for the sake of their country, they ought to employ their bodies and minds in the service of the commonwealth, otherwise foolish statesmen and magistrates will make such disorder as no particular family or man could live safely, much less plentifully, for peace and plenty would be utterly destroyed with civil wars, were there no foreign enemies; whereas wise men can keep peace and make a commonwealth or kingdom flourish: for it is as difficult and hard to keep a commonwealth in peace and order as it is easy to cause wars and ruin, and more difficult to make peace when war is begun. Wherefore, the best way to keep a commonwealth in order, peace, and plenty is to choose wise and able magistrates, and not to let the wise men follow their own pleasures and delights, but to imploy them in the service of the commonwealth.[19,20]

34 *An Excusing Oration in Answer to the Former*

*Noble Citizens,*

I am come here at this time to speak for my self, and to tell you I deserve not to be punished either in my estate or person for refusing a charge

---

[19] The public duty of citizens is a popular theme in Renaissance and early-modern political theory. Writers often cite or allude to Cicero, who argues that 'we are not born for ourselves alone, but our country claims a share of our being', *De Officiis*, Book I. 7. 22.

[20] This Platonist reply to Cicero is rehearsed, for example, in More's *Utopia*, ed. George M. Logan and Robert M. Adams (Cambridge: Cambridge University Press, 1975), Dialogue I.

and employment I am not capable or fit to be employed in; for I confess I am naturally dull and lazy, no ways busy or active, and therefore unfit for state employments; and since it is a natural imperfection, I ought to be free from punishment, for the fault lies in nature not in me, and it would be a great injustice to lay nature's fault to my charge, and to punish me for that I cannot help; but perchance you will say this is only an excuse, and I may help this defect; but put the case it were so and I could help it, yet I do not find in myself such a supreme wit, judgement, understanding, knowledge, contrivance, prudence, patience, experience, and the like above other men, but that there be other men far beyond me; for though the orator that spake the last speech said I am a wise man, yet it is more than I know, and probable he says more than he believes; for it is the nature of some men to praise other men to their ruin, and praise in some cases, and at some times, and to some assemblies or persons, doth more hurt to the praised than all the dispraises could have done, nay, sometimes men receive a benefit by being dispraised, whereas praises would utterly ruin them. But as I said, put the case I were a wise man and could discharge the office of a magistrate as a wise man should do, yet if a company of fools or knaves join together to oppose my orders or power I can do little good, nay, had I other wise men joined in power and authority with me, yet we should do little good, for fools and knaves are too strong for honest and wise men because they are far more in number, and so much odds there is, as there are thousands of fools for one wise man; wherefore it is fortune, or chance, or some particular favour from the gods that govern commonwealths, and not those they call wise men; for the wisest men in the world cannot keep a people in peace if they be resolved and set to rebel; for when the generality is up in arms it is a folly for particular persons to oppose them; and when the generality will pull down particular persons from their power, particular persons can not stand; and when the generality will alter a particular government, the government must change; wherefore, the only and best means to keep up the commonwealth is to pray to the gods for peace, and to keep the people as much as may be to religious ceremonies, that they may fear the gods, which fear and devotion will make them obey their magistrates, which I wish, and leave them.[21]

---

[21] Compare the policy of the Empress of the Blazing World.

35 *An Oration against some Historians or Writers of State Affairs or Policy*

*Fellow Citizens,*

We have some men amongst us that seem to desire to be statesmen, and because they are not statesmen in practice they are statesmen in books, writing of state affairs. But how do they write? Not like wise, but like learned men; not to teach men what is best to be done but what evil hath been done, which is a relation of past, not an instruction to future actions. The truth is, they make an hash of many several authors, taken out of several pieces, to make up a dish to present to their readers, in hope they may enrich their host, if not with preferment yet with praise; but surely those are hungry, half starved guests that can feed with a *gusto* on such broken meat, although skilfully drest; and these cooks of other men's meat which are writers out of other men's works are not only unprofitable, but cumbersome in the state or commonwealth, filling our libraries and heads with repetition of old authors in new styles. Yet were they the authors or first writers of such books as treat of state affairs, they would do more hurt than good, and rather make division than unity, warr than peace; for instead of declaring the policy of state, they teach men to be politick against the state; and it is to be observed that much writing of that nature makes much trouble, wherein the pen doth more mischief than the sword, witness controversies that make atheism; for the more ignorant a people are, the more devout and obedient they are to god and his deputies, which are magistrates; wherefore it were very requisite that all such books should be burnt and all such writers silenced, or at least none should write of states-affairs but those the state allows or authorises.[22]

36 *An Oration Concurring with the Former*

*Fellow Citizens,*

I am of the former orator's opinion, that all books of politics, state affairs or national histories should be burnt, and none suffered to write any more books of that nature; otherwise not only every writer, but every

---

[22] Cf. *Newcastle's Advice*, p. 21. After the restoration of Charles II in 1660, the government curbed the power of the press by passing a Licensing Act (1662), and the volume of publications dropped sharply. It also limited freedom of discussion in an Act against Tumults and Disorders. See Paul Seaward, *The Cavalier Parliament and the Reconstruction of the Old Regime, 1661–1667* (Cambridge: Cambridge University Press, 1988), pp. 72f.

reader will pretend to be statesmen, which will bring an infallible ruin to the commonwealth, having more politicians than business, which will produce more faction than reformation. The truth is, many politicians will be apter to dissolve than agree to make good laws, and will sooner cause a destruction than govern a commonwealth; for every several politician would have a several policy; but could or would they all agree in their opinions, yet if every man were a statesman all particular affairs would be laid aside, which particular industries make up a general commerce, trade and traffick in the commonwealth: Wherefore take the former orator's advice, for the peace and preservation of this state, and suffer none to write or read any books but what recreates the mind, as poems, what increases their stores, as husbandry, what restores health, as medicines, what exercises the body, as arts, and what improves the understanding, as sciences; all which may be allowed without danger; but for divinity and state, let those be particular and not general, and rather be in the breast or brain of some than in the books or studies of many, and let them continue in tradition, but not in print. So will the people obey and not dispute, they will be practisers and not preachers, and will be content to be subjects and not endeavour to be soveraigns.

37 *An Oration somewhat Different from the Former*

*Fellow Citizens,*

I confess it is dangerous in a state when as some men think they are wiser than really they are, but more dangerous when as every man thinks himself wiser than his neighbour, for those thoughts make them proud, ambitious, and factious, and in the end mutinous and rebellious, and of all self-conceited persons, the self-conceited statesmen are the most dangerous, and oftentimes the most foolish; the greatest danger is that there are more fools than wise men, through which general defect a self-conceited statesman may be the head of fools, although but the tail of wise men, and head to tail is disproportionable; but it may be that this disproportion may make them unactive, by which they become less dangerous; wherefore I am not of the former orator's opinion, as to have all such books as treat of state affairs burnt, for the burning of such books may advance their authors' fame, but not advance the public good; neither do such books public hurt, by reason none but some few private persons read them, for the generality delights not in such studies; so as they will partly die in oblivion, especially if you take no notice of them.

38 *An Oration against those that lay an Aspersion upon the Retirement of Noblemen*

*Noble Citizens,*

We have some ill-natured people amongst us, that endeavour to turn all other men's actions but their own to the worst sense or construction; as for example, some of our nobles retire to their country habitations, for which those ill-natured or foolish persons exclaim against them, both in books and speeches, as that they retire through pride, ambition, and revenge, being discontented they are not the chief ministers of state, rulers in government, or counsellors for advices; also they would make their harmless country recreations, as hunting, hawking, racing, and the like sports, as also hospitality, dangerous designs, which is unjustly censured and wickedly wrested, to pull out the right and truth, to place falsehood, when as it may be easily known that most of our nobles which retire out of this metropolitan city to their country houses, retire either for pleasure, profit, quiet, or health, or all; for it is manifest that in a very great and populous city there is nothing but trouble, expenses, noise, and oftentimes malignant diseases, all which some ill-natured men and pretending politicians would have them suffer rather than to avoid.[23] But those men that are so wise to choose the best are not afraid of a bawling pen or tongue, and seldom consider or regard what they write or speak, and if they do, they only give such find-faults a pity or a scorn. But put the case, *Noble Citizens,* that some noblemen did retire out of some just discontent, as for example, imagine this kingdom or monarchy had been in a long civil war, and some noblemen had not only been so loyal as never to adhere to the rebels, but had served their prince to the last of their power, ventured their lives, lost their estates, and had endured great misery in a long banishment, and after an agreement of peace, and the proof of their honesty and loyalty, should be neglected or affronted instead of reward and favour; if these forsaken and ruined, although honest persons, should retire from court and city into the country, to bewail their misfortunes in solitary groans, or to pick up their scattered goods, broken inheritance, and tattered states, or to restore their half-dying posterity to some time of

---

[23] Margaret Cavendish's husband retired to his estate at Welbeck Abbey shortly after the Restoration, protesting to King Charles II that he was not displeased with the way Charles had treated him. See Introduction, p. xvi. The hypothetical nobleman discussed here has Newcastle's history, as his wife describes it in her *Life of . . . William Cavendish.* Newcastle, however, was not the only rejected Royalist. See Seaward, *The Cavalier Parliament,* p. 54.

life, should they be railed and exclaimed against? Can heaven bless a state or kingdom that will suffer such uncharitableness and inhumanity? Or can nature suffer her most noble-minded creatures to stay in the presence of public affronts, disgraces, and neglects, and not humbly turn their faces from them, or honestly endeavour not to trouble those, that have a desire to please? And if by their wise prudence, those retired persons can afford themselves some harmless recreations to mix and temper their over-careful and industrious labours, they ought not to be condemned for it; for God and nature mixes good and evil, and the greatest grief hath some refreshment of ease, and the hardest labours some rest, but only these find-faults are restless through envy and ambition, hoping by their busy heads, restless pens and abusive exclamations to rise to promotion and preferment, and though they pretend to discover seditions, they are the only authors of factions and seditions. Wherefore it would be very fit, *Noble Citizens*, that our ministers of state and magistrates should silence such bold persons that dare censure our nobles private and particular actions; for if they should have that liberty, they would in time censure this government and our governors of state and commonwealth, and who can foresee but that the common rout or people might take their factions or ill-natured or meddling dispositions for wisdom?

39  *An Oration for Liberty of Conscience*

*Fellow Citizens,*
It is very probable we shall fall into a civil war through the divers opinions in one and the same religion; for what hath been the cause of this hash in religion but the suffering of theological disputations in schools, colleges, churches, and chambers, as also books of controversies? All which ought not to have been suffered, but prohibited, by making laws of restraint; but since that freedom hath been given, the inconveniency cannot be avoided, unless the magistrates will give, or at least not oppose a free liberty to all; for if the people of this nation is so foolish or wilful or factious or irreligious as not to agree in one opinion and to unite in one religion, but will be of divers opinions, if not of divers religions, the governors must yield, or they will consume the civil government with the fire of their zeal; indeed they will consume themselves at last in their own confusion. Wherefore the best remedy to prevent their own ruin, with the ruin of the commonwealth, is to let them have liberty of conscience, conditionally that

they do not meddle with civil government or governors; and for security that they shall not, there must be a law made and enacted that whosoever doth preach, dispute, or talk against the government or governors, not only in this but of any other nation, shall be punished either with death, banishment, or fine; also for the quiet and peace of this kingdom there ought to be a strict law that no governor or magistrate shall in any kind infringe our just rights, our civil or common laws, nor our ancient customs; for if the one law should be made and not the other, the people would be slaves and the governors their tyrants.[24]

40 *An Oration against Liberty of Conscience*

*Fellow Citizens,*

I am not of the former orator's opinion; for if you give liberty in the church, you must give liberty in the state, and so let every one do what they will, which will be a strange government, or rather I may say, no government; for if there be no rules there can be no laws, and if there be no laws there can be no justice, and if no justice no safety, and if no safety no propriety, neither of goods, wives, children nor lives, and if there be no propriety there will be no husbandry and the lands will lie unmanured; also there will be neither trade nor traffic, all which will cause famine, war and ruin, and such a confusion as the kingdom will be like a chaos, which the gods keep us from.

41 *An Oration proposing a Mean betwixt the two former Opinions*

*Fellow Citizens,*

I am not of the two former orators' opinions, neither for an absolute liberty nor a forced unity, but between both, as neither to give them such liberty as for several opinions to gather into several congregations, nor to force them to such ceremonies as agree not with their consciences; and if those sects or separatists disturb not the canon, common,

---

[24] See Introduction, pp. xxvi–xxvii. In 1661, Parliament restored bishops to the House of Lords and revived ecclesiastical courts. In 1662 it passed an Act of Uniformity designed to expel Presbyterians from the clergy. The Conventicle Act (1664) and Five Mile Act (1665) imposed further restrictions on nonconformists. See Seaward, *The Cavalier Parliament*, pp. 56f, 162–95. These measures disappointed many people who had expected greater religious toleration.

or civil laws, not to disturb their bodies, minds, or estates: for if they disturb not the public weal, why should you disturb their private devotions? Wherefore, give them leave to follow their several opinions in their particular families, otherwise if you force them you will make them furious, and if you give them an absolute liberty you will make them factious.

42 *An Oration Reproving Vices*

*Noble Citizens,*

Being a fellow citizen with you, I ought not to forbear from persuading you to reform the disorders of this city, as not to suffer loose and idle persons to live without employment, or to pass by their abuses without punishment; also to reform the excess of vanity, luxury, drunkenness, and adultery, of which the chiefest are most guilty; for the poor and inferior sort hath not means to maintain those vices, although they endeavour to the utmost of their abilities; and as they have not means, so they have not that courage or rather impudence to act vices so publicly as the richer sort doth; for poverty is humble, which makes it modest, when as riches is proud and bold; the truth is, this city is like a surfeited body full of diseases, and I fear easy remedies, which are persuasions, will not cure you, except wars, plagues or famine come amongst you or be applied to you, for they may cure some although they will kill most: but one thing I wonder most at, that you send your children to school to be instructed in divinity and morality, which is to teach them to pray and to fast, to be humble and charitable, to be prudent and temperate, yet at home they have leave and liberty to be vain, idle, and expensive, to feed luxuriously, to play wantonly, and to live riotously, so that what good their tutors teach them by reading and preaching, their fathers corrupt them by example and precepts; they go forth to be schooled and come home to be fooled. Wherefore I cannot imagine why you should put your selves to that charge, to have your children taught and instructed to that which is good, and yet suffer them to do what is bad, unless you desire to see whether god or the devil be strongest in them; but if you cannot live more soberly, moderately, orderly, and honestly, the best way were to send your children so far from you as not to hear of you until you die, so that the next generation may be better, unless by nature you leave your sons to inherit your vices as they do your goods by birth, and then there is no hopes of amendment. It is likely you will say, why I stand here talking to you, and exhorting you? I answer, that Saint Paul sayeth, *by the foolishness of preaching men may be saved*: so I hope my words may work upon your hearts, as to persuade you not to spend your wealth, to waste your time, to end your lives so unprofitably, as neither to serve your god, your country nor your friends.

43 *An Oration concerning the Foreign Travels of Young Gentlemen*

*Noble Citizens*,

You think your sons not well bred unless you send them to travel into foreign nations, to see and understand fashions, customs, and manners of the world, by which they may learn the better to know themselves and to judge of others; but though you send your sons abroad in hope they will profit by their travels, yet you are for the most part deceived in your hopes and expectations: for our young men in this age get nothing by their travels but vanity and vice, which makes them fools; for they gain not any profitable understanding or knowledge to make them wise men; the truth is, they go forth of their own country civil men, but return brute beasts, as apes, goats, and swine, and some few return foxes, so that their travels metamorphose them from men to beasts; and as for their learning of several languages, give me leave to tell you that they learn more words than wit, which makes them speak much but not well. But to come to the drift of my speech, since our travelling gallants bring home only vanity and vice, as more prodigality than frugality, more luxury than temperance, more diseases than health, more extravagancy than discretion, more folly than experience, and more vice than virtue, it were better they should stay at home than travel as they do; for their travels are not only unprofitable to themselves and their country, but destructive; for their vices and vanity doth not only corrupt their own natures and civil manners, and waste their bodies and estates, but it corrupts all good government in the weal public; for which reason I think it most requisite and fit that none should travel without leave of the state or public counsel, and at their return should be accountable to the state and public counsel of their travels and the advantages they have made. Thus their travels would be profitable both to themselves and to their country; for they would be as a nursery and school to breed up youth to be wise men.[25]

---

[25] As a young man, William Newcastle had accompanied Sir Henry Wotton on an embassy to Savoy. The grand tour was *de rigueur* for young men of the Cavendish family. For

44  *An Oration concerning Plays and Players*

*Noble Citizens,*

Here is a company of players, which are for pleasure and pastime to those
that have nothing to do and money to spend; but give me leave to tell you,
you mis-spend your time and also your money, unless the players were
better actors and their plays better plays; for as their plays have no wit in
them, so the actors have no grace nor becoming behaviour in their actions;
for what is constraint is misbecoming, as being not natural, and whatsoever is unnatural is deformed: but pray, mistake me not, as believing I am
an enemy to plays or players, for I am an enemy only to foolish plays and
ill-actors, but for good plays well acted, I am so far from being an enemy
to them as I think there is nothing so profitable for youth, both to increase
their understanding and to fashion their behaviour; and for those that have
spare time, they cannot pass it more pleasingly; therefore let me advise you
that are magistrates of this city, to set up a company of players at the common charge, and to maintain some excellent poet to make good plays, and
certainly you will be no losers in so doing, but gainers, being the best and
readiest way of education for your children: for the poet will inform them
both of the world and the natures and humours of mankind, an easier and
delightfuller way than the school-men; and the actors will show them to
behave themselves more gracefully and becomingly than their dancing-
masters. Thus they will learn more both for their bodies and minds of
the poet and players than of their tutors and governors, or by studying
or travelling, which is expensive, laborious, and dangerous, whereas the
other is easy, delightful, safe, and profitable. Also one thing more I must
advise you, that you provide a practick judicious man to instruct the players to act well; for as they must have a poet to make their plays, so they
must have a tutor to teach them to act those plays, unless the poet will take
the pains to teach them himself, as to humour the passions and to express
the humours naturally, and not to act after the French fashion with high
strained voices, constrained motions, violent actions, and such transporta-
tion as is neither graceful, becoming, nor natural; but they must make love
soberly, implore favour humbly, complain seriously, lament sadly and not
affectedly, fantastically, constraintly, ragingly, furiously, and the like; all

example, Hobbes accompanied the 2nd and 3rd Earls of Devonshire on their European
travels. Cavendish's is an old-fashioned complaint, made, for example, in Roger Ascham's
*Schoolmaster* (1570). See John Walter Stoye, *English Travellers Abroad 1604–67. Their
Influence in English Society and Politics* (London: Cape, 1952).

which in my opinion they do senselessly, foolishly, and madly; for all feignings must be done as naturally as may be, that they may seem as real truths.[26]

---

[26] See Introduction, p. xviii, and compare the policy of the Emperor of the Blazing World. Compare, too, Hamlet's advice to the players. William Shakespeare, *The Tragedy of Hamlet, Prince of Denmark*, Act III, Scene 2. On Shakespeare, see *Sociable Letters*, cxxiii.

# SEVERAL CAUSES PLEADED IN SEVERAL COURTS OF JUDICATURE

## PART IV[27]

45  *Accusing and Pleading at the Bar before Judges, for and against a Woman that hath Killed her Husband*

*Most Reverend Judges,*

*The Plaintiff*: This woman, who is accused not only for killing a man, but her husband, we have for this grievous and horrid fact brought before your honours, to be judged according to the laws, delivering her to your justice and judgement.

*Defendant: Most Reverend, and Just Judges*, 'Tis true that this unhappy woman hath unfortunately killed her husband, but heaven knows, it was against her will, and as I may say against her knowledge: for her husband and she being lovingly together, not mistrusting any danger, on a sudden came a man who, as it seems, was her husband's enemy, for he assaulted her husband with a drawn sword; this woman seeing her husband in danger, as being unarmed and defenceless, was so afrighted as she knew not what she did; wherefore, she having got a dagger which lay in the room they were in, and thinking to thrust it into her husband's enemy, unawares thrust it into her husband's body, wherewith he fell down and immediately died, which when she saw and perceived the mistake, she was as distracted and at last fell into a trance, but being recovered out of that faint fit, she hath since remained a most sorrowful and lamenting widow; I express her sorrow, to prove her innocence from all evil constructions; for the death of her husband was not designed or intended by her, but by Fate and Fortune; and it is the duty of a loving wife, to defend her husband's honour, person, and life with all her endeavours, and if the success of her honest, loyal, and loving endeavours falls out unfortunately she ought not to be punished for her misfortune; for misfortune is no crime, but rather to be pitied and comforted, neither can justice make misfortune a law to condemn to die; and shall duty and loyalty be made traitors? Shall honest love be punished with torments and death? No, *Most Reverend Judges,*

---

[27]  The orations in Part IV resemble a model familiar from Sitvayn's *The Orator*, which contains speeches pro and con on a wide range of dramatic conflicts. See *The Orator: handling a hundred several discourses, in forme of declamations, some of the arguments being drawn from Titus Livius and other ancient writers, the rest of the author's own invention, parts of which are matters happened in our age.* Written in French by Alexander Sitvayn and Englishd by L. P. [Lazarus Piotte] (London, 1596).

love and loyalty ought to be honoured with praise and respect, and not with torments and death, and the death of this woman's husband was caused by a maskered[28] fear proceeding from an extraordinary love. Thus his death was a chance, not an intended murder.

*Plaintiff: Most Reverend Judges*, there can be no witness of the intention but her own knowledge and conscience, which are invisible and not provable, and therefore insufficient to acquit her; but that which is a sufficient witness against her intention, and may lawfully condemn her, is her endeavour to resist the judgement and sentence of death; for all good, loyal, and loving wives ought, nay, desire to live and die with their husbands when as they be free from all suspect, wherefore much more ought they to accompany their husbands in death who are liable to be judged and condemned for treason and murder; for as it is unlawful and irreligious for to act her own death, so it is dishonourable and impious to endeavour to resist the judgement of death by lawful authority, pleading by her lawyers most shamefully for life.

*Defendant: Most Reverend Judges*, it is not that she desires to live, but not to die infamously, as to die as a murderer of her husband; for though her husband was killed by her hand, yet he was not killed by her intention but by chance, which misfortune makes her life a torment to her, for being so unhappy as unwittingly to destroy him which her life did most delight with; but yet she would, if she could, rather live miserably than die dishonourably; for in her dishonourable death, both she and her husband doth doubly die.

*Plaintiff: Most Reverend Judges*, it were better two persons should dye four times over, than such a crime should be once pardoned; for the example will be more dangerous, than to have an innocent condemned would be grievous: but it is most probable, she is guilty.

46 *A Cause of Adultery Pleaded at the Bar before Judges*

*Most Reverend Judges,*

*Plaintiff*: Here is a man and a woman that were taken in adultery and brought hither to be judged, that they may suffer according to the law, which is death.[29]

---

[28] Bewildered or disoriented.

[29] Mosaic law had prescribed the death penalty for adulterous women and adultery was made a felony in 1650. The law was not strictly enforced – only seven people were indicted for

*Defendant: Most Reverend Judges*, This adulteress and adulterer, (for so in truth they are) although the woman is ashamed to confess in words, only in silent tears, yet the man confesseth his fault publicly and asks pardon, only he says it is a natural fault: for the desire of procreation is born and bred in all nature's animal creatures; it is an original appetite, but whether it be an original sin, he says, he doth not know; yet if it be, it may more justly be pardoned than gluttony, which was the cause of man's fall, witness *Eve* and the forbidden fruit; and that damnable sin, gluttony, that destroys many lives through surfeits, the law takes no notice of, but procreation that begets and makes life is punished by the law, which seems strange to reason, that cursed gluttony should be advanced and loving adultery hanged. Indeed, it is a great injustice, at least a grievous law; and surely our forefathers that made that law were defective either in bodies or minds, or at least in judgement; and though I confess it is not fit we should break or dissolve those laws, howsoever erroneous they are, that our predecessors made; yet we, their posterities and successors, may sweeten or qualify the extreme rigour of their laws, as in this case of adultery, to punish the bodies but to spare their lives; or to fine their estates and spare their bodies; for if the rigour of the law should be put in execution in all cases and to all persons, there would no man be free, either in his estate, person or life; but howsoever, this male-offender my client says that if he must die, yet he shall not die basely or dishonourably, by reason he shall die love's martyr; as for the female offender, she says that she was seduced by nature, as *Eve* by the devil, and women being of soft and tender dispositions do easily yield to an enticing appetite; besides, men being eloquent in persuading, prevalent in flattering, free in protesting, and earnest in vows and promises, all which hath such force with females who are credulous and believing creatures, as she had no power to deny him his desire. But both these lovers desire these most noble and just judges to consider, their crime is not caused through spite, envy, malice, revenge, scorn, pride, hate or the like sins, but through love, kindness, friendship, charity, generosity, humility and such like virtues, which caused this crime, namely adultery, so that it is the only sin that is built upon virtues: besides, this sin, namely adultery, hath a well-pleased countenance, a courtly behaviour, and an

adultery in Essex during the 1650s – and was repealed at the Restoration, although in 1675 an anonymous tract pleaded to have it reinstated. See Margaret R. Somerville, *Sex and Subjection* (London: Arnold, 1995), pp. 90–1; Jacqueline Eales, *Women in Early Modern England, 1500–1700* (London: UCL Press, 1998), p. 103.

eloquent speech, which is the cause most men and women are in love with this sin, the Gods forgive them for it; for this sin doth not appear with terrible and horrid aspect as murder, as to cause the very soul as much as the senses to be maskered[30] with fear; nor it doth not appear of so foul an aspect as gluttony and drunkenness, as to cause hate or aversion, but it hath so amiable an aspect as to cause love, and so fruitful an effect as to cause life and living creatures. They implore mercy and beg your favourable sentence, and since it is a natural effect for males and females to be adulterers, at least lovers, you may as soon destroy all animal creatures as this sin, if it be one; and if there be some men and women purely chaste, those are of divine compositions and not perfect naturals, their souls and bodies having more of the purity of the gods, than the gross corporeality of nature; but these two offendants confess they have proved themselves nature's creatures, and the woman says she is *Eve*'s daughter, but if you will spare her life she hopes to be as great a saint as *Mary Magdalene*; for she will beg pardon by repentance and wash out her sin with her tears.

*Plaintiff: Most Reverend Judges*, This pleader ought to be condemned, not only for a corrupt lawyer but a wicked man, and may very well be believed to be guilty of the same crime he pleads so well for; for if he were not guilty of the crime, he would not plead for a pardon.

*Defendant: Most Reverend Judges*, I am no more guilty of the sin than the interceding saints in heaven for sinners on earth; but if the pleader should be condemned for the cause of his client, neither truth would be heard nor right decided, so that all justice would be overthrown with malicious accusers and false witnesses. But howsoever, *Most Reverend Judges*, I am not to decide the cause, though I plead in the behalf of my clients, and it is the profession of a lawyer to speak for his clients and not against them, whatsoever their cause be; for this is the part of their opposites and I am not to fling the first stone.

*Plaintiff: Most Reverend Judges*, Howsoever he be affected, whether evil or not, yet the cause [he] pleads is a wicked cause, and the offender ought to be severely punished according to the punishing laws for such offences and offenders; and if adultery should be suffered, propriety and the right of inheritance would be lost in the obscurity of hidden adultery, or in the uncertainty of the right children or fathers.[31]

---

[30] Bewildered.      [31] Cf. Sitvayn, *The Orator*, Declamations 28, 36, 65.

47  *A Cause Pleaded at the Bar before Judges concerning Theft*

*Most Reverend, and Just Judges,*

*Plaintiff*: Here is a man which is accused for stealing privately and robbing openly, against all law and right, the goods of his neighbours, for which we have brought him before your Honours, appealing to the laws for satisfaction of the injuries, wrongs, and losses, leaving him to your justice and judgement.

*Defendant: Most Reverend Judges*, I am come here to plead for this poor man, my client, who is accused for stealing, which is a silent obscure way of taking the goods of other men for his own use; also this poor man (for so I may say he is, having nothing of his own to live on but what he is necessitated to take from other men) is accused for robbery, which is to take away the goods of other men in a visible way and forcible manner; all which he confesseth, as that the accusation against him is true; for he did both steal and rob for his own livelihood and maintenance of his old parents, which are past labouring, and for his young children, that are not able to help themselves, and for his weak, sick wife, that labours in child birth; for which he appeals to Nature who made all things in common, she made not some men to be rich and other men poor, some to surfeit with overmuch plenty and others to be starved for want: for when she made the world and the creatures in it, she did not divide the earth, nor the rest of the elements, but gave the use generally amongst them all.[32] But when governmental laws were devised by some usurping men, who were the greatest thieves and robbers, (for they robbed the rest of mankind of their natural liberties and inheritances, which is to be equal possessors of the world), these grand and original thieves and robbers, which are called moral philosophers or commonwealth makers, were not only thieves and tyrants to the generality of mankind, but they were rebels against Nature, imprisoning Nature within the jail of restraint, keeping her to the spare diet of temperance, binding her with laws, and enslaving her with propriety, where as all is in common with Nature. Wherefore, being against Nature's laws for any man to possess more of the world or the goods of the world than another man, those that have more wealth or power than other men ought to be punished as usurpers and robbers, and not those that are poor and powerless. Therefore, if you be just judges of Nature

---

[32] Cavendish may have associated these views with Gerald Winstanley. See 'A New-Yeers Gift for the Parliament and Armie' (1650) in David Wootton ed., *Divine Right and Democracy* (Harmondsworth: Penguin Books, 1986), pp. 321–3.

and not of art, judges for right and not for wrong, if you be judges of the most ancient laws and not usurping tyrants, you will not only quit this poor man and set him free from his accusers, which are his and such poor men's abusers, but you will cause his accusers, who are rich, to divide their wealth equally with him and all his family; for which judgement you will gain Nature's favour, which is the empress of mankind, her government is the ancientest, noblest, generousest, heroickest, and royalest, and her laws are not only the ancientest, (for there are no records before Nature's laws, so that they are the fundamental laws of the universe, and the most common laws extending to all creatures), but they are the wisest laws, and yet the freest; also Nature is the most justest judge, both for rewards and punishments; for she rewards her creatures that observe her laws as they ought to do with delight and pleasure, but those that break or abuse her laws, as in destroying their fellow creatures by untimely deaths or unnatural torments, or do riot and oppress her with excess, she punishes them with grief, pains, and sicknesses, and if you will avoid the punishment of remorse, grief, and repentance, save this poor necessitated man from violence and the cruelty of these inhuman, unnatural, destroying laws.

*Plaintiff: Most Reverend Judges,* This man, who is Nature's lawyer and pleader, ought to be banished from this place, and his profession of pleading out of all civilest governments; for he talks he knows not what of Nature's laws, whereas there is no law in Nature, for Nature is lawless, and hath made all her creatures so, as to be wild and ravenous, to be insatiable and injurious, to be unjust, cruel, destructive, and so disorderous that, if it were not for civil government ordained from an higher power, as from the creator of nature her self, all her works would be in a confusion, and sow their own destruction. But man is not all of Nature's work, but only in his outward frame, having an inward celestial and divine composition and a supreme power given him by the Gods to rule and govern Nature; so that if your Honours submit to the plea of this babbler you will make the rulers and governors of Nature the slaves of Nature; wherefore, if you be celestial and not natural judges, and will give divine judgement and not judge according to brutal senses, you will condemn this notorious thief and wild robber to the gallows, that his life may be the satisfaction for the wrongs, and his death an example for a warning to prevent the like crimes.[33]

---

[33] Cf. Sitvayn, *The Orator*, Declamations 14, 84.

48  *A Cause Pleaded before Judges betwixt two Bastards*

*Most Reverend Judges,*
*Plaintiff*: There be two laws in this kingdom which seem to be very unjust; the one is that if a woman be got with child by one man, and marries another before her child is born, that child must inherit her husbands estate if it be a son, so that one man's son comes to be an other man's heir by the law. The other is that if a man begets a son before marriage and he marries not the woman till after his son is born, and though the marriage cancels the fault of adultery and is an atonement for the sin or crime, both to God and the law, yet the innocent child that was in no fault is put by the inheritance by the law; indeed, the son so born inherits only the disgrace of a bastard, but not his fathers estate; and thus if the woman be incontinent, a man's own begotten son shall not inherit, and another mans bastard be his heir. The same case is brought to be pleaded before your honours, for two sons of one woman, but not of one father, the eldest being her husbands, begotten and born before marriage, the other begotten by an other man, but born a month after her marriage with the first sons father. The son born after marriage claims his mothers husbands estate as inheritance by law, the other claims the estate as a natural right.
*Defendant: Most Reverend Judges*, the son born to inherit claims the estate by the right of birth, and hopes your Honours will not suffer his birthright to be taken from him.
*Plaintiff: Most Reverend Judges*, the right begotten son doth not challenge his father's estate as his right by birth, but as his right by gift; for his father by deed gave him that which the law took from him; for his estate being not entailed, he might give it to whom he would, and he could not give it more justly, honestly, and lovingly, than to his own son; but had he not a child of his own to have given it to, yet surely he would never have left it, if he had power to dispose of it, to a son of his inconstant wife or friend, which bore him to his shame and dishonour; but the case is so clear for his true begotten son as it needs no more pleading.[34]

49  *A Cause Pleaded before Judges between an Husband and his Wife*

*Most Reverend Judges,*
*Plaintiff*: Here is a woman born of good parents, brought a great portion, and makes a chaste wife, yet her husband is so unkind and so cruel as he

---

[34] Cf. Sitvayn, *The Orator*, Declamations 29, 35, 51.

doth not only beat her often, but so grievously and sorely as she is weary of her life, and therefore she beseeches your Honours to take so much commiseration of her cause as to bind her husband to a good behaviour, or to grant her a bill of divorce and some allowance from him, that she may live absent in peace.[35]

*Defendant: Most Reverend Judges*, A husband's anger, nor yet his corrections, is not a sufficient plea for a wife to part from her husband; for a woman when she marries makes a promise before God and his divine minister in the sacred temple, that she takes her husband to have and to hold, for better for worse, and that she will be dutiful and obedient, as also constant to him so long as life lasts, and so plights her troth; wherefore it is against the laws of God and his Church to sue for a divorce; also it is against her duty to complain; wherefore she ought by the laws of God, and consequently by all other laws, to suffer patiently, did she give her husband no cause to use her so severely.

*Plaintiff: Most Reverend Judges*, A wife is not bound by any laws but religion to hazard her life, and she fears he will kill her in his fury, and therefore for the safety of her life she desires your Honours will quit her of the danger.

*Defendant: Most Reverend Judges*, A wife is bound both by the law of Nature and God to hazard her life, not only for her husband's safety, honour, and pleasure, but for his humour; for a wife is bound to leave her parents, country, and what else soever, to go with her husband wheresoever he goes and will have her go with him, were it on the dangerous seas, or into barren deserts, or perpetual banishments, or bloody wars, besides child-birth; all which is more dangerous and painful than blows; but howsoever, it is as lawful for an husband to govern, rule, and correct his wife, as for parents to rule, govern, and correct their children, or for masters to rule, govern, and correct their servants or slaves.

*Plaintiff*: But parents ought not strike or cruelly use their children, nor masters their servants or slaves, without faults committed.

---

[35] On attitudes to wife-beating see Somerville, *Sex and Subjection*, pp. 90–7; Elizabeth Foyster, 'Male Honour, Social Control and Wife Beating in Late Stuart England' in *Transactions of the Royal Historical Society*, vol. VI (Cambridge: Cambridge University Press, 1996), pp. 215–24; Anthony Fletcher, *Gender, Sex and Subordination in England, 1500–1800* (New Haven: Yale University Press, 1995), ch. 6. Spouses could sue in the church courts for a separation on grounds of ill-treatment, and an informal system of separation existed when husband or wife simply left the marital home. However, the church courts could prosecute women who did not live with their husbands. See Eales, *Women in Early Modern England*, p. 68. On the theme of domestic violence cf. Sitvayn, *The Orator*, Declamation 16.

*Defendant*: Parents, masters, and husbands in the case of ruling, governing, correcting, punishing or using their children, servants, slaves, and wives, ought to be their own judges, and no other. But, *Most Reverend Judges*, she is not free from fault, for though she be chaste, yet she is a scold, she gives her husband more unkind words than he gives her unkind blows, and her tongue provokes his hand to strike her; but as she is lavish of her words, so she is of his estate, not so much with what she spends as with that she spoils, and though he can keep her from the one, he cannot hinder her from the other; for she is not only unhuswifely and careless of the main stock, but she breaks, rends, and spoils all his goods out of a malicious revenge and evil nature; yet howsoever, were she the best wife that could be and he the worst husband, the law hath no power to mend him and help her, for the law ought not to intermeddle in their quarrel, as having no more power to take away the prerogative of a husband than the prerogative of parents and masters; for whensoever the law takes the part of a servant against his master, a subject against his prince, a child against his parents, or a wife against her husband, the law doth unjustly usurp on their rights and privileges, which rights and privileges they received from Nature, God and morality.

## 50 *A Widows Cause Pleaded before Judges in the Court of Equity*

*Most Reverend Judges*,
*Plaintiff*: Here is a poor widow of a rich husband, who in his lifetime did allow her little, and at his death left her less; for he only left her a small annuity during her life, which is so small as cannot maintain her, neither like his widow, nor indeed in any decent fashion; for she having no jointure, he to bar her of her widows share gave her this small annuity, knowing that otherwise she should have had the third part of his estate during life, but he by a deed and gift of a little hath cast out her claim from the common law, wherefore she doth appeal to this court of equity and conscience, hoping to have justice accordingly.
*Defendant: Most Reverend Judges*, there is no reason, equity, nor conscience that the widow should carry away during her life so great a part of her husband's estate as to impoverish his children and ruin his family; besides, it hinders the paying of debts, and there be very few families that have not debts as well as children, which creditors ought to be paid as well, as children to have portions: and were there no debts, yet many children's

portions, although but small, would shrink a great estate almost into nothing; but if a widow carries out the third part, there will be little left for after posterity when every child hath had their portion, indeed so little as after posterity will have nothing to live on, nor to be bred up with, which is the cause there are so many noble, honourable, and right worshipful beggars; nay, it makes them not only beggars, but base and wicked, for having not means according to their births, nor minds according to their means, despising their fortunes they take desperate courses, or else their minds are so dejected as they degenerate from their births and do base actions.

*Plaintiff: Most Reverend Judges*, It is against conscience and equity that the mother that bred and bore her children, with fear, sorrow, pain, and danger of her life, should be left poorer than the children that were born from her.

*Defendant: Most Reverend Judges*, It is against all reason, equity, and conscience that parents should get and bring forth children and not provide for those children; for if they give them no means to live, as neither by education to get means, nor some allowance or means to live, their children will have small reason to thank their parents, or natural affection to be dutiful to them, for giving them a miserable life, which deserves no thanks, nor can challenge a duty; for as children are bound by the laws of nature to assist their parents, so parents are bound by the laws of nature to provide for their children's subsistence, and when the bonds are broken of one part, the other part is free. But, *Most Reverend Judges*, I do not plead against the mother's or wife's livelihood; for it is not that mothers and wives ought not to be provided for, for a man ought to be a kind husband as well as a loving father, but a wife ought not to be the ruin either of her own or her husbands children, and if she be a natural mother she ought to spare for her children and not to spend what her children should have, but most women do not only spend what their children should have but give it away to a second husband, to the ruin of the first husband's children and family; for this reason, wise men that are husbands, not knowing what their wives will do when they are dead, leave them as little as they can, securing their own estates and families as much as they possibly can from the spoils and ruins which strangers, as second husbands, make; for it were more conscionable not to leave a wife any maintenance than too much, and better one should suffer than many perish, at least it is better that a widow should live poorly all her life than that an honourable family should be poor to all succession: wherefore this widow in conscience ought to have no more out of her dead husband's estate than what he hath left her, which is enough for necessity though not for vanity, enough to live a solitary widow as she ought to do, although not enough to enrich a second husband which a hundred to one but she would do if she had it; but her husband was a wise man, a careful father, and a prudent husband in not giving his wife the liberty to play the fool.

51 *A Cause Pleaded before Judges betwixt a Master and his Servant*

*Most Reverend Judges,*

*Plaintiff*: Here is a poor servant, which served his master honestly, and his master hath turned him out of his service without his wages, which are due unto him by right of bargain and agreement made betwixt them, which bargain and agreement he hath broken, and unjustly detains his wages.

*Defendant*: *Most Reverend Judges*, this servant accuses his master falsely, and challenges that which he ought not to have, as so much for his wages, for the bargain was that his master would give him so much wages to do so much work, he did not hire him to be idle, so that a master is not bound to keep a lazy servant, nor to pay him his wages, unless he had done the work he was hired to do, and not only to do it, but to do according to his master's will and good liking.

*Plaintiff*: *Most Reverend Judges*, If a master's finding fault shall be sufficient to bar a servant of his wages, no servants could live by their labours, for masters would find faults a purpose to save their hire.

*Defendant*: *Most Reverend Judges*, If servants should live idly or disorderly or disobediently, or make waste and spoil of their masters' goods and estate, and be maintained with meat, drink, lodging and wages, their masters would become poorer than their servants, and live in more subjection; rather than so, the masters would serve themselves and keep no servants; for surely, men will rather be their own servants than to be servants or rather slaves to their servants, so that servants would not only want wages but food, and starve for want; for if they gain nothing by their labour and have no means of their own, they must upon necessity perish; and for example's sake, as well as justice, this servant ought not to be paid his wages, for he doth not deserve it and therefore 'tis not his right nor due to have it.

52 *Two Lawyers Plead before Judges a Cause betwixt a Father and his Son*

*Most Reverend Judges,*

*Plaintiff against the father*: Here is the son which ought to be his father's heir, whom for marrying against his fathers consent his father hath disinherited, which is against all law or right, both of God, nature, and man.

*Defendant*: *Most Reverend Judges*, disobedient children ought to have no part nor parcel of their parents' estate, as lands, goods, or whatsoever; for if the parents have no duty nor obedience from their child, their child can challenge no part of their parents' estate, and since he hath married disobediently he ought to live poorly, or to get his living by his own labour or industry.

*Plaintiff*: *Most Reverend Judges*, there is no reason nor law that if one man commit a fault to another, that man should commit another to be quit with him; and put the case the son were unnaturally disobedient, must the father be unnaturally cruel to be revenged of him?

*Defendant*: *Most Reverend Judges*, Parents are the fittest judges of their children's faults and crimes committed against them. But howsoever, parents cannot be thought cruel or unnatural to punish the crimes of their children, no more than God can be said to be cruel or unjust to punish sinners; for God who made creatures may do what he pleases with them; for being his own work, he may dispose or order them as he thinks best, or as he pleaseth: so parents that begot their children may do the like in things concerning themselves.

*Plaintiff*: But God is merciful, wherefore parents ought to be natural.

*Defendant*: God is just, and therefore children ought to be dutiful.

*Plaintiff*: But if God should punish his creatures according to their desert, no man would be saved.

*Defendant*: And if children should do what they list, there would be no government; for parents would be made slaves and their children masters: so if God should not punish some of his creatures, all would be damned, and to make up the fullness of their sins they would despise his love and not fear his power, and so they would neither love nor fear God; so children would have neither duty nor obedience to their parents: but to prove it a clear cause, his estate is free from all entails, and wholly in his own power to dispose of it as he pleases, and to give it to whom he will, and therefore his son can challenge nothing by law or right.[36]

---

[36] Cf. Sitvayn, *The Orator*, Declamations 37, 62, 67, 71.

# SPEECHES TO THE KING IN COUNCIL
## PART V

53  *A Privy Councillors Speech to his Sovereign*

*Dread Sovereign,*
Here are many of your noble subjects chosen out to be, I cannot say privy councillors, by reason there be too many to keep secrets of state, which shows we are rather councillors for form than for business, councillors in name rather than councillors in nature; wherefore we shall not need to trouble your Majesty or ourselves, the one to hear, the other to speak long *orations* or tedious *speeches*; for should we speak, we should rather speak like fools than wise men, by reason we are not acquainted with your Majesty's cabinet designs or intrigues; and so being your Majesty's general and not particular councillors, must needs speak at random: wherefore we beseech your Majesty not to censure our judgements, but our ignorances in not knowing your Majesty's most private, as cabinet desires, designs, and intrigues.[37]

54  *A Petition and Plea at the Council Table, before the King and his Council, concerning two Brothers Condemned by the Laws to Die*

*May it please your Most Sacred Majesty,*
I am come here to your Majesty's council table to plead the cause of two brothers whose cause hath been heard, judged, cast, and condemned by the judges of the laws of this land, and must suffer death unless your Majesty acquit or pardon them; indeed their cause is hard, for they were forced either to offend the laws of government or the laws of honour; the laws of government threatened bodily death, the laws of honour threatened infamy, and being worthy persons they chose rather to venture life than

---

[37] Cf. *Blazing World*, n. 178. Newcastle advised Charles II to keep his Privy Council small, and urged that councillors should speak briefly and clearly. 'Long orations at Council, one to speak like Tully and the other like Tacitus is very ridiculous.' See *Newcastle's Advice*, pp. 54–5. In 1679, Charles did in fact dissolve his Privy Council and replace it with a smaller one. At the Restoration, the King was felt to be in need of reliable councillors. E.g., 'There was in no conjuncture more need ... than that all who were eminently trusted by him should be men of unquestionable sincerity, who with industry and dexterity should first endeavour to compose the public disorders, and then to provide for peace and settlement of the kingdom, before they applied themselves to make or improve their own particular fortunes.' *The Life of Edward Hyde, Earl of Clarendon*, 2 vols. (Oxford, 1857), vol. I, pp. 273–4, quoted in Seaward, *The Restoration*.

to live dishonourably; but their crime, or (it may rather be called) their justice, which the laws of the land have condemned them for, is for killing, or rather punishing their sister for the impurity, immodesty, dishonesty, and dishonour of unchastity, which was an offence to the Gods, a reproach to her life, a disgrace to her race, a dishonour to her kindred, and an infamy to her family; as for the sin, they passed that by, to be judged of by the Gods, her own reproach they regarded not, the disgrace of her race they endeavoured to obscure; but as for the dishonour to her kindred and infamy to her family, her brothers were resolved to wash off the dishonour with her blood, and to rub out the black spot of infamy with her death, which resolution they put in execution, forcing a surgeon to open an artery vein through which she bled to death. Besides, had they let her have lived, the laws of the land would have punished her, which would have been a double dishonour and a recorded infamy, receiving as much dishonour by her public punishment, as her private crime. Wherefore, to prevent as well as to take off all disgrace, they were her executioners, by forcing the surgeon to strike an artery, a very easy death for so great an offender: but the natural affections from brothers to a sister did desire she might die with as little pain as might be: now dead she is, and they condemned to die for her death unless your Majesty will pardon them, and it will be a gracious act to pardon worthy men, such men as preferred honour before life.

55 *A Speech of one of the Privy Councillors which is an Answer to the former Plea and Petition*

*May it please your Majesty*

To give me leave as one of your Council to answer this man. As for parents to kill their children, for children to kill their parents, for brethren to kill each other, and sisters their brothers, or brothers their sisters, or nieces or nephews their uncles or aunts, or uncles and aunts to kill their nephews or nieces or cousins german,[38] is unnatural, or to be the cause of their death is unnatural, I may say a great sin in nature; wherefore these two brothers that were the cause, indeed the actors in effect of their sisters death, have sinned against the Gods, Nature, and the laws of good government, for which they deserve punishment, both in this world and in the world after this life; and as for that which is called honour, it is but the opinion of some men, a mere fancy, not any real good, only a name to persuade men

---

[38] First cousins.

to do evil actions, as to fight duels, to make wars, to murder friends, nay, to murder themselves; all which is against Gods, men's, and Nature's laws, which is inhuman, uncharitable, unnatural, and impious.

## 56  *The Petitioners Reply*

*Most Dread Sovereign,*
Since your Majesty is pleased to hear the suits of humble petitioners, and the causes of pleaders, and the defences of condemned persons, as your condemned subjects, at your Council Board, their last refuge in extremity, appealing to your Majesty's self where your Majesty sits in person to hear not only counsels but complaints, I shall answer this Privy Councillor, whose judgement is more severe than I hope your Majesty will be in your sentence; he says it is inhuman, uncharitable, unnatural, and impious for near allies to kill each other; but neither your Majesty, nor your most loyal subjects, should nor would think nor believe so if your Majesty had a civil rebellious war, which I pray the Gods to keep you from; yet in all civil wars near allies fight against one another and kill one another, believing they do not only their King but God good service in so doing; for what pious men or loyal subjects would not kill their fathers or their sons, that fight against their King or do but oppose his will and pleasure? Nay, those that speak against it ought to be accounted traitors; and as for honour, which is said only to be an opinion and fancy of some men, yet it is such an opinion and fancy that without it men would neither be generous nor valiant, just nor grateful, faithful nor trusty, but all men would be sordid, covetous, cowards, false cheats, unthankful, and treacherous; besides, wit and learning would be quite abolished or buried in oblivion, and if men care not for esteem, respect, and praise, men would not care to do that which is good, but on the contrary would do all the hurt and evil they could; for praise keeps men from evil more than laws or punishment, and praise is more powerful to persuade and to allure men to good than strength or authority hath power to enforce men to good, and honour lives in praise, and praise lives in worthy acts, which worthy acts fame records, that after-ages may know what just, valiant, generous, wise, learned, witty, ingenious, industrious, pious, faithful, and virtuous men lived in former times, which knowledge will make posterity desirous and industrious to do as their forefathers have done. Thus do good and honourable acts beget their like in after-ages, which is a race of worthy deeds. Wherefore, your Majesty for the good of the present and future times will favour these men

that love honour more than life, and fear disgrace more than death, which
is the cause of the two brothers for whom I plead and beg your Majesty's
pardon.

## 57  *The Kings Answer*

I neither ought to approve the act of those two brothers concerning the
death of their sister, nor to obstruct or oppose my laws in their condemnment: yet since their act was to take away disgrace, and not out of malice,
and through a hate to the crime not to the person, I am not willing to leave
them to the punishment, and the laws being satisfied by their arraignment,
judgement, and condemnment, I will give them their lives, lands, goods,
and liberties which the laws took from them, and so leave them to God's
mercy for grace to repent their sin.

## 58  *A Privy Councillors speech at the Council Board to his Sovereign*

*Most Gracious Sovereign,*
This your city, wherein your majesty doth chiefly reside, grows too big
for the rest of your kingdom, indeed so big as it will be too unruly and
unwieldy to be governed, and being fully populated it will not only be
apt to corrupt the air, and so cause often and great plagues[39] which may
infect the whole kingdom; for where many people are, there is much
dung and filth, both within the streets and houses, as also foul bodies and
corrupt humours, which of necessity must be very unwholesome; but it
will devour the rest of the kingdom, for it is the mouth and belly that
devours the fruitful increase of the land, yet labours not to husband the
ground: besides, the richest and noblest of your subjects residing for the
most part in the city, as being the chief city, rob the country and enrich
the city; for what they receive in the country they spend in the city, so
that they feed on the labours of the poor countrymen, and are enriched
by the vanities of the nobles. Thus they thrive by vanity and live by spoils,
wasting the plenty, beggaring the gentry, and ruining the country and
so the kingdom. Also too great and populous a city is not only a head
too great for the body of the commonwealth, but like a head that is full

---

[39] Cf. Oration 122. There were outbreaks of plague in London in 1603, 1625, and again in
1665, three years after *Orations* was published. See Roy Porter, *London. A Social History*
(London: Hamish Hamilton, 1994), pp. 80–4. See also *Blazing World*, n. 97.

of gross humours, indeed a great city is a head filled with evil designs, and not only a head with evil designs, but it is the tongue of detraction, the heart of civil war, the magazine of warring arms, and the treasury to maintain rebellious armies; for though they are more apt to mutiny than to fight, and more apt to rise in tumults than in arms, yet more apt to take up arms than to keep peace; and though they have neither conduct nor courage, yet they will destroy with force and fury whosoever will offer to oppose them; and their great plenty will make them more apt to rebel than if they were pinched with necessity; for their wealth makes them proud, their pride makes them ambitious, their ambition makes them envious, their envy makes them factious, their faction makes them mutinous, and in a tumultuous mutiny they will endeavour to pull your majesty from your throne, break your laws, and make havoc and spoil of all the goods and lives of your loyalest ministers of state and noblest persons about you, and for the most part, the most honest and worthiest persons they can come to they will destroy. Thus a great city is too rich to be obedient, too proud to be governed, too populous to be quiet, and too factious to live peaceably.[40]

59  *A Privy Councillors Speech to his Sovereign, concerning Trade*

*Dread Sovereign,*

I think it my duty to inform your Majesty that trade is so decayed as it will in a short time ruin your kingdom if not timely repaired; for this kingdom being an island, trade is the foundation to uphold it, without which foundation it will fall to ruin; and the chief persons of and for trading in an island are merchant adventurers, which are both foreign and home traffickers. These merchants your Majesty should assist and defend to the utmost of your power. As for the advancing of trade, there be three things; the first is easy taxes for customs; the second is to secure them from enemies at sea; the third is not to suffer your neighbour nations to

[40] Charles I had lost control over London at the beginning of the Civil War. After the Restoration, Charles II was careful to re-establish control over the towns (The Corporation Act, 1661) and particularly over the military forces of London (An Act for Ordering the Forces in the Several Counties of this Kingdom, 1662). This speech echoes *Newcastle's Advice*, where he advises the King to re-establish control over the towns, and especially over London's 'trained bands', *Newcastle's Advice*, pp. 6–7, 9. The same view is expressed by Hobbes in *Leviathan*, vol. II, ch. 29. See Valerie Pearl, *London and the Outbreak of the Puritan Revolution. City Government and National Policy, 1625–43* (Oxford: Oxford University Press, 1961).

encroach upon their privileges or to take the trading from them: as for the first, to lessen your customs will lessen your revenue, and that ought not to be, by reason your revenue is not so great as to admit of any diminution, your charge being extraordinary great; but your Majesty may secure them at sea by your shipping, and maintain their privileges abroad and at home by your power, which actions will not only cause your neighbours to fear you but your subjects to love you, the one for your force, the other for your favour. And give me leave, *Dread Sovereign*, to inform you that the more merchant adventurers you have, the more power and strength at sea you have; for shipping increases with their trade, in so much as your merchant adventurers will both increase your power and wealth; for if they be rich, the kingdom cannot be poor, and if the kingdom be rich, your Majesty cannot be poor; besides, their ships of burden are an assistance to your ships of war, both which I beseech the Gods to increase for your Majesty's, and your subjects' security.[41]

60 *An Oration to his Majesty for Preventing imminent Dangers*

*Dread Sovereign,*

I think it my duty, being one of your Privy Councillors, to give your Majesty advice, lest sudden dangers may surprise you, or at least great disorders may give you great troubles; for certainly, if your Majesty take not a speedy course to rectify some errors, you will soon have a civil war, which I pray the Gods to avert: the first error is that justice is corrupted; the second that vanity is excessive; the third and worst that your treasury is empty: to rectify injustice is to suffer no offices to be sold nor bribes to be taken; to rectify the excess of vanity is to see that a law be made that every degree or quality is to be known or distinguished by their habits, and to set a stint or proportion in feasting,[42] as that the greatest feast shall not exceed such a price or charge as your Majesty and your Great Council shall think fit; and to rectify your empty treasury is to provide that first your Majesty's expenses must not be above your revenue; also to take great care that your officers and receivers do not cozen[43] your Majesty; for if your expenses

---

[41] This again echoes *Newcastle's Advice*, pp. 19, 36–7. Charles II's government inherited a large burden of debt, and sought to raise revenue through customs and excise taxes. See Seaward, *The Restoration*, pp. 103–10. This was one important reason for encouraging trade.

[42] On sumptuary laws see Introduction, p. xxviii; Orations 118 and 119; *Blazing World*, n. 23.

[43] Cheat.

be above your revenue, and that your officers and receivers deceive you, your Majesty must be necessitated to tax your people, which will so much discontent your subjects in general as will cause them to murmur and make them apt to rebel, and if they should rebel, your Majesty for want of money would not be able to resist them or to help yourself; also for want of money, your Majesty's magazines are as empty as your treasury. Wherefore, your Majesty must be industrious to fill the one and to store the other, that your majesty may have arms and ammunition for your use if need require.

61 *A Privy Councillors Speech to the King at the Council Board*

*May it please your Majesty,*
There are some needy, or rather spending or wasting unthrifts that have got from your Majesty leave for monopolies,[44] not caring what harm they do your Majesty so they may reap a profit to themselves; but were they as meritorious subjects as any your majesty hath, yet they cannot be so deserving as to displease many thousands of your other subjects, to favour and reward some few particular persons, and for the advancing and enriching of those persons, many hundreds, nay thousands, are ruined, at least impoverished; but if your Majesty were any ways the better, or received any profit, either by increasing and enriching your treasures or for the service of your wars, or that it were any ways beneficial for your government, or that you did receive any pleasure or delight thereby, monopolies ought not to be spoken against; but it is so far from that, as it impoverishes your Majesty's store by impoverishing your subjects, by their engrossing and then enhancing particular commodities, and when the generality of your subjects are poor, your Majesty cannot be rich; for your revenue comes or is drawn from the generality throughout your whole kingdom, and not from some particular persons; for though particular persons may make your Majesty poor by receiving from your majesty

---

[44] Opposition to monopolies, and anxiety that the King might use his prerogative to grant patents in defiance of the law, continued during the 1660s. In a Parliamentary debate about the Canary Company, a speaker argued that 'If the king can in one particular destroy by a patent this highest and most sacred security . . . by the same rule he may certainly take away the lands, privilege or rights of the subjects whatsoever', quoted in Seaward, *The Cavalier Parliament*, pp. 285–6. Many Royalists, including Newcastle and Hobbes, opposed monopolies and regarded them as destructive of the commonwealth. See *Newcastle's Advice*, p. 37; *Leviathan*, vol. II, ch. 22.

great gifts, yet particular persons cannot make your Majesty rich with particular presents or assessments. Thus particular persons may drain your treasury but not fill it. Neither can monopolies nor monopolizers serve you in your wars; for though monopolies and monopolizers may be the cause of civil wars by discontenting the people, yet they cannot maintain your wars, nor defend your person nor pacify the people unless by the sacrifices of their lives, and those will not always satisfy them; for whensoever a rebellion is raised and civil wars begun, it is a long time before there can be peace again. Neither can monopolies be beneficial to the commonwealth, for the commonwealth thrives in equal distributions, whereas encroachments, engrossings and hoardings of several and particular commodities impoverish the commonwealth, like as when some men hoard up corn it causes a dearth, enhancing the price so high as the poorer people are not able to buy it, or at least not so much as daily to feed them; the like for money, when rich miserable men hoard up money it makes such a scarcity of it that the poor people, although they labour painfully, yet cannot get enough to maintain themselves, their wives, and children; for the scarcer money is, the cheaper is their work, in so much as poor labouring men cannot get half the worth of their labour: neither doth your Majesty receive any pleasure or delight by granting monopolies or monopolizers; for what pleasure can it be to hear the murmurs and complaints of your poor subjects? What pleasure can it be for your Majesty to have monopolizers to spend what they get by their monopolies on mistresses, luxury, and vanity? They are not to entertain your Majesty with masques, plays, shows, sports and pastimes, for you pay dear for those delights without their assistance. The truth is that those monopolizers get more than they ought to do that way, and yet not so much as the people loses; like as those that plunder a city, the city loses more than the soldiers get by their plunder, for they can make little profit of those commodities that the citizens grew rich by, and the soldiers do not only take the goods but spoil the trade; the like do monopolizers; indeed they are devouring worms in a commonwealth, eating out the very bowels, which is trade, for without trade a commonwealth cannot well subsist; for how should men live by one another, but by trading? But we are sure that your gracious Majesty did not know or think what a mischief monopolies are in a commonwealth, otherwise we your Majesty's councillors know, your Majesty would never have granted or suffered such sores upon your loyal subjects.

62 *A Privy Councillors Speech to his Majesty at the Council Board*

*May it please your Sacred Majesty,*
These petitioners that petition for reformations of government, and complain for the breach of their privileges, and exclaim against their magistrates and your Majesty's ministers of state, are to be considered as dangerous persons, for their petitions are forerunners of civil wars if not timely prevented; for though they cloak their treacherous designs under fair and humble words at the first, yet no doubt but they will persist and go on in a rough and rude manner; for what they call in their petition their humble complaints are factious and seditious murmurings, and what they name their humble desires of redress are presumptuous demands, and the number of the petitioners are a rebellious insurrection, for which they ought to be severely punished, some of them with imprisonment and some with the loss of their goods, others to be punished with death and others with banishment, and their privileges ought utterly to be taken from them, as that they have forfeited them to your Majesty. Thus shall you raise money from mollits, strength from traitors, and peace from war.[45]

63 *A Privy Councillors Speech to his Majesty at the Council Table*

*May it please your Majesty,*
That I say I am of the opinion that the counsel of the lord *N. N.* is too severe, and that it is dangerous to inveterate a discontented people, but rather they should be palliated and qualified with some condescendence, as also to put out some declarations in their favour, which will be a means to pacify them, and to allay their discontents, and hinder their evil designs; for if you rub a sore it will fester and may make it gangrene, and cause a part to fall from the whole: so to enrage a people may make them rebel and fall from their allegiance, which otherwise it may be they would not do; and he is an ill surgeon that will make a wound instead of healing a wound; so it were not well to make traitors that would be loyal subjects, or to make wars instead of keeping peace, and when war is begun, it is not likely there will be any good agreement until most of the kingdom is ruined, in which ruin your Majesty will be a loser; for he is the greatest

---

[45] Disagreements between king and Parliament about the balance of their powers continued, amidst suspicion on both sides, throughout the early 1660s. See Seaward, *The Cavalier Parliament*, pp. 131–61.

king that hath the most flourishing and populous kingdom, and he is the happiest king that hath the most peaceable subjects.

64 *A Privy Councillors Speech to his Majesty at the Council Board*

*May it please your Majesty,*
That I say I am neither of the lord *N. N*'s opinion, as to put your justice against your offending subjects presently in execution, nor of the lord *S. Y*'s opinion, to let your offending subjects go unpunished, and worse to flatter them, for that will make them proud, and pride will make them stand upon high terms; nay, it will make them insult so imperiously as not any condescendence will satisfy them; for when as the people perceives their sovereign is afraid of them, they become unruly, but when they fear their sovereign, they are obedient; for it is impossible to work upon their good nature as to make them obey through love and good will, because they have no good natures to work on; wherefore, there is none other way but force, to make them loyal and to keep them to their allegiance; and my advice is to your Majesty, to make yourself strong before you appear either to favour them or disfavour them,[46] but to be so long in your results as your Majesty hath gathered up your strength and settled your power and secured your person; otherwise you may declare what you will, but you shall have but few partakers whilst you are weak and powerless; for men listen not so much to words as they are afraid of what they see; for power increases power, whereas words do but multiply words and lessen power; but when your Majesty hath got a sufficient power to oppose them or to command them, then declare your will and pleasure and put your justice in execution. Wherefore it is requisite that your Majesty should store your magazines, man your forts, make garrisons, rig your navy, and get what money you can to raise an army if need require; also your Majesty must take great care that you employ and entrust honest men and loyal subjects, such as have been always obedient, otherwise you will be betrayed and your own designs will be turned against you; for your Majesty's affairs require now rather honest than subtle men, and wise rather than crafty men.

---

[46] Cf. *Newcastle's Advice.*

# ORATIONS IN COURTS OF MAJESTY, FROM SUBJECTS TO THEIR KING, AND FROM THE KING TO HIS SUBJECTS

## PART VI

### 65 *Complaints of the Subjects to their Sovereign*

*Most Gracious Sovereign,*

We are come here not as mutinous rebels, but humble petitioners to implore your favour, as to redress our grievances and to take off our heavy oppressions; for all the profit of our labours, which should maintain our lives, wives and children, is forcibly taken from us, and we do not only pay taxes, but intolerable prices for all commodities and necessaries, occasioned by monopolies and projects which engross all particular commodities, so that we are forced to buy our liberties to sell, and sell our liberties to buy; but if your Majesty were a gainer by our loss and were enriched by our poverty, we could be well contented to be miserable for your Majesty's sake, either for your profit or pleasure, but your Majesty enjoys it not, but other men which are called courtiers, promotors and projectors, spend it idly, vainly, riotously, and we fear wickedly; so that what we get with labour they spend with idleness, what we get with care they spend with carelessness; the truth of it is, they wear our lives upon their backs and feed upon our bowels; but the worst is, that if we be poor and half starved, we shall neither be able to serve your gracious Majesty either in peace or war, and therefore we beseech your Majesty for your own sake as well as for ours, you would be pleased to redress our grievances.[47]

### 66 *The Subjects Complaint to their Sovereign of the Abuses of their Magistrates*

*Most Gracious Sovereign,*

As all creatures make their complaints to God, as the highest and most powerful in heaven, so we your humble and obedient subjects make our

---

[47] At the Restoration, Parliament granted the government substantial revenues to deal with a burden of debt, but they proved insufficient and further taxes were soon imposed. Parliament was also suspicious of the corruption and extravagance of government. For example, in 1663 MPs criticised the granting of Crown lands to courtiers. See Seaward, *The Restoration*, pp. 19–20.

complaints to your Majesty, as the highest and most powerful being, God's vice-regent on earth; but though your Majesty is loving and careful of your poor subjects, making judges, magistrates, and officers to keep order, to do justice, to give right, to rectify errors, and to punish crimes, that your subjects might flourish in peace and plenty, yet they are so far from doing justice as they make wrongs and do injuries; and instead of giving every one their right they take away our rights from us, and instead of order they commit disorder, and instead of rectifying errors they make errors, and instead of punishing crimes they are the greatest criminals themselves, and those that are the most honest and peaceable of your subjects are most sure to be worst used by them, because they have not that profit by them as by those that are disturbers, destroyers, or deceivers, for when they have committed faults they get money for their pardons, whereas those that commit no fault need no pardon: and as for justice, or rather injustice, it is sold at the bar or on the bench; for causes or cases are not pleaded or decided for truth or right, but for bribes or favour; also the magistrate doth not set the poor awork, but takes away the poor's work, I mean not their labour, but their getting, as the profit, and so leaves them not anything to live on; also they do rob the subjects in general, and your Majesty in particular; for though they take away much from us, yet they pay your Majesty but little in comparison of what they take, and they use or rather abuse your Majesty's name, to the ruin of your subjects; for they extort by your Majesty's name, and when we hear your Majesty's name we humbly submit and yield to all they demand; for not only your person but your name is sacred to us: but give us leave to tell your Majesty that they are so unsatiably covetous as all the wealth of your other subjects will not satisfy them, and their covetousness makes them so unbelieving and hardhearted, as when they have taken all from us they put us in prison because we have nothing left to give them, and if we be not put in prison we are put to slavery, and many times our wives and our children are abused; and this is the lamentable condition of your poor subjects; for which we implore your Majesty's redress, knowing it is not your Majesty's pleasure we should suffer so miserably.[48]

---

[48] The corruption of officials remained an issue throughout the 1660s. Cf. Oration 125 and *Newcastle's Advice*, pp. 23–33. Seaward, *The Cavalier Parliament*, argues that loyal Royalists who expected to be rewarded by Charles II, but were disappointed, tended to accuse the government of corruption.

67 *A Kings Speech to his Rebellious Rout*

*Beloved Subjects,*

What is the reason or cause you gather together in such rebellious tumults? Is it for fear of your lives or liberties? Which you have no cause to fear, for I am not your enemy but your gracious King; or is it that you are my enemies, and throng to dethrone me? Or is it that you would have the absolute power amongst you? Which absolute power cannot be divided amongst many; for if every one hath liberty to do what he list, not any man will have power to do what he would; for liberty will be lost if every man will take upon him to rule, and confusion will take place of government. Thus, striving for liberty you will thrust yourselves into slavery, and out of ambition to rule you will lose all government, and out of covetousness to be rich you'll make yourselves miserably poor; for if there be no government there can be no order, if there be no order there can be no justice, and if no justice there can be no safety, if no safety no peace, if no peace no trade, and if no trade there will be no riches. Wherefore your best way is to submit and obey, to be content to be ruled and not seek to govern, to enjoy your rights and to revenge your wrongs by law and justice, and not to make war and confusion to destroy yourselves.

68 *A Kings Speech to Rebellious Subjects*

I may call you well-beloved subjects, but cannot call you loving subjects; for although I have been careful, watchful, prudent and just for your safeties, peace, prosperities and rights, yet you regard not my safety, my peace, nor my rights; neither can I call you good, for you are factious, complaining, and full of malice; nay, it may be a question whether I may call you subjects, for you disobey all authority, resist the laws, and will obey no command unless you be forced; and though you have not actually rebelled, yet you are in the way to it, for you dispute my power, and would if you could take away my prerogatives,[49] but will not quit any of

---

[49] The royal prerogative was a central issue in the struggle between Charles I and Parliament. On the background to their dispute see J. P. Sommerville, *Royalists and Patriots*, 2nd edition (London: Longman, 1999), pp. 96–100; 126–30; 134–75. Newcastle argues that one of Charles I's main errors was to allow Parliament to bring his prerogative into dispute, and warns Charles II to avoid this. See *Newcastle's Advice*, pp. 24–5. After the Restoration, legislation which had drastically reduced the power of the royal prerogative was repealed, and a series of Acts defining the extent of royal power were passed in its place. See Seaward, *The Cavalier Parliament*, pp. 131–61.

your privileges, which shows your unconscionableness, ungratefulness, and unkindness to me, your *Sovereign*; besides, you are so unreasonable and so evil, as you murmur at my harmless and lawful pleasures but will abate none of your own vanities, vices, and wickednesses. The truth of it is I have done like an over-fond father, who through extreme love and tenderness to his children hath given them their wills and liberties so much as they forget their duties, and become disobedient through wantonness; but had I used severity instead of clemency, and had rigorously kept you in fear, and had exacted more from you, and had yielded less to you, and had I curbed your liberties, you had been more obedient, which would have been more happy both for me and for you; for then you would have been governed easily and obeyed willingly, by which we should have lived peaceably, whereas now we are like to ruin each other with civil wars, unless heaven open your eyes of understanding, to see your faults, errors, and dangers you are like to fall into; but I hope heaven will give you grace to reform your lives, and conform your manners to live peaceably.

## 69 *A Kings Speech to Discontented Subjects*

*Beloved Subjects,*

I perceive frowning countenances amongst my people, which doth portend a storm, but let me advise you from raising a storm lest you shipwreck the whole kingdom and be drowned your selves in the waves of rebellion; the truth of it is, raging men are worse than raging billows, and worse, more devouring than the sea. Yet if you are resolved to make war, rather make war in foreign nations than in your own country, and on strangers rather than on your friends; for to make war on me, your *King*, and your *Sovereign*, is against the laws of God; to make war on the protector of your liberties and father of your country is unnatural; to spill your friends' blood is ungrateful and inhuman; to ruin your native country is barbarous; by which actions you will become worse than beasts and as bad as devils; but if you be so possessed with fury as no intreaties will dispossess you, you must be scourged with misery: the truth is, you seem by your rebellious actions to be mad, and then there is no cure for you but to be let blood in the discontented veins, and I will be your surgeon, on whom I'll try my skill and power to bring you into a perfect obedience; besides, I will bind you with bonds of slavery, and whip you with rods of afflictions, unless you presently conform your selves to peace, law, and government, and humbly crave pardon for your faults.

70  *A Kings Speech to his Rebellious Subjects*

Proud, presumptuous subjects, for so you are, that dare bring your *Sovereign's* prerogatives in question, and to dispute his power; but who gave you that authority? Not my ancestors nor your own; for my ancestors conquered your ancestors and made them slaves, in which slavery you ought to have been kept, and not to have such liberty as now you have, in so much as to come so near and so high in your demands as to jostle me in my throne; only you cast a veil of pretence over your wicked designs, the pretence is your rights and privileges; but what rights had you, when you were conquered? And what privileges have you, but what the conqueror gave? He gave you not the privilege to dispute my power or to bring my prerogatives in question; neither have you privilege to disobey my command, to resist my authority or to break my laws; and know, rather than I will quit my rights, my birth, or my power, I will die first; but my death will not serve your turn, for I have successors; and though your idle thoughts and vain hopes persuade you you shall get more liberty by rebellious actions, yet you may be deceived, and in the end thrust yourselves in absolute slavery; but it seems you had rather be base slaves than loyal subjects, or else you would not be so apt to mutiny as you are, yet if you once rebel, I will endeavour to destroy every man that opposes me or stands neuter, and if I cannot destroy you with that power I have, I will call in foreign nations that shall devour you; for believe, I will not be ruined alone, but the ruin of the whole kingdom shall accompany me.

71  *A Recantation of the poor Petitioning Subjects*

*Most Dread Sovereign,*
Your most sorrowful and poor petitioning subjects, hearing your Majesty was displeased at their complaints, and angry with them for coming in a company together, imploring your Majesty's favour and redress of their poor condition, not imagining that their complaints would be taken as factious and seditious murmurings, or their desires of redress as presumptuous demands, or that their petitioning in a company together would be taken for a rebellious insurrection, they have sent me, a poor man, not daring to come together as they did, to let your Majesty know how much afflicted they are for your displeasure, which displeasure they are more grieved for than for any other affliction that could come either upon their lives, bodies, goods, wives, or children; for they do assure your Majesty,

and call heaven to witness for them, that they came not for any evil design to your Majesty nor your Majesty's government, but only out of a good intent, believing your Majesty did not know what they did suffer; but if they had known, or but imagined, it had been your Majesty's will and pleasure they should suffer, they would never have complained, and rather have starved or endured any torment than opposed your Majesty in anything: and if your Majesty thinks their ignorant fault is beyond a pardon, they are ready and willing to endure any punishment or to die at your Majesty's command.

72 *Repenting Subjects to their Sovereign*

*Most Gracious Sovereign,*
We your most penitent subjects crave pardon for our faults, not only with tears in our eyes, but sorrow in our hearts, for our murmuring speeches and rebellious actions, for which we confess we deserve to die, or worse, as to endure great and grievous torments; but if your Majesty's clemency spare our bodies from pain and our lives from death, we are doubly, nay trebly bound to your Majesty, first by our duties, next for your mercy, and last for our pardon, to be not only your Majesty's loyal subjects but loyal slaves; and since there is no man so perfect but is subject to offend, and not in light or small offences, but great and grievous, as not only against man and man, or against nature, but against God himself; we hope your Majesty will consider our frail natures and will rather blame Nature for making us so, than us for being so. But since repentance is the way to forgiveness, and absolution follows contrition, we with contrite hearts and humble spirits crave your mercy.

73 *A Kings Speech to his Good Subjects*

My beloved and most loving subjects, (for so you are), I have required your assembling together that I may see you and you me; for I do not love to be as a stranger to my subjects, nor I would not have my subjects as strangers to me; and if it were possible, I would be acquainted with their faces, degrees, qualities, and professions, and not only be their king but their friend, not to govern them in general but to counsel and advise in particulars. Indeed, I have reason to give you often public visits, as also public thanks, for your loyalty and love; for your obedience seems such as you seem to watch for my commands, and your love is such as you seem to prefer my safety before your own lives and my pleasures before your own profits, in so much as you seem you did desire only to live to serve me; for which I thank the Gods for making me so happy to be a king of such subjects, whose only strife is for my favour, who are ambitious only for my fame and take a pride in my glory, whose valours enlarge my dominions, whose industries enrich my treasuries, whose delights are my pleasures, whose love protects my person, and whose prayers are for my health and long life; I can only say that your loyalty, obedience, and love, is not to a king that doth not regard it, nor to a tyrant that had rather be feared than loved; but assure yourselves, my affection to my people is such as a fond fathers to his only son, who had rather die for his son's good, than live to his own pleasure, and that all the endeavours of his life are for his sake, as to make his son rich, noble, and powerful, that he may have respect, renown, and fame amongst strangers; the like do I for my subjects. Indeed, a king is the common father of his people, and I rejoice to see you as a loving father doth his children, and so I pray the gods to bless you.

# SPEECHES OF DYING PERSONS
## PART VII

74 *A Kings Dying Speech to his Noble Subjects*

Faithful counsellors, just magistrates, loving friends, noble men, and loyal subjects, you see me here Death's prisoner; yet though I must part with my subjects, they shall not part with their sovereign, for I shall leave them a king, though I die. I have been your crowned king this thirty years, a heavy weight and a long time of trouble; but a king hath more title than power, and more power than pleasure: for were all his subjects slaves and all did obey his will, yet to order and govern them to his will requires pains, care, and study; but my desire and will was to make my subjects happy, to which end I bent all my industry, the which I wish my successor may do the like, for good subjects deserve a good sovereign; indeed, all good subjects have not at all times good sovereigns, nor all good sovereigns good subjects, for all sovereigns are not wise, nor all subjects loyal; for though good men make good subjects, yet good men do not always make good sovereigns, as being not piety nor moral honesty that makes good kings, but industry, observation, understanding, judgement, wit, prudence, and courage, that makes kings wise rulers; also counsels, experience, and practice, which makes an old king a better governor than a young king, and yet all subjects for the most part grow weary with their sovereign's age, and so consequently with their own happiness; but their folly and ingratitude is often punished in having their desires. Indeed, most of mankind through ignorance and inconstancy desire their own hurt, which when they feel, they are displeased with the Gods for granting that they were earnest with the Gods to give them, so that they are seldom contented: but I wish they may have good desires, contented minds, and happy lives, and I pray the Gods they may flourish with my successors in peace and plenty, as they have done with me, to whom I leave you, and him to you: farewell.

75 *A Daughter's Dying Speech to her Father*

Father, farewell! And may that life that issues from my young and tender years be added to your age! May all your grief be buried in my grave, and may the joys, pleasures and delights that did attend my life be servants unto yours! May comfort dry your eyes, God cease your sorrows, that, though I die, you may live happily. Why do you mourn that Death must be your son-in-law? Since he is a better husband than any you could choose me or I could choose my self, it is a match that Nature and the Fates have made; wherefore be content, for it is not in your power to alter the decrees of Fate, for destiny cannot be opposed, but if you could, you would rob me of the happiness the Gods intend me; for though my body shall dwell with death, my soul shall dwell in Heaven, and holy angels that are my marriage guests will conduct it to that glory, for which you have cause to joy and not to grieve, for all creatures live but to die, but those that are blessed die to live, and so do I. Farewell.

76 *A Soldiers Dying Speech to his Friends*

*Dear Friends,*
You are come to see me die, but I am sorry you shall see me die in the bed of sloth and not in the field of action; for now I shall die like a coward, whereas had I died in the field of war I should have died as a valiant man; indeed the field of war is the bed of honour wherein all valiant and gallant men should die; but Fortune hath denied me that honour, she hath spared my life to my loss, for those that die in the wars have greater renowns and gloriouser fame than those that die in chambers of peace; for whatsoever heroic acts men have done for the most part die if they out-live them; for such actions live by the deaths of the actors, I do not say always, but for the most part, which makes me fear the service I have done my king and country will die with me and be buried in oblivion's grave, yet should the service I have done be quite forgotte I should not repent my actions; for honourable persons and gallant men should do what they ought to do although they were certain never to be rewarded; for though few men are rewarded according to their merits, and many have favour that did never merit a reward, (so unjust is the world, Fortune, and fame), yet their injustice must not make men unworthy; but I have done my part, and death will do his. Farewell.

77 *A Dying Speech of a Loving Mistress to her Beloved Servant*

Servant, this day I should have been your wife, and so your servant, as you have been mine, but Death hath robbed *Hymen*[50] of his rights, and

---

[50] The God of Marriage.

now he fights with Life, which he will overcome; for Death is conqueror of all and triumphs in his spoils: yet Death by taking my life prisoner will set your person free to choose another mistress to make a wife, in whose embraces I shall be buried and utterly forgotten. I speak not this in envy to her happiness nor yours, for envy dwells with Life, and not with Death; nor am I loath to die, nor grieve to be forgotten, no, not by those that I loved most and equal with my soul; for those I love, I would not have them mourn in melancholy thoughts and sad remembrance of my death, I only wish that she that you love next may return love again with as much truth, constancy, and purity as I have loved you, and may she be the glory of her sex and honour of her husband, and may you live to love each other, and love to live for one another's sake; may Nature, Time, Fortune, Fate, and the Gods join in your happiness. Farewell.

78 *A Foreign Travellers Dying Speech*

*Dear Friends,*
I have travelled far, and have seen much of the world, and have gone round about the world, but now I shall travel out of the world, from which I shall bring no news, I shall not come back to relate my journeys, or to tell you what strange creatures there are in the other world, or what dangers I escaped, or what adventures I have made, or what several countries there are, and which is good for plantation, or what commodities there are, or what traffic there is or may be; for though all creatures are transported, yet no returns are sent back in lieu of them, unless we believe new-born creatures are sent out of the other world into this, but that is not probable because they are made in this world and of the same substances of the world: but howsoever, those that are sent thither, as by sickness, casualties, Fortune, and age, return no more; wherefore I must take my last leave of you; for though I have been at the confines of death and am returned to my friends again, yet I never was in the region of death, a place I never was ambitious or desirous to go to; for though I had the curiosity to see the several countries, kingdoms, and places in the several parts of the world, yet I never had the curiosity to travel into Death's kingdom, no nor to see the mansions of the Gods, which may be accounted a sin. Indeed travellers are accounted atheistical, but if they were, yet when they come to die they would change those atheistical opinions: and as bad as they are thought to be, yet they are not afraid of Death; for then they would not venture their lives so often as they do; indeed travellers have as great courage as

soldiers have, and 'tis believed as little religion, but not so much hate, envy, malice, revenge, nor covetousness, unless they be merchants; nor they are not robbers and murderers, they do not take away men's lives nor goods, as soldiers do; but of all men, travellers have most reason to adore and worship God best, for they see most of his wonderful works, which show his power, might, wisdom, and majesty, the which makes his creatures admire him, praise him, fear him, love him, and pray to him as the great, omnipotent, infinite, eternal, incomprehensible, and everlasting God, to whom I resign my soul, and leave my body to death. Farewell.

79 *A Lovers Dying Speech to his Beloved Mistress*

*Dear Mistress,*
Though I must die, I leave my life to live with you, for you are the life of my love and the love of my life; you are the palace of my soul wherein it lives and will remain, though Death doth take my body hence; for souls live though bodies die; yet do not drown my soul in tears, nor cloud it with your sorrows, but give it light of joy, and please it with your kind remembrance. But O my jealous thoughts do torture more my mind than pains of death do torture my weak body, lest you should banish the love of me to entertain a stranger, which if you do, the Gods will punish you for your inconstancy; but pardon this my jealousy, for doubts proceed from love, and your virtue is the anchor of my hopes and haven of security, in which my love lives safe. Farewell.

80 *A Sons Dying Speech to his Father*

Father, I have been an unprofitable son, for I shall die a bachelor and so leave you no posterity to keep alive your name and family, which is a double grief, both to yourself and me, indeed to me it is a treble grief, because the fault is only mine, loving vain pleasures and liberty so much as made me unwilling to be bound in wedlock bonds, believing that a wife would be a hindrance to those delights that pleased me; besides, I trusted to my youth and health, thinking I had time enough to marry and increase; also I thought that very young men's children would prove but weak and sickly in body and mind; thus did I bring many arguments to live a bachelor until such time as I had more maturity of years, and then I did intend to choose a wife with your consent, or else consent to marry whom you pleased; but Death will alter that design, and you and I must both submit to Heaven's decree. Yet have I this to comfort me, that you did never command me to marry, wherefore my fault was not a fault of disobedience, for I never disobeyed you all my life, which makes me die in peace. Farewell.

81 *A Young Virgins Dying Speech*

*Dear Friends,*
I do perceive that holy angels hover about my soul to bear it to the Gods when parted from my body, a virgin's soul it is, clothed with white innocency and so fitter for their company, as also for the robe of glory which the Gods will give me. As for my body, though it be young, yet is it only fit for Death, as being due to him, for that was made of earth, and Death is lord of all the earth doth form, breed, and bring forth; but souls being of another nature, those that are celestial, proceeding from the Gods, do to the Gods return; whereas wicked souls that are damned, and proceed not from the Gods but from the damned spirits, return to the damned crew again: for all is good that doth proceed from God, and though the best of souls doth sin, yet God doth give them purging grace, that cleanses them from evil, which grace hath purified my soul and made it fit for heaven, where I do wish all souls may come. Farewell.

82 *A Husbands Dying Speech to his Wife*

Wife, farewell; for Death will break our marriage knot and will divorce our persons, but not dissolve our love, unless you be inconstant; for Death hath not that power to disunite our souls, for they may live and love eternally; but if you marry a second husband, you separate our loves as Death will separate our bodies, for in that marriage bed you will bury all remembrance of me; and so shall I doubly die, and doubly be buried; for your second husband will be my second death; but if you live a widow you will keep me still alive, both in your name and memory, where I desire to live until your body dies, and then our souls will meet with joy, delight, and happiness; till then farewell.

83 *A Common Courtisans Dying Speech*

Kind Friends, and Wanton Lovers, when I was in health you came to view my beauty, to hear my voice and to enjoy my person in amorous embraces, and all for your own pleasures and delights, but I did entertain such visitors more for the lucre of profit than for the pleasures of love, more for your presents than your persons; the truth is, I was more covetous of wealth than amorously affected; not but that I took pleasure in seeing my beauty admired and hearing my wit praised, and took delight to ensnare men's affections with my attractive graces, and was proud of the power I had by Nature's favour, yet that power I only employed to enrich my self, that I might live bravely and luxuriously, or to hoard up to maintain me when I was old. But O those covetous desires and vain delights have ruined both my body and soul, in grievous pains I live, and should despairing die but that the Gods are merciful, and pardon penitent sinners, for if I were to live I would not live that life I have done, not only for my soul's sake, but for my body's; for had I thought of Death, or could imagine the pains that now I feel, the pocky, rotting pains that torture my weak body, I should have been less covetous of wealth and more careful of health, I should not have made my beauty, wit, and becoming graces and adornments to intake customers to buy sinful pleasures; or had I thought of the joys in Heaven, I should have despised all worldly delights; or had I feared the torments of Hell, I should have spent my time in prayers, and not in courtships: but life is almost passed with me, for Death hath stricken me with his wand so that I cannot live to mend, but die to be forgiven, for I do truly and unfeignedly repent. Farewell.

84  *A Vain Young Ladys Dying Speech*

*Dear Friends,*
You are charitable in visiting the sick, a charity that I did seldom practice, for when I was in health I was so taken up with vanities and worldly pleasures as I could never spare so much time as to visit a sick friend; neither was I charitable to the poor, as to help to relieve their wants, for I spent so much on my breviaries as I left not anything to give unto the poor; indeed, I did shun visiting the sick, because they put thoughts of death in my mind, which thoughts did disturb my mind and obstruct my delights; but if I had thought of death more, and had visited the sick oftener, I had never lived so idly, nor spent my time so unprofitably, nor had been so foolishly vain as I have been; for I regarded nothing but beauty, fashions, dressing, dancing, feasting, courtships, and bravery, I never thought of Heaven, nor read holy books of divinity, but only lying romances, and my contemplation was all of wanton love. 'Tis true, I went often to church,

but not to pray, but to be prayed to, not as a saint but as a mistress, I may say as a sinner; for I went not to church for instruction but for destruction, more for to show my beauty than to reform my life, more to get wanton lovers than to get saving grace; I listened not to what the preachers taught, but looked which of the gallants eyed me. Thus did I increase and multiply sins under the veil of devotion, for which I deserve great and grievous punishments; but the Gods are merciful and will forgive me, for now I do more hate vanities than ever I did love them, and all my evil thoughts are banished from my mind; indeed death hath frighted all such thoughts away and pious thoughts do take their place, and as the Gods come near, the world shrinks from me, as guilty of these sins, and millions of other sins besides: but death will stay no longer, for blessed angels bear away my soul. Farewell.

85 *A Fathers Speech to his Son on his Deathbed*

*Son,*

I have lived a long time, so long that were not you a good son, you would have wished my death before Nature had ordained me to die; but as Heaven hath blessed me with long life, so with a good, loving, and dutiful son, which hath been a help and comfort to my old age; and as Heaven hath given you grace, and Nature a good disposition to love and obey your father, so Heaven and Nature hath given you health and ability to beget posterity, in which I shall live in name and fame, though I die in body. But son, as you have been a helpful and dutiful son, so I have been a loving and careful father; for I have been more prudent for my son's good, than vain for my own pleasure; I have been more industrious to advance and enrich my son than to please or delight myself, and I have thought myself happier in my son's life than I have done in my own. Thus, Son, I have and do love you better than my self, and all the desire and request I have to you is that as I have been a father to you, so you to be a father to yours, and so I pray the Gods to bless you, Fortune to favour you, Wisdom to help you, Nature to strengthen you, Time to prolong you, and when your time comes to die, that we may meet in the other world with joy and happiness; the Gods have mercy of me, and bless you. Farewell.

# FUNERAL ORATIONS
## Part VIII

86 *An Oration to the People concerning the Death of their Sovereign*

*Dear Countrymen, and Loyal Mourners,*

We may see our loss by our love, and our love by our grief, and our grief by our tears; but we have reason for our general mourning and sorrow in every heart, that our dread *Sovereign* is taken from us. He was our earthly god, as our protector, defender, assister, subsister, ruler and governor; he protected us with his justice, defended us with his arms, assisted us with his prudence, subsisted us with his love, ruled us with his power and governed us by his laws; and such a prince he was, as he was dreadful to his enemies, helpful to his friends and careful of his subjects; he hath enlarged his dominions with the sword and enriched his people with the spoils, and hath increased his power both by sea and land, and so strengthened and fortified his kingdoms as his subjects have no cause to fear any foreign invasion, but may safely sit with pleasure under their own vines: and so wise and good a prince he was, that though he be gone, yet he hath left peace and plenty amongst his people, and power, dominion, and strength to his successors, with which Heaven grant they may inherit his wisdom, moral virtues, divine graces, heroic spirit, good fortunes, and great fame, that though our old *Sovereign* is gone to the Gods above, yet our new *Sovereign* may be as a God to us here; for which let us pray to our *Sovereign* saint, to intercede for us to the Gods on high, to endue their deputy on earth with divine influences and humane wisdom, to govern and rule us as he did.


87 *A Young Noblemans Funeral Oration*

*Beloved Brethren,*

We are met together as funeral guests to a dead man, who died in the flower of his age, and whilst he lived was favoured of nature, birth, breeding, and fortune; for he was handsome of body, understanding in mind, noble of birth, knowing in learning, and rich in wealth. He was generous, valiant, and courtly; he had a pleasant speech, and a graceful behaviour; he was beloved of the Muses, admired by the Sciences, and attended by the Arts; he was entertained with the pleasures of the world, and feasted with the varieties of pleasures; yet all could not save him from death. Indeed death appears more cruel to youth than to age, because it takes youth from the most flourishing time of their life, although youth fears death less than age, not that youth hath more courage, but youth doth not think of death so often as age doth, for if youth had death in their mind, they would fear death more than age doth, by so much more as they are younger and know the world less; but youth thinks death a long time off from them, although to many he is so near as ready to seize on them; wherefore if those that are young did think they should die soon, they would not be so eager and fond of the world as they are, nor be so vain and intemperate as many young persons be; the brave gallants would take little pleasure in new modes, gay clothes and fair mistresses; a young gallant would be but a dull courtier, a melancholy lover, not melancholy for his mistress disfavour but at death's approach, not for love but for life; neither would he take pleasure in music or dancing, for the thoughts of death would make him dance false and put his hearing out of tune, and the music would sound to his ears as his passing bell; neither would he eye beauty, but if he did the freshest beauty would appear faded; in truth all his senses would be as rough and troubled waters, disturbed by the storms of fear raised in his mind; for the most valiant minds are somewhat disturbed with the thoughts of death, by reason the terrors of death are natural to all mankind, not so much to feel as to think of, not only for the parting of soul and body and the dark oblivion in death, but for the uncertain condition after death; for though death is not sensible of life yet life is sensible of death; so that it is the thoughts of death that are fearful, and not death it self that is so terrible, as being neither painful to feel nor dreadful to behold because invisible and insensible, having neither shape, sound, scent, taste, nor touch; but this noble person is past thinking, and therefore past fearing, also past wishing; for he doth not desire to live in this world again, he thinks not of the world or of any thing in the world, he is free from all trouble of mind or body; in which happiness let us lay him in the tomb with his forefathers, there to rest in peace and ease.

## 88  *A Generals Funeral Oration*

*Beloved friends,*

This noble person that lies here dead was once our general; a valiant man he was, a skilful soldier, a wise commander, and a generous giver; he loved his soldiers more than spoil and fame more than life, he was full of clemency and mercy, he would give his enemies their lives freely when he had overcome them valiantly, and he was so careful of his own soldiers lives as he would never adventure or put them to the hazard but when he saw great probability of victory; yet this gallant man, this excellent soldier, whom his enemies could never overcome, Death hath taken prisoner, with whom he shall have but a dark lodging and cold entertainment. Thus Death is the most absolute conqueror that is, for no creature is able to resist or defend themselves from Death, whose uncontrolling power makes him dreadful even to the most valiant men, not that they fear Death's dart, but Death's oblivion; for valiant men love life, and fear death more than cowards, or else they would not venture their bodies so often, were it not out of love to life and fear of death; yet is it not that life which cowards are so fond of, nor that death which they are so afraid of, but 'tis the life of their fame and death of their name that honourable and valiant men so much love and fear, insomuch that to gain the one and to shun the other they will sacrifice their bodily life, and embrace their bodily death with more delight and pleasure than the beautifulest woman that ever nature made; and they are to be commended for it; for it is life that the Gods themselves take delight in; for the Gods are pleased to live in the minds of their creatures and are angry if their creatures think or speak not of them, as well as to them: so all worthy men desire and endeavour to live in the minds of their own kind, and to be praised, at least spoken of; for they desire and endeavour to live both in the thoughts and words of men, in all ages, and in all nations, and by all men, if it were possible; it being as natural for worthy men to desire to be remembered as for all men to desire to live, and as natural for men to desire to live as to love themselves. But some say it doth a man no good to be remembered when he is dead: it may be answered that then it doth a man no good to be remembered whilst he lives, for remembrance lives in the absent, and absence is a kind of death, but he is as evil a natured man that cares not to be remembered by his friends as those that never remember their friends; also he is unnatural to his kind, and it may be said that such men are ungrateful monsters, or monstrous unnatural: but this noble person was remembered and spoken often of by his absent friends, and did remember and spoke often of his friends in their absence whilst he was living, and his worthy and valiant actions will be remembered and spoken of now he is dead, in which remembrance and words he may live so long as the world lasts, as being the only reward this world can give to worth and merit, as piety, moral virtue, valour and generosity, wit and learning; for there is no other reward in this world but remembrance and praise, which remembrance and praise all good men will give him as his due. Thus will the tongues and minds of living men build him a monument of fame wherein all his worthy acts will be kept in remembrance, though his body be dead and buried in earth, in which let us put it with devout ceremony.

## 89  *A Judges Funeral Oration*

*Dear Friends,*

We are met together to see judge *N*. *N*'s body laid into the grave, who in his lifetime was an upright judge, for he judged according to truth and right, and not for fear nor favour; he was free from covetousness or corrupting bribes, he was both a good and a wise judge, for he would never judge over-hastily any cause for or against, until he had heard all sides; neither would he retard or delay suits over-long, but in all causes he was very attentive, and in doubtful causes very cautious how to judge, and in all criminal causes, or on life and death, he would be very inquisitive to know the truth, for he would not judge rashly, as to judge before he had examined strictly and had sufficient proofs and witnesses, or at least very great probabilities of the truth; also he was neither a temerarious nor an over-bold judge, neither cruel nor foolishly pitiful; for as he would not pardon so much nor so many as to encourage men to offend or commit crimes, so he would not condemn so much nor so many as to make a kind of a massacre of lives; all which made him live with a good conscience and die with a good courage, not fearing a condemnation, neither in this world nor the next, but desired to be summoned to God's tribunal, there to be tried and judged of the course of his life in this world, to which divine judge we leave him, bearing his body to the grave there to leave that, but not to leave the remembrance of him, nor the due praise his memory deserves.

## 90  *A Sergeants or Barristers Funeral Oration*

*Dear Friends,*

You see the body of sergeant *N*. *N*. lies dead, ready to be put into the grave, which shows that he would not plead for life, or else Death had no ears to hear his suit; but if he pleads as well for himself at God's tribunal as he did for his clients at the bar, he will get judgement on his side; the truth is, nature as well as education made him a pleader; for naturally he had a flowing speech and a fluent wit, to turn, wind, and form any cause as he liked best; for his wit and eloquence was such as to make a doubtful cause seem clear, and had he not known by learning the laws so well as he did, yet his wit and eloquence would have covered his ignorance and supplied the defect of his learning, but he was as good and learned a lawyer as an excellent pleader, and as honest a man as either, for he took more pains to plead his clients' cause than pleasure to take from his clients' fees; neither would he prolong his clients' suit to drain their purses, nor yet make his clients' cause more doubtful than it was, to make them more fearful of the success of their suits than they had reason to fear, and all this to get more fees; for fears and desires are prodigal givers as well as promisers; but rather he pleaded *gratis* for his poor clients, wherein he showed more charity to the poor than covetousness to the rich. Thus he was a good and generous lawyer, a witty, ingenious, eloquent pleader; the truth is he did not only take pains for his clients but pleasure in his own wit, for he had more delight than profit by his pleading, and yet he did not take so much pleasure in his own wit and eloquency as others did which heard him, insomuch as more went to hear him plead than those that had causes to be pleaded; he reproached not any man nor used railing speeches or violent actions in his pleading, as many, nay most pleaders do, but his behaviour was civil, his wit sweet and his speech gentle; for though his wit was quick, ready, and free, yet it was neither salt, sour, nor bitter; and though his speech was flowing, yet it was not rough, for it ran in a smooth though full stream; and his behaviour or demeanour was so graceful and becoming as the one delighted the eyes of the beholders as much as the other the ears of the hearers; but though his body be dead, yet his wit, eloquency, elegancy, honesty, and abilities are living in the memory of living men, which will live by tradition as long as there are men to remember or speak: wherefore let us keep his living parts in our minds and bury his dead parts, as his body in the grave, there to remain in peace, as the other in fame.

91 *A Magistrates Funeral Oration*

*Beloved Brethren,*
We are met here together to mourn for our loss; for the death of this man is not only a loss to every particular man but to the whole commonwealth; for he was a wise man and an upright and just magistrate, he did not serve the commonwealth to enrich himself as most magistrates do, but took

pains to enrich the commonwealth; nor did he sell justice for bribes, but punished bribe-takers; neither was he partial, either to the rich or poor, but judged according to right and truth, at least to great probability: also he kept the rich from riot and the poor from idleness, and he took away superfluities to help necessities, not that he troubled any man for living to their degree and quality, but he would not suffer any man to live above their degree and quality; neither would he hinder men from their lawful pleasures and delights, but he would not connive at their disorders and misrules, neither would he pardon their wickednesses: he regarded not the slanders of his enemies, nor was he revengeful, for he suffered not his enemies to be injured but gave them all the justice he could; neither was he unjust to his foes nor ungrateful to his friends, he had a tender regard to the old, sick, poor, and shiftless; indeed he was such a magistrate as he was a father, a husband, a brother, a friend, a master, a servant, a slave for the commonwealth, all which adds to our loss and grief, but not to his happiness; for his happiness admits of no addition, he being as happy as can be, in which happiness let us leave him after we have interred him with his forefathers.

## 92 *A Funeral Oration of a Student*

*Fellow Students,*
We are met together to wait upon the dead body of our worthy brother in learning, to be laid in peace into the bed of earth, whose life was so studious, as we may say he was partly dead whilst he lived, for the most of his conversation was with dead authors, and his study was as his grave, so that our learned brother hath only changed his habitation and landlord, as from his study to the earth, from his bodily life to death; I confess, his landlord, Death, is covetous, for Death exacts or extorts the flesh from the bones as his due, yet the body is more happy, dwelling more peaceably with Death than with life; and as his body hath made a happy change, so hath his soul, but his soul dwells not now with his body, for the soul is an enemy to Death and flies from it, neither can the soul live in the body when as the body is turned into insipid earth, for the soul being of a celestial nature cannot live in a terrestrial place, but when separated, being pure in it self, it is light, and being free, as having liberty, it is agile, through which propriety it ascends unto the Gods on high and lives with them eternally. Thus our learned brother's body resting peaceably, and his soul living blessedly, both shall meet gloriously,

and so let's lay his corpse into the grave humbly, ceremoniously and piously.

## 93  *A Funeral Oration of a Divine*

*Beloved Brethren,*
This our dead brother was an holy man, both in profession and life; as for his profession, he was a divine, and his practice was as pious as his profession was pure; he was blessed of the Gods, for they endued him with spiritual graces, enabled him with spiritual knowledge, and enabled him with spiritual eloquence, to inform, reform, and perform the Church of God, according to the word of God amongst men; but though his time of life is expired, yet his true doctrine will remain for the satisfaction, comfort, and salvation of the souls in living bodies. Wherefore let us lay his body into the grave, and leave it to the time of glorification.

## 94  *A Funeral Oration of a Poet*

*Beloved Brethren,*
Our brother, whose body is dead and is brought to this place to be inurned, was the most fearful man that ever nature made, not to die, but to be forgotten; also he was the most ambitious man, not for wealth, title, or power, but for fame; in truth, he was so ambitious as his body and mind was restless, endeavouring to live like as nature or the Gods of nature, which live and are partly known in their works and by their works, which are their creatures, especially the chief of their creatures, which are mankind; for we cannot perceive but that the chief habitations of the Gods are in the minds of men, with which habitations they are so pleased and delighted as they punish those men that neglect or forget them; nay, the Gods made men, or such kind of creatures, to remember them, as to speak of them, think of them, and to admire them in their praises, contemplations, and adorations; also to have visible worship to their invisible deities, as to have altars, priests, and sacrifices, to offer praise, prayers and thanksgiving: so that the Gods are not satisfied to live only to or in themselves, but in their creatures; wherefore those men resemble the Gods most that desire fame, which fame is to be remembered and praised by all men in all ages throughout the world; whereas on the contrary, those that slight, neglect, or speak against fame as being a foolish vain-glory in that it doth a man no

good to be remembered and praised after the bodily life, are irreligious, ungrateful, and unnatural: irreligious, not desirous to imitate the Gods; ungrateful, not divulging natures gifts; and unnatural, caring not for the memory of their own kind, as not caring to live with them, which is to live in their minds: also they are unjust to themselves, not desiring their own good, as their perpetual name, memory, and fame. But this our brother was not of that sort of mankind as to be contented to be buried in a terrestrial oblivion, but would have a celestial remembrance, which the Gods perpetuate for a reward to his merit. So let us lay his body in the grave, and let his praise ring out his peal.

95 *A Funeral Oration of a Philosopher*

*Beloved brethren,*
This our dead brother, when he had bodily life, he was a close student and had a great library, wherein were more works than he had time to learn, and they were of more several languages than he was capable to understand; but he endeavoured, and was advanced far in knowledge; his study was natural and moral philosophy, his library the universe, and his several books the several creatures therein. As for moral philosophy, he knew well how to compose commonwealths and to settle and govern them; also he knew well the natures, humours, passions, and appetites amongst mankind, as also to divide and distinguish them, and to order, form, and reform them. As for natural philosophy, he did not only study the outward forms of several creatures but their inward natures. In truth, his conception was so subtle and piercing, his observation so dilative, his reason so strong, his wit so agile, his judgement so solid, his understanding so clear, and his thoughts so industrious as they went to the first cause of several effects, and he did not only converse with the body but the soul of Nature, indeed he was Nature's platonic lover, and she rewarded him in discovering to him her most hidden and obscure secrets by which he begot great wisdom and everlasting fame; for though his body be dead, yet his good laws, wise sciences, profitable arts, witty experiences, graces, virtues, and eloquence will live for the benefit and delight of living men in all nations and ages; and though we have great reason to mourn for his bodily death, yet we have more reason to rejoice for his glorious fame; but leaving his merits to life and his body to death, let us lay him into the grave, to transmigrate as Nature pleases.

96  *A Funeral Oration of a Dead Lady, spoken by a Living Lady*

*Dearly Beloved Sisters in God,*

We are met as sorrowful mourners, to attend this dead lady's corpse to the grave; she was in her life the rule of our actions, and will be in her fame the honour of our sex; she was favoured of Nature, the Gods, and Fortune; Nature gave her wit and beauty, the Gods gave her piety and charity, and Fortune gave her wealth and education; she was adorned by the Graces, beloved by the Muses, and attended by the Arts; she was sociable in her conversation, just in her promises, and generous in her gifts; she was industrious in all good actions, helpful to all distressed persons, and grateful for all sorts of courtesies; she was humble in her own prosperities, and full of magnanimity in her own adversities; her mind had no passage for any evil, nor no obstruction against any good; but to repeat or sum up the number of this lady's merits is beyond my rhetoric or arithmetic; for certainly she was composed of the purest essence of Nature, and the divinest spirits of Heaven; she had the piety of saints, the chastity of angels, and the love of the Gods, in which love let us leave her soul and lay her body in the grave, till the time of glorification.

97  *A Foreigners or Strangers Funeral Oration*

*Beloved Brethren,*

You show your charity and humanity, and that they are not bound up to particulars, or to your friends and countrymen, but that they extend to strangers, in coming to see this stranger who died out of his native country, decently to be buried in a foreign land, I mean foreign, as from his native country, although the truth is that all the world is common to mankind, for Nature hath not assigned men to any particular place or part of the world, but hath given all the world freely to them, as if she made the world and all other creatures only for man's sake; for all other creatures are not so generally dispersed, or rather so spreading and branching throughout the world as mankind is, by reason they belong, breed, prosper or increase in particular climates, as some in cold and others in hot, and some in one part of the world and some in another, for some creatures will be so far from increasing in some particular climates as they cannot live in them, but in all parts of the world that are habitable there be men. 'Tis true, different climates may cause men to be of different complexions, but what complexions soever they have, they are all of the same kind as mankind, and of the same sort of animals; for though all beasts are of beast-kind, yet a fox and an ass is not one and the same sort or kind of beast; but there is no such different sort amongst mankind, for there is no difference of men in their natural shapes, proprieties, qualities, abilities, capacities, entities, or the like, unless some defects to some particulars, which is nothing to the generality, for all the kind of mankind is all alike both in body and mind, as in their shapes, senses, appetites, speech, frowning, laughing, weeping and the like, as also alike in their rational parts, as judging, understanding, conceiving, remembering, apprehending, considering, imagining, desiring, joying, grieving, loving, hating, fearing, doubting, hoping, believing and the like;[51] and therefore, since not any man can be accounted as a stranger in any part of the world, because he hath by Nature a right as a natural inheritance to inhabit what part or place of the world he will; but all mankind are as brethren, not only by kind but by inheritance, as being general sharers and possessors of the world, so this dead man ought not to be accounted as a stranger but a brother; wherefore let us mourn as we ought to do for a dead brother and accompany his hearse to the grave with religious ceremony, there leaving it in rest and peace.

## 98  *A Post-riders Funeral Oration*

*Beloved Brethren,*

You have expressed your humanity and charity in coming to this poor, unfortunate man's burial, which though he was a poor man yet he was an honest man, and therefore is much the more worthy to be praised; for poverty and necessity is a great temptation to knavery, as much as riches is a temptation to foolery, which is vanity, nay, riches is not only guilty of vanity, but vice, as luxury, pride, and wantonness, whereas knavery is cheating, cozening, stealing, and the like, of all which this poor man was free; and as he was an honest man, so he was a laborious man, for his profession of life was a post-rider, an unfortunate profession for him, for he riding fast upon a stumbling jade, fell down and broke his neck. Thus we see that misfortunes as well as sicknesses bring many to their lives ends, and many times to a miserable end, for misfortunes take life away unawares, and sometimes unprepared to die; so this man did not think when he got on the horse's back, he should ride post to Death, for had

---

[51] See *Blazing World*, nn. 26, 28.

he thought so he would have chosen to run afoot, a safer, though a slower pace: but could his soul ride post on Death to heaven, as his body rid post on a horse to death, he might out-strip many a soul that is gone before him; for though his soul, as all souls are light, and of no weight, yet Death is no nimble runner, being cold and numb and nothing but bare bones, a hard seat for a tender soul: besides, the way to heaven is so narrow and steep as Death cannot get up, for should he venture, his soul would be in danger to be overthrown and cast into hell, which is a deep, dark, terrible and dreadful pit, wherein is no hope of getting out: the truth is, Death carries many evil souls down into hell, but good souls he leaves at the bottom of the hill that leads up to heaven, from which those souls climb and clamber up with great difficulty; for whatsoever is excellent is hard to get or come to, whereas that which is bad is easy to be had. But howsoever, this poor man is dead, and we shall see him buried, leaving his soul in its journey and his body in the grave.

## 99 *A Young Virgins Funeral Oration*

*Beloved Brethren, and Sisters in God,*

We here meet, not only as funeral mourners, but as marriage guests, to attend and wait upon a young virgin, to see her laid into her nuptial bed, which is the grave; 'tis true, her husband, Death, is a cold bedfellow, but yet he makes a good husband, for he will never cross, oppose, nor anger her, nor give her cause of grief or sorrow, neither in his rude behaviour, inconstant appetite, nor lewd life, which, had she married any other husband, might have made her very unhappy, whereas now she will know no sorrow; for there is no whoring, gaming, drinking, quarrelling nor prodigal spending in the grave, for Death banishes all riot and disorder out of his habitations; there is no noise nor disturbance in his palace; indeed Death's palace is a place of peace, rest, quiet, and silence, and therefore all are happy that dwell there, for there is no envy, malice, slander, nor treachery; there men are not tempted with beauty, nor women flattered into wantonness, they are free from all temptation or defamation, neither are they troubled or tormented with pain or sickness, for Death hath a remedy for all diseases which is insensibility; the truth is, Death is not only charitable to help all creatures out of misery, but generous, as to be so hospitable that he sets open his gates for all comers, insomuch, as the meanest creatures that are have a free entrance and the same entertainment with the noblest, for there are no ceremonies of state, all is in common; there is no pride nor

218

ambition, no scorn nor disgrace; and Death's palace is so spacious as it is beyond all measure or circumference, being sufficient to receive all the creatures Nature makes; and since there is such store of company in death, and Death so generous and hospitable, why should we fear or be loth to die? Nay, why should not we desire to die and rejoice for those friends that are dead, especially considering the unhappiness of life, wherein man is most miserable because he is most sensible and apprehensive of what he suffers, or what he may suffer? But this young virgin is happier by Death than many others are, because she hath not lived so long to suffer so much as those that are older have done, or as those that live to be old will do. Wherefore let us rejoice for her happiness, and put her into the grave, the bed of rest, there to sleep quietly.

100 *A Young New-married Wifes Funeral Oration*

*Beloved Brethren,*

We are met together at this time, to see a new-married wife, which is here dead, to be buried; she hath made an unequal change from a lively hot husband to a deadly cold lover, yet will she be more happy with her dull, dumb, deaf, blind, numb lover, than with her lively, talking, listning, eyeing, active husband, were he the best husband that could be; for death is far the happier condition than marriage; and although marriage at first is pleasing, yet after a time it is displeasing, like meat which is sweet in the mouth but proves bitter in the stomach; indeed, the stomach of marriage is full of evil humours, as choler and melancholy; and of very evil digestion, for it cannot digest neglects, disrespects, absence, dissembling, adultery, jealousy, vain expenses, waste, spoil, idle time, laziness, examinations, cross answers, peevishness, frowardness, frowns, and many the like meats that marriage feeds on: as for pains, sicknesses, cares, fears, and other troubles in marriage, they are accounted as wholesome physic which the Gods give them; for the Gods are the best physicians, and Death is a very good surgeon, curing his patients without pain, for what part soever he touches is insensible. Death is only cruel in parting friends from each other, for though they are happy whom he takes away, yet those that are left behind are unhappy, living in sorrow for their loss; so that this young new-married wife that is dead, is happy, but her husband is a sorrowful widower; but leaving her to her happiness and him to be comforted, let us put her into the grave, there to remain until the day of judgement, which day will embody her soul with everlasting glory.

101 *A Widows Funeral Oration*

*Beloved Brethren,*

This widow, at whose funeral we are met, lived a very intemperate and irregular life all the time of her widowhood, for which not only Nature, but the Gods might be angry with her; for though she did not surfeit with feasting, yet she starved herself with fasting, and though she did not drink her self drunken as many women in this age will do, yet she did weep her self dry; she grew not fat and lazy with overmuch sleeping, but became lean and sick with overmuch watching; she watched not to dance and play but to mourn and pray, nor did she waste her wealth in vanities, but she did waste her life in sorrow; she sat not on the knees of amorous lovers but kneeled on her knees to God; her cheeks were not red with paint but pale with grief; she did not wear black patches on her face but black mourning on her body; she was adorned with no other jewels than her tears; she had no diamond pendants in her ears but transparent tears in her eyes, no oriental pearls about her neck but drops of tears lay on her breast; thus was she dressed in tears. She suffered not painters to draw the picture of her face, but her thoughts did form her husband's figure in her mind; she hung not her chamber with black but her mind with melancholy; she banished all stately ceremonies and ceremonies of state, and set herself humbly on the ground; she passed not her time with entertaining visitors, but entertain'd her self with the remembrance of her husband; she did not speak much, but think much. In short, she was so intemperate in her grief as her grief killed her; it may be said she was murdered with grief, and no kind or manner of murder is acceptable either to Nature or the Gods, but some sorts of murders are hateful to both. Yet this widow, howsoever she offended in her over-much grieving, she had pardon for her praying, and to prove the Gods did pardon her, they granted her request, which was to take her out of this world without painful sickness, and so they did; for she was so free from pains as she parted with life with a smiling countenance, and lay as still as if she lay to sleep, she breathed out her last breath so softly as those that stood close by her bed could not hear her sigh, and when she was dead, her beauty, that all the time of her mourning was obscured in her sorrows, appeared in her death, only the gloss of her eyes were covered with their lids, for Death had shut her eyelids down and sealed up her lips, which lips seemed as if they had been sealed with red coloured wax although Death had kissed them cold; for now Death is her lover, not an amorous but a deadly lover,

to whose embraces we must leave her body after we have laid it in the bed
of earth.

102  *Another Widows Funeral Oration*

*Beloved Brethren,*
We are met as funeral or rather marriage guests of a dead widow, who is now
re-married to her husband in death, and no question, but their souls will
joy in the knowledge of each other; for though bodies dye, yet souls do not,
but live for ever, death having power only over the sensitive, not over the
rational life; for knowledge lives, though senses dye; and if the soul lives,
no question, but all that is inherent in the soul lives, as all the passions,
affections, thoughts, memory, understanding, judgement, conceptions,
speculations, fancy, knowledge, and the like, which are the parts and
ingrediences with which the soul is composed, formed, and made; thus
the soul being made of such thin, fine, pure, and rare matter, death can
take no hold of it, for death's power is only on gross corporeal substances
or matter, not on celestial bodies, but terrestrial; but this widows soul
was purer than other souls usually are, (for there are degrees of purity in
souls as well as degrees of grossness in bodies), the truth might easily be
perceived in her life, for there was as much difference between her soul
and other souls, as between souls and bodies, at least as much difference as
between a glorified soul, and a soul imbodied; nay, her soul was so pure, as
it did purify her body, for it did refine the appetites, which cleared the
senses; besides, her soul did instruct the senses, which made them more
sensible, so that they were kept clean, clear, and healthful by temperance,
and made apt, quick, and ready by reason, insomuch, as time had but a
little power to hurt them, and was not able to destroy them without the
help of death, had she lived long, but death to show his power, destroyed
her body without the help of time, for she lived not to be so old as for
time to make a trial; yet her body lived longer than she was willing it
should have done, desiring it might have died when her husband died,
but the gods forbade it; for though any creature, especially man, may call
death when he will, and force him to take his bodily life away, yet the gods
are angry, if any man will not stay whilst death comes of himself without
enforcement. Nevertheless, death did favour this widow; for though he
did not take her so soon as she would have died, yet he suffered her not
long to live a weary life, for which favour she received death with joy, and
a smiling countenance, whereas death for the most part is received with

fear and sadness; and since she rejoiced at her death, we have no reason to mourn now she is dead, especially in that she lived and died virtuously, and piously, for which the gods will advance her to everlasting glory; for this glory let us praise the gods, and bury her body in her husbands tomb or grave, that their dust or ashes may lye together.

103 *A Young Childs Funeral Oration*

*Beloved Brethren,*
We are the funeral guests to a young male child, an infant, who died soon after it was born, and though all men are born to live, and live to die, yet this child was born to die before it had lived, I mean in comparison of the age of men; thus this child was born, cried, and died, a happy conclusion for the child that he had finished what he was made for in so short a time, for he could not have had less pain, less trouble, nor less desires to have left the world had he lived longer, for life is restless with desires, sickly and painful with diseases, troublesome with cares, laborious with labour, grievous with losses, fearful with dangers, and miserable in all; which misery this child hath escaped, but had he lived he could not have avoided it: besides, he is not guilty of self-acting sins and so deserves no punishment, for neither commission nor omission can be laid to his charge, having no time for either, so that he is free from both, as also from suffering either in this world, or the next, unless there be such a severe decree as the child shall suffer for his parents' faults, which faults he could neither hinder nor annul, neither did he approve nor allow them, nor assist them in evil; but it is not probable he shall suffer, being innocent; and death that is accounted the wages of sin may rather be taken as a gift of mercy; also death might be said to be a purifier from sin as well as a punisher of sin; wherefore this child is past the purgatory of death and is in the heaven of peace, rest, ease, and happiness, in which let us leave him, after we have covered his corpse with earth.

104 *An Old Ladys Funeral Oration*

This old lady was favoured by nature, fortune, and time, nature in her youth gave her beauty, fortune gave her wealth, and time and nature gave her long life; she was courted in her youth for the pleasures of her beauty, and flattered in her age for the profit of her wealth, but being chaste and wise, she was neither corrupted with the one nor deluded with the other, not tempted with courtship nor cozened with flattery; and as she was chaste and wise, so she was pious, for the Gods gave her grace to bestow her wealth to charitable uses; thus what she got by Fortune she gave to Heaven, indeed she bought Heaven with Fortune's gifts, for none can get into Heaven but by faith and good deeds, and her faith did believe that her good works would be as an advocate to plead for her, and no question but they have gotten her suit, and her charity will live here on earth though she be dead, and those she relieved will make her their saint; thus she will be sainted both on earth and in Heaven, which is as great an honour and a more blessed condition than the Emperors had with all their conquests, power, pride, and vanity, for the height of their ambition was to be deified on earth, and to be sainted in as much; they were worshipped for fear, she prayed to for love; they had idolatrous worshippers, she sanctified petitioners; their idols lasted but a time, she shall be blest for evermore.

105  *An Ancient Mans Funeral Oration*

*Beloved Brethren,*
Age hath ushered our friend to death, and we are here met to attend him to the grave; it is an human, charitable, and pious service to see the dead laid decently and ceremoniously into the earth, and it is an happiness for the dead to be inurned with their forefathers; for who knows to the contrary, but that there may be a natural sympathetical intermixing with their dust, and an earthly pleasure in their mixture? For certainly there is a mutual society in the earth as well as on the earth, and why may not the earth have a sympathetical intermixing and conjunction as well as the other elements? I perceive no reason against it; but whether there be an incorporating, associating, and friendship, as dust with dust, I know not, surely there is a peaceable abiding, having not a sensible feeling or knowledge, whereas life, wherein sense and knowledge dwells, is restless, full of troubles, misfortunes, pains, and sicknesses to the body and perturbations in the mind, so that the body is seldom at ease or the mind at quiet; but life hath tried the patience and death the courage of our friend, for he was neither impatient with life nor fearful of death; he had such great experience living so long, as to know there is neither constancy, certainty, nor felicity amongst or with the creatures in this world, and time had made him so wise a man, as he knew by himself that there was no man perfect nor truly happy, for happiness and imperfection

cannot associate together: yet by his wisdom, he did inform, reform, rule and govern himself as well as nature and the world would give way or leave to; for he would never command any but those that were willing to obey, and he did obey those he could not command; he would never make a fruitless opposition, but was free from faction and sedition, ambition and covetousness, for he knew there is not any worldly thing worth an over-earnest desire, nor any thing so permanent as could be kept long; he would temperately make use of what he had, and what he wanted for his use he did honestly endeavour for it, and what he could not have easily and freely he was content to be without; moreover, he was so moderate in his desires as he did scarcely desire what was necessary, and oftentimes he would part from his own maintenance to relieve the distresses of others, believing he could suffer want more patiently; indeed, he had such a power and command of himself, as the appetites of his body and passions of his mind were as obedient to his will as saints on earth, or angels in heaven, are to the Gods; and this wise government of himself made him fit for the company of the Gods, with whom we leave his soul, and will inter his body as we ought.

106  *An Old Beggar-Womans Funeral Oration*

*Beloved Brethren,*
This woman, that is here to be buried, was old when she died, very old, and as poor as old, and though she was old, yet she had longer acquaintance with her poverty than age, being always poor from her youth, indeed so poor as she was forced to beg for her livelihood: thus she was a double beggar; but now she is gone to beg at Heaven's gate, both for food and raiment, where, if Heaven's porter lets her in, she will be fed with beatifical food and clothed with celestial glory, a great and good change, for here she was fed with nothing but scraps and clothed with rags, and much ado to get them, not without long stay and earnest intreaties; so hard are men's hearts, and cold are men's charities; the truth is, men in prosperity feel not the misery of adversity, and being not sensible of their want are not ready in their relief: besides, they think all that is given from their vanities and luxuries is a prodigal waste, and it is to be observed that those that are richest are the most uncharitable, whereas those that have but little yet will give to those that have nothing to live on, feeling in some sort what want is; and to show the hard hearts of mankind to their own kind, this woman, although she had begged almost fourscore years, yet she got so

little as she had nothing to leave, not so much as to bury her. But as she lived on cold charity, so now she lies with cold death, a cold condition both alive and dead; the first cold she felt to her grief, this last cold she is insensible of to her happiness, in which happiness we will leave her, and put her into the grave of peace.

107 *A Young Brides Funeral Oration*

*Beloved Brethren,*
This young virgin, that lies here dead, ready to be buried, this very day had she lived she had been married, for so her lover and she had designed, at which designed time she little thought Death should have been her bridegroom, and that her winding sheet should be her wedding smock, and her grave her bride-bed, there to lie with Death, but doubtless Death was as far from her thoughts as her lover near to her heart: for had she believed she should have died so soon, or but feared it, she would not have made such preparations as usually young maids do for their wedding days; indeed young maids have reason enough to esteem much of that day, for it is the only happy day of their life; it is a day which is wholly consecrated to love, joy, pleasure, bravery, feasting, dancing, mirth and music; on that day their hearts are merry and their heels are light, but after their bridal shoes are off, their dancing days are done, I mean they are done in respect of happiness; for though married wives keep more company, and dance and feast oftener than maids, having more liberty, yet they are not so merry at the heart, nor have they so lively countenances, nor are so galliard[52] after they have been married some time as they were before they were married, or as they were on their wedding day, for their mirth is forced, and their actions more constrained, though not so much restrained; whereas maids and brides, their very thoughts as well as their persons dance, sport, and play in their minds: but this young virgin and dead bride can neither dance nor be merry, neither hath she cause to weep or be sad, nor she hath no amorous thoughts towards her bridegroom; she takes no notice of him, his kind embraces do not make her blush, neither doth she hate or fear him; she grieves not for the change, nor thinks she of her living lover, that should have been her living husband but is now her living mourner, whose tears like raining showers have all bedewed her hearse; and though she was not led with bridesmaids to the church, yet

[52] Lively, high-spirited.

she is brought by virgins to the grave; her hearse is crowned, though not her head, and covered with white satin like as a marriage gown, and all her tomb is strewed with flowers sweet like to a bridal-bed, in which tomb let us lay her, and then sing anthems instead of epithalamiums,[53] and so leave her to her rest.

108 *A Child-bed Womans Funeral Oration*

*Beloved Brethren,*

We are met together to see a young dead woman, who died in childbed, to be laid into the bed of earth, a cold bed, but yet she will not take any harm there, nor we shall not fear she will catch her death, for death hath caught her; the truth is that although all women are tender creatures, yet they endure more than men, and do oftener venture and endanger their lives than men, and their lives are more profitable than men's lives are, for they increase life when men for the most part destroy life, as witness wars, wherein thousands of lives are destroyed, men fighting and killing each other, and yet men think all women mere cowards, although they do not only venture and endanger their lives more than they do, but endure greater pains with greater patience than men usually do: nay, women do not only endure the extremity of pain in childbirth, but in breeding, the child being for the most part sick and seldom at ease; indeed, Nature seems both unjust and cruel to her female creatures, especially women, making them to endure all the pain and sickness in breeding and bringing forth of their young children, and the males to bear no part of their pain or danger; the truth is nature hath made her male creatures, especially mankind, only for pleasure, and her female creatures for misery; men are made for liberty and women for slavery, and not only slaves to sickness, pains, and troubles in breeding, bearing, and bringing up their children, but they are slaves to men's humours, nay, to their vices and wickedness, so that they are more enslaved than any other female creatures, for other female creatures are not so enslaved as they; wherefore those women are most happy that never marry, or die whilst they be young, so that this young woman that died in childbed is happy in that she lives not to endure more pain or slavery, in which happiness let us leave her after we have laid her corpse to rest in the grave.

[53] A nuptial poem or song in praise of the bride and bridegroom.

109 *A Soldiers Funeral Oration*

*Beloved Brethren,*
This dead man whom you attend to the grave was, whilst he lived, a valiant,
gallant man, and an excellent soldier, for that was his profession in times of
war; a noble profession, for all valiant soldiers are Honour's sons, Death's
friends, and Life's enemies, for a soldier's profession is to destroy lives to
get honour and fame, by which destruction Death is a gainer; in truth,
Death is a soldiers companion, comrade and familiar acquaintance, but
not a soldiers friend, though soldiers be Death's friends; he is no stranger
to soldiers, for they see him in all shapes, postures, and humours; yet the
most terrible aspects of Death could not affright nor terrify this soldier,
nor cause him to remove an inch back, for he would venture to the very
jaws of Death. Thus bold, adventurous soldiers do more affright Death
than Death doth affright them, insomuch that Death for the most part
runs away from valiant men and seizes on cowards, and daring not assault
valiant men in the forefront, he steals upon them as it were unawares,
for he comes behind valiant men when he takes hold of them, or else he
seizes on them by treachery, or weakens their bodies so much by sickness
as they are forced to yield; indeed there was no other way for Death to
take this valiant soldier but by sickness, for he could never take him in the
field; but Death is of the nature of ungrateful men who endeavour to do
those most mischief that have been most bountiful to them, and are ready
to take the lives of those they were most obliged to; for valiant men give
Death thousands of lives to feed on, yet he is like some gluttons, the more
they eat, the leaner they are; nay, Death is so lean as to be only bare bones,
and by his empty skull he may be thought a fool, having no brains, though
he be rather a knave than a fool, for he deceives or robs Nature and Time
of many lives, taking them away before Nature and Time had ordained
them to die; but leaving Death to ingratitude, cheats, and robberies, we
must also leave him this dead soldier's body for to feed upon, for all heroic
men are Death's most nourishing food, they make him strong and lusty;
and since there is no remedy, let us place this dead *Hero* on Death's table,
which is to put him into the grave, and there leave him.

110 *An Oration concerning the Joys of Heaven, and Torments of Hell*

*Beloved Brethren,*
You have heard of Heaven and Hell, Gods and devils, damnation and
salvation, and that you shall have a fullness of bliss in Heaven and be

everlastingly tormented in Hell; also you have heard Hell and Heaven described to you, as that Heaven is composed and built all of precious stones and rich metal, as gold, diamonds, rubies, pearls, sapphires, and the like; as also what degrees and powers there be; and for Hell, it is described to be dark as night, and yet great elemental fires in which the damned shall be tormented, the like for other torments that devils use as their rods and scourges to punish the damned; also that the devils do curse and the blessed sing and rejoice; moreover, you have heard by your teacher, and seen painted in pictures, both the shapes of devils and angels, the angels with wings and the devils with horns and cloven feet like beasts; all which may be true, for any thing we sensibly know to the contrary, and yet perchance all these relations may be false, as the relation of the situation of Heaven and Hell, and the architecture of either, or the shapes of devils or angels, or the manner and ways of their pleasures and delights, and their pains and torments; all which may not be so as they are usually described to us, but made by men's fancies, for no mortal man is come either from Heaven or Hell to tell us punctually of every particular truth. Yet a Heaven and Hell, good and bad angels, pains and torments, joys and pleasures there are, for both reason and faith informs us, also God himself tells us in his holy writs, and by his inspired priests and prophets, that there is reward for the good in Heaven, and punishment for the bad in Hell; but if we will give our imaginations leave to work upon that we cannot know whilst we live here in this world, let us imagine what is most probable; and first for the situation of Heaven and Hell, or the architecture of either, or the shapes of devils or angels, it is beyond my imagination; yet some imagination may beget a belief, at least some probability, of the joys in Heaven, and the torments in Hell; wherefore I'll begin with the glorified bodies in Heaven, which bodies in their glorified condition shall have their senses more perfect and their appetites more quick, the body being purified into a celestial purity, than when their bodies were clogged with a terrestrial grossness, which made their senses weak and their appetites dull; these glorified bodies shall have their senses filled and their appetites satisfied in a spiritual manner, as thus: the sight shall have the most beautiful, splendorous, pleasant, and glorious objects, not that those objects are corporeally without them, but only in their sight; and such varieties of such sights, as they shall see each sight fully to admire them, but not to tire them, and being satisfied, they shall have new, and with every new sight a new admiration, and after every admiration a new sight: the like for the sense of hearing, which shall be filled sometimes with eloquent language, witty expressions, and fancy, expressed both in verse and prose, sometimes rational discourses, wise sentences, oratory speeches and learned arguments, also harmonious music, melodious voices and pleasing vocal sounds, with such variety and delight as art nor nature never knew; yet nothing shall come from without to the ear or be conveyed into it, but be within it: and as for the sense of scent, such sweet perfumes and ravishing sweets shall it smell as every scent shall breed a new desire, and every desire a new scent, and have in all a satisfaction; yet nothing of these various sweets, or sweet perfumes, shall enter from without into the nostrils, but be within them: and as for taste, deliciously and with *gusto* shall it feed and satisfy the stomach, not with food, but taste, for taste shall be the food, and every appetite shall bring a new taste, and every taste a new appetite, and every appetite shall be satisfied, yet in the mouth shall not any meat be: the like for touch, which is a kind of taste, there shall be a feeling pleasure, where every touch shall be a new pleasure, and every pleasure shall bring a new touch, there shall touch feel a comfortable heat from a freezing cold, and a refreshing cold upon great sultry heats, and yet no fire nor frost shall touch their bodies; there shall it feel a scratching pleasure, to take off itching pain, yet nothing hurt the body; there shall it feel a soft and downy touch, as from a hard rough pain, yet nothing press the body, and all the body shall feel such ease as if it came from hard labour, and such rest as from a tedious travelling, and infinite of other pleasurable and delightful touches as are not to be expressed. Thus every sense shall be satisfied in a spiritual way, without a gross corporeal substance, and the blessed souls of these glorified bodies, and spiritual satisfactions of glorified senses and appetites, shall be filled with all perfection, as a clear understanding, a perfect knowledge, a pure wit, a sound judgement and a free will, and all the passions regulated and governed as they ought to be, into love and hate, as hate to the wicked and damned, and love to the blessed and glorified; and such delights shall they have not only in the pleasures of their glorified bodies, but in themselves, such as God himself enjoys; thus shall souls and bodies be blessed and glorified in Heaven. And after the same manner and way as blessed souls and bodies have delight and pleasure and fullness of joy in Heaven, so shall the souls and bodies of the damned have terror and torments and fullness of horror in Hell; for as the senses and appetites have variety and satisfaction of pleasures in Heaven, so shall the senses and appetites have variety of terror, dread, and horror, and be surfeited with aversion, loathing and reluctance, and filled with misery and evil: as for the sense of touch in damned bodies, it is not probable they are burnt with elemental fire, as many think, but their sense of touch hath such a burning feeling as is so far beyond the elemental burning as that burning is a pleasure to it, and such excessive variety of pains it is probable they have, as art could never invent, nor nature make, nor sense feel in this world, nor thought of man imagine: and for the sense of scent, it is not probable there is the smell of brimstone and sulphur, for that may be endured without a great dislike, but it is probable and to be believed that their sense of scent smells varieties of filthy stinks, yet not from without them, as of the devils making, but within themselves: and as for their sense of hearing, it is not probable that the devils do vocally roar or verbally curse, but that the damned have in the sense of hearing infinite, confused, fearful, and dreadful noises, reproaching, exclaiming, and cursing words and speeches: and as for the sense of sight, it is not so much the devils' ugly and monstrous shapes which they see, but their sense of sight is filled with infinite varieties of ugly, deformed, monstrous, and terrible sights. Thus it is probable the damned are tormented. Also 'tis probable that both the damned and blessed are fixed to their places; for the blessed having fullness of joy and a fruition of desire, have no occasion or desire to wander from place to place, for it is restless desire and unsatisfied appetite that moves and removes, seeking for that they would have and cannot get, or for something, they know not what, for which the damned may desire to remove; but as the blessed saints are fixed with a fullness of joy and admiration, not caring to remove therefrom, so the damned are so stricken with fear and terror as they dare not remove if they could; and as the satisfaction, variety, pleasure, delight and joy of the blessed begins and continueth without end, so the variety of aversion, terror, and torments begins and continues for ever; but the most probable opinion is that the fullness of joy is the love of God, and the fullness of pleasure the glory of God, and the horror and torments of the damned is the want of that love and glory.

111  *An Oration to a Congregation*

*Dearly Beloved Brethren,*
Man hath not only vain or erroneous imaginations or opinions, but beliefs, being without ground or foundation, which is without sense and reason; for what sense and reason hath man to imagine or believe that Heaven, which is celestial, should be composed of terrestrial materials, as of pure gold, crystal, and precious stones, and not rather believe it to be only

the beatifical vision of God? And what sense and reason hath man to believe that Hell is Hell for want of the presence of God, whereas the omnipotent God must necessarily be all fulfilling? And is it not a strange contradicting opinion or belief that Hell is dark, and yet that in Hell is elemental fire and terrestrial brimstone? And what sense and reason hath man to believe that celestial bodies have terrestrial shapes, whereas we may easily perceive that all outward shapes, forms or figures are according to the degrees of the purity or grossness of the substance or matter they are composed of? Wherefore man hath not any reason to believe that angels, which are celestial substances, can have terrestrial shapes; and what reason hath man to believe that angels in Heaven have the shapes of men on earth; but if they should believe they have terrestrial shapes, why should they believe them to have men's shapes and not the shapes of other creatures? It might be answered, the belief proceeds from the Son of God, who did take upon him the shape of man, but then we may believe that angels are of the shape of doves, because the Holy Ghost, which is co-equal and co-eternal with the Son, did take upon him the shape of that bird. Also what reason hath man to believe that the devils' shapes are partly of the shape of beasts, as to have tails, horns, claws, and cloven feet? Do they believe that the shape of beasts is a more wicked or cursed shape than any other animal shape? But these opinions or beliefs proceed from gross conceptions, made by irregular motions in gross terrestrial bodies, or brains in mankind, who make Hell and Heaven, God, angels and devils, according to their fancies, and not according to truth; for man cannot know what is not in his portion of reason and sense to know, and yet man will judge and believe that which he cannot possibly know, which is ridiculous even to human sense and reason. But to conclude, *Dearly Beloved*, men's thoughts are too weak, their brains too little, their knowledge too obscure, and their understandings too cloudy to conceive Gods celestial works or workings, or his will or decrees, fates or destinies; wherefore, pray without forming, obey without censuring, fear his power, love his goodness, and hope in his mercy, and the blessing of God be amongst you.

112 *An Oration to a Sinful Congregation*

*Beloved Brethren*,
You live so lewdly, riotously, and wickedly, as if you did not believe there are gods or devils, Heaven or Hell, punishment or bliss, and as if there were none other life after this life, but you will find you shall be so punished for

your wickedness unless you amend, as you will curse your birth, life, and death; for so bad and wicked you are that the seven deadly sins are not sins enough for you, but daily, nay hourly, you study to make more deadly sins, nay you are so ingenious in devising sin as you are the most subtle artisans therein that ever were; you are a *Vitruvius* for designing sins, a *Pygmalion* for carving out sins, an *Apelles* for painting out sins, a *Galileus* for espying out sins,[54] an *Euclid* for numbering and multiplying sins, so that your sins are now past all account, an *Archimedes* for inventing sins, an *Aristoteles* to find out sins, a *Cicero* in pleading for sins, an *Alexander* in fighting for sins, an *Homerus* in describing sins,[55] and your lives and actions are the foundations and materials, the stones and chisels of sins, the boards and planks, the light, shadows, and colours of sins, the perspective glasses of sins, the figures of sins, the instruments and engines of sins, the lines, circles, and squares of sins, the bodies, parts, and lives of sins, the tongue and speech of sin, the arms of sin, the brains and wit of sin: thus you are nothing but sin within and without, for life, soul, thoughts, bodies and actions are all sin; indeed you seem as if you were neither made by Nature nor God, but begotten or produced from devils; for Nature exclaims against you, and God abhors you, the devils will own you, but God of his mercy give you grace to repent and amend your lives, that what sin is past may be blotted out, and that your lives, thoughts and actions may be such as may gain upon eternal blessedness and everlasting glory, for which let us pray.

113  *An Oration which is an Exhortation to a Pious Life*

*Beloved Brethren,*

You come here to be instructed, but yet you do not amend your lives, for you live idly and wickedly; you make no profit of your instructions or exhortations, for it seems by you that the more you are taught, the more ignorant you are, like those that become blind or their sight dazzled with too much light; indeed you live as if you had not rational souls, or that you thought souls die as bodies do, but you will find you have souls that shall

---

[54] Vitruvius was a Roman architect, Pygmalion of Paphos was a sculptor and Apelles was a Greek painter. Galileo was famous for astronomical observations made with the help of telescopes. See *Blazing World*, n. 36.

[55] Archimedes was a Greek mathematician, Euclid a Greek geometer, Aristotle a Greek philosopher, Cicero a Roman orator, Alexander a Greek conqueror. The poet Homer is the author of the *Iliad* and the *Odyssey*.

live to endure torment if you do not reform your lives: 'Tis true, many
have strange, and some atheistical opinions concerning the soul, for some
have had opinions that man hath no other soul but such as beasts have,
and others that the souls of all creatures go out of one body into another
and that death doth but change the soul's lodging; and some have had an
opinion that there is no such thing as a soul, but that which is called a
soul is only animal life; and others believe there be souls, but they die
as bodies do; others, that there is but one great soul which is the soul of
the world; but the right and truth is that men have particular souls which
not any other creature hath, which are called rational souls, and shall live
for ever, either in torment or bliss, according to their merit; but the best
and wisest men make no question of the rational soul of mankind, though
many learned men trouble their heads to prove what the soul is, for some
believe the soul is corporeal, others it is incorporeal. Also many trouble
themselves to know when the souls of mankind enter into their bodies;
some think before the body is born, others hold it enters not until the
body is born; and some think that the body receives the soul so soon as
it receives life in the womb; and some think before, as when it is newly
conceived: but those that are of an opinion that life and soul enters into
the body together, believe their departs together by death; and those that
think the soul enters not into the body until it be born believe the soul is
but a weakling at first, and grows stronger as the body grows older. Thus
they trouble their heads and exercise their wits concerning the soul, to
know what it is, and how it is, but never take thought as how it will be when
they die, like the dog that left the substance to seek for the shadow, so men
leave the salvation and dispute about the creation: but my exhortation
is that you would pray more and dispute less; for what shall we need to
trouble our minds, whether the soul be corporeal or incorporeal? Or if
corporeal, of what matter it is made of, so that it be capable of glory?
Nor shall we need to trouble our minds when it enters the body, so it
enters heaven. Wherefore those that are truly wise, and wisely devout,
will endeavour with all their power, faith, and industry of their minds,
thoughts, and life, to do such charitable deeds, and to think such pious
thoughts in holy contemplations, and pray with so much zeal and faith,
penitence and thanksgiving, as God may be so well pleased with them
as to glorify their souls in Heaven, where there is all joy and happiness,
which joy and happiness I pray the Gods may give you.

# MARRIAGE ORATIONS
## Part IX

114  *A Marriage Oration to a Congregation, and a Young Bride and Bridegroom*

*Beloved Brethren,*
We are met together as bridal-guests to see this young man and woman married, who are to be bound, tied, and manacled with holy ceremony, vows and promises; yet all too little to tie some couples fast, for many do not only loosen those bonds with taking unlawful liberty, but quite break them by divorce, which shows the unruliness and untowardness of married people, or else it shows the insufferable condition of a married life; and yet for all the proofs, trials, and examples of the evils that are in marriage, men and women will take no warning, for not only maids and bachelors, but widows and widowers run head-long into the noose or marriage halter; I do not say this to discourage this young couple, but to advise them when they are married to live temperately, prudently, lovingly, and peaceably, that they may not surfeit their fond and eager appetites, which causes the sickness of aversion and death of affection, or prodigally waste their maintenance, or idly spend their time, for poverty breaks friendship and turns near friends to foes; nor live inconstantly, for that makes jealousy and jealousy hate; nor live quarrelsome, for that makes faction, faction division, and division divorce; whereas temperance makes constancy, prudence plenty, love keeps peace, and peace makes happiness, which happiness I wish this young couple, and so I will join their hands, praying that God will join their hearts with an united love and felicity.

115  *A Marriage Oration to a Congregation, and an Old Bride and Young Bridegroom*

*Beloved Brethren,*
We are met together as marriage-guests to see this couple married together, although it be an unequal match, the bride being aged and the bridegroom young, she too old for him and he too young for her; which shows as if she wanted wit and he wealth; but I hope neither of them will want that love which ought to be betwixt a man and wife: I say not this to hinder their marriage, for if they do agree, every one ought to approve it, and if they should not agree, none will suffer but themselves, either in the opinion of their neighbours and friends or in their own discontents; for

their neighbours will censure both, as if she was too amorous for her age and he too covetous for his youth, and that time will cool the one and riot consume the other; which if it prove so, you will wish one another dead, but not love one another living; whereas when you agree kindly, and live orderly, you will be praised worthily, and so much the more as being unusual, and therefore not expected: for who would not believe but that an old wife should be jealous and a young husband wanton? Or who will believe an old wife to be pleasing and a young husband continent? But this true pleasure and constancy I wish you, and will join your hands, praying for your happiness.

116 *A Marriage Oration to a Congregation, and a Young Bride and Aged Bridegroom*

*Beloved Brethren,*
Here is a loving aged man and a chaste young woman to be joined in holy matrimony, which shows the man to have courage, the woman to be prudent; for surely it is very dangerous for an aged man to marry a young woman, especially an handsome young woman, not only that youth is apt to be inconstant and loves variety, but youth and beauty is a temptation to amorous lovers which will lay siege and make assaults, endeavouring with all their flattery, bribes, vanity, and prodigality to corrupt, betray, and win her; but she is prudent to choose an experienced man, preferring wisdom before youth, wit before beauty, love before courtship, and temperance before pleasure: all which foreshows she will make a chaste wife which will keep her husband's love and her own reputation, which love and chastity will make them happy, and both will make them honourable, to which respect and happiness I join them inseparably.

117 *A Marriage Oration of two Poor Servants*

*Beloved Brethren,*
You have attended these two poor servants to the church, as their bridal-guests, to witness their lawful marriage, by which you do them honour, and if you will also do them good you will bestow on them an offering, for though each person should give but a small gift, yet in the whole sum it will be great to them, so that it will not be missed in your purses, and yet be a benefit to their lives, for it may make them rich, and yourselves not poor; but if you give them not any, they may nevertheless by their industry

thrive, for as they have wrought honestly for their master and mistress, so they will labour honestly for themselves, and as their master did thrive by their service, so they hope to thrive in serving themselves, and so in time they may become master and mistress to servants as they were servants to master and mistress; for prudent industry and thrifty sparing makes the poor rich, and riches doth advance them to honour, whereas carelessness, riot, and vain expenses make rich men poor and noble men mean, so that in time labouring peasants' and thriving citizens' posterities come to be rich men and great lords, when as the posterity of rich men and great lords, through their prodigality comes to be poor labouring men and slaves, for Heaven blesses the industry of the poor but punishes the riot of the rich; which blessing be upon this couple, and so let us join their hands with holy ceremony, and Heaven join their hearts with love.

# ORATIONS TO CITIZENS IN THE MARKET PLACE

## PART X

118 *An Oration against Excess and Vanity*

*Fellow Citizens,*

I observe great excess in stately and chargeable buildings, rich and costly furnishings, vain adornings, wasteful feasting, idle entertaining and unprofitable attendances, and the like vanities. First for your building, you build not only for conveniency and decency, but for state and magnificence, and you build not only large and high, as if you would spread to the circumference of the earth and ascend to the mansions of the Gods, but you endeavour to work beyond nature for curiosities in cutting, carving, engraving and painting to the life; also you dig to the abyss, as to the centre of the earth for several materials, as diverse sorts of stones and metals, and endeavour to make your palaces to outshine the sun with gold; wherein you waste so much gold and silver in vain and unprofitable gilding and inlaying, that there is not enough left to make coin for traffic: also your stately building doth not only ruin your posterity, leaving them more houses than land, but you ruin the poor, enclosing the land with your walls and filling up lands with houses, whereas corn and fruits should grow; thus you tread upon the bellies, backs and heads of the poor. And as for your rich and costly furniture, it costs much and wears out soon, yielding no profit, for the principal of so much money is wasted and no use made thereof. Secondly, for your feasting, wherewith you eat rather to be sick than to prolong life, you spoil more than you eat and eat more than you have appetite; you are like misers in your feeding, stuffing your stomachs with meat as they do their trunks and bags with money, and the superfluity of meat destroys the gluttonous eater with surfeits. Thirdly, your adorning or rather deforming yourselves in antic fashions and toyish vanities, which sheweth your heads to be brainless, and sometimes your purses to be moneyless, for spending so much on your backs, you cannot keep anything in your coffers nor for your necessary use. Fourthly, your idle visits and unprofitable discourses, wherein is more words than wit, and more time lost than knowledge gained, for you become more ignorant with talking than learned with contemplating, for brains are not manured with foolish discourses but wise considerations. Lastly, your numerous trains, which are unprofitable servants, being maintained for show and not for use, they spending much and doing little service, is the cause not only of great disorders, but the ruin of many noble families. The short is, you drink to be drunk, eat to be sick, live to be idle, spend to be poor, and talk to be fools: thus you lose time, waste your estate, trouble your minds and shorten your lives, living with more cost than worship, and more worship than pleasure; for you are stewards for your servants, hosts for your guests, and slaves to your vain humours.

119 *An Oration Contradicting the Former*

*Noble Citizens,*

The former oration was against the lawful delights and pleasures of our *citizens*, nay, of all mankind, which expresses the orator either to be so poor of means as he cannot attain to such delights and pleasures, or that his senses are imperfect as not capable to receive them, or that he is of so evil a disposition as to desire all men to be miserable, or that he is a fool as not knowing how to speak or live wisely, whereas had he spoken against hurtful and destroying vices he had spoken as a good man ought to do, for vices are vices no otherwise but that they are hurtful or destructive to mankind, which makes them vices, for the Gods forbid them because of the evil effects; as drunkenness, which disorders the reason, distempers the brain, and obstructs the senses, making men senseless or to be as mad, and causes oftentimes quarrels, wounds, and death, at least breaks peace and makes enemies of friends; besides, drunkenness makes men sick, and is apt to shorten their lives, all which makes it a vice and so a sin; but did drunkenness cause no evil effect, it ought not to be forbidden, nor could it be accounted a crime. The like I may say for gluttony, for would men eat only to please them, and not so much as to disease them, it would be no fault to eat well or to please their palate, but it is the surfeits, sickness, and oftentimes untimely death that makes gluttony a vice; and for adultery, it would be so far from a crime as it would be a virtue in the increase of mankind, were it not for the loss of propriety, in that no man would know his own child, nor be sure to enjoy his own wife, or that woman he makes choice of. As for theft and murder, they are not of that sort to be named vices only, but damnable sins, wherein can neither be society, safety, nor security of life, for thieves and murderers endeavour an utter destruction without mercy or remorse; wherefore, since vices and sins are vices and sins for their hurt and evil effects, those things that are called vanities, which produce pleasure and delight without death and destruction, ought not to be spoken against; for vanities are profitable to the poor, and not hurtful to the rich; but yet moralists and divines plead, preach and write, rail and exclaim against all honest, harmless delights and pleasures, as if they were sins to God and Nature, as if nature and the God of nature should make senses and appetites in vain, or only to the hurt and dislike of the creature and not for their good and pleasure, as to make a body for pain and sickness and not for health and ease, and to make a mind for trouble and discontent and not for peace and tranquillity, to make desires but not fruitions: indeed nature and the God of nature is more just to mankind; for as they have made eyes and seeing, so they have made light, splendour, and beauty to be seen; and as they have made ears to hear, so they have made harmony to be heard; and as they have made nostrils to smell, so they have made perfumes to be smelt; and as they have made taste, so they have made relishes; and as they have made hunger, so they have made food; and as they have made appetites, so they have given satisfaction or satiety. Thus we may perceive that every particular sense is fitted or matched to particular pleasures; but because nature hath made some aversion, therefore moralists and divines would not have men enjoy the pleasure in nature, whereas the most rational men perceive that aversions were only made to heighten and redouble the pleasures and delights both of body and mind; but these men are so rigid in their doctrine, (I will not say, in their own particular practice), as they would have men choose the worst part and refuse the better, and would have all mankind struggle, strive, and oppose all nature's delights and benefits; the truth is, they seem to desire a perpetual war between the senses and the objects, as also between the mind and the body, as between the reason and sense; but in my opinion, their doctrine hath neither sense nor reason, and their authors would have as little if they should practice what they preach. Wherefore, *Noble Citizens*, my advice is that you take your pleasures, yet so as you may enjoy them long, as to warm your selves not to burn your selves, to view the light but not to gaze out your sight, to bathe your selves but not to drown your selves, to please your selves but not to destroy your selves with excess.

120 *An Oration against Usurers and Money-hoarders*

*Noble Citizens,*
We have some citizens amongst us that are rich, and yet miserable; they covet much, yet enjoy but little, for they hoard up their wealth and starve

themselves; and if they did starve none but themselves it were no great matter, being fitter for death than life, but their hoards impoverish the commonwealth, and so starve the poor; for there cannot be a greater evil in a commonwealth, set aside war, than to have many rich usurers, as covetous getters, and spare spenders; for their great wealth is like as a great dunghill, which whilst it lies on a heap together doth no good, but hurt, whereas if it were dispersed and spread upon the barren lands, it would enrich much ground, producing increase and plenty. The like should money or such sort of riches be spread equally, to make a commonwealth live happily; indeed, a prodigal is more beneficial and profitable to a commonwealth than a usurer, for a prodigal makes only himself poor and the commonwealth rich, whereas a miserable man makes only himself rich and the commonwealth poor. 'Tis true, riches is accounted a great blessing, and surely it is so, but I take riches to be only a blessing in the use, and not barely in the possession, for riches is not what we have but what we enjoy; for he that hath delicious fruits and will eat sour crabs; hath reviving wines and will drink insipid water; hath stately houses and will live in a thatched cottage; hath store of fuel and will freeze with cold; and hath great sums of money but will spend none, those are poorer than they that have but a little and will spend according to their estate; yet these miserable men that live starvingly, slovenly, and unwholesomely are commended by the moralists, and accounted wise men, as not taking pleasure in that they call vanities, which is to make use of their riches, as to live plentifully, pleasantly, gloriously, and magnificently, if they have wherewithall to live so, pleasing themselves with what good fortune hath given them. I for my part, I had rather live rich and die poor, than die rich and live poor, and leave my wealth to those that will be so far from acknowledging my gifts with thanks by praising me for them, as it is likely they would rail on my memory, so that my wealth would only build me a tomb of reproaches and a monument of infamy, which would be a just judgement for being so unnatural to my self. But miserable men believe they are masters to their wealth, because they have it in keeping, when as they are slaves, not daring to use it unless it be in getting ten in the hundred: I confess, if such men had children, being for the most part childless, there were some excuse for them, but yet fathers should not make themselves miserable to make their sons prodigal, for a rich son of a miserable father is commonly a spendthrift; and as fathers are bound by nature to provide for their children in a wise proportion, so they are bound by nature to maintain themselves so plentifully as to enjoy a happy life. But to conclude, those that are miserable hoarders, or unconscionable usurers, are like as weasels or such like vermin; for as these suck out the meat of an egg, so they suck out silver and gold, and leave the commonwealth like as an empty egg shell, which is a penniless purse or treasury.

121 *An Oration concerning the Education of Children*

*Fellow Citizens,*
I commend your love and care, which you seem to have of your sons, as to have them taught and instructed in arts and sciences, as also when they are grown up towards manhood to send them abroad to see foreign and several nations, for to be acquainted with their fashions, manners, and behaviours, and to learn their several languages, all which is profitable, and will make them worthy men if they profit;[56] yet though I commend your love, I cannot commend your judgements for putting your sons to be instructed by young pedants and to be guided by young governors, which are but boys themselves in comparison of experienced, understanding, knowing, wise men, that is aged men who have seen, heard, and learned much and so know much, whereas young men have not had time to hear, see, and learn much, and so cannot understand nor know much, but must of necessity be ignorant. Wherefore it is not to be wondered at that fathers reap not the profit, or have not the return of their care and expenses in their sons educations; for youth breeding up youth makes many men to be boys all their lifetime, and being not instructed as they ought, become wild, like plants that want manuring; and fathers, mistaking the cause through long custom, think it is the incapacity of their sons, and not the insufficiency of their tutors and governors, if they prove not according to their hopes and expectations; but most fathers, being bred as ignorantly as their sons, think their sons completely bred if they have been some time at the university and have made some short time of travel, although without profiting either in knowledge or manners. Thus it may be thought that one fool begets another; but the truth is that one fool breeds an other, for the fault is not in nature, but in education, at least not so generally and constantly, for nature doth not commit so many errors, and make so many defects, as breeding doth.

[56] Cf. Oration 43.

122  *An Oration concerning the Plague*

*Fellow Citizens,*

I shall not need to tell you that the plague[57] is in this city, or that it increases daily, I may say hourly, or that this city hath been formerly infested or infected with this disease, in so much as sometimes it hath almost made a depopulation; but by reason it is such a deadly destroying disease as to sweep thousands into oblivious death, and not only a destroying, but a murderous disease, for it takes men suddenly, unawares and unprepared, being in perfect health and full strength, and wounds so deadly as to be past remedy, not to be cured either by medicines or salve when it hath strongly seized on the body; wherefore, to hinder it from such a strong assault and ruin, let me advise you, *Citizens*, especially the magistrates who have power and authority to order and govern this city, as they shall think good and expedient for it; first, to set out a declaration to all house-holders, upon paying a fine if neglected and not performed, to cleanse their houses, pumps, springs, sinks, gutters, and privy-offices; also that officers in every parish, and other particular persons, may be authorized for that employment, to see the streets, lanes, and out-corners in and of the city cleansed from dunghills, and dung of men and beast, and from carrion, mud, and such like filth; also to have the common sewers, sinks, channels, wells, as also the lakes, ponds and such like places without the city near adjoining, well cleansed, and all this foul filth buried deep in the earth, that no ill savour or vapour may ascend therefrom; for foul, gross, stinking vapours arising, especially from several places, as several houses, streets, ditches, sewers, and the like, dispersing corruption about, infect the air, which spreads far and enters into the very bowels and inward parts of men, nay, it doth not only poison the bodies of men, but all other animal creatures, as also the fruits of the earth; and so strong it is that it bursts forth in sores, ulcers, and spots on the bodies of men and beasts, inflaming their spirits and consuming their lives in a moment; wherefore, to help to purify the air, let there be pitch and tar burnt in the open streets, and frankincense, storax[58] and benzoin[59] in the houses, or at least juniper; and after the city is thus cleansed and the air purified, you must endeavour to cleanse and purify the bodies of the inhabitants by commanding every one to be purged with drugs or simples, and to be let blood, or else it will

---

[57] Cf. Oration 58.    [58] A fragment of resin from the tree *Styrax officinalis.*
[59] A fragrant resin obtained from the *Styrax benzoin*, a tree found in Sumatra and Java.

be a vain work, as to cleanse their houses from filth and let their bodies be full of foul humours, to cleanse their sinks and gutters and let their veins be full of corrupted or inflamed blood; yet must the bodies of men not be cleansed until the city be cleansed, lest the infected air from without should more easily get into them and kill them. But I hope I shall not need much rhetoric to persuade you to take a care of your own lives, for life is sweet and death is terrible; although I have observed that men, though they desire to live, nay, are afraid to die, yet are so careless, obstinate and confident as not to endeavour to prolong their lives, or to defend their lives from diseases, which are death's sergeants; for although all creatures were made to consume into other forms, and men are born to die, yet no creature was made to die and be consumed or transmigrated before their natural time, for nature hath given her creatures defences and remedies against the spoilers and destroyers of life, which spoilers and destroyers, as also their remedies and defences, are not easily to be numbered; but men are often their own lives' enemies, killing themselves with riot and excess, or being over-bold in adventuring or entering into dangers, or so careless as to pass by remedies: yet I hope you will be careful and speedily industrious to prevent, if possibly you can, the increase and fury of this plague.

123 *An Oration against Idle Expenses*

*Fellow Citizens,*
I observe great excess and luxury in this city, prodigally spending your estates and wasting your lives with riot, which I cannot enough won-der at, that although men will hazard their lives to get wealth and to keep it from those that would take it from them, yet will spend it lav-ishly, as extravagantly and vainly, nay, more readily to make them sick than to make themselves well when they are sick, for they will spend it freely in luxury and be sparing to a physician, which shows men love pleasure more than health, whereas health is the greatest pleasure, for sensual pleasures are always followed with sickness and pain, which lasts long, even so long as many times they do accompany them to the grave; and as pains and sickness follow sensual pleasures, so poverty and scorn follows vain expenses, all which makes a discontented mind: wherefore, what man, if he were wise, would destroy his body, disquiet his mind, and ruin his estate for that which is called pleasure? Which is nothing

but sensual appetites that are no sooner enjoyed but are forgotten or loathed with the fruition; and for pleasures of the mind, those are only opinions, which are nothing in substance and therefore not to be truly or really enjoyed. But as temperance is the greatest bodily pleasure because it gives health, so judgement is the minds physic, purging out vain opinions, idle thoughts and restless desires, which give it the health of peace and tranquillity. Thus your body and mind will live healthfully, happily, and honestly, employing their time and labours in the service of God, their country and friends, living wisely, parting with the world willingly, leaving a good fame behind them, and ascend to a crown of glory and eternal life.

124 *An Oration for Men to Please themselves*

*Fellow Citizens*,

Give me leave to tell you that moral orations are more proper to be spoken in schools than in the market-place, where they will sooner spoil young students than reform old citizens; but those that speak against pleasure speak against the darling of life, and therefore I do not wonder at any for taking his pleasures, but at those that speak against it, since it is the quintessence or elixir of Nature, as we may know by the scarcity of it; for Nature being just in all her works, hath ordered them so as what is curious, excellent, and good, she hath sparingly made, but what is indifferent and bad she hath made plentifully, countervaluing the worth of the one sort with the quantity of the other; as we may observe, she hath made more iron than silver, more silver than gold, more stones than diamonds, more weeds than flowers, more beast than men, and of men she hath made more fools than wise men, more cowards than valiant men, more bad men than good men, more enemies than friends, and so more pains than pleasures; but because there is but a little of that which is good, shall not we enjoy it? Shall we refuse the best because we have not so much as we would? That would be unreasonable; but as men will give a great quantity of lead for a little gold, so men will endure a great deal of pain for a little pleasure, and they have reason, for a little pleasure is of great value, being the most delicious sweets in nature; but you will ask what is the delicious pleasure? I answer, all that is pleasure is delicious, yet every man is to judge of pleasure by his own delectation, for pleasures are as different as men; for although all men are of mankind, yet every man is not alike, neither in mind nor body, so although all pleasure is pleasure, yet not one and the same.

125 *An Oration against Vice-Actors*

*Noble Citizens,*

Our city doth so increase with vice, as I fear the numerous vices will be like as the plagues of *Egypt*[60] to destroy our city, if you do not use speedy remedy to punish the vice-actors; but we are so far from punishing them as we admire, applaud, and advance such, as have most vices, or least honesty; the truth is that vice and injustice is the only way or means to advance men to office, power, authority, respect, and credit in our city, for those men that are temperate, honest, and just are thought fools and unprofitable drones, and those that are wisely provident and not vainly prodigal are believed to be miserable men, which know not how to live; and as for our grand magistrates, they have more formality than reality, more good words than good deeds, more covetousness than justice; they regard not the poor man's cause but the rich man's money; for they decide causes not according to right but according to bribes, humility, and honesty are strangers to them, they study their self interest but regard not the public good, all which will bring a confusion and so a dissolution to this commonwealth, if that you do not carefully and suddenly choose wise and conscionable men for magistrates, to wit, such as will punish extortions, wrongs, and injuries, suppress pride, vanity, and luxury, banish quarrels, put away idleness, and administer right and justice for right and justice's sake, as also do as they would be done unto.

126 *An Oration against a Foolish Custom*

*Worthy Citizens,*

There is an unjust and unhandsome custom in this city, and therefore ought to be abolished, which is that whensoever a wife beats her husband, the next neighbour rides through the city disgracefully, not only striding upon a horse with his face towards the tail, or sitting astride upon a staff, but having foul things flung at or on him, and all the vulgar people

---

[60] In the Bible, God visited Egypt with plagues because Pharaoh would not release the Israelites from slavery. Exodus, 7–8.

follows with shouts, and all this to shame an innocent person who hath not committed a fault, whereas the fault-makers are neither troubled nor disgraced, which is a great injustice, that those escape that ought to have the punishment; for the foolish husband of such a wife rampant should ride in disgrace, scorn, and pain, by reason he suffers himself to be degraded of his masculine authority; yet is this not the only foolish and unjust custom, but we have many more, which ought not to be suffered in a peaceable and well-governed commonwealth; wherefore the public magistrates, that are the public fathers, should order private families that they may not disorder the public tranquillity.

127  *An Oration against the Liberty of Women*

*Citizens of N. N.,*

Although I am sure to be hated of all the women in this city, and perchance elsewhere, yet by reason I think it fit to reprove their liberties, vanities, and expenses, I shall not be silent, although I were sure to be tortured with their railing tongues and to be exclaimed in all their female societies, which societies ought to be dissolved, allowing no public meetings to that sex, no not child-bed gossipings, for women corrupt and spoil each other, striving to out-brave, out-beauty, and out-talk each other with their vanities, paintings, and gossipings; wherefore it were fit that women should be restrained not only from the company of men, but their own sex, unless it be those they have near relations to, and not to suffer them to make acquaintance with strangers; this would cause moderation, sobriety, and silence amongst them; also it would cause them to be housewifely in their families, obedient to their husbands and careful of their children; but liberty is an enemy to women, nay it is an enemy to men, not only to fathers, husbands, and sons but even to wanton lovers, or rather courtiers, making them as vain and expensive as women, to gain their mistresses favours, knowing women, especially amorous women, are soonest won with gayes,[61] toys, and shows; but women are so far from being restrained in this age, and in these nations round about, that they have liberty to spend what they will, to keep what company they will, and to use their husbands and natural friends as they please; the truth is, liberty makes all women wild and wanton, both maids, wives, and widows, which defames

---

[61] Things that are bright and showy.

themselves and their families. Thus in short, women are the chief ruiners of men in their estates, fortunes, and honours, and so I leave them.

128 *An Oration for the Liberty of Women*

*Noble Citizens,*
It is not only uncivil and ignoble, but unnatural, for men to speak against women and their liberties, for women were made by Nature for men, to be loved, accompanied, assisted and protected; and if men are bound to love them by Nature, should they restrain them by force? Should they make them slaves, which Nature made to be their dearest associates, their beautifulest objects and sweetest delights? And shall man restrain them of their harmless pleasures, chaste societies, and gentle conversations? And as it is natural for men to love women, so it is natural for love to please what they love, and not to cross, oppose, or restrain them, but to grant them all their lawful requests and desires, as far as lies in their powers; for can men dispose of their estates more generously than to women? Or think any fortune better than when they can serve them? Or is there a greater happiness than to be beloved of them? Whereas they are the chiefest good that Nature hath made for men, and the greatest delight she hath given to men; for can there be any sound sweeter than their voices? Any object brighter than their beauties, or any society more divine than theirs? Yet these celestial creatures a terrestrial man in the former *oration* did plead against them, persuading you, O horrid persuasions, to use them as your slaves which ought to be your goddesses on earth, for Nature made them to be beloved, admired, desired, adored, and worshipped, sued and praised to by our sex.

# FEMALE ORATIONS
## Part XI

129

Ladies, Gentlewomen and other Inferiors, but not less worthy, I have been industrious to assemble you together, and wish I were so fortunate as to persuade you to make a frequentation, association, and combination amongst our sex, that we may unite in prudent counsels to make ourselves as free, happy, and famous as men, whereas now we live and die as if we were produced from beast rather than from men; for men are happy, and we women are miserable, they possess all the ease, rest, pleasure, wealth, power and fame, whereas women are restless with labour, easeless with pain, melancholy for want of pleasures, helpless for want of power, and die in oblivion for want of fame; nevertheless, men are so unconscionable and cruel against us, as they endeavour to bar us of all sorts or kinds of liberty, as not to suffer us freely to associate amongst our own sex, but would fain bury us in their houses or beds, as in a grave; the truth is, we live like bats or owls, labour like beasts, and die like worms.[62]

130  *ii*

Ladies, Gentlewomen, and other Inferior Women, the Lady that spoke to you hath spoken wisely and eloquently in expressing our unhappiness, but she hath not declared a remedy, or showed us a way to come out of our miseries; but if she could or would be our guide, to lead us out of the labyrinth men have put us into, we should not only praise and admire her but adore and worship her as our goddess; but alas, men, that are not only our tyrants but our devils, keep us in the hell of subjection, from whence I cannot perceive any redemption or getting out; we may complain, and bewail our condition, yet that will not free us; we may murmur and rail against men, yet they regard not what we say: in short, our words to men are as empty sounds, our sighs as puffs of wind, and our tears as fruitless showers, and our power is so inconsiderable as men laugh at our weakness.

[62] These orations rehearse a set of arguments which were debated in the so-called *querelle des femmes*. See Ian Maclean, *Woman Triumphant: Feminism in French Literature, 1610–1652* (Oxford: Clarendon Press, 1977).

131 *iii*

Ladies, Gentlewomen, and other more Inferiors, the former *orations* were exclamations against men, repining at their condition and mourning for our own; but we have no reason to speak against men, who are our admirers and lovers; they are our protectors, defenders, and maintainers; they admire our beauties, and love our persons; they protect us from injuries, defend us from dangers, are industrious for our subsistence, and provide for our children; they swim great voyages by sea, travel long journeys by land, to get us rarities and curiosities; they dig to the centre of the earth for gold for us; they dive to the bottom of the sea for jewels for us; they build to the skies houses for us; they hunt, fowl, fish, plant and reap for food for us; all which we could not do ourselves, and yet we complain of men as if they were our enemies, when as we could not possibly live without them: which shows we are as ungrateful as inconstant; but we have more reason to murmur against Nature than against men, who hath made men more ingenious, witty, and wise than women, more strong, industrious and laborious than women, for women are witless and strengthless and unprofitable creatures, did they not bear children. Wherefore, let us love men, praise men, and pray for men, for without men we should be the most miserable creatures that Nature hath or could make.

132 *iv*

Noble Ladies, Gentlewomen, and other Inferior Women, the former oratoress says we are witless and strengthless; if so, it is that we neglect the one and make no use of the other, for strength is increased by exercise, and wit is lost for want of conversation; but to show men we are not so weak and foolish as the former oratoress doth express us to be, let us hawk, hunt, race, and do the like exercises as men have, and let us converse in camps, courts, and cities, in schools, colleges, and courts of judicature, in taverns, brothels, and gaming houses, all which will make our strength and wit known, both to men and to our own selves, for we are as ignorant of ourselves as men are of us. And how should we know ourselves when as we never made a trial of ourselves? Or how should men know us when as they never put us to the proof? Wherefore my advice is, we should imitate men, so will our bodies and minds appear more masculine, and our power will increase by our actions.

133  *v*

Noble, Honourable, and Virtuous Women, the former oration was to persuade us to change the custom of our sex, which is a strange and unwise persuasion, since we cannot change the nature of our sex, for we cannot make ourselves men; and to have female bodies, and yet to act masculine parts, will be very preposterous and unnatural; in truth, we shall make ourselves like as the defects of nature, as to be hermaphroditical, as neither to be perfect women nor perfect men, but corrupt and imperfect creatures; wherefore let me persuade you, since we cannot alter the nature of our persons, not to alter the course of our lives, but to rule our lives and behaviours as to be acceptable and pleasing to God and men, which is to be modest, chaste, temperate, humble, patient, and pious; also to be housewifely, cleanly, and of few words, all which will gain us praise from men, and blessing from heaven, and love in this world and glory in the next.

134  *vi*

Worthy Women, the former oratoress's oration endeavours to persuade us that it would not only be a reproach and disgrace, but unnatural for women in their actions and behaviour to imitate men; we may as well say it will be a reproach, disgrace and unnatural to imitate the Gods, which imitation we are commanded both by the Gods and their ministers, and shall we neglect the imitation of men, which is more easy and natural than the imitation of the Gods? For how can terrestrial creatures imitate celestial deities? Yet one terrestrial may imitate another, although in different sorts of creatures; wherefore since all terrestrial imitations ought to ascend to the better and not to descend to the worse, women ought to imitate men, as being a degree in nature more perfect than they themselves, and all masculine women ought to be as much praised as effeminate men to be dispraised, for the one advances to perfection, the other sinks to imperfection, that so by our industry we may come at last to equal men both in perfection and power.

135  *vii*

Noble Ladies, Honourable Gentlewomen and Worthy Female Commoners, the former oratoress's oration or speech was to persuade us out of ourselves, as to be that which Nature never intended us to be, to wit masculine; but why should we desire to be masculine, since our own sex and condition is far the better? For if men have more courage, they have more danger; and if men have more strength, they have more labour than women have; if men are more eloquent in speech, women are more harmonious in voice; if men be more active, women are more graceful; if men have more liberty, women have more safety; for we never fight duels nor battles, nor do we go long travels or dangerous voyages; we labour not in building nor digging in mines, quarries, or pits for metal, stone, or coals; neither do we waste or shorten our lives with university or scholastical studies, questions and disputes; we burn not our faces with smith's forges or chemist furnaces, and hundreds of other actions which men are imployed in; for they would not only fade the fresh beauty, spoil the lovely features, and decay the youth of women, causing them to appear old whilst they are young, but would break their small limbs and destroy their tender lives. Wherefore women have no reason to complain against Nature, or the God of Nature, for though the gifts are not the same they have given to men, yet those gifts they have given to women are much better; for we women are much more favoured by Nature than men, in giving us such beauties, features, shapes, graceful demeanour, and such insinuating and enticing attractions, as men are forced to admire us, love us and be desirous of us, insomuch as rather than not have and enjoy us, they will deliver to our disposals their power, persons, and lives, enslaving themselves to our will and pleasures; also we are their saints, whom they adore and worship, and what can we desire more than to be men's tyrants, destinies, and goddesses?

# ORATIONS IN COUNTRY MARKET TOWNS, WHERE COUNTRY GENTLEMEN MEET

## PART XII

136

*Noble Gentlemen,*

Who are ennobled by time and not by favour, give me leave, since we are sociably met here in this town, that I remember you of our happy condition of life we live in, as on our own lands, amongst our own tenants, like as petty kings in our little monarchies, in peace, with moderate plenty and pleasure; our recreations are both healthful and delightful, which are hunting, hawking, and racing, as being far nobler pastimes than carding, dicing, and tennis-playing; for whereas gamesters meet for covetousness, we meet for love, they leave most of their gettings to the box, we bring most of our gettings to our tables, and whereas we make ourselves merry with our games, they make quarrels with theirs. Thus we live more friendly than gamesters and more happily than great monarchs, we neither quarrel, nor fear usurpers.

137 *ii*

*Noble Gentlemen,*

The Gentleman that formerly spoke said we were petty kings, making our tenants our subjects; but if they be as subjects, they are rebellious subjects, not paying us our rents duly nor truly; besides, they are apt to murmur at the least increase of our farms, although they sell their commodities they get out of our lands at a double rate; and as for our pleasures, as hawking, hunting and racing, they may be sociable, but they are very chargeable, for hawks, hounds and horses, with their attendance, will devour a great estate in a short time, besides open house keeping in *Christmas* time; all which makes gentlemen beggars and beggars gentlemen, for the servants and tenants grow rich but their masters and landlords become poor, the one sort buyeth, the other sort selleth, and the title of a gentleman is buried in the ruin of his estate.

138 *iii*

*Noble Gentlemen,*

The Gentleman that spoke last spoke rather like a cottager than a gentleman, or rather like a miser than a noble hospitable person, for he spoke as if he would have gentlemen rather to follow the plough than the race, the cart rather than the deer, the puttuck[63] rather than the hawk, to eat cheese instead of venison, sour curds instead of partridge, fried peas for young leverets,[64] rusty bacon for chines[65] of beef, rye bread instead of white manchet:[66] all which is to live like a clown and not like a gentleman, burying his birth in the dung of his earth. But, *Noble Gentlemen,* I have observed that a gentleman, although of small fortune, if he live wisely, may live plentifully and honourably, without his own personal drudgery; the wisdom is to look into his own estate industriously, to know and understand the value of his lands justly, to endeavour to have his rents paid duly, and not suffer his servants to cozen him either by flattery or excess; all which will cause a country gentleman to live as the first gentleman said, like a petty king, yet not like a tyrant but like a generous prince, with delight and pleasure, generosity and magnificence, amongst his tenants, servants, and acquaintance; also he will be an assistance to travellers and a relief to the poor, and his fame and name will not only sound loud, but long.

139 *iv*

*Noble Gentlemen,*

The Gentleman that spoke last spoke well for those gentlemen that can content themselves in that condition their forefathers left them in, but gentlemen of great estates desire great titles, offices and authorities, which cannot be had in the country, but from the court, which ambition persuades them to leave the country to live near the court, where they may be seen and known unto the grand monarch, in which courts are such delights and pleasures as the country is not capable to have, as masques, plays, balls, braveries and courtships, which ravish and transport their thoughts beyond the country region; indeed, they are as if they were transported into the third heaven, until such time as their money is spent, their land sold, and their creditors are numberless, and then they are cast

[63] A kind of hawk, usually a kite or common buzzard.    [64] Young hares.
[65] The back.    [66] The finest kind of wheaten bread.

out as evil angels into the hell of poverty, and become poor devilish sharks living upon their wits, which is to live upon their cheats, which cannot last long. Thus gentlemen in the country are proud, in the court vain, in the city base and at last unfortunate, as being much indebted and miserably poor.

140 *v*

*Noble Gentlemen,*
The Gentleman that spoke last declares our ambitions at court, but not our luxury in the country, and though we have not court ladies and city dames to our mistresses, yet we have country wives and tenants daughters for our wenches, and we eat and drink our selves into surfeiting diseases, and our expenses are far more in riotous hospitalities than the courtiers in their foolish flattering vanities: for the natures of gentlemen and noble men are for the most part prodigal, whether they be in court, city or country, and they will never rest until such time as their money is spent and their land sold, and then they become idle drones for want of stings, which is wealth, to employ them.

141 *vi*

*Noble Gentlemen,*
We have argued much of our humours, actions and estates, of our follies, vanities and vices, but we have not concluded what is best for us to settle in: as for the course of our lives, there are but three ways, as to be either mere clowns, or perfect gentlemen, or between both; to be mere clowns is to be drudges in our estates, to be perfect gentlemen is to be careless of our expenses, and to be between both is to be careful overseers and moderate spenders, and of these three I judge the last best, as not to be so much a gentleman as to be a beggar, nor so much a clown as to be a beast.

142 *vii*

*Noble Gentlemen,*
We agreed to meet in this town for pastime and mirth, and not for study and disputation; we came not hither to learn good husbandry, but to spend our money freely; our intention was not to meet with formality and gravity, but with freedom and jollity; our design was not to return to our

dwelling houses with heavy hearts, but light heads; wherefore leave off arguing and settle to drinking, and let our tongues cease, and the music play, and when we are dead drunk let the fiddles ring out our knells, and let our coaches as our hearses carry us to our home beds as to our designed graves, where after our long sleeps we may rise, and in our resurrections be like either saints or devils; in short, let good wine and good brains be our good fortune.

143 *viii*

### A Speech of a Quarter Drunk Gentleman

*Noble Gentlemen,*
You have made eloquent *orations* before you did drink, but let that pass, for now you must speak only witty expressions, and give me leave to tell you that logic and wine are as great enemies as poetry and water; wherefore let the orators drink water and poets wine, for wine begets fancy and water drowns reason, which is the cause orators speak so much and long until they speak nonsense: but O divine wine, whose sprightly vapour doth manure the brain to a just height of wit, it is the serene air of wit, the quintessence of wit, the sun and light of wit, the spirit and soul of wit; for were it not for wine, the mind would be as in a dark hell of ignorance, and the brain would be lethargically stupefied for want of lively heat; for wine is the food of vital life and animal reason.

144 *ix*

### A Speech of a Half Drunken Gentleman

*Noble Gentlemen,*
You have made eloquent speeches, but of what I am a rogue if I can tell, but that they were full of words: I did hear many words, but I do not remember any sense or reason in them; the truth is that the spirits of wine have burnt out the sense of your discourse, and have rarified my memory so much as no substantial matter will remain therein, so that your oratory is dead and buried in the vapour of wine, a blessed death and a happy funeral, and may it rest in peace and silence, and not rise to disturb our drinking, to which wish and hope I begin a health, and desire you all to pledge it.

# ORATIONS IN THE FIELD OF PEACE
## PART XIII

145 *A Peasants Oration to his Fellow Clowns*

*Fellow Peasants,*

For we are all fellows in labour, profit and pleasure, though not fellows in arms, spoils and danger, and though we live in the fields of peace and not in the fields of war, yet our fields of peace resemble the fields of war, for we are an army of clowns though not of soldiers, and our commanders are our landlords, who often deceive us of the increase of our labours as the warring commanders deceive their common soldiers of the profit of their spoils; also we have our infantry and our cavalry, for all those that belong to the keeping and breeding of beast, as shepherds, graziers, herdsmen, goatherds, swineherds and carters, are of the cavalry, but all they that belong to the earth, as sowers, planters, reapers, threshers, hedgers, ditchers, diggers, delvers, are our infantry; also we have arms and ammunition, for we are armed with our beast skins, and our arms of use are pikes, forks, cutting sickles, mowing scythes, pruning knives, threshing flails, ploughshares, shepherd's hooks, herdsmen's staves and the like, and our match, powder, and bullets, are puddings, peas, and porridge, and our granadoes[67] are eggs of all sorts and sizes, our carts are our wagons, our cottages our tents, and our victuals and country housewives our bag and baggage, and the lowing of our herds and bleating of our sheep are our drums and trumpets, not to alarm us to fight, but to feed; also we have enemies, which are unseasonable seasons, rotting moistures, drowning showers and over-flows, chilling frost, scorching heat and devouring worms, all which we fight against, not with force but with industry. And our army of clowns is more skilful to destroy our enemies than an army of soldiers is to destroy their enemies, nay, our army is an army wherein is peace and plenty, whereas in their army is war and want: we become rich with safety, they become poor with danger; we be gentle to beast, they be cruel to men; they thrive by blood, we by milk; we get health by our labours and long life by our temperance, and they get diseases in their riots and death in their wars: thus they live painfully, die violently, and only leave their bare name to their posterity and beggarly race; we live healthfully, die peaceably, and leave our goods to our posterity, who by their wealth come to be gentlemen.

[67] Grenades.

146  *A Peasants or Clowns Oration spoken in the Field of Peace, concerning Husbandry*

*Fellow Peasants,*

I must tell you we live in a happy age, where peace sows, and plenty reaps, for whereas wars destroy our increase, now peace increases our stores; also I would have you know that our profession which is husbandry, is one of the noblest and generousest professions, which is to employ ourselves like as the Gods and Nature; for though we cannot create creatures as Nature doth, yet we by our industry increase Nature's creatures, not only vegetables, that we produce in our fields and store in our barns, but animals, which we breed in our farms and feed in our fields; but as Nature commits errors and defects in producing her creatures, so we for want of knowledge have not the good effect of our labours; for though we are bred up to husbandry, yet we are not all so knowing in husbandry as to thrive and grow rich by our labours; for as all scholars are not learned, that have lived and spent most of their time in studies in universities, but are mere dunces; or as artisans are not all excellent workmen, although they have been bound to their trade and have wrought long in it, yet are but bunglers: so for husbandry, all husbandmen are not so knowing in their profession as to thrive, but they labour at random without judgement or observation, and like those that learn to read by rote, may understand the words or letters but not the sense and meaning: so we may be brought up to labour, but not understand to make a profitable increase, not knowing the nature of the several soils, as what for pasture, or meadow, or tillage; nor to foresee the change of weather, nor to take the most seasonable times, nor to observe the course of the planets, all which is very requisite for the breed of our animals and increase of our vegetables. Wherefore, in my opinion, it were very necessary for us to choose the most observing and experienced men amongst us that understand husbandry best, to be our public and general teachers, instructors, informers, and reformers in our profession of husbandry: for as there are divine teachers for the souls of men, moral teachers for the manners of men, human teachers for the bodies of men, and physicians for the lives of men, so there should be natural teachers and informers for the profitable increase for men, such as have not only experience by practice and judgement by observation, but have both learning and conceptions of natural philosophy, as to learn and search into the causes and effects of Nature's works, and to know and observe the influences of the heavens on earth, and on the diverse and sundry creatures in and on the earth; also the sympathies and antipathies of the several creatures to each other, as also the natures and proprieties of every kind and sort of creature; so shall we know how to increase our breed of animals and our stores of vegetables, and to find out the minerals for our use; for as learning without practice is of no effect, so practice without knowledge is of small profit; yet many will take upon them to instruct others that want instructions themselves, but such instructors' instructions are more in words than for use, as *Plutarch*'s Commonwealth or *Virgilius' Georgics*,[68] two famous men, the one a moral philosopher, the other a poet; the one did form such a commonwealth as men would nor could not live in it, and so not fit for use; the other could better set his wit to work than his hands, for if *Virgil* had left his husbandry in verse to practice it in prose, he had lived poorly and died obscurely, as having more wit and fancy to write of husbandry in his *Georgics*, than knowledge or experience to practice it in his farms; thus poets get fame and farmers wealth, the one by their wit, the other by their experience, the one by imagination, the other by practice, for a clown or peasant gains more knowledge by his practice than a poet by his contemplations; but when practice and wit are joined together, they beget wisdom and wealth, the one being adorned with gold, the other enthroned with fame, for emperors have ascended from the plough, and kings from the sheep-cots, converting their ploughshares to thrones, their sickles to crowns, and their sheep-hooks to sceptres. Thus clowns, boors or peasants by name, are become princes in power, and princes in power are become beasts by name and nature, witness *Nebuchadnezzar*.[69]

## 147   *A Peasants Oration to his Fellow Peasants*

*Fellow Peasants*,

Give me leave to tell you, we are the most unhappy people in the world, for we live to labour and labour to live; and we are not only the unhappiest,

---

[68] Plutarch, Greek biographer and moralist (*c.* 50– *c.* 125 CE). Cavendish mentions several of his *Lives*, which were translated into English by Thomas North in 1579, and could have read his *Moralia*, translated by Philemon Holland as *The Philosophy Commonly called Moral written by the Learned Philosopher Plutarch* (London, 1657). Neither contains a work entitled 'Commonwealth'. Perhaps she means Plato's *Commonwealth*, i.e. *Republic*. Virgil, or Publius Virgilius Maro (70–19 BCE), Roman poet and the author of *Georgics*, a panegyric to rural life.

[69] When God humbled the proud Nebuchadnezzar, King of Babylon, 'his heart was made like the beasts, and his dwelling was with the wild asses', Daniel 5.

but the basest men in the world, for we are not only bred with beasts, and live with beasts, and die like beasts, but we are the bawds and pimps too, to bring beasts to act bestially together; also we are the dungers of the earth, to carry and spread the several excrements of several creatures thereon, which makes us not only to have a continual stink in our nostrils, but to be a mere stink ourselves; thus we are beastly within and without, for all our thoughts are employed on our labours, which labours are brutish; neither have we such fine and pleasant recreation as other men, for our recreation is only to whistle, pipe, and sometimes to dance in a crowd together, or rather jump and leap together, being ignorant of dancing measures; and the only pleasure we have is to rumble and tumble our country lasses, who being more foul than fair, more gross than fine, more noisome than sweet, we soon surfeit of them, and then they become a trouble instead of a delight, a disease instead of a pleasure, a hate instead of a love; and as they are to us, so no doubt but in the end we are to them, a loathing surfeit; for we meet wildly, associate brutishly and depart rudely; and as for our profits, though we labour, yet our landlords have the increase. In short, we are slaves to beasts, and beasts in comparison of other men.

148 *A Peasants Oration to prove the Happiness of a Rural Life*

*Fellow Peasants,*
The peasant that formerly spoke hath rather shown his ungratefulness to Nature and his unthankfulness to the Gods by his complaining speech, than the truth of our condition and life, for he says we are the unhappiest, miserablest, and basest men in the world; all which is false; for can there be more happiness than peace and plenty? Can there be more happiness than in the repose of the mind and contemplations of thoughts? Can we associate ourselves more contentedly than with innocent, harmless, and sinless creatures? Are not men more stinking, foul, and wicked than beasts? Can there be more odoriferous perfumes than the sweet vegetables on the earth? Or finer prospects than stately hills, humble valleys, shady groves, clear brooks, green hedges, cornfields, feeding cattle and flying birds? Can there be more harmonious music than warbling nightingales and singing birds? Can there be more delightful sounds than purling brooks, whispering winds, humming bees, and small-voiced grasshoppers? Can there be a more delicious sweet than honey? More wholesome food than warm milk, fresh butter, pressed curds, new laid eggs, seasoned bacon,

savoury bread, cooling sallets,[70] and moist fruits? Or more refreshing drink than whey, whig[71] and buttermilk? Or more strengthening drink than ale, meath,[72] perry and cider? And are not we at our own vintage? Nay, should we desire to feed highly, we may, for we are masters of the beasts of the field and the poultry in the grange, and know well how to catch the fowls of the air. Can we have warmer and softer garments than cloth spun from the fleece of our flocks, to keep out freezing cold? Or can we be cooler than under shady trees, whose waving leaves are fans to cool the sultry air? Or can we lie softer than on the downy feathers of cocks and hens? And can we be happier than to be free from stately ceremony, court envy, city faction, lawsuits, corrupt bribes, malice, treachery and quarrels? And as for our recreation, although we do not dance, sing and play on music artificially, yet we pipe, dance and sing merrily; and if we do not make love courtly, yet we make love honestly; and for our women, whom our fellow peasant doth disgracefully, scornfully and slanderously speak of, although they are but plain country housewives and not fine ladies, yet they be as honest women as they, for they spend their time in housewifery, and waste not their time in vanity; and as for their beauty, their faces are their own as Nature gave them, not borrowed of art; and if they be not so fair, yet they are as lovely, and as they use no sweet perfumes, so they use no stinking pomatum,[73] and though their hands be not smooth, yet they are clean, they use no oiled gloves to grease them but rub their hands, when washed, with coarse cloth to cleanse them; and as for their garments, they are plain, yet commodious, easy, and decent, they are not ribbed up with whale-bones nor encumbered with heavy silver and gold laces, nor troubled with new fashions; they spend not half their time in painting and dressing, and though they patch their clothes sometimes out of good housewifery, yet they patch not their faces out of vanity as ladies do; neither do our women sweat to make their faces fair, but sweat for their children's livelihood, and though they breed not their children curiously, yet they breed them up carefully: but our discontented and ambitious peasant would turn from a clown to a gallant, as to waste lavishly, to spend prodigally, to live idly, to be accoutred fantastically, to behave himself proudly, to boast vaingloriously, to speak words constraintly, to make love amorously, to flatter

---

[70] Salads.    [71] A beverage of whey, fermented with herbs.
[72] Mead.    [73] Pomade, a scented ointment originally made with apples.

falsely, to quarrel madly, and to fight foolishly, but not to thrive prudently, to employ time profitably, to spend wisely, to live temperately, to speak truly, to behave himself friendly, to demean himself civilly, to make love chastely, to live peaceably, innocently, and safely, as we that are of the peasantry do.

# ORATIONS IN A DISORDERED AND UNSETTLED STATE OR GOVERNMENT

## PART XIV

149  *An Oration against Taxes*

*Fellow Citizens,*

This city is taxed to pay a great sum of money, which tax is more than we are able to pay without being impoverished, yet if it were all that would be laid upon us, there were some comfort, but that is not likely unless our ministers of state and magistrates were less covetous to get, and more sparing to save; for though they get much, they spend much, or rather spoil much in luxury, vanity, and bravery, which makes them always needy, and though they pretend that their taxing is for the service of the commonwealth, yet most of it is employed in their common expenses, or hoarded up to buy lands and build stately palaces for their posterity to enjoy and live in; thus they build upon our stocks and buy lands with our labours, so that we take pains for their pleasure; but if they tax us often, we shall be so poor as we shall not only have nothing to pay, but nothing to live on, which poverty will either starve us, or force us to be their slaves for maintenance, for when they have engrossed all the wealth they will become lords of the people, or rather their tyrants.[74] Thus if we part with our wealth, we part with our liberty, but to keep both, let us not part with our money until we know how it shall be employed, for if it be employed in the service of the commonwealth, it will return to our profit, which will be as traffic to enrich and not as robbery to impoverish us, but if they rob the commonwealth, employing our money to their own use, we are doubly robbed, like as men should take our fathers' goods, which is our inheritance, and also that we have gotten by our own industry; and if it be requisite for us to part with our money, it is requisite they should give us an account of the distribution; for as the magistrate or ministers of state are the commonwealth's stewards, so the people ought to be their overseers, lest they cozen the commonwealth, by which the commonwealth will thrive and become so rich as to keep the natives from beggary and slavery.[75]

---

[74] Cf. nn. 37, 47.

[75] In 1661 the government offered to let Parliament view royal accounts. At the end of 1667, the court had to accept a parliamentary commission to examine its accounts. See Seaward, *The Restoration*, pp. 21–2.

*An Oration contrary to the Former*

*Fellow Citizens,*

The last oration that was spoken concerning taxes was a factious oration endeavouring to bring in innovation, and the orator that spoke that mutinous oration spoke not for the public good, but his own advancement, hoping by this oration to be a popular man, embroiling the commonwealth in a civil war to work out his own designs; thus men for private respects would make a public ruin, and the people through ignorance do never perceive them, but rather do applaud and praise them for good commonwealth men, when they are oftentimes the occasion of a commonwealth's destruction; but if you should follow his instructions you would not only lose all your wealth, which is worse than to part with some on necessary occasions, but you would part with lives or liberties, for he advises you to rebel against your magistrates and ministers of state by calling or forcing them to give a public account of the state's private affairs: but to show you how foolishly he hath advised you, give me leave to speak to your sense and reason, in hope you are not void of either, for in sense and reason a commonwealth cannot be guided, ruled, and governed without a sovereign power, which sovereign power is in the magistrates and ministers of state; they are the head to the body of the commonwealth, and to have a body without a head is against nature, and your reason and sense shows you that if you take off or divide the head from the body, both will die, rot, and consume: so if you take a sovereign power from the commonwealth, it dies, dissolves and consumes with disorder, war, and ruin, and if your sense and reason perceive a commonwealth must of necessity have a supreme power, your sense and reason will show you that you must trust that supreme power, otherwise it would not be a supreme or sovereign power, which power is to command, order, and dispose of all as it shall think fit, or as it pleases, without giving any account; for giving an account makes it of no force or effect; for a commonwealth cannot be governed without subtlety and secrecy, which is called policy, which policy, if divulged, is no policy, wherefore a public account ought not to be given of that which is not fit publicly to be made known; and give me leave to tell you that policy is chargeable, not only that it costs much study and labour of the brain, but it requires much money, or money's worth, to execute the designs; for though it be the chief design of policy to be a gainer in the end, yet it is but a contriver in the beginning, a worker in the continuance or execution, and a possessor in the end, and whilst it works it must have something to work with, for the old philosophers say out of nothing, nothing can be made; neither is it fit they should give an account of the receipts or expenses they receive or distribute of the commonwealth, for much money must be employed to have intelligence from foreign parts and nations, for fear of surprisals, and perchance great sums of money are required to corrupt some enemies to betray the rest, and so to prevent danger, if not ruin; besides many other ways, abroad and at home, which expenses are not fit to be made known, or an account given for; for wise ministers of state make use of all passions, appetites, vices and vanities of mankind, as well as of their virtues, courages, generosities, ingenuities, abilities, and the like; for that which would be base, foolish, dishonourable, and wicked for private and particular families, persons, or acts, is honourable, justifiable, and wise in the public-weal.[76] Wherefore let me persuade you to pay the taxes willingly and readily, for money is the materials to repair, strengthen, enlarge, enrich and adorn a commonwealth, that you may live safely, magnificently, plentifully and pleasantly, which otherwise you will not do, but ruin your selves, at least make your lives unhappy through covetousness; which to avoid, part with some of your wealth or profit contentedly, that you may enjoy the rest quietly, peaceably, and freely, and follow not the advice of the former orator whose speech, although it was plausible to you, yet you might easily perceive his design was dangerous, not only to the magistrates which are your fathers, but to the whole state or kingdom, endeavouring with his speech to embroil the whole state in a civil war, persuading you to be the first risers, stirrers and disturbers. Thus through private, particular, and self respects, men oft times make general wars, but I hope you will live in peace, and so I'll leave you.

151 *An Oration against Collectors*

*Fellow Citizens,*
There ought some order to be taken, to rectify the abuses and cozenages of the collectors and receivers of assessments, contributions and the like;

---

[76] This oration offers a standard Royalist defence of the royal prerogative, including the right to raise taxes in emergencies, which was used under James I and Charles I. See Sommerville, *Politics and Ideology*, pp. 149–53. The extent of the royal prerogative continued to be debated under Charles II.

for they collect and receive much more than is paid into the common treasury, so that they rob both the people and the common treasure, impoverishing the commonwealth, and disabling the rulers in the discharges of necessary expenses, which thefts they secretly hoard up, so that in the end, if they be suffered, there will be such a scarcity of money as there will be none to pay nor none to receive, and like as those that hoard up corn make a dearth, so those that hoard up money make a mutiny, so that money-hoarders cause civil wars, as corn-hoarders cause famine; for when there is but little money stirring in the kingdom, they that have any are so loath to part with it as they will rather part with their lives, and those that have none are so greedy to have some as they will venture their lives to get it; and if the common treasure be empty and the people be poor, we cannot live in security; if we have no means to provide for our safety, the kingdom will lie open to the enemy, for money or money's worth is a ward that locks up a kingdom in safety, and is a key to unlock the gates of our enemies, and sets them open for our entrance, and money or money's worth is so subtle and insinuating, as it enters into the most privy counsels of our enemies, brings us intelligence of all their designs, or makes them advise treacherously and give counsel even against themselves, such power hath riches! It buys out honesty, corrupts justice, betrays lives, nay, even souls, for men will venture damnation for the sake of money; wherefore it is necessary that the common treasure should be well stored; good commonwealth men should be not only industrious to enrich the common treasure, but sparing in spending the common treasure, and severely punish those that endeavour to cozen and rob the common treasure; and none should be suffered to hoard up riches but in the common treasure, which is to be spent generally for the good of all the whole kingdom in time of necessity, as in the times of plagues, famines and wars, as also for the strength and power of the kingdom, for the reward of merit, advancing of trade, and such like ways of expenses, not in gay shows and idle pastimes, nor in vain or unprofitable buildings, or the like. But if we suffer the people to be impoverished by these cheating, cozening purloiners, we shall never fill the common coffers, for to cozen and rob the people is to cozen and rob the common treasure, which is the general store of the whole people, filled and enriched by them, to be profitably laid out for them.[77]

---

[77] This emphasis on money as the basis of security echoes *Newcastle's Advice*, pp. 36–40.

152  *An Oration for Taxes*

*Fellow Citizens,*

I perceive a discontent amongst you, by your murmuring, at the tax that is laid upon you, which murmuring is dangerous, for many men's murmurs may in a short time amount to the sum of rebellion, which will make a civil war, in which war you will lose more than you are now required to pay: but give me leave to tell you that you are both unreasonable and unjust, for you will live in the commonwealth and yet not help to maintain or uphold it; also you are ungrateful, as not to return a small gratuity to the commonwealth, for the many and great benefits you have received therefrom; indeed, in denying this tax you seem as unnatural to your country, as children who should suffer their parents to starve whilst they surfeit, which causes both their untimely deaths through want and excess; so rather than you would abate your idle expenses and vain pleasures to pay necessary taxes, you would suffer the kingdom to be defenseless, and open for an enemy to invade and destroy it and yourselves. But if words cannot persuade you, surely your rational understanding, wise prudence, careful providence, honest minds and natural affections will not only make you willing and ready to pay this tax, but any other tax at any time you are taxed, which is for the common benefit, good and safety of your country, wherein you desire to live safely and to die peaceably, and to lie in the graves with your forefathers.

153  *An Oration to hinder a Rebellion*

*Noble Citizens, and Dear Countrymen,*

I perceive by your humours, dispositions, factions and speeches that you intend to rebel against your king and noble governors, endeavouring to alter the ancient government of this flourishing kingdom, that hath continued in and under the reign and rule of kings these many hundred years, which time hath confirmed so strongly in the monarchical power as you cannot easily make a change; yet if you could, the action would be very unjust, unnatural, wicked and damnable; unjust to force away the rights of your king; unnatural as not to live under the same government your forefathers did; wicked to spill the blood of your nobles; and damnable to spill the blood of your sovereign. Thus it will be evil and dangerous, for you cannot think they will part peaceably from that power their ancestors left them; they will not become your slaves if they can help it, nay, they will sooner part with their lives than their honours, and you are not sure of victory, for all honest men will be of their party; yet put the case you should have victory, you will sooner make a confusion than settle the kingdom into a republic, for the nature and constitution is not for it, as having been bred up a long time to monarchy, so that you may sooner change the nature of man into a beast than the government of this kingdom into a republic;[78] and could you make it a republic, you would not be so happy as you are now, for now you are governed easily, without troubling your selves, but then you would be troubled, not knowing how to govern your selves as also the commonwealth, for you must be forced to set up some to govern you; and is it not better to be governed by your superiors, than your equals? Which equals would rule you by corrupting flattery, or terrify you with reports of dangers, and so rule you by fear. Thus, by insinuations or terrors, you would be more enslaved than you are now, and poorer than you are now; for though you commons have not power to rule as a king, yet you have wealth to spend on what you please, witness your luxuries and vanities, which if you were poor you could not exceed in plenty as you do, insomuch as you can hardly afford God some fasting days. Besides, those sycophants and cheats which persuade you to this change would not only spend your wealth but waste your lives, for they would persuade you to make wars abroad to keep you in subjection, for in wars they command you, and in time of peace they are afraid you will command them, and rather than you should live in peace they would corrupt your neighbours with bribes, or provoke them with injuries to make war with you. Thus you would be enslaved by being outwitted by those that have more brain than your selves. O foolish people that will quit your present happiness for a voluntary slavery! And as for a monarchical government, which you seem to be weary of, it is the most ancient and divinest, as being an imitation of God and his angels in Heaven, wherein are degrees, as higher and lower, from and to his throne; but as God had evil angels, so our king hath evil subjects, which ought to be cast out of the kingdom like devils, as they are.

---

[78] The period in which there was no English monarch only lasted from 1649 to 1660. In 1649 Parliament declared England a commonwealth and a free state; in 1653 Oliver Cromwell was made Lord Protector under a new constitution.

*An Oration against Civil War*

*Noble Auditors,*

I perceive this kingdom hath two faces like a *Janus*, and both look with a lowering and frowning countenance, which doth fore-show a storm, and by your accusations and factions your hearts seem full of malice, and your heads full of design, as if you did intend each others ruin, and so the kingdom's destruction by a civil war, not considering that a civil war is far worse than a foreign war, for against a foreign enemy the whole strength of a kingdom is united to defend it self, but in a civil war the strength is divided to destroy the whole kingdom, and so much difference there is between each war that a foreign war is but like an outward sore on the body, but a civil war is as an inward disease even in the vital parts, which causes a consumption; indeed, I may similising say that in a civil war the kingdom doth as if it did spit up its lungs, for civil wars oftentimes cause famine and plagues, which is to a kingdom as a hectic leanness, heat and corruption in a man's body, which causes death and destruction. But *dear Countrymen*, what can you propound to yourselves in a civil war? Can any man be happy when injustice reigns and force rules? Or can any man hope to enrich himself when fury and malice makes a spoil of all? Or can any man think to advance himself, when as every particular desires and endeavours to be superior? For though authority may be pulled down, yet where no single authority is suffered by the power of many, no particular person can be advanced, they must all continue equal or be all destroyed to one man, and that man will only be superior in his single person and life, but not have authority or power over other men; for if there be none to be governed, it cannot be said he governs, and when there is none to obey there is none to command; but should several parties choose chiefs, yet if one party should get the better of the other parties, 'tis probable the chief of that party could not rule long, for there would be always divisions between the head and the body of that party, and every several party of that body would be the head; so that in effect there would neither be head nor body, but in the end the whole would be destroyed: and as for spoils, if any be gotten in civil wars, the possessors have not assurance to enjoy them, for spoils in civil wars are tossed from man to man, where every one striving to have them not any one can keep them: and as for lands, though they cannot be removed, yet several claimers will move to them, and every one strive to possess them. Thus civil wars do level power and wealth, and in the end destroy them; and since men can neither have rest, safety, plenty, honour, or authority in civil wars, it were a madness to make such wars wherein they are sure to be losers, at least no gainers; nay, were there any thing left to be enjoyed, those that never ventured in the wars would go away with the spoils; for the ruins of a civil war are left to succeeding ages, the quarrellers and fighters being for the most part destroyed in the war. In truth, there is nothing, so miserable, hateful, cruel and irreligious as civil war, for it is an enemy against law, nature, and God, it pulls down the seats of justice, throws down the altars of religion, digs up the urns of their parents, disperses the dust and bones of their dead ancestors, spills the blood of their fathers, sons, brethren, friends and countrymen, and makes a total destruction and dissolution, or at least their country so weak as it becomes a prey to foreign enemies, and the remainders of the natives become slaves; so that civil war begins with liberty but ends in slavery. Wherefore, those turbulent spirits that will not live in peace, but endeavour to make civil war, ought to be hanged to prevent it, so shall the peaceable and innocent live in safety, which otherwise will be devoured and destroyed by the merciless men in arms.

155  *An Oration against a Tumultuous Sedition*

*Fellow Citizens,*
I observe a turbulent spirit, or rather a spirit of fury, hath possessed most of this city, to rise tumultuously and mutinously, as some against others and they against them; but what can you propose to yourselves in this civil broil, or rather war, but ruin, death, and destruction? And by what authority do you thus? For common, canon, and civil laws forbid you, the like doth humanity, morality, divinity, and charity; also nature forbids you, for what is more unnatural than for *Fellow Citizens* and *Countrymen* to spill each others' blood? And if injuries have been done and faults committed, this is not the way to rectify them, but to the contrary, to heap faults upon faults and injuries upon injuries; and if it be for justice, certainly you ought not to claim justice in an unjust way; and if for right of privileges, let me tell you you have no privilege to make civil war of disorders in this city, and so consequently through the kingdom, by your ill examples; and if it be several factions of several parties that cause this disorder, know, you may sooner destroy each others parties than either party be victor; and if it be through the poverty of some and envy of others, in hope to plunder the rich and pull down the powerful, though your designs should

have success for the present, you may chance to suffer for this disorder in the end, so as neither to enjoy your plundered goods, nor to save your own lives, for plundering is robbing and killing in a mutiny is murder, so that unless you can get above the laws, the laws will accuse you; wherefore if you be wise, you will moderate your covetousness, qualify your spleens, cast your arms away and crave pardon for your faults whilst you may have it; but if you consider not your own lives or tranquillities, yet have pity and compassion of your old parents, young children, chaste wives, dear friends, brethren and country, wherein infallibly many must suffer in this great disorder and outrage; but if nothing can persuade you, Heaven protect the innocent and lay a heavy punishment upon the guilty, to which I leave you, whether I live or die.

156 *An Oration to Mutinous yet Fearful Citizens*

*Fellow Citizens,*
Give me leave to tell you that I did not wonder more at your sudden courages in your sudden rebellion than I do now at your sudden fear and sudden obedience to those you rebelled against, obeying whatsoever they command, delivering up your purses and arms in hope to get pardon for your lives; for your fear was such as you no sooner saw an army come towards your city as an enemy, but you presently drew up your bridges, shut fast your gates, chained up your streets, and ran to your prayers for heavens help; I confess you had great reason to fear when as a sharking[79] needy army was at your gates, which would have fought more valiantly to get into the city to plunder, than you to keep them out from plundering; besides, there is a castle or fort that is built so near your city, and stands so advantageous as the canons placed thereon can easily beat down your city over your heads; but these things at the first you did or would not consider, resolving madly to rebel, having at that time neither fear nor wit, for before such time as you saw the army, believing it was far off from you, a stranger had he seen and heard your boasts, brags and bravadoes, your arming, drumming and trumpeting, might have believed, at least thought, you had both valour and power equal with the old *Romans* that conquered all the world; but you appeared more terrible than you were, for your deeds were not answerable to your words and behaviour, and your countenances did change with your fear; the truth is, your courage was a rebellious

---

[79] An army that cheats and oppresses by extortion.

courage, and your fear seems as a loyal fear, for before your enemies did appear you did boast like soldiers, but now you ask pardon, you flatter like courtiers, yet for all your flattery you must pay for your disorders and buy your peace with a huge sum of money: and if I should ask you why you did put yourselves into a warring posture without leave or command from your king or ministers of state, you will answer me, for the defence of some of your privileges, so that for the sake of some you endangered all, for the readiest way and surest means to lose your privileges was to rebel against your sovereign, all which shows your ignorance, folly and great simplicity; wherefore by this rebellious stir you have not only lost your privileges, but you are forced to pay more than your privileges are worth, might you enjoy them, so that you must lose the one and pay the other; and all this loss and charge is caused through your factious humours and restless natures, being unprofitably busy. Indeed, you are like troubled waters, muddy and foul, yet it is likely, at least hoped, that the fine that is set upon you will draw you clean, making you clear and smooth, which is to be loyal and peaceable; only the chief misery is that in the loss of your privileges, and payments of money, good men (for all were not traitors, though most were) must suffer with the bad, the fine being generally laid upon the whole city wherein every particular must pay his share, and the loss of the privileges falls upon all, by which we may observe that peaceable men suffer with troublers, and honest men with traitors, and it cannot easily be avoided, not only that the few that are good, are obscured and hid amongst the many that are bad, and so cannot be easily culled out, but in cases of taxes and privileges, it would make a confusion in levies and partments;[80] thus neither good nor wise men can suddenly avoid those misfortunes that fools and knaves many times bring upon them; but wise men did see at your first rising, arming and soldiering, that you would sooner yield to your opposers than fight them, and rather pay for your follies than dispute for your privileges; for you were all body and no head, and so consequently no brains; but that I wonder at most is that so great a body as you were should not only be headless, but also heartless, as having neither wit nor courage. Wherefore, to conclude, let me persuade you, having never a head of your own, to send to your gracious sovereign to send you a head, and he will not only send you a head, but a wise head to rule and govern you, and as for a heart, Fortune in time may give you one.

[80] Payments.

157  *An Oration concerning Trade and Shipping*

*Dear Countrymen,*

For some small errors in the former government, and for some few oppressions by our former governors, we were discontented, and through
a discontent began to murmur, then to complain, and at last to rebel,
in which rebellion we entered into a civil war, wherein Fortune was our
friend, for Fortune for the most part is a friend to fools and knaves; and
though we were honest men, fighting only for our liberties, yet our enemies say we fought for their lands and riches, having none of our own; but
let them say what they will since we have what we desire; the misery is only
that now we have both their wealth and power, we know not how to use it,
a shrewd sign, that we are more covetous than provident, more ambitious
than wise, for every man striving to make a particular profit to himself,
we shall at last bring the whole state or commonwealth to a confusion;
the truth is that striving to make particular profits, you make a general
spoil, for you cut down woods, pull down houses, set open enclosures, live
idly upon the fundamental riches of the commonwealth, not labouring to
manure the land; but if you take not care of two things, your ruin will be
sooner than you imagine; these two necessary considerations and actions
are trade and shipping; as for trade, you give your neighbours leave to take
part of it away from you, and that you trade your selves in is so ill managed
as it brings but small profit or advantage to this kingdom; for you trade
rather like as peddlers than great merchants; besides, you send out of
the kingdom the most profitable commodities, as those that are called sta-
ple commodities, and bring in the most unprofitable commodities, such as
are only for vanities, and not such as are for necessary use; also, you raise
your customs to so high a rate as the custom is beyond the profit of trade;
but could merchants gain, yet, if the gain of their far-fetched commodities be uncertain and the customs for those brought home commodities
certain, few would venture or be merchants, so that trade upon necessity
must fall, and then the kingdom cannot be rich;[81] and as the kingdom
cannot be rich without foreign trade, so it cannot be safe without home
shipping, which is the other necessary consideration and action; but you
do not consider enough of it, as being blinded with covetousness, regarding your particular profits more than the general safety, cutting down and
making a spoil of all such woods as should repair and increase shipping,
which wood is oak, whereof this island had the best in the world; indeed,

---

[81] See n. 41.

there is no such oak in any part of the world but in this kingdom, which is the reason there are no such ships in the world as do belong to this island, for one of our ships is able to vanquish two or more ships of other nations, by reason our oak is not apt to cleft or splinter, being smooth, sound, and strong, besides close, not porous or spongy; but we, for the covetousness or present gain, cut down this excellent full-grown timber to be burnt into coals for iron forges, whereas our ancestors were so careful as they would not cut more than was for necessity, although there was great store of it; for by reason this sort of wood requires above a hundred years growth to be tall, firm, strong, close, and free from splintering, they would not cut it before age made it fit for use, nay, our ancestors did oftener plant young than cut down the old, and all for the sake and safety of their posterity; but we do not consider posterity, for if we did we should not do as we do; wherefore, what with a standing army, no trade, and daily spoils, the kingdom will be impoverished, and of necessity fall to ruin.[82]

158 *An Oration for the Disbanding of Soldiers*

*Senators, and Citizens,*

If I might, I would counsel you to disband most of the soldiers, since we perceive no visible enemy; for we have more reason to fear our own soldiers than any other power, by reason they are become so proud and insolent with their victories that we, that were their masters, if not speedily prevented, may chance to become their slaves, at least their servants, as their stewards and purveyors to get them money and provision; but were they as obedient as insolent, yet it were fit that most of them should be disbanded, otherwise they will impoverish the commonwealth; for there is no greater expense and charge than to maintain an idle army that feeds upon others' labours and is clothed upon others' cost; besides, they are not only unprofitable through their idleness, and chargeable to be maintained, but they are great destroyers with the spoils they daily make; for their idleness makes them mischievous, so as they are insolent and proud as we, their masters, dare not speak roughly to them; but when they are disarmed they will be humble, and the common soldiers will follow their former trades and several occupations: thus the charge and expense of maintaining the army will not only be taken off, but trading will then increase, by

---

[82] See *Blazing World*, n. 166.

273

which the commonwealth will be unburdened and enriched, and we ourselves out of danger and fear of being dispossessed of our power.

159 *A Soldiers Oration for the Continuance of their Army*

*Fellow Soldiers,*

Those that would be our masters, if you will give them leave will disband us, turning us out of our power by their authority, but if we submit and yield thereto we shall not only lose our pay, at least part of it, but we shall be subject to their tyranny, ruled by their laws, and commanded by their power; in short, we shall be their slaves, which are now their masters, our arms being stronger than their laws; wherefore let us keep our strength and pull down their authority, for it were a shame for sword-men to yield to gown-men, which only love to talk, but dare not fight; and shall their tongues wrest out the swords out of our hands? Shall their gowns pull off our arms? Shall they give law to us that are victorious? Or shall we suffer them to make ill laws, that broke good laws? Or shall we be governed by them that cannot govern themselves? Shall they, that have sit in safety when we ventured our lives, reap the profit of our victories? Shall we, that have conquered with our swords, be conquered by their words? Shall we, that have fought for our liberty, be subject at last to their commands? No, *Fellow Soldiers*, let us subject them to our commands, as being their betters, and let not us, that have made ourselves gentlemen by arms, noblemen by victories and kings by absolute conquest, and so absolute power, be subject to the common cowardly rout, to parish officers with their tip-staves, to unjust judges, corrupt magistrates, babbling lawyers, foolish councillors, city sergeants, tub-preachers, and the like; no, we will preach, teach, decide, rule and give the law our selves, and we having absolute power can command our pay, for every man's purse is ours; but it is best, if it can be, to have our pay gathered a legal way; wherefore let me advise that these men that are our seeming masters be made our real servants and officers, to raise us money and to collect it from every particular throughout the whole nation, whereby they will only get the hatred of the people, and we their money.

160 *Another Oration against the Former*

*Senators and Citizens,*

We that were the first studiers and stirrers to alter the government of the commonwealth, we that have prayed, preached and pleaded down tyrannical power which was in monarchical hands, we that have pulled down the nobles and have advanced the lowly, enriched the poor and impoverished the rich, shall we now be subjected and ruled by those we employed in our service, as to lead our armies, to fight our battles and to keep our cities, towns, and forts? Shall these, I say, command us, when we at first commanded them? For you well know, this army that is now in this kingdom was raised, armed, and paid by our order and industry, for it was we that combined, joined, plotted, and contrived this war, and by our subtlety, policy and wisdom we made factions and divisions, drawing thereby numbers to our party, and by our ingenuity we drained their purses as well as drew their persons to maintain this war, and yet now this our army disputes with us, and are disobedient to our command; nay, they threaten to overthrow our counsels and to put us out of our authorities, forcing the supreme power from us, which ought not to be suffered, but seriously considered how we may disband them, for it is dangerous to let one and the same men continue long in arms, especially commanders, but rather to change their commanders often, lest they may gain so much the love and obedience of their soldiers as to make them absolute; yet I leave all to your better judgements.[83]

161 *A Soldiers Oration concerning the Form of Government*

*Fellow Soldiers,*

Now we are absolute masters of this kingdom, having cast out the gown-men out of their power and authority, the question will be what kind of government we shall settle this kingdom in, as in a celestial, aerial, or terrestrial; the celestial is monarchy, the aerial is aristocracy, the terrestrial is democracy; the first is to be governed by one, the second by few, the third by many; the first is to be governed by a king, the second by nobles, the third by commons; but one of these governments we must settle in, otherwise all the kingdom will be in a confusion; for if there be no order and method, there will be no rule nor government, since everyone will do what he list, and then none will take care of anything, so that there will be neither tillage nor trade, and if there be no tillage nor trade there will be neither food nor money, for where there is no government there can be no assurance, and who will take pains for that they are not sure to keep, or rather I may say, they are sure to lose? Wherefore some government

---

[83] Charles II disbanded much of the army in 1660 and 1661.

we must choose, and all kinds of governments are divided into these three I have mentioned; as for democracy, I like that the worst, for the common people is not only insolent when they have power, commanding imperiously, condemning unjustly, advancing unworthily, but they are so inconstant as there is no assurance in them, and so foolish as they know not what to choose, only like little children they will be persuaded with a flattering tongue, sometimes to reason, but oftener against reason and sometimes against all reason and sense; the truth is, though they seem to govern, yet they are ruled by some particulars, as first by one and then another, as those that can flatter best, or rather most, by which they become slaves to an insinuating tongue; wherefore it is no fit government for us, for we are soldiers and not pleaders, we are fighters and not flatterers; the truth is that a pure democracy is all body and no head, and an absolute monarchy is all head and no body, whereas aristocracy is both head and body, it is a select and proportional number for a good government, which number being united, represents and acts as one man, for like as many men's voices agreeing and consenting make it as one man's decree, so a proportional number makes it as one man's ruling or governing: wherefore this is the best kind of government for us, for so all the chief commanders in our army, being united together, may be this whole person in this aristocratical government, in which the whole power of the kingdom will be in us and so we may govern as we shall think good.

## 162 *An Other Soldiers Oration Contrary to the Former*

*Dear Countrymen and Fellow Soldiers,*

We are disputing with ourselves what government we shall agree upon, whether democracy or aristocracy or monarchy, and I perceive you are inclined to aristocracy because that government gives room for all the chief commanders to share in the government; but give me leave to tell you that we shall never agree in that government, for though we should be fellow statesmen as we be *Fellow Soldiers*, yet if we be fellow governors we shall ruin the commonwealth and ourselves; for we shall be like as a kingdom divided in itself, which the Holy Writ says cannot stand, so we shall be divided amongst ourselves, striving which shall bear sway; wherefore I am of the opinion that monarchy is the best and safest government; for as there be many dangers and but one courage, many miseries and but one patience, many appetites and but one temperance, many injuries and wrongs and but one justice, many cheatings and cozenages and but one honesty, many falsehoods and but one truth, many creatures and but one creator, so where there are many subjects there ought to be but one governor, which is a king, and he to have the sovereign power.

163 *Another Oration Different from the two Former*

*Fellow Soldiers,*

The two former orations were one for aristocracy, the other for monarchy; but I am of an opinion as to have neither an absolute aristocracy, nor a monarchical government, but a government that shall be mixed of the two former, as neither to have it perfect monarchy nor perfect aristocracy, but mixed of both; for as the nobles are as the head, to guide, direct, rule and govern the common people, which are as the body; so a king or a chief governor is as the brain to that head, for without a brain the head would be but as an empty skull, and without a head and brain the body would be but as a senseless block; wherefore a king or chief ruler, joined to a grand council, is the best government of all, for the grand council is the eyes, ears, nose, mouth and tongue for and in the commonwealth, to spy our errors, to see advantages, to hear complaints, to smell out dangers, and to advise, counsel, and speak for and of that which will be best for the commonwealth. The king, as the brain, is to consider, reason, judge, approve, and conclude of what the council hath seen, observed, heard, found, and spoken; wherefore let us choose out one amongst us to make an elective king, and he to give judgement, drawing all the several opinions, debates and disputes to a conclusion, otherwise we shall have a division amongst us, for we shall reason and discourse of many things, but conclude not any.

164 *An Oration which is a Refusal of an Absolute Power*[84]

*Kind Countrymen,*

You have expressed not only your good opinion of me, but your extra-ordinary love, by the honour you intend me in making me your absolute governor and ruler, which is to be your king in effect, though not in name,

---

[84] In 1657 Parliament presented a Humble Petition and Advice in which it offered the pro-tector, Oliver Cromwell, the title of king. In a series of speeches made between March and May (when he refused the crown), Cromwell emphasised the burdens of office. The reasons he gave for refusing were not those of Cavendish's speaker. See Wilbur Cortez Abbott ed., *The Writings and Speeches of Oliver Cromwell*, 4 vols. (Oxford: Clarendon Press, 1988), vol. IV, pp. 399–514.

which honour I neither desire nor deserve, for I never did my country so much service as to merit such an honour, neither have I those abilities or capacities of knowledge, understanding, ingenuity and experience as are required for to manage and govern a kingdom, and to conform the divers and different humours, extravagant appetites, unruly passions, various dispositions and inconstant natures of a numerous people and head-strong multitude to a settled order and obedience, as which is apter to set up authority and pull down authority than to obey authority; but had I those abilities and wisdom to govern, and were the whole nation as ready and willing to obey, and as industrious and careful to perform all my commands, and were devoted wholly to my rule and government, yet considering the trouble and continual labour in the employment and affairs of the state, and the cares and perturbations in the mind concerning those affairs, as the maritime, martial and judicial, as also the civil, common and canonical, besides the foreign and home affairs, as trade and intelligence and the like; I should not willingly take upon me that power, for a kingly power is a slavish life, especially if he governs as he ought to do, as to be the chief actor and overseer himself, not trusting those affairs to the government and ordering of some whom he favours, only keeping the name and title to himself, quitting the labour and trouble to others; for he will not have much spare time for himself, either for soul or body; the truth is, a good governor is to be a trusty, industrious, laborious royal slave; but if he be a tyrant he enslaves the people; and though I am willing to take any pains and to employ all my time, or to lose my life or liberty for the sake or service of my country, yet, by reason I am not capable to govern, nor fit to rule so large a nation and many people, I cannot take this great charge upon me, but most humbly desire you to excuse me, and choose some other, who may better deserve it, and may more wisely govern it, that it may flourish in itself with peace and plenty, and be renowned and famed through all the world, to which end let me advise you to choose one that is born a king and bred a king, who will rule and govern magnificently, majestically, heroically, as a king ought to do.

165 *An Oration concerning Disorders, Rebellion, and Change of Governments*

*Dear countrymen,*
You know well, without my repeating, that monarchy is a government of one, aristocracy of some, and a republic of most, or rather all; also you have found by woeful experience that this kingdom hath been tossed

from one sort of government to an other, that it is now so exhausted as to be almost expired: it was at first monarchical, where in a long peace flattery, vanity, and prodigality got into the monarchical court, all which caused poverty, and so injustice, (for poverty and necessity is all times a page to prodigality), which caused the selling of all offices and places of judicature, for those that buy dear are forced to sell dear and this caused exactions and extortions, besides bribes given and bribes taken, insomuch that no justice was done for justice's sake, but bribes' sake, and they who gave the greatest bribes had their suit or cause judged of their side, whether right or wrong; nay, many judges and officers were so ignorant as they knew not how to judge rightly, or execute any public affairs as they should have done had they a will to do honestly; but how should they do either wisely, knowingly or honestly, being not chosen for parts, abilities, understanding or merit, but by paying so much money? This fault in government was a great grievance; also monopolizers engrossed several and almost all commodities in the kingdom, heightening their price as they pleased, which hindered the general trade and traffic, and this was another great grievance; also there were great taxes laid upon the people and kingdom, which was an other grievance; moreover, needy poor courtiers would beg that which ought not to be granted, or accuse some rich men to get some of their estates, at least to get a bribe to be freed; all which begot such dislike and hatred that the whole kingdom rebelled with such a fury as they pulled down monarchy, and after much blood was spilled in the war, they set up a republic, in which government the commons chose the magistrate and officers of state, for which the commons were grossly flattered by the nobler sort, which vice of flattery became a studied and practised art, by which the chief men became most elegant and eloquent orators, every man striving to out-speak each other; but this practice and strife begat ambition and envy in the better sort, and pride in the commons, which pride was heightened by their power to make peace or war, to choose magistrates and officers, to pull down or advance, to give life or death, to banish or recall, to condemn or reprieve; and all this power lay in their voices. O powerful voice of a headless monster! This power caused the brainless people to be so proud, and withal so envious, as also malicious to those men that had merit and worth, having none themselves, as they would often banish if not put to death their generous nobles, valiant commanders, and wise magistrates, as also those that were more rich than their neighbours; besides, they would advance mean and worthless men such as were of their own degree and quality to places and offices of dignity, which discontented the nobles, and that discontent bred a faction betwixt the commons and nobles, which faction being increased by the friends of the banished or executed persons, brought forth a civil war; long was the strife, but at last the nobles got the better, and then the state or government became aristocracy, in which government for some time they lived agreeable, and governed justly and orderly; but by reason aristocracy is a government of some of the nobles, and not of one, they could not long agree, every one striving to be chief and most powerful, insomuch that through envy and ambition they would cross and oppose each other; for some would keep peace with their neighbours, others would make war, and some would have such or such laws made, others would not, some would have some old laws abolished or dissolved, others would oppose them; neither was justice executed as it ought, for some would punish those that others would save, some would reward those that others would disgrace: thus every one was striving for supreme power, although they did hinder one another, and by the means of doing and undoing, decreeing and opposing, the people could not tell whom to address their suits, causes and grievances to, for what one spake for another would speak against, till at last by their pulling several ways the aristocratical government broke in pieces, and then those nobles set up each one for himself, and so there became another civil war; long was that war, for sometimes one had the better, and then another, and some times two or three sides would join against the rest, and then most against one, but now at last they being weary with war, yet know not how to agree in a peace, insomuch as we have neither war nor yet peace, nor any settled government; the truth is, the kingdom is like as the chaos and confused substance, and there is no way to bring it to an orderly form but to have a native king to bring light out of darkness, that we may see our own errors and reform our faults, and hereafter live happily under the government of a good and wise king, which I pray the gods to send you.

## 166 *An Oration to a Discontented People*

*Noble Citizens and Dear Countrymen,*
After many disorders, several governments, cruel wars, much losses, and almost absolute ruin, we desire to associate and agree in a peace with our first government, which was monarchy, a government our forefathers chose for the best; but our natures, I may say mankind, are so restless

as never to be contented with what we have, were it the best; for should the Gods reign and rule visibly upon earth we should find fault and be apt to murmur, if not rebel against them; wherefore I fear we shall never continue long in peace, if a celestial power cannot persuade us, a terrestrial will never be able to keep us in order; for if mankind desire to be above the Gods, a fellow creature will never be satisfied with any power, nor the rest of men will never be satisfied with any government, so as we shall never live in a settled peace in this world, nor never dwell peaceably but in the grave, nor never be happily governed but by that grim and great monarch, Death.

167 *An Oration in Complaint of the Former*

*Noble Citizens and Dear Countrymen,*
The former orator's oration, although it was short, yet it was sharp, for though it was but a dagger for length, yet it was a sword for Death, for he partly persuaded men to die voluntarily, to dwell in the grave peaceably, a cruel persuasion and a wicked one, for death is the punishment of sin, and shall we embrace our punishment without hopes of redemption? Shall we die before a repentance and amendment? But surely he believes after this life there is none other, but that is more than he knows or can prove, for I am confident he hath no intelligence from Death, for Death is so obscure that there is not any that goes to him which ever returns from him into this world; but setting aside the former orator and his oration, give me leave to tell you that you are in the way of being happy, in that you are resolved to agree peaceably under a monarchical government, and to have a king who shall have absolute government, which government, king and power is a type of Heaven, God and his omnipotency, and I hope we shall all prove as angels and saints, for which I pray God to grant that we may live in unity, peace, and love.

168 *A Kings Oration or Speech to his Subjects*

*Beloved Subjects,*
And I hope you will prove such, you are returned to your obedience, and I to my rights after a long absence the one from the other; but since your loyalty and my royalty have been parted, we were never happy, nay, we were never out of misery, and whose fault was it that caused such miseries?

You in the time of rebellion laid the fault on me and I on you, which was a sign we were of either side guilty, but of your side most; for though a king may err in his government, yet a people errs more in their rebellion, for the greatest tyrant that ever was was never so destroying or cruel as a rebellion or civil war, for this makes a dissolution, whereas the other makes but some interruptions; but now we have found our errors we shall mend our faults, I in governing, you in obeying, and I pray the Gods to bless us with industry and uniformity, unity and love, plenty and tranquillity, that this kingdom and people may flourish in all ages, and have a glorious fame throughout the world.

169 *A Generals Oration to his Chief Commanders*

*Fellow Soldiers and Gallant Commanders,*
I have required your assembly at this time, to persuade you to practice both riding and fencing when you have spare time from fighting; for it is impossible you should achieve any brave or extraordinary actions by your single persons in the day of battle unless you be excellent and skilful in the manage of your horses and in the use of your swords, for [if] your horses [are] well managed and well ridden, [you] shall not only overthrow your opposites as man and horse, that are ignorant in the art, but any one of you will be able to disorder an enemy's troop; 'tis true, an ignorant horse commander hath less assurance than a foot commander, besides it is a double labour and requires a double art as to manage a horse and to use a sword skilfully at one time, but then he hath a double advantage if he can ride well and hath a good managed horse, that obeys well the hand and the heel, that can tell how to turn or to stop on the haunches, or to go forward or sideways and the like: the truth is, a good horseman, although not so well skilled in the use of the sword, shall have advantage of an ignorant horseman, although well skilled in the use of the sword; but to know both arts is best for a good horse soldier. As for foot commanders, they must chiefly, if not only, practise the use of the sword, for it is the sword that makes the greatest execution; for though neither horse nor sword is either defensive or offensive against canon bullets, yet they are both useful against bodies of men; for all sorts of bullets, either from canons, muskets or pistols, will miss ten times for hitting once, whereas an army when joining so close as to fight hand to hand, the sword is the chief and prime executor, insomuch that a sword skilfully or artificially used hath the advantage over the strength of clowns or their clubs, or the butt ends

of their muskets. Wherefore a complete soldier should be as knowing and well practised in the use of the sword and the management of his horse as in drawing up a body of men, and setting or pitching an army in battle array; for by the forementioned arts you will make a great slaughter, and a quicker despatch to victory, and gain a great renown or fame to each particular person, that are so well bred or taught to be horsemen and swordsmen.

# SCHOLASTICAL ORATIONS

## Part XV

170 *A Sleepy Speech to Students*

*Fellow Students,*

Who study to think, and think to dream; as there are three sorts of worlds, so there are three kinds or sorts of life, viz. the material, poetical and drowsy world, and the dreaming, contemplating and active life; but of all these three worlds and three lives, the drowsy world and dreaming life is most wonderful, for it is as a life in death and a death in life; and this drowsy world and dreaming life is a type of an unknown world and an unknown life, for sleep is a type of death, and dreaming is a type of the rewards and punishments in the other world; good dreams are like as the rewards for the blessed, and bad dreams are like as punishments for the wicked, the one receives pleasure and joy, the other fear and torments, and these joys, pleasures, fears and torments are as sensible to the senses, and as apparent to the understanding and knowledge, as when awake; also memory and remembrance, and the same appetites and satisfactions are as perfect in dreams as when awake, the passions of the mind as forcible, the dispositions and humours of the nature as various, the will as obstinate, the judgement as deep, the wit as quick, the observation as serious, reason as rational, conception as subtle, courage as daring, justice as upright, prudence as wary, temperance as sparing, anger as violent, love as kind, fear as great, hopes and doubts as many, joys as full, hate as deadly, faith as strong, charity as pitiful, and devotion as zealous in perfect dreams as awake: also they are as uncharitable, wicked, foolish, cowardly, base, debased, furious and the like in perfect dreams as awake; but dreams in sleeping senses are shorter than the actions of waking senses, and not so permanent, for they suddenly fade and their sudden fading oftentimes makes a confusion and more disorder than in the waking and active life; but to speak of the sleeping senses generally and particularly, have we not the same appetites and satisfactions? Are not we sensible of dying, living, suffering, enjoying, mourning, weeping, rejoicing, laughing? Are we not as sensible of pain and ease? Of accidents, misfortunes, dangers and escapes, in dreams as in active life? For if we dream of thieves and murderers, are not we sensible of the loss of our goods, and of our bonds and wounds? Do we not see our loss, feel our bonds, and the smarts and pains of our wounds as much as if we saw and suffered awake? And do not we endeavour to help ourselves? And do not we beg for life, call for help, and strive with resistance as much in dreams as awake? Though not vocally, verbally, locally, nor materially yet spiritually, for it is the sensitive spirits and not the senses' gross bodies or parts that travel into foreign countries and unknown lands, and make voyages by sea in dreams; do not we hear and see in dreams lightning, thunder, wind, storms and tempest, seas, billows, waves, ships, shipwrecks? And are not we drowned in dreams? And do not we see huge precipices, barren deserts, wide forests, and wild beasts and serpents, and other hurtful creatures, and endeavour to escape and avoid the danger? Do not we feel stinging serpents and flies, striking, tearing, clawing, biting beasts, as sensibly in dreams as awake? Do not we see flowery meadows, low valleys, high hills, cornfields, green meadows, grazing pastures and beasts, clear springs, fruitful orchards, and small villages, labouring husbandmen, great cities and many people? Do not we see light, colours, sun, moon, stars, clouds, rain, frost, snow, hail, shade, dawning mornings and closing evenings, in dreams as awake? Do not we see fish swim, birds fly, beasts run, worms creep, in dreams as awake? Do not we see our friends living and our friends dying, and those that be dead, in dreams as awake? Do not we feel drought, wetness, heat, cold, itching, scratching, smarting, aching, biting, sickness, in dreams as awake? Do not we hear all warring sounds, and see all warring actions, and feel all warring miseries? Do not we see courts, balls, masques, beauties, plays, and pastimes? Do not we see musical instruments and hear harmonious music, and several tunes, notes, airs, words, voices, distinctly? Do not we see feasts and banquets, and do not we taste the several meats distinctly, not only fish, flesh, and fowls, but distinctly every sort and particular taste of every part, also the ingredients of the sauces and their particulars in them? And do not we taste bitter, salt, sour, sharp and sweet distinctly in dreams, and the several sorts of them? And do not we smell the several perfumes that are by art and nature made, as also the several stinks, in dreams as awake? And for desires and ambitions, would we have our dead friends living, have we not them in dreams? Or can we see and converse with them, or they to us, as if they were alive, but in dreams? Nay, in dreams we may rejoice with them, feast with them, sport and play with them, ask their advice or give them advice, and the like; would we have a beautiful mistress, or many several mistresses of different beauties, behaviours, births, fortunes, wits and humours, have not we them in dreams? Would we enjoy a mistress, do not we so in dreams? Would we be rich, noble, generous, valiant, are not we so in dreams? Would we see the ruin of our enemies, do not we so in dreams? Would we have our enemies die or be killed, do not they die or are slain in dreams? Would we have stately palaces, have not we so in dreams? Would we feed luxuriously, do not we so in dreams? Would we live riotously, do not we so in dreams? Would we view ourselves, as to see our faces and bodies, do not we so in dreams? Would we ride, race, hunt, hawk, and have the like pastimes and exercises, do not we so in dreams? Would we win at cards, do not we so in dreams? Would we fight duels and battles and have victory, have not we victory in dreams? Would we conquer all the world, do not we so in dreams? Would we be emperor to rule and govern all the world, do not we so in dreams? But as I said that there are pleasing and delightful dreams, so there are displeasing and fearful dreams, and there is as much trouble, disorder, and opposition in the sleepy or drowsy world, and as much discontent, faction, detraction, defamation, troubles and the like in this dreaming life, as there is method, order, agreement, praise, trust and the like therein; yet for all that, this drowsy world and dreaming life is the best of the three; for can there be greater pleasure in the material world and active life than rest to the weary limbs and sleep to the tired senses, which have been overpowered with gross objects which have laid heavy burdens on them? Or can we enjoy anything so easily, freely, suddenly, without actual trouble, as we do in dreams? Or can we be quit of all sorts and kinds of trouble and labour, but by sleep? Wherefore, if dreams were but more constant and of longer continuance, and that we should always dream pleasing dreams, the greatest happiness, next to the blessed life in heaven, were to sleep and dream, for it would be much more pleasant than the Elysian Fields. The next world and life that were to be preferred were the poetical world and contemplative life, but all the senses are not sensible in the contemplative life, whereas all the senses are as sensible in the dreaming life as awake; the truth is, the poetical world and contemplative life is rather a world for the thoughts, and a life for the mind, than the senses, yet if the senses were as sensible in contemplation as in dreams, it would be the best life of all, because it might make the life what it would, and the pleasures of that life to continue as long, and to vary as oft as it thought good, and for the poetical world or rather worlds, they would be a delight to view as well as to live in.

171 *A Waking Oration of the Former Sleepy Discourse*

*Fellow Students,*
Our brother in learning, or rather dreaming, hath commended that which
is an enemy to study, viz. sleeping and dreaming, wherefore in the drowsy
world and dreaming life there be no scholars, for they cannot sleep to
study, nor dream so much as to be very learned; neither are there poets,
for poets live altogether in their own poetical world and contemplative
life; neither are there eloquent orators, for dreams will be faded before
an oration is half spoken, or else the subject of their oration will be lost
in the variousness of dreams; neither can there be pleaders at the bar nor
preachers in the pulpit, for their text and cases may be altered in a moment
of time, from Gospel to a romance from law to riot; neither can there be
justice on life and death, for by the alteration of dreams the thief may
escape and the honest man hang, or the judge may hang himself; neither
can there be a settled government in dreams, for the government may end
in a piece of a dream, or instead of a commonwealth of men be a forest of
wild beast; neither can there be wise councillors or grave statesmen, for
their grey faces and grey beards may be changed into monkeys faces and
goats-beards, and the wise councillors in the midst of their serious advices
may on a sudden sing a wanton song, or else there may suddenly appear
a tumultuous monster or a monstrous tumult, where in a great fright
they will run from their council board or senate house; and as for school
arguments and disputations, they are quite banished, and for lovers, a
hundred to one that when a dreaming lover is embracing a young fair
lady, she suddenly turns into an old ill-favoured witch, or for a plump,
smooth, smiling Venetian courtesan, he chances to embrace grim Death's
bare rattling bones, which will fright a lover more than a fair mistress
can delight him: and as for dancing balls and French fiddles, when the
gallants in dreams are dancing in smooth measures and with fair ladies,
and the music keeping tune to the dancing time, on a sudden the courtly
dancers or dancing courtiers turn topsy turvy, dancing with their heads
downward and heels upward, a very unbecoming posture for fair-faced
ladies; and as for the music, that is quite out of tune, and the fiddle-strings
broken, and the musicians as mad as March hares, and many other such
like disorders, confusions and extravagancies, as asses' heads or bulls'
horns set on men's bodies, or a woodcock's head to an asses tail, as also
men turned to beasts, birds and fish; also walking woods and trees; but
set aside the extravagances, deformities and monstrosities in dreams, yet

there are more bad dreams than good, more fearful than delightful, more troublesome than quiet, more painful than easy; wherefore the dreaming life is a worse life than any, and the drowsy or sleepy world is only good for dull, lazy, unprofitable creatures; and as the dreaming life is the worst, so the contemplating life is the best, and the poetical world the pleasantest, for all wise, witty, learned, ingenious, good and pious men dwell all in the contemplative life, and for the most do lovers of all sorts, especially amorous lovers, for they take more pleasure to think of their mistresses than to speak with their mistresses, for they can entertain the idea of their mistresses a long time with great delight, whereas they grow soon weary of their real persons. Thus the contemplative life is best, for true pleasure and delight is not in the senses, but in the mind, for delights and pleasures are but passengers through the senses and inhabitors in the mind; besides, whatsoever the senses have enjoyed lives in the mind after their enjoyment, and though the like is for pains and surfeits, yet the mind may fling them out, or if it fling them not out, yet it may fling them aside from troubling it, and though the mind cannot satisfy the gross appetites of the senses, yet those satisfactions live in the mind, when as the senses, though they would, cannot longer enjoy them; the truth is that the senses are but as hired labourers, not owners, they are actors, not possessors, for the mind is the lord of all, and not only possessor and lord of all the satisfactions of the appetites and the objects and subjects of the senses, but it is lord of that which the senses cannot know, being beyond their capacity, having a power of forming, composing, altering, changing, making, continuing, prolonging, keeping, putting away or destroying whatsoever it pleases: all which makes the contemplative life the best, being happiest and pleasantest; and as for the poetical world, it is the most splendorous world that is, for it is composed of all curiosities, excellencies, varieties, numbers and unities: in short, it is a world that is extracted out of infinite wit, ingeniosity, judgement, experiences, understanding, knowledge and good nature, it is the heaven, and contemplation is the spiritual life in this poetical world.

172 *Of Parts and Wholes*

*Fellow Students,*

The question in the school at this time is whether a part taken from a whole remains a part after the dividing or separating, or becomes a whole of itself when it is divided; some are of the opinion that after a part is divided from the whole it is no longer a part of such a whole, either of figure or matter, but is a whole of it self; but if it be as we believe, that the bodies of men shall have a resurrection, then it proves that the several divided, separated and dispersed parts, with their joining and consistent motions and essential powers, shall meet and join to make the whole body; which proves that although parts be separated, yet they are parts of such or such a whole body or figure; also they remain distinctly in nature as parts to such a body, otherwise they could not return at the Resurrection so readily, to compose the whole by the joining and uniting of every part into one whole body. But to conclude, as all creatures are parts of infinite matter, so the divided parts of every creature are parts of the whole figure or body of every creature, and as there is infinite matter, so infinite creatures, and infinite parts, and infinite figures of every and in every part and whole.

### 173 *Another of the same Subject*

*Fellow Students,*

The former student endeavours to prove that parts pertain to their wholes, and I may endeavour to prove that wholes pertain to parts as much as parts pertain to wholes, for there can be no whole without parts, nor no part without a whole; but howsoever, all parts and wholes of every creature were from all eternity, and so consequently shall be to all eternity, for as they were, so they will be; for if such matter, motions, powers, creatures, parts, and figures had not been formerly in nature, they would, nor could not have been in nature's power at this time to produce them: but some might question what nature is? I might answer that nature is matter, motion and figure: then some might question, what power nature hath? It might be answered, nature hath power to create and uncreate: again, others might ask who gave nature that power? It might be answered, that natures power proceeds from infinity and eternity, and that it is not a gift: and some may question how infinity and eternity came? But that is such an infinite question as not to be answered: for whatsoever is infinite and eternal is God, which is something that cannot be described or conceived, nor prescribed or bound, for it hath neither beginning nor ending.

### 174 *Of the Soul*

*Fellow Students,*

The argument at this time is to prove whether the soul be a thing or nothing, a substance or no substance; some of our *Fellow Students* endeavour to prove the soul nothing, as not to be a substance, but, as they call it, an incorporeal thing, because it alters or forms everything to its own likeness, or as it pleases; for say they, whatsoever the senses bring corporeal, the soul makes incorporeal; but it may be answered that fire makes all things or at least most things or substances, like itself, so long as it works on combustible matter; and shall we say, or can we believe, that fire is an incorporeal thing because it transforms most things into its own likeness? Wherefore my opinion is that the soul is a substance, yet such a substance as to be the rarest and purest substance in nature, which makes it so apt to ascend as to make the brain the residing place; it is the celestial part of man, whereas the body is but the terrestrial part.

175 *A Speech concerning Studies*

*Fellow Students,*

We study to argue and argue to study, for the chief design of our study is only to dispute, either by the tongue, or pen, or both; but all disputes are more full of contradictions than informations, and all contradictions confound the sense and reason, at least obstruct the understanding and delude the judgement; for it keeps the one from a clear insight, and the other from a settled conclusion; so as we argue rather to make ourselves fools than to make ourselves wise.

176 *Another of the same Subject*

*Fellow Students,*

The former student speaks against arguing and disputing, and so in effect against study and learning; but to what purpose should we study or learn if we did not inform each other of our conceptions, or at least our opinions, which are bred or learned by our studies? Also what advantage should wise or subtle or eloquent orators, or great schoolmen have, if they had not studious disciples to follow them, admire, praise, and imitate them? But as it is honourable to be learned, so it is wise to learn, for knowledge is gotten by information and the best informers are wise books, which books must first be read and studied before they can be understood; also arguing and disputing is a great increase of knowledge, for it distinguishes truth from falsehood, clears the understanding, quickens the wit and refines the language; it exercises the memory, makes the tongue voluble and the speech tunable; and if it were not for study, learning and practice, there would neither be religion, law nor justice, neither would there be preachers, pleaders nor general orators; for should study be neglected and arguments rejected, men would in time degenerate their kind from being men to be like beasts, whereas learning makes men divine, as to resemble God and nature in knowledge and understanding; also it makes men in some things creators, as in conceptions, imaginations, fancies, arts and sciences.

177 *Another Concerning the same Subject*

*Fellow Students,*
The former student contradicted the first student's speech, and if I should contradict this second student's speech, as he did the first, it would be the perfect figure, picture or character of controversy and controversers; and if every disputant or arguer should contradict each other, in time there would be a great confusion, not only in the Schools, but in the minds of men, and not only in the minds, but in the souls of men; for if every controverser or disputer were of a several opinion, and those opinions should be concerning religion, there would be more several religions, than the Son of God, as he was man, could decide or judge at the Last Day; but all controversers in divinity are apt to breed atheism; wherefore it were very necessary that all divine scholars, or scholars in divinity, should agree on one ground and substantial belief, otherwise the world in time will be confounded in factions, and damned through atheism.

178 *Another concerning the same Subject*

*Fellow Students,*
Our former fellow in learning persuades us to an impossibility, as that all men should agree in one opinion or belief, but how can that be? Since by, and in nature, all men, especially scholars, are so opinative and conceited of their own wit and judgement, as that every man thinks himself as wise as his neighbour, and that his opinion may be as probable and his belief as well grounded as an other man's; and they have reason, for why may not I think I am as wise as another, and why may not another think himself as wise as I, and yet be both of different opinions? And though our opinions be different, yet our degrees of judgement may be equal; for I do not perceive that nature hath made any one man to transcend all other men in wisdom, for nature's gifts are general and not particular, and if any

one man should say he is inspired from heaven, how can we believe him, when as we cannot tell whether he be so or not? Also it is as difficult to find out another man to judge of his inspiration, as to know whether he be inspired. Wherefore, to conclude, all mankind will never agree of one teacher or judge, and so not of one opinion or belief.

179  *Another of the same Subject*

*Fellow Students,*

We complain of the differences in our arguments, disputes and opinions, but we never complain of the subjects of our studies, arguments or disputes, for we spend our time and wear out our lives in our studies and discourses to prove something nothing, as witness, motions, notions, thoughts, and the like; nay, all scholars and students endeavour to make, or at least to persuade us to believe, that our rational souls are nothing, as incorporeal, which is to have a being, but not the substance of a body, which is as impossible as to be a body and no body; also they endeavour to make the matter of the universe to be nothing, as that it is made of nothing and shall return to nothing; the worst of all is that they dispute so elevating, as to make all divinity like as a logistical egg, which is nothing; but if they could make sin and punishment nothing, their arguments would be something, whereas now their arguments are empty words without sense or reason, only fit for fools to believe and wise men to laugh at; but I wish that our studies and arguments may be such as to benefit our lives, and not such as to confound our saving belief.

# Index

# Index

# Cambridge Texts in the History of Political Thought

*Titles published in the series thus far*

Aquinas *Political Writings* (edited by R. W. Dyson)
0 521 37595 9 paperback
Aristotle *The Politics* and *The Constitution of Athens* (edited by Stephen Everson)
0 521 48400 6 paperback
Arnold *Culture and Anarchy and other writings* (edited by Stefan Collini)
0 521 37796 X paperback
Astell *Political Writings* (edited by Patricia Springborg)
0 521 42845 9 paperback
Augustine *The City of God against the Pagans* (edited by R. W. Dyson)
0 521 46843 4 paperback
Augustine *Political Writings* (edited by E. M. Atkins and R. J. Dodaro)
0 521 44697 X paperback
Austin *The Province of Jurisprudence Determined* (edited by Wilfrid E. Rumble)
0 521 44756 9 paperback
Bacon *The History of the Reign of King Henry VII* (edited by Brian Vickers)
0 521 58663 1 paperback
Bagehot *The English Constitution* (edited by Paul Smith)
0 521 46942 2 paperback
Bakunin *Statism and Anarchy* (edited by Marshall Shatz)
0 521 36973 8 paperback
Baxter *Holy Commonwealth* (edited by William Lamont)
0 521 40580 7 paperback
Bayle *Political Writings* (edited by Sally L. Jenkinson)
0 521 47677 1 paperback
Beccaria *On Crimes and Punishments and other writings* (edited by Richard Bellamy)
0 521 47982 7 paperback
Bentham *Fragment on Government* (introduction by Ross Harrison)
0 521 35929 5 paperback
Bernstein *The Preconditions of Socialism* (edited by Henry Tudor)
0 521 39808 8 paperback
Bodin *On Sovereignty* (edited by Julian H. Franklin)
0 521 34992 3 paperback
Bolingbroke *Political Writings* (edited by David Armitage)
0 521 58697 6 paperback
Bossuet *Politics Drawn from the Very Words of Holy Scripture* (edited by Patrick Riley)
0 521 36807 3 paperback
*The British Idealists* (edited by David Boucher)
0 521 45951 6 paperback

Burke *Pre-Revolutionary Writings* (edited by Ian Harris)
  0 521 36800 6 paperback
Cavendish *Political Writings* (edited by Susan James)
  0 521 63350 8 paperback
Christine De Pizan *The Book of the Body Politic* (edited by Kate Langdon Forhan)
  0 521 42259 0 paperback
Cicero *On Duties* (edited by M. T. Griffin and E. M. Atkins)
  0 521 34835 8 paperback
Cicero *On the Commonwealth* and *On the Laws* (edited by James E. G. Zetzel)
  0 521 45959 1 paperback
Comte *Early Political Writings* (edited by H. S. Jones)
  0 521 46923 6 paperback
*Conciliarism and Papalism* (edited by J. H. Burns and Thomas M. Izbicki)
  0 521 47674 7 paperback
Constant *Political Writings* (edited by Biancamaria Fontana)
  0 521 31632 4 paperback
Dante *Monarchy* (edited by Prue Shaw)
  0 521 56781 5 paperback
Diderot *Political Writings* (edited by John Hope Mason and Robert Wokler)
  0 521 36911 8 paperback
*The Dutch Revolt* (edited by Martin van Gelderen)
  0 521 39809 6 paperback
*Early Greek Political Thought from Homer to the Sophists* (edited by Michael Gagarin and Paul Woodruff)
  0 521 43768 7 paperback
*The Early Political Writings of the German Romantics* (edited by Frederick C. Beiser)
  0 521 44951 0 paperback
*The English Levellers* (edited by Andrew Sharp)
  0 521 62511 4 paperback
Erasmus *The Education of a Christian Prince* (edited by Lisa Jardine)
  0 521 58811 1 paperback
Fénelon *Telemachus* (edited by Patrick Riley)
  0 521 45662 2 paperback
Ferguson *An Essay on the History of Civil Society* (edited by Fania Oz-Salzberger)
  0 521 44736 4 paperback
Filmer *Patriarcha and Other Writings* (edited by Johann P. Sommerville)
  0 521 39903 3 paperback
Fletcher *Political Works* (edited by John Robertson)
  0 521 43994 9 paperback
Fortescue *On the Laws and Governance of England* (edited by Shelley Lockwood)
  0 521 58996 7 paperback

Fourier *The Theory of the Four Movements* (edited by Gareth Stedman Jones and Ian Patterson)
0 521 35693 8 paperback
Gramsci *Pre-Prison Writings* (edited by Richard Bellamy)
0 521 42307 4 paperback
Guicciardini *Dialogue on the Government of Florence* (edited by Alison Brown)
0 521 45623 1 paperback
Hamilton, Madison, and Jay (writing as 'Publius') *The Federalist* with *The Letters of 'Brutus'* (edited by Terence Ball)
0 521 00121 8 paperback
Harrington *A Commonwealth of Oceana* and *A System of Politics* (edited by J. G. A. Pocock)
0 521 42329 5 paperback
Hegel *Elements of the Philosophy of Right* (edited by Allen W. Wood and H. B. Nisbet)
0 521 34888 9 paperback
Hegel *Political Writings* (edited by Laurence Dickey and H. B. Nisbet)
0 521 45979 3 paperback
Hobbes *On the Citizen* (edited by Michael Silverthorne and Richard Tuck)
0 521 43780 6 paperback
Hobbes *Leviathan* (edited by Richard Tuck)
0 521 56797 1 paperback
Hobhouse *Liberalism and Other Writings* (edited by James Meadowcroft)
0 521 43726 1 paperback
Hooker *Of the Laws of Ecclesiastical Polity* (edited by A. S. McGrade)
0 521 37908 3 paperback
Hume *Political Essays* (edited by Knud Haakonssen)
0 521 46639 3 paperback
King James VI and I *Political Writings* (edited by Johann P. Sommerville)
0 521 44729 1 paperback
Jefferson *Political Writings* (edited by Joyce Appleby and Terence Ball)
0 521 64841 6 paperback
John of Salisbury *Policraticus* (edited by Cary Nederman)
0 521 36701 8 paperback
Kant *Political Writings* (edited by H. S. Reiss and H. B. Nisbet)
0 521 39837 1 paperback
Knox *On Rebellion* (edited by Roger A. Mason)
0 521 39988 2 paperback
Kropotkin *The Conquest of Bread and other writings* (edited by Marshall Shatz)
0 521 45990 7 paperback
Lawson *Politica sacra et civilis* (edited by Conal Condren)
0 521 39248 9 paperback

Nietzsche *On the Genealogy of Morality* (edited by Keith Ansell-Pearson)
0 521 40610 2 paperback
Paine *Political Writings* (edited by Bruce Kuklick)
0 521 66799 2 paperback
Plato *The Republic* (edited by G. R. F. Ferrari and Tom Griffith)
0 521 48443 X
Plato *Statesman* (edited by Julia Annas and Robin Waterfield)
0 521 44778 X paperback
Price *Political Writings* (edited by D. O. Thomas)
0 521 40969 1 paperback
Priestley *Political Writings* (edited by Peter Miller)
0 521 42561 1 paperback
Proudhon *What is Property?* (edited by Donald R. Kelley and Bonnie G. Smith)
0 521 40556 4 paperback
Pufendorf *On the Duty of Man and Citizen according to Natural Law* (edited by James Tully)
0 521 35980 5 paperback
*The Radical Reformation* (edited by Michael G. Baylor)
0 521 37948 2 paperback
Rousseau *The Discourses and other early political writings* (edited by Victor Gourevitch)
0 521 42445 3 paperback
Rousseau *The Social Contract and other later political writings* (edited by Victor Gourevitch)
0 521 42446 1 paperback
Seneca *Moral and Political Essays* (edited by John Cooper and John Procope)
0 521 34818 8 paperback
Sidney *Court Maxims* (edited by Hans W. Blom, Eco Haitsma Mulier and Ronald Janse)
0 521 46736 5 paperback
Sorel *Reflections on Violence* (edited by Jeremy Jennings)
0 521 55910 3 paperback
Spencer *The Man versus the State* and *The Proper Sphere of Government* (edited by John Offer)
0 521 43740 7 paperback
Stirner *The Ego and Its Own* (edited by David Leopold)
0 521 45647 9 paperback
Thoreau *Political Writings* (edited by Nancy Rosenblum)
0 521 47675 5 paperback
Tönnies *Community and Civil Society* (edited by José Harris and Margaret Hollis)
0 521 56119 1 paperback